REFEREEING IDENTITY

D1521063

Refereeing Identity

The Cultural Work of Canadian Hockey Novels

MICHAEL BUMA

McGill-Queen's University Press
Montreal & Kingston • London • Ithaca

© McGill-Queen's University Press 2012

ISBN 978-0-7735-3987-7 (cloth)
ISBN 978-0-7735-3988-4 (paper)

Legal deposit second quarter 2012
Bibliothèque nationale du Québec

Printed in Canada on acid-free paper that is 100% ancient forest
free (100% post-consumer recycled), processed chlorine free

This book has been published with the help of a grant from the Canadian
Federation for the Humanities and Social Sciences, through the Aid to Scholarly
Publications Program, using funds provided by the Social Sciences and
Humanities Research Council of Canada.

McGill-Queen's University Press acknowledges the support of the Canada
Council for the Arts for our publishing program. We also acknowledge the
financial support of the Government of Canada through the Canada Book
Fund for our publishing activities.

Library and Archives Canada Cataloguing in Publication

Buma, Michael, 1979–
    Refereeing identity: the cultural work of Canadian hockey novels /
    Michael Buma.

    Includes bibliographical references and index.
    ISBN 978-0-7735-3987-7 (bound). – ISBN 978-0-7735-3988-4 (pbk.)

    1. Hockey stories, Canadian (English) – History and criticism. 2. Hockey
in literature. 3. National characteristics, Canadian, in literature. 4. Hockey –
Social aspects – Canada. I. Title.

PS8191.H62B84 2012   C813'.54093579   C2011-907841-4

This book was typeset by Interscript in 10.5/13 Sabon.

To Selena, for sitting with me "up there in the blues," and to Mom and Dad, for early-morning practices and everything else.

Contents

Acknowledgments

A book such as this is inevitably a team effort (hockey pun intended), and I'm very grateful to the many people who have contributed along the way. Manina Jones oversaw this project during its first iteration as my doctoral thesis, and has been enormously encouraging, insightful, and gracious throughout the entire process. She is truly the Scotty Bowman of academic advisors. Joe Zezulka served as second reader, and set me straight on everything from commas to cross-checking. Don Morrow gave generously of his expertise in sport literature, connected me to the Sport Literature Association, and sometimes passes me the puck in Saturday morning shinny. Jamie Dopp went above and beyond the duties of an external examiner, and has helped with both the literary and hockey aspects of this study at many points along the way. D.M.R. Bentley was involved from day one, and provided valuable feedback at several stages of the manuscript and impeccable wisdom on grant applications. Thy Phu served as a departmental examiner, and was especially helpful in clarifying some theoretical issues in the introduction. Mary-Lynne Ascough and James Thomas from McGill-Queen's University Press have been excellent editors, and have guided me ably and efficiently through the publishing process. Finally, a little more than a decade ago Ron Wells let me study the Summit Series for my undergraduate senior seminar, then challenged me to write a paper casting Phil Esposito as a Foucauldian hero when I got to grad school. That paper never materialized, but I guess this study is close enough.

A few more general acknowledgments are due. I would like to thank my fellow hockey scholars, particularly those who attended the Plymouth, Victoria, and Buffalo conferences, for helping to shape my understanding of the game's cultural and political contexts and for validating my belief that hockey is indeed worth studying. I'm also grateful to my students, who constantly remind me why research is important in the first place. Special thanks are due to Ricki-Lee Gerbrandt for sharing her experience in the game and as a reader of hockey novels. Thanks are also due to my grad school colleagues, especially the members of the Habs–Leafs (or Leafs–Habs) Ultimate Mortal Street Fight Combatant Club: Andrew Moore, Kaya Fraser, Sean Henry, Michael Kightley, Laurel Ryan, and Karis Shearer. Watching hockey and playing video games with you helped me stay sane. Finally, I'm especially grateful to my wife Selena and son Logan, my parents Paul and Clara Buma and in-laws Don and Tilda Dam, and my brother and sister, Alisa and Nick Buma, and brothers- and sisters-in-law, Mike and Annie Dam (and daughter Elly), Ken and Claire Dam, and Aaron Dam. I can't thank you enough for your love and support. Any failings in the book are entirely my own.

Parts of this work were included in "'Save Our Team, Save Our Game': Identity Politics in Two Canadian Hockey Novels," published in *Now Is the Winter: Thinking About Hockey*, ed. Jamie Dopp and Richard Harrison (Hamilton, ON: Wolsak & Wynn Publishers, 2009), 39–49; "John Richardson's Unlikely Narrative of Nationhood: History, the Gothic, and Sport as Prophecy in *Wacousta*," published in *Studies in Canadian Literature/Études en littérature canadienne* 36, no. 1 (2011): 142–61; and "Review of Jason Blake's *Canadian Hockey Literature*," published in *Aethlon: The Journal of Sport and Literature* (2009/2010, fall/winter) 17(1/2). They are in each case reprinted with permission.

REFEREEING IDENTITY

Introduction

I don't think I've ever felt so Canadian as on 24 February 2002. The men's hockey finals were taking place at the Salt Lake City Olympics, Team Canada versus Team USA, and I was watching the game from Port-au-Prince, Haiti, with an exuberant group of fellow expatriates. The tension in the room was palpable when the Americans scored first; it was as if the goal had thrown a blanket on the fire of our collective hopes, reinforced our doubts about Canada's chances against a strong American team. But then it happened: only minutes after the American goal, Canada's Chris Pronger made a cross-ice pass to team captain Mario Lemieux. As if by clairvoyance or extrasensory perception, Lemieux somehow sensed teammate Paul Kariya directly behind him and in better position to get a shot away. As the puck sped toward Lemieux, the captain opened his legs and allowed it to glide through to Kariya, who converted the pass for a game-tying goal. I'll never forget the split second before the room erupted into cheering, screaming, and applause. It was a moment of mutual understanding, an awareness among everyone present that we had witnessed an act of inimitable athletic brilliance. Certainly our shouts and cheers paid tribute to Lemieux's remarkable unselfishness and astonishing hockey sense, but the moment felt bigger than simply this; in a way, we were celebrating our shared capacity to perceive such brilliance and be thrilled by it. What was most striking about this feeling of unity and togetherness, however, is that it somehow brought us closer to home. It was as if Kariya's goal had connected us to our fellow Canadians, whoever they were and wherever they were watching from. After that there could be no doubt that Canada would win, and the simmer of our enthusiasm was carried to full boil by four more Canadian goals before the game was over. The final score was 5–2, and Team Canada brought home Olympic gold for the first time in fifty years.

When I think back on my reaction to Canada's 2002 gold-medal win, I'm struck by how much the way I felt resembled the way I was *supposed to* feel. In other words, my reaction fell almost perfectly into line with certain cultural expectations and assumptions about what it means to be Canadian. Canadians are bombarded by cultural representations of hockey that encourage them to think about the game as contributing to national unity and identity. Hockey has been seen by many commentators as "Canada's game," and has frequently been mobilized in the rhetoric of identity discourse and cultural nationalism.[1] In this configuration, the game purports to unify diverse internal populations while at the same time marking Canada as symbolically different from external others such as the United States. In other words, hockey has often been represented in popular culture as an expression of Canadian character, unity, and identity. Much of the basis for such nationalistic representations has arisen from hockey's purportedly "natural" connection with Canada's northern setting, as well as from the idea that Canadians symbolically possess hockey in a way that other nations don't (we invented it, are best at it, care most about it, etc.). As Jamie Dopp and Richard Harrison suggest, "investigating hockey critically is to think of it not as expressing some real connection between nature and culture, but to see it as carrying a story, often expressed in mythic terms, that people desire to be true about themselves and their place in the world" (2009, 9). In addition to its long-standing association with national identity, hockey has often been represented in Canadian culture as expressing a version of masculinity that is contingent on physical toughness. We have entered a time in which such representations have, paradoxically, never been more abundant or less true. While globalizing processes, new technologies, alternative recreational options, changing ideas about gender, and the emergence of a post-industrial economy have worked in various ways to diminish the essential Canadianness and assumed masculinity of hockey, representations of the game that propose and encourage these traditional identities have never been more plentiful or pronounced.

Taking this paradox as a starting point, this study examines representations of nation and gender in Canadian hockey novels. As the title suggests, particular attention will be given to the cultural work of hockey novels, the ways in which fictive representations of the game work to rehearse and/or referee certain identities and derive their significations within larger networks of cultural meaning. Stephen Greenblatt identifies several questions that are useful to the study of cultural work in literary texts: "What kinds of behaviour, what models of practice, does this work seem to enforce? Why might readers at a particular time and place find this work compelling? Are there differences between my values and the values implicit in the work I am reading? Upon what social understandings does the work depend? Whose freedom of thought or movement might be constrained implicitly or explicitly by this work? What are the larger social structures with which these particular acts of praise or blame might be connected?" (1990, 226). Such questions inform this study and provide the underlying basis for its claims about hockey novels. Simply put, this book argues that the novels it discusses typically work in the service of homogenizing nationalism and traditional masculinity, and that this is precisely their appeal. It is no coincidence that hockey novels attempt to reinforce these concepts at an historical moment when they are frequently perceived to be in crisis.

CANADA'S HOCKEY MYTH

The accumulated pool of cultural meanings and significations that have become attached to hockey in Canada might be referred to as the "hockey myth." Roland Barthes defines myth simply as "a system of communication ... a message" (1972, 109). Barthes argues that myth is a "second-order semiological system" (114), meaning that it functions using another linguistic system as its basis. He deploys the terms *form*, *content*, and *signification* to connote a *signifier*, *signified*, *sign* pattern in the metalanguage of myth. The form of the myth is supplied simply by the object of its conveyance: a television commercial, for instance, or popular song, or, in the case of this study, a scene or passage from a novel. The content of the myth is supplied by the vast network of pre-existing cultural meanings already associated with its subject. Signification, then, forces a potentially nebulous field of content into a hollow specificity of form, producing a "myth-meaning" by filtering, condensing, or distorting its subject.

For Barthes, myth works by "transforming history into nature" (140), thus presenting what is actually socially particular and historically specific as natural and inevitable. In other words, a myth works to naturalize its own assumptions in the mind of the perceiver by appearing commonsensical, self-evident, and innocent, a fair and accurate representation of reality.

Benedict Anderson has famously suggested that modern nation-states such as Canada tend to be "imagined communities" in that "the members of even the smallest nation will never know most of their fellow-members, meet them, or even hear of them, yet in the minds of each lives the image of their communion" (1991, 6). This is accomplished largely through what Eric Hobsbawm has referred to as "the invention of traditions," the creation of symbolic cultural practices that "seek to inculcate certain values or norms of behaviour by repetition, which automatically implies continuity with the past" and thereby gives the appearance of naturalness (1983, 1). The process of national imagining, then, involves constructing shared mythologies that appear to be both objectively real and grounded in history. In Canada, hockey has been one such vehicle for imagining national community and establishing what Eli Mandel, borrowing from Hobsbawm, has called a "usable tradition" (1977, 81).

According to a speculative, yet compelling, argument by sport sociologist Michael Robidoux, hockey first became associated with national identity in Canada because of its symbolic connection to lacrosse, a game that was invented and played by First Nations peoples before the arrival of Europeans in North America. For the First Nations, lacrosse had spiritual significance and was played to honour members of the community, decide disputes between nations, factions, or cultural groups, or simply as a ritual celebration of life. According to Robidoux, early European accounts of lacrosse emphasize the "remarkable sportsmanship and respect" displayed by the players for their opponents, which were made all the more striking by the "violent nature of the sport" (2002a, 212–13). It was this violence that initially attracted many seventeenth- and eighteenth-century French settlers to lacrosse, and for a "certain sector of French Canadian males … the First Nations male provided an alternative model of masculinity to what they had known in France, one where physicality, stoicism, and bravado, were valued and celebrated, not repressed, as was the typical Christian model of masculinity" (214). To borrow a term from Terry Goldie's analysis of the indigene in Australian and Canadian literatures, lacrosse also presented the French with an opportunity to "indigenize," a means by which the colonists could conceive of themselves as naturally connected to Canadian space by participating in an important element of Native culture. According to Goldie, "the indigene is often used [in Australian and Canadian literatures] to present the possibility of nature in a human form" (1989, 19). The elision between Native and nature, then, results in European appropriation of Native culture as a "metaphorical attempt ... to achieve root in the new land." This process is one of "acquisition" rather than "becoming," however, in that the "indigene is acquired, [but] the white is not abandoned" (215).

Although lacrosse supplied a means by which the French colonists could imagine their connection with the land, it was first conceived of as a national game by an Englishman, George Beers, a Montreal dentist and ardent Canadian nationalist, in the mid-nineteenth century. According to sports historian Don Morrow, Beers was utterly instrumental in standardizing the rules of lacrosse and spreading the popularity of the game. Throughout the 1860s Beers wrote several articles in Montreal newspapers arguing that lacrosse should be adopted as the Canadian national sport rather than the "imported" British game of cricket: "As cricket, wherever played by Britons, is a link of loyalty to bind them to their home so may Lacrosse be to Canadians. We may yet find it will do as much for our young Dominion as the Olympian games did for Greece or cricket for our Motherland" (quoted in Morrow 1989, 49). Part of the rationale for Beers' claim was that the Native game of lacrosse most closely reflected the experience of Canadian peoples, especially the First Nations and settler French. According to the director of the North American Indian Travelling College, Mike Mitchell, "Beers clearly understood and accepted the role of sport in integrating the disparate aspects of the new Canadian society, and his love of the new country demanded that the symbolic sport through which this nationalism be channelled would be wholly and uniquely Canadian" (1995). By the end of 1867 Beers had largely achieved his goal: "[lacrosse] was indeed surrounded by a 'national' aura; for example, the formation and acceptance of the name National Lacrosse Association had its own connotation; and the Association's provision of a banner for 'championship' play bore the slogan 'Our Country and Our Game'" (Morrow 1989, 54).

As attempts were made to modernize lacrosse – that is, to standardize the rules and market the game to a wide audience – accompanying efforts were made to divest the game of its violence and physical intensity. To accomplish this, the National Lacrosse Association introduced rules that would effectively limit the participation of Natives and working-class whites. Barred from lacrosse, many of these working-class players turned to other sports, especially hockey: "Unlike baseball or football, hockey was seen as uniquely Canadian in origin and character. An amalgam of modern and vernacular sporting pastimes, hockey resembled lacrosse in design and in the manner it was played. Play was aggressive and often violent, providing men the opportunity to display this emergent notion of masculinity. At a symbolic level, it was played on a frozen landscape, perfectly embodying what life as a Canadian colonialist was supposed to be like" (Robidoux 2002a, 218). It was the rugged masculinity-cum-nationalism of lacrosse, then, as well as the game's apparently "natural" connection to the Canadian landscape, that initially infused hockey with its nationalistic overtones. By exemplifying "images of masculinity valued in First Nations culture, and later by early Canadian settlers" hockey provided "Canadian males with an identifiable image outside of a British Victorian framework" (220–1). The result of this was that "hockey became a vehicle of resistance against British and American hegemony, something that Canadians continue to call on in periods of political uncertainty" (221). In other words, hockey came to be seen as a uniquely Canadian institution, something that demonstrated national particularity and cultural distinction against the perceived threat of external influence.

Hockey's growing prominence in Canada throughout the late nineteenth century – and its reputation as a national sport – can be attributed in large part to the Governor General Sir Frederick Arthur Stanley's suggestion that teams should vie for an official "Dominion Challenge Trophy." Stanley donated just such a trophy in 1893 with the intention of drawing teams from across the nation to compete. The Stanley Cup, as the trophy came to be called, allowed for a series of essentially local hockey dramas to be enacted on the national stage. Any team from anywhere in the nation could make a Cup challenge, though their bid had to be accepted by designated trustees. To be accepted, at least in the early days, a team would have to win a significant local championship. Challenges were played at the home rink of the defender as a best of three series, which, according to sports historian Wayne Simpson, "proved both workable and successful in enlisting the participation of teams from much of the country" (1989, 179). As Michael McKinley puts it in his popular history of the game, *Putting a Roof on Winter*, Lord Stanley's scheme quickly "ensured that regional rivalries would develop," and "by virtue of making the teams travel, Stanley made Canadians go with them, or at least go with them in their hearts" (2000, 24). The Stanley Cup challenge format, then, was vastly successful in creating Canadian community, both real and imagined, and as a result "hockey began to earn its reputation as Canada's 'national game'" (Simpson 1989, 179).

Although hockey was frequently mobilized in the service of nation throughout the late nineteenth and early twentieth centuries, by the end of the Second World War Canada remained in many ways "colonial in psychology as well as in mercantile economics," as Northrop Frye describes it in one of his "essays on the Canadian imagination" in *The Bush Garden* (1971, iii). In *The House of Difference: Cultural Politics and National Identity in Canada,* Eva Mackey observes that one of the principal activities of nation-building is "the perceived necessity of [creating] a differentiated and defined national culture" ([1999] 2002, 70), and throughout the 1950s and 60s the Canadian government instituted a series of programs and inquiry commissions intended to accomplish just this. The result was a period of concerted national "imagining" which sought to justify the Canadian polity by establishing and recovering a distinctly Canadian history, tradition, and cultural identity. Myths of national character and identity are often disseminated through what Louis Althusser has called "Ideological State Apparatuses" (ISAs) (1971, 136), the various means by which people make sense of themselves and their place in the world. For Althusser, human beings are shaped as social subjects by the frequent repetition of material rituals and through constant exposure to certain ideological positions and assumptions. By rehearsing these models of identity and opinion, Althusser suggests, people eventually come to occupy them or acknowledge them as "true." Throughout the 1950s and 60s, the cultural work of Canadian ISAs such as radio, television, newspapers, and magazines achieved a "near national consensus in which the core assumptions of Canadian hockey mythology were felt viscerally and rarely questioned" (Whitson and Gruneau 2006, 4).

According to Whitson and Gruneau, the tenets of this "consensus" were that "*hockey is our game; it expresses something distinctive*

about how we Canadians have come to terms with our unique
northern environment and landscape; it is a graphic expression of
'who we are'; the game's rough masculinity is a testament to the
distinctive passion and strength of the Canadian character; we are
better at it than anyone else in the world; and the National Hockey
League is the pinnacle of the game – as well as a prominent Canadian
institution" (2006, 4; italics in original). Foster Hewitt articulates
many of these ideas quite clearly in one of the first-ever Canadian
hockey novels, *Hello, Canada and Hockey Fans in the United States*
(1950), a children's novel that fictionalizes Canada's hockey performance in the 1952 Olympics and argues the importance of maintaining hockey dominance on the international stage: "hockey means
more to Canada than it does to any other people in the world. We
wrote the rules, made the skates and pads and sticks, taught the
game to Europe and won all the championships. Everywhere our
teams appeared, Canadians were respected as strong, sturdy, sports-
loving people. In fact, hockey and Canada were so close to each
other that our national coat-of-arms could have included a hockey
puck along with a beaver and a maple leaf. Now, Canada's population ... is not large when compared with that of many other countries. So we need hockey's prestige to give us a national lift, to make
us look big, confident and powerful in the eyes of other people.
Hockey has already sold Canada to at least twenty-five other
nations" (15). Again, hockey is seen as an expression of Canadian
character and a definitively homegrown national institution. Broadly
speaking, the cultural work of Canadian hockey novels is to confirm
such ideas about the importance and significance of the game. Given
the hockey myth's insistence that hockey guarantees Canadian cultural distinctiveness, it is in some ways hardly surprising that the
heyday of the hockey myth throughout the 1950s and 60s coincided
with Canada's wider push to define itself as a culturally viable polity.
In other ways, however, this fact appears remarkably paradoxical.

The central tenet of the identity shift that the Canadian government worked to implement throughout the 1950s and 60s was a
movement from "Britishness" to multicultural pluralism. In 1971,
the Canadian government implemented a policy of "Multiculturalism
within a Bilingual Framework," which stated that although Canada
would have two official languages (French and English) there was to
be no state-sanctioned culture and no preference afforded to any
ethnic group over another. Throughout the 1960s and 70s the idea

of the "pluralist cultural 'mosaic'" replaced "cultural policies that centred on maintaining British cultural hegemony" as a way of imagining the nation as "distinct and differentiated from external others such as the United States" (Mackey [1999] 2002, 50). The paradox of hockey's imbrication in this identity shift is that the two appear to be mutually exclusive. While the "Multiculturalism within a Bilingual Framework" act sought to ensure, at least on paper, the viability of pluralism as the central tenet of Canadian identity, the myth of hockey offered unity and identity based on cultural homogenization.[2] In simplest terms, the idea of the cultural mosaic argues that Canadian identity is rooted in our ability to get along despite the fact that we have nothing in common. The hockey myth, however, maintains we actually do have something in common, our shared cultural obsession with hockey. These seemingly incompatible identity configurations have been curiously accommodated by the apparatus of state. Although the "Multiculturalism within a Bilingual Framework" Act (the Canadian Multiculturalism Act) clearly stated that Canada would have no official culture, Parliament passed Bill C-212 (Canada's National Sport Act) in 1994 to officially "recognize Hockey as Canada's National Winter Sport and Lacrosse as Canada's National Summer Sport" (quoted in Mitchell 1995). Sports, of course, are inevitably cultural constructions, and as such the idea of sanctioning two official national sports would seem fundamentally incompatible with the governmental pledge to recognize "no official culture." In other words, the rhetoric of hockey nationalism and the passage of Bill C-212 suggest the insufficiency of multiculturalism as a way of imagining the nation as "distinct and differentiated from external others." As will be seen, the perceived need to identify Canada as culturally distinct underwrites many of the novels discussed in this study, especially in the context of increased globalization, continental monoculture, and increased internal instability since the 1970s. The hockey myth, then, paradoxically objects to globalizing processes that efface cultural difference, while contradicting multiculturalism's insistence on a Canadian identity grounded in difference rather than similarity. We need to distinguish a distinctly Canadian culture, these novels seem to suggest, but the way to do so, they further suggest, is by focusing on our similarities rather than our differences.

As the Centennial-era drive to define a "usable Canadian tradition" receded in other areas of culture, various commentators persisted in vehemently asserting the "Canadianness" of hockey. Published in 1972, Bruce Kidd and John Macfarlane's *The Death of Hockey* is dedicated to "the rightful owners of hockey, the Canadian people" and opens with the suggestion that "hockey is the Canadian metaphor, the rink a symbol of this country's vast stretches of water and wilderness, its extremes of climate, the player a symbol of our struggle to civilize such land" (4).[3] Kidd and Macfarlane see the major challenge to hockey's Canadianness as the "American" drive to accumulate wealth, manifested in the slick commercialism of the National Hockey League (NHL) and the now defunct World Hockey Association (WHA), as well as in the inability of small-market Canadian teams to compete in the North American hockey market. To address this problem, Kidd and Macfarlane propose the creation of an all-Canadian hockey league based on reasonable player salaries, community-based franchise ownership, and government subsidies to help cover operating costs. Kidd and Macfarlane, then, essentially challenge one of the peripheral tenets of the hockey myth (the idea that the NHL is an important Canadian institution) on the basis that it jeopardizes the core assumption that the game "belongs" to Canadians and functions as a symbol of Canadian identity.

Kidd and Macfarlane's *The Death of Hockey* was written in the same year as Canada's most monumental hockey event, the Summit Series victory over Russia, which in the minds of many confirmed hockey's status as "Canada's game." The Summit Series was an unofficial eight-game challenge that pitted the best Canadian professional players against the best Russians, the first four games to be played in Canada and the last four in Russia. Team Canada was expected to dominate, but when they posted a meagre record of one win, two losses, and a tie during the first leg of the series, disillusion swept the nation. Canadian hopes sank even lower when Team Canada lost the first game of the Russian leg, but managed to rally in the next two games, winning both on goals from a rather unlikely recruit, Paul Henderson of the Toronto Maple Leafs. By the final game the series had reached a fever pitch, the cultural dimensions of which appeared to extend well beyond the hockey rink. Occurring at the height of the Cold War, many Canadians had come to perceive the Series as a clash of cultures, a battle of free-market capitalism versus communism. Game 8 of the Summit Series drew the largest television audience in the history of Canadian broadcasting to that point (CBC 2009). When Paul Henderson scored yet another winning goal with less than a minute left, the victory seemed to vindicate both the myth of hockey and the Canadian "way of life." The magnitude of the Summit Series is such that Ken Dryden and Roy MacGregor refer to it as the only "wholly Canadian event" (1989, 193) and Gruneau and Whitson suggest that the victory "mobilized patriotic interest among Canadians like no other cultural event before or since" (1993, 249).

Despite the momentary feeling of unity brought about by the Summit Series, the 1970s witnessed an escalation of tensions between Canada's French and English and an increasing amount of instability between the nation's different levels of government. This resulted in a "strong sense of [the] diffusion and decentralization ... of what had once been perceived as a monolithic cultural establishment" (Bumsted 1998, 397). As it seemed more and more apparent that the once-stable centre could no longer hold, "Anglo-Canadian nationalism in particular ... seemed to embrace hockey with a sense of urgency" (Whitson and Gruneau 2006, 9). It was against a backdrop of cultural and political uncertainty, then, that the next round of hockey-as-identity salvos were fired throughout the 1980s. The first of these was Peter Gzowski's *The Game of Our Lives* (1981), which provided a symbolic answer to Kidd and Macfarlane's call to repatriate hockey, casting the budding success of Wayne Gretzky and the Edmonton Oilers as a triumph for Canadian possession of the game. A more generic version of the hockey myth was articulated by Doug Beardsley in *Country on Ice* (1987), which sees hockey as an authentic and autonomous expression of Canadian culture and identity. Beardsley situates hockey within the Canadian myth of the north, constructing a "unity by setting" version of nationhood in which a mythologized version of a natural northern landscape acts as an actively unifying and homogenizing cultural force: "Ice binds us together, shapes and defines both our style and our substance. It informs us, connects us rink by rink to ourselves. In the Canadian psyche, the motion we create on our national icescape is the nearest we come to permanence" (185). Beardsley's idea of a "national icescape" is particularly interesting for its multi-layered implications of naturalness; nationalist sensibility appears here as both organically related to the soil (or, more specifically, the frozen water) and existing *ex nihilo* without context or history. For Beardsley, hockey "created our history" (a curious inversion of the actuality that history creates hockey), "is an allegory for life in Canada as Canadians," and "represents the most important aspects of the national spirit in that it mixes the right amounts of innocence and integrity in a character mould that is elementally Canadian" (36–7). Beardsley again suggests the "natural" relationship between hockey, identity, and landscape by punning the word "elemental," which signifies here as both "inherent" and "relating ... to a great force of nature" (*Merriam Webster's Collegiate Dictionary*, 10th ed., defs. 1d and 2). For Beardsley, hockey is one of Canada's "greatest national – even natural – resources" (1987, 184), and his constant elision between the two attempts to efface the cultural work that necessarily underwrites any such yoking of nature and nation.

Less mythopoeic than *Country on Ice* but equally nationalistic is Ken Dryden and Roy MacGregor's *Home Game: Hockey and Life in Canada* (1989), which sees the game as a grassroots expression of Canadian unity, community, and identity. For Dryden and MacGregor, lives of citizens that are otherwise divided by "age, income, status, neighbourhood, technology, distance, language, [and] culture" (10) are intangibly united by hockey in that "hockey helps us express what we feel about Canada, and ourselves. It is a giant point of contact, in a place, in a time, where we need every one we have – East and West, French and English, young and old, past and present. The winter, the land, the sound of children's voices, a frozen river, a game – all are part of our collective imaginations. Hockey makes Canada feel more Canadian" (19). Like Gzowski and Beardsley, then, Dryden and MacGregor attempt to mobilize hockey in the service of cultural nationalism at a time when "we need every point of contact we have," at the end of a decade characterized by divisive political squabbles such as the constitutional and Free Trade debates, and in which "everything, from the economy to the very nation itself, suddenly seemed to be in a state of disintegration bordering on confusion" (Bumsted 1998, 365). While hockey novels are more likely to address the issue of Free Trade than the constitution (and do so circuitously by lamenting the plight of small-market NHL teams in the economic climate created in part by Free Trade), they tend to propose the game as an immutable constant in Canadian life, a national stay against the forces of confusion that confound us in an era of heightened diversity and increased globalization. For many of the novels discussed in this study, hockey is a cohesive connection that appears to safeguard Canadianness during a time of instability and, especially in English Canada, the one remaining social institution that guarantees some basic level of unity.

Buoyed by David Cruise and Alison Griffiths' *Net Worth: Exploding the Myths of Pro Hockey* (1991) and Gruneau and Whitson's *Hockey Night in Canada: Sport, Identities and Cultural Politics* (1993), a critical atmosphere arose during the early 1990s that began to question and challenge the hockey myth as never before. Cruise and Griffiths' *Net Worth* cemented Canadian distrust of the "big business" end of professional hockey, exposing the fact that "no sport has controlled its athletes as effortlessly and totally as hockey. Though fabulously profitable over the long term, the NHL has always been able to convince the players – in good times or bad – that the clubs couldn't afford the salaries, benefits, and working conditions they demanded, and that if they persisted, the players would kill the sport" (1991, 5). In other words, the abstract "purity" of the game was perceived as being contaminated by contemporary economic conditions and institutional forms. Around the same time, Gruneau and Whitson's *Hockey Night in Canada* offered the first comprehensive cultural analysis of Canadian hockey, premised on the idea that "the centrality of hockey in Canadian cultural life has never been inevitable or predetermined ... [but] rather ... has emerged out of a series of clashes of cultures and traditions that have occurred against the backdrop of Canada's development as an industrial and consumer society" (1993, 6). Gruneau and Whitson, then, directly oppose the tendency to see hockey as inherently linked to Canadianness. More recently Whitson and Gruneau have employed the metaphor of "artificial ice" to expose the game as "a human social and cultural product, something that we Canadians have 'made' over a period of years" (2006, 2).

As a result of heightened critical attention throughout the 1990s and certain significant cultural and economic changes, Canada's symbolic possession of hockey was less certain during this period than at any other time. By the time of the 2004–05 NHL lockout, many Canadians "found that they got on just fine without [professional] hockey and did not really miss it much" (Whitson and Gruneau 2006, 13). As Whitson and Gruneau note, part of Canada's waning interest was surely the deterioration of "the NHL 'product'" into "a grinding, boring, defensive game, filled with obstruction, and played over such a long season that regular matches often seem meaningless" (13). But deeper structural changes to the fabric of Canadian society had affected cultural attitudes toward hockey far more than the deterioration of the game: "Canada today has become a very different country from the Canada of the 1960s and 1970s. We are now a much more urban and multicultural country, and many of our most recent migrants have come from societies in which professional sport scarcely exists. Even among multi-generation Canadians, moreover, the range of interests available to young people (including other sports, as well as artistic pursuits and new forms of electronic entertainment) has become so great that hockey at any level is now just one recreational or consumer choice among many, as opposed to the ritual of winter life that many middle-aged Canadian men recall" (13–14). Simply put, we have entered a time in which heightened critical attention to the cultural work of hockey has coupled with increased urbanization, growing multiculturalism, and a flourishing of alternative recreational pursuits that have called into question the myth of hockey more than ever before. Paradoxically, we have also entered a time in which cultural representations of hockey that portray, propound, and enforce the myth have never been so abundant.

One unabashed apologist for Canada's hockey myth in recent years has been novelist David Adams Richards, whose *Hockey Dreams: Memories of a Man Who Couldn't Play* ([1996] 2001) is a nationalist polemic which one reviewer went so far as to characterize as the literary equivalent to a conversation with the brashly outspoken hockey commentator and Canadian cultural icon, Don Cherry. Like Kidd and Macfarlane, as well as Beardsley, Richards sees American cultural imperialism and profit motive as ruining Canadian hockey. *Hockey Dreams* begins with the assertion that "there are two *theirs* in the game, and ... *our* game doesn't seem to count anymore" (11; italics in original). The first "their" is American capitalism ("business interests in the States" [11]), and the second "their" is the "supposedly more *moral* and *refined*" European game (11; italics in original), contrasted with the more physical, rough-and-ready playing style associated with the Canadian game. Richards positions both of these "theirs" in opposition to the Canadian "our." They are seen as outside interests trying to "defeat" a uniquely Canadian way of thinking, living, and playing. Richards dismisses would-be critics of such arguments as elitist, overly academic, and too consumed by the perennial sense of crisis that has structured Canadian identity debates.[4] Another recent commentator to suggest Canadian symbolic possession of the game has been Roch Carrier, the author of Canada's most widely read and cherished piece of hockey fiction, "The Hockey Sweater," and, latterly, director of the Canada Council for the Arts and national librarian of Canada. Writing on behalf of Library and Archives Canada for a hockey retrospective web page, Carrier argues that "hockey is Canada's game ... [and] surely the most Canadian of metaphors" (2003). Furthermore, "hockey is also the history of Canadians" because it "reflects the reality of Canada in its evolution, ambitions, character, tensions and partnerships" (Carrier 2003). As with Beardsley, Carrier's configuration of the relationship between hockey and history connotes naturalism, ignores context, and assumes that the "reality of Canada" exists (and indeed can be known) as a monolithic and homogenous whole. More prominent than either Richards' or Carrier's accounts, however, has been the Canadian Broadcasting Corporation's (CBC's) *Hockey: A People's History* (2006), a television documentary modelled on an earlier series in 2000, entitled *Canada: A People's History* (note the simple substitution of "hockey" for "Canada"). *Hockey: A People's History* works in the service of the hockey myth by portraying the game as "born of survival against the snow and ice of a Canadian winter," "[uniting] us like nothing else can," and as having "captured the soul of [the] nation" (CBC 2006).

One of the most emblematic moments of the hockey myth's apparent resurgence in recent years has been Canada's double gold-medal performance at the 2002 Winter Olympics. Writing in *Maclean's*, Robert Sheppard cast the victory as a "passing of the torch, not just from hockey legends of 50 years ago to the greats of today, but from one generation of fanatics to the next" (2002, 27). The thrill of 2002 was arguably surpassed at the 2010 Winter Olympics in Vancouver, where Canada repeated its double gold-medal hockey performance on home soil. When Sidney Crosby scored his now-famous golden goal to win the 2010 men's tournament for Canada, Canadians across the country and around the world celebrated with an outburst of flag-waving, anthem-singing, and beer-drinking. "This is the best day of my life," one reveller told a *Toronto Star* reporter: "I think we are going to party all night!" (Aulakh 2010). The proof that hockey continues to resonate deeply with Canadians can be found in the ratings: 26.5 million (approximately 80 per cent of the nation) watched at least part of the 2010 men's gold-medal game, and 16.6 million tuned in for the entire match, making it the most-watched broadcast in Canadian history (TSN 2010). Furthermore,

the 2002 men's Olympic gold-medal game and the final game of the
1972 Summit Series currently rank third and fourth, respectively, in
all-time Canadian ratings, exceeded only by the 2010 men's gold-
medal game and the closing ceremonies of the Vancouver Olympics
(CTV 2010; TSN 2010). More generally in the area of viewership,
Hockey Night in Canada remains the CBC's most consistently well-
watched program (Morrow and Wamsley 2010, 5).

Indeed, Canada's myth of hockey remains alive and well and has
been increasingly mobilized by various ISAs in the service of identity
over the last several years. Recent CBC offerings such as "The
Tournament" (a satirical look at minor hockey culture), *Making the
Cut* (a reality show in which amateur players compete for a chance
at an NHL tryout), *Kraft Hockeyville* (in which Canadian communities compete to demonstrate their hockey spirit in order to win
upgrades to the local arena and host an NHL exhibition game),
Hockey Day in Canada (a documentary celebration of Canadian
hockey that is aired in conjunction with coverage of the one day on
which the six Canadian NHL teams play against each other), *MVP:
The Secret Lives of Hockey Wives* (a prime-time soap opera based
on the lives of professional hockey players and their wives), and,
most recently, *Battle of the Blades* (a reality show that pairs former
professional hockey players with prominent female figure skaters in
a figure-skating competition) have all worked in some way to reinforce the hockey myth. Networks other than the state-funded CBC
have also participated in this trend, as evidenced by Showcase's
"Rent-a-Goalie" (a hockey sitcom set in Toronto) and Global's
acquisition of "Making the Cut" for a second season in 2006.
Television advertisements have also gone along for the ride, perhaps
based on the success of the much-discussed Molson Canadian
"Rant" advertisements (beer commercials appearing in 2000), which
featured an average "Joe Canadian" character delivering an impassioned speech about what it means to be Canadian, the content of
which prominently included hockey. Molson's major Canadian com-
petitor, Labatt's, quickly followed suit with its own hockey-themed
ads, and Tim Horton's, Coca-Cola, Gatorade, and MasterCard (to
name only a few) have also recently mobilized the hockey myth in
their attempts to appeal to Canadian consumers.

The political ISA has also been involved in propounding the hock-
ey myth in increasing and unprecedented ways. The very fact that
Prime Minister Stephen Harper consented to an interview as part of
TSN's coverage of the 2007 International Ice Hockey Federation's

(IIHF's) World Junior tournament conveys both the cultural relevance of hockey (hockey is worth the prime minister's public time) and the "natural" connection between hockey and nationhood (the prime minister is an appropriate choice to offer thoughts and commentary). It would hardly be conceivable for a Canadian prime minister to conduct a similar interview on the occasion of, say, an international volleyball competition. A little more than a month after the World Junior tournament, Harper travelled to Plaster Rock, New Brunswick, to attend the World Pond Hockey Championship, an annual event that draws teams from across Canada and the United States and from as far away as Europe and the Cayman Islands. Harper, whose presence marked the first prime ministerial visit to Plaster Rock since Confederation, dropped the puck for the tournament's ceremonial opening faceoff and attended several of the games. The apparent importance of hockey to Canadian politics is further underscored by the success of several former hockey players as politicians. A former goalie for both Team Canada and the Montreal Canadiens, Ken Dryden, served as a Liberal member of parliament (and at one time was a candidate for leadership of the party) from 2004 to 2011, while a former Toronto Maple Leaf, Frank Mahovlich, was appointed to the senate by Prime Minister Jean Chretien (this after another former hockey star, Jean Beliveau, respectfully declined the honour). Perhaps in an effort to counter Dryden's success as a Liberal, Prime Minister Harper reportedly attempted to recruit Don Cherry to run as a Conservative in the 2008 federal election. The efforts of government to associate hockey with national identity, however, are perhaps most evident on the redesigned five-dollar bill (first appearing in 2001), which now depicts a young boy playing pond hockey and quotes a passage from Carrier's iconic short story "The Hockey Sweater." Although these are only a few such examples, it should be abundantly clear that the political utility of hockey far exceeds that of other Canadian sports, a fact which is further demonstrated by the 2006 World Lacrosse Championship: despite being held in Canada and representing the highest level of international competition in our other official national sport, the tournament went essentially ignored by politicians and pundits alike.

THE CANADIAN HOCKEY NOVEL

Following Anderson and others, this study sees the "political 'rationality' of the nation as a form of narrative – textual strategies,

metaphoric displacements, sub-texts and figurative stratagems"
(Bhabha 1990, 2). Because the "nation [is] conceived in language"
(Anderson 1991, 145), literature has frequently been a site of national imagining. Furthermore, this study focuses specifically on novels
because they allow for a depth and sophistication of representation
that poetry, drama, and short fiction arguably do not. In the words
of literary critic and theorist Jonathon Culler, the novel has been the
literary form that most consistently serves as "the model by which
society conceives of itself, the discourse in and through which it
articulates the world" (1975, 189).

Despite a small but growing number of "non-normative representations of ice hockey in popular culture" (Hewson 2009, 198), several of which will be discussed in this study as a frame of reference,
the vast majority of representations of the game in recent years – be
they in advertising, journalism, television, politics, or elsewhere –
have worked in some way to reinforce the hockey myth. One might
reasonably expect Canadian hockey novels to defy this trend.
Canadian fiction in the last sixty or so years has generally refused to
participate in the exercise of nation-building, to the point where
Imre Szeman has claimed that "there is *nowhere* in Canadian fiction
after World War II a national literature that aspires to write the
nation into existence" (2003, 162; italics in original).[5] Rather than
following the literary mainstream, however, Canadian hockey novels actively involve themselves in the imagining of national community. Almost invariably, the content of this national imagining is
supplied by fidelity to the hockey myth's insistence on hockey-as-
identity and masculinity-as-toughness. Even within the narrower
field of Canadian sports novels and novels that make significant reference to sport, the hockey novels discussed in this study are exceptional in their attempts to foster a monolithic national identity and
safeguard traditional masculinity. Several of these non-hockey sports
novels will be discussed throughout this study to illustrate the relatively unique cultural work that Canadian hockey novels undertake
in the areas of nation and gender.

Canadian hockey fiction has only recently begun to be seen as a
unified genre. To call it this raises immediate questions about inclusion and exclusion. Does the mere mention of hockey in a novel
qualify it as a "hockey novel"? For the purposes of this study, the
answer is no, although several Canadian novels that deal with the
game but shouldn't be considered hockey novels per se are discussed

(Hugh MacLennan's *Two Solitudes*, Mordechai Richler's *The Apprenticeship of Duddy Kravitz*, Morley Callaghan's *The Loved and the Lost*, Ralph Connor's *Glengarry School Days*, Richard Wagamese's *Keeper'n Me*, and Lynn Coady's *Saints of Big Harbour*, among others). The two most important American hockey novels, Don DeLillo's *Amazons* (which was written under the pseudonym Cleo Birdwell; 1980) and Jack Falla's *Saved* (2007), are also discussed as a frame of comparison.[6] A "Canadian hockey novel," then, is one that employs predominantly Canadian characters and/or settings, and in which hockey provides a central basis of plot action and/or a central theme or motif. For reasons of manageability and in the interests of covering a relatively unified field, this study is limited to Canadian hockey novels written in English. Although its intent is not to define a canon or to cover the novels with equal weight, it does attempt to consider most of the available novels in the genre. To set forth this body of literature as a "genre" in the first place is a distinction of subject rather than form, as hockey novels are not governed by expectations of convention or tone to the extent that, say, detective or romance novels seem to be.

Furthermore, this study is focused primarily on adult-oriented hockey novels but draws frequently on children's hockey novels as a frame of comparison. When authors such as Foster Hewitt, Scott Young, and Leslie McFarlane began producing hockey novels for children in the 1950s, 60s, and 70s, they established a tradition that later writers of hockey novels would both work within and react against.[7] There is a great deal of continuity between adult-oriented hockey novels and their juvenile counterparts; for instance, one of the first authors to attempt an adult-oriented hockey novel, Roy MacGregor, whose *The Last Season* essentially created the genre in 1983, went on to become Canada's most commercially successful author of children's hockey fiction with his *Screech Owls* series about a children's hockey team that also solves mysteries and gets into off-ice adventures. But there is an important distinction to be made between children's hockey novels and those that target an adult audience as well. When McClelland & Stewart approached MacGregor in the mid-1990s about creating a children's hockey series to appeal to the "reluctant reader" audience of nine- to -thirteen-year-old boys, they did so on the premise that "nothing's been done for nearly 50 years since Scott Young sat down and wrote *Scrubs on Skates*" (MacGregor 1998). Despite ignoring a significant number of children's hockey novels that were produced around the same time as Young's iconic contributions to the genre, this claim suggests a useful distinction between what might be called a first wave of children's hockey novels – those produced throughout the 1950s, 60s, and 70s by writers such as Hewitt, Young, and McFarlane – and a second wave of children's hockey novels that appeared throughout the 1990s and 2000s by MacGregor, Gordon Korman, Sigmund Brouwer, Jacqueline Guest, and others. Although the second wave of children's hockey novels are exactly contemporary with the rise of adult-oriented hockey fiction, they tend to be more progressive, especially on issues of gender, than both their adult counterparts and their children's antecedents.[8]

Canadian hockey novels are predominantly realist in mode, a fact that both occasions and justifies this study's interest in the ways that hockey is represented. When we encounter hockey in a realist novel, we are really encountering a likeness or an interpretation that inevitably conveys a certain statement, account, or perspective on the "reality" or cultural significance of the game.[9] Commentators on Canadian hockey fiction have notoriously attempted to distance themselves from this fact. For example, Steven Galloway (himself the author of the hockey novel *Finnie Walsh*) writes in his review of John Degen's *The Uninvited Guest* (2006) that Canada has produced "precious few [hockey novels], and even fewer good ones," but that "of the good ones, it is often said that they're not really about hockey at all, that hockey is simply the backdrop for what the story's actually about" (2006, D4). Similarly, Michael P.J. Kennedy begins an academic article in which he surveys the field of Canadian hockey poetry and prose by suggesting that "hockey plays an integral part in the development of plot conflicts, characters and themes which transcend sports" in the texts he discusses, and "can even illustrate the vicissitudes of life" (1998, 81). Putting aside, for a moment, the literary value judgments of "good" and "bad" raised by Galloway, it is striking how thoroughly these commentators attempt to distance themselves from the idea of hockey as being a legitimate subject matter of hockey fiction. Canadian hockey fiction is, in many ways, about hockey: it burgeons with representations of the game that naturalize, normalize, and (albeit less frequently) problematize the range of meanings and identities that hockey has come to encapsulate in Canadian culture (i.e., the hockey myth). The tendency toward realism, then, the primary effects of which are verisimilitude and perceived accuracy of representation, works to further normalize the assumptions and omissions of the hockey myth as it is enacted throughout these novels.

In addition to being predominantly realist, most hockey novels are directed to a popular audience. This is to say that they are, for the most part, relatively absent of "high literature" aspirations such as self-reflexivity, metafictionality, and narrative experimentation. Although they don't aspire to be "high literature," Canadian hockey novels do ask to be taken seriously, a fact that helps to account for both Galloway and Kennedy's effacement of hockey as an actual subject of hockey fiction. Despite the formal entrenchment of cultural studies as a bona fide area of academic research over the past several decades, perceptions of illegitimacy still seem to haunt non-traditional or traditionally "low culture" areas of research. In the case of Kennedy, the argument that hockey fiction deploys the game as an effort to "transcend sports" seems to function as a legitimating strategy for his own critical enterprise: hockey as metaphor is an acceptable configuration in traditional literary criticism, while hockey as subject is not. For Galloway (the actual author of a hockey novel), the pressure to be perceived as legitimate must be even more intense, and helps to account for his separation of "good" hockey novels from "bad" by the degree to which hockey is diminished or posed as "simply the backdrop for what the story's actually about." In other words, hockey fiction is more respectable (read: more literary), when it appears to be about something other than hockey.[10]

Although some hockey novels are more sophisticated than others in terms of narrative complexity, depth of characterization, degree of plot construction, and deployment of techniques such as symbolism, imagery, foreshadowing, irony, etc., the purpose of this study is not to make value judgments, either aesthetic or literary. In the words of Roger Rollin, "to judge a work of Popular Art can only be a way of knowing oneself, which unlike true criticism is a personal rather than public *desideratum*" (1989, 22). On this issue, however, it is worth noting that the novels discussed in this study can be generally divided into one or other of two categories: those that employ irony and those that don't. Novels such as Eric Zweig's *Hockey Night in the Dominion of Canada* (1992) and Don Reddick's *Dawson City Seven* (1993) appear entirely earnest and straightforward in their claims and convictions about the game, while novels such as Wayne Johnston's *The Divine Ryans* (1990) and Paul Quarrington's *King*

Leary (1987) are more ironic and represent the game in ways that alternately work to challenge and reinforce the myth. The latter category are more complex in their representations of the game, in that they simultaneously resist and affirm the myth in various ways; accordingly, this study attempts to acknowledge the possibilities of resistance offered by hockey novels whenever useful and applicable. It is also worth noting that the apparently earnest intentions of a text do not circumscribe the possibilities of reader response, and that some readers may react ironically to a straightforward and affirming treatment of the hockey myth. Nevertheless, earnestness remains a defining feature of many hockey novels, to the point that one novel which particularly attempts to theorize literary hockey writing, Bill Gaston's *The Good Body* (2004), valorizes earnest straightforwardness as the genre's defining characteristic (more on this in chapter 5).

Finally, this study assumes that we have reached a point at which hockey no longer needs to be defended as a worthwhile subject matter for academic inquiry. Admittedly, this is a fairly recent development. According to MacGregor, when *The Last Season* was first published in 1983 "booksellers didn't seem to know where to place it. 'Is it a juvenile book?' 'Is it a sports book?' No one thought to take the damn thing and put it out with new fiction" (1998). MacGregor explains this uncertainty by suggesting that "there has been no acceptance of hockey as part of CanLit" because "CanLit is dominated at an academic level, and academia and sports have never been a congenial mix" (1998). Writing in 1993, Gruneau and Whitson corroborate MacGregor's assessment and identify a sense among academics that "one's work should be about more 'important' things [than hockey]: the constitution, the fur trade, social inequality, poststructuralism, the Canadian novel" (1993, 4). This "higher earnestness" (4) has dissipated somewhat in recent years, as scholars from various disciplines have increasingly turned their attention to the ways in which hockey functions in Canadian culture and society. In fact, with a series of academic conferences and a spate of new scholarly and critical writing on the game over the last decade, hockey scholarship has blossomed into an emerging interdisciplinary field which historian Andrew Holman has referred to as "hockey studies" (2009b, 7).

Despite the modest flourish of hockey scholarship over the past decade or so, relatively little has been said about the ways in which hockey has been represented in Canadian cultural texts. Perhaps this lack of critical perspectives can be attributed to the perceived need to promote and establish the genre of literary hockey writing. Whether or not this is the case, it would be a mistake to presume that criticism and support are mutually exclusive. This study, then, adopts a posture of "critical support" (Kidd 1983, 42), a belief that the best way to encourage the growth and development of Canadian hockey writing is by addressing its ideological shortcomings head-on. This perspective follows several commentators who have challenged the national and masculine identities that traditionally attend the game itself (Gruneau and Whitson 1993; Theberge 2000; Avery and Stevens 1997; Scanlan 2002; Kidd 1983), as well as several commentators who have challenged specific popular and filmic representations of the game that promote certain racial and/or class-based exclusions and stereotypes (Genosko 1999; Gittings 2002; Beaty 2006; Shehid 2000).

Prior to this point there have been two sustained examinations of hockey's representation in Canadian cultural texts. Chronologically speaking, the first of these is Patricia Hughes-Fuller's 2002 doctoral dissertation, "The Good Old Game: Hockey, Nostalgia, Identity." Hughes-Fuller offers readings of texts that have "constructed narratives, created images, and otherwise engaged in discursive practices having to do with the game," from fiction to memoir to television to journalism and beyond (2002, 3). For Hughes-Fuller, the dominant theme in Canadian representations of hockey is nostalgia. The idea of nostalgia factors significantly into this study as well, particularly as it relates to the themes of coming of age and small-town hockey. But while Hughes-Fuller's readings are often valuable and instructive, this study doesn't share her optimism that by participating in the nostalgia of popular hockey texts we are "creating ideal worlds inside our heads" and thus "keeping the possibility of better worlds alive, at a time when there is almost no remaining public or psychic space available to us" (231). Nostalgia, especially as enacted in hockey texts, has a way of glorifying the idealized and simplified past at the expense of the messy and conflicted present. There's a great deal of truth in Ken Dryden's oft-quoted adage that the golden age of hockey was whenever you were twelve years old. But to suggest that a twelve-year-old's beautiful idolatry for Maurice Richard in the 1950s was somehow more pure or authentic than my own childhood adulation of Wayne Gretzky, or that of today's youngsters for Sidney Crosby, is to diminish the wonder and magic that continues to pervade the game for many. As Richard Harrison suggests in the updated edition of his hockey-poetry classic, *Hero of the Play*, "the game just keeps producing image after image" (2004, 13).

More serious than its tendency to efface the present, however, is nostalgia's ability to replicate the assumptions of the past. While Hughes-Fuller's desire to make something productive out of the nostalgia that surrounds Canadian hockey is certainly appealing, doing so seems to wilfully ignore the problems of the hockey myth. We human beings glory in our heroes and legends, our telling of tall tales and lore, and all of these are legitimate functions of hockey writing. But to celebrate hockey in this simple sense of the word "myth" has often meant forgetting or ignoring the fact that hockey also works in the Barthesian sense as a vehicle for ideology. Canadian hockey novels frequently work to normalize and naturalize harmful masculine identities and homogenizing nationalisms that – despite their seeming best intentions – inevitably end up as exclusionary or hierarchical. The way forward toward imagining a "better world" isn't through myth-making or idealizing an imperfect past, but through demystification and commitment to an attainably better present. This study, then, participates in the growing critical project of freeing the game from the harmful and homogenizing assumptions that have often attended it. This does not, as some might conclude, mean divesting hockey of its glorious intensity, nor calling into question the legitimacy of exhilaration it summons in a crowd upon, say, Mario Lemieux's almost magical awareness of an unseen teammate behind him.

The other sustained analysis of Canadian hockey novels is Jason Blake's *Canadian Hockey Literature* (2010), a groundbreaking survey of the genre of literary hockey writing in Canada. Although Blake focuses particularly on novels and short stories, his study covers poetry, drama, and memoirs as well, and frequently branches out into Canada's literary mainstream for relevant tie-ins and examples. Blake's discussion focuses largely on the genre's major themes, all of which are dealt with to some degree in this study as well: national symbolism and identity, the hockey dream, violence, nostalgia, and the game's mediation of family relationships. Although Blake's analysis is generally very good, he often supposes that merely by nature of their fictionality the texts he discusses work to create critical distance between reader and subject. This distance, Blake supposes, inherently illuminates the more sordid aspects of hockey culture, especially the problem of excessive violence, in such a way as to consistently differentiate hockey literature from punditry and juvenilia. Literary hockey writing, however, is an emerging genre and has yet to fully outgrow its adolescence. As noted above, hockey novels employ irony to varying degrees and in some cases see earnestness about subject matter as definitively important. Furthermore, it appears from customer reviews on the Amazon.ca and Chapters. Indigo.ca bookseller websites that many readers take hockey novels at face value in their portrayals of the game and its place in Canadian culture. For instance, a reader named Vanessa (2001) suggested that Galloway's *Finnie Walsh* (2000) "makes me proud to be Canadian" while another reader named Brenda Rigby (2001) stressed the accuracy of the novel's hockey content: "as the mother of two young hockey players – one of which is a goalie – I could appreciate all the stuff the two main characters got up to … I would strongly recommend this book to anyone who appreciates hockey." Readers of other hockey novels emphasized their perceptions of accuracy as well. Referring to Johnston's *The Divine Ryans* a reader named James Carraghe (2001) suggested that "the memories of the Canadiens and the other original NHL teams before expansion, and the frigid days and nights of street hockey are exactly right." Similarly, a reader named Ron (1999) wrote that *The Divine Ryans* "contains truths that's [*sic*] sure to bring back childhood memories of all Canadians." Another reader named Chris Stoat (2007) suggested of Gaston's *The Good Body* that "the [hockey] context is so genuine … particularly for those of us who grew up in the Canada of this era." And these are only a few such examples. Whether or not hockey novels approach their subject with ironic distance, then, many readers seem to accept the representations and values they convey as accurate, appropriate, and distinctively Canadian.

Because *Canadian Hockey Literature* is a broad genre survey that attempts to cover the entire field of literary hockey writing, it is more concerned with breadth than depth. This observation is not intended as a criticism, although the need to cover a large field results in certain surprising omissions such as John Degen's *The Uninvited Guest* (2006) and Judith Alguire's *Iced* (which, as the first adult-oriented hockey novel written by a woman and featuring a female protagonist, is quite significant; 1995). By doing the important work of surveying the broad field of literary hockey writing, Blake's book allows this study to focus particularly on hockey novels. As Angie Abdou

(2010) notes in her review of Jamie Dopp and Richard Harrison's (2009) collection of critical essays *Now Is the Winter: Thinking about Hockey*, the time has come for a book-length study "that provides a deep and extended analysis of the great Canadian hockey novels." Given the recent proliferation of material in this relatively new genre (at least four new hockey novels have appeared since Blake's book went to press), as well as the fact that a hockey novel, Quarrington's *King Leary*, won the 2008 edition of Canada Reads (CBC 2008a), it is safe to say that the genre has come into it's own.[11] Indeed, the popularity of many hockey novels suggests that they are no longer just niche reading. Hockey novels such as *The Divine Ryans*, Bill Gaston's *The Good Body*, Steven Galloway's *Finnie Walsh*, Mark Anthony Jarman's *Salvage King, Ya!* (1997) and Roy MacGregor's *The Last Season* have all been through multiple print runs and at least two editions, and according to the somewhat unscientific sales rankings posted on the Amazon.ca website, *King Leary*'s success in the Canada Reads competition has propelled Quarrington into the company of best-selling authors such as Margaret Atwood and Yann Martel.[12] Furthermore, several Canadian universities and colleges offer hockey literature courses, and Galloway's *Finnie Walsh* has been taught in enough Canadian high schools to justify a teacher's guide published by Raincoast Books in 2005.

A few more words are necessary by way of context. More than 80 per cent of Canada's adult-oriented hockey novels were written after 1990. Of these, more than half were written after 2000. What this means is that the genre of adult-oriented hockey fiction developed largely over the period of time in which Canada's hockey myth was never more widely challenged or less demographically true. Hughes-Fuller refers to this seemingly paradoxical phenomenon as a "return of the nationalist repressed" (2002, 48), which she understands as a sort of "local" backlash against globalization and increased transnationalism. While "the dominant discourse insists we are living in a globalised 'post-nationalist' era," Hughes-Fuller maintains that "nationalistic beliefs and attitudes are still in force" (2002, 51). What follows from this is that "cultural practices, including sport in general and hockey in particular, are as available for deployment in support of nationalist interests as they were in previous periods of history" (51).[13] This explanation certainly seems reasonable, especially in the Canadian context where issues of national identity have been particularly uncertain. As sport-and-recreation scholar Daniel Mason suggests, "in some instances, a consequence of globalizing processes can be the reassertion of local/national cultures" (2002, 140).[14]

For many Canadians, the 1972 Summit Series seemed to confirm Canada's symbolic possession of hockey and cement the incipient spirit of patriotism that was awakened a few years earlier during the nation's Centennial celebrations. But this groundswell of popular nationalism was ultimately to be short-lived; already in 1972 the "imaginary unity" occasioned by the Summit Series was "on the verge of collapse" (Hewson 2009, 190). Perhaps more than anything else, Canada's last-minute victory in the Summit Series illustrates that even the most popular and powerful congruence of nationalistic energies through sport can't provide the basis for a unified and cohesive political vision or sustain the idea of the nation as a monolithic whole. Even as Canadians revelled in the afterglow of Henderson's dramatic goal, "the deconstruction of the post-war Canada that the hockey players defended so fanatically was well under way" (Dowbiggin 2008, 16). With the onset of globalization from without and bilingualism, multiculturalism, and feminism from within, much of what had appeared stable about both Canada and masculinity during the Original Six era heyday of the hockey myth was increasingly called into question in the 1970s and beyond. As the old totalizing conceits of Canadian identity appeared to give way, they were replaced with more diffuse and decentralized notions such as pluralism, diversity, tolerance, and the belief that Canada is an exemplary postmodern or post-national state. The free trade debates of the late 1980s made clear "how deeply fractured the conscious cultural views of Anglophone-Canadian[s]" had become (Davey 1993, 5), and the constitutional squabbles and Quebec sovereignty referendums throughout the 1980s and 90s called into question the continued existence of the Canadian polity itself. In hockey terms, Stephen Hardy and Andrew Holman refer to these years as the "Rise of Corporate Hockey" and note several developments within the game that mirror the larger trends in Canadian society during this time: the internationalization of hockey, the NHL's rise to dominance, the rapid growth of the women's game throughout the 1980s and beyond, and the creation of a "[hockey] world much more fluid and connected than ever before" (2009, 30).

While hockey wasn't immune to the social and cultural changes that shattered the perception of a Canadian monolith throughout the 1970s and beyond, it is nonetheless seen by many as the last

remaining "constant in Canadian life" (Dowbiggin 2008, 19).
Hockey novels are heavily invested in this idea, and suggest that if
any sense of national cohesiveness and distinction remains it is in
our collective obsession with the game. Although most hockey
novels aren't explicitly concerned with the issue of Quebec separatism, they react broadly against the sense of identity crisis this movement has helped precipitate and the attendant suspicion that
national instability might result in heightened cultural susceptibility
to globalization and/or Americanization. Many hockey novels convey the idea that the game ensures a necessary commonality among
Canadians, and cling to the tenets of the hockey myth as a final rem-
nant of stability or as a nostalgic longing for an era in which national and gender identities appeared more certain. As Kelly Hewson
notes, "where the discourse of heritage in Canada proper, with its
official multicultural policies, seems to suggest that 'heritage' always
means coming from somewhere else, heritage in the hockey nation
seems to mean nostalgic repetition" (2009, 194). Steven Jackson
and Pam Ponic have similarly noted that "the increasing impact of
globalization on economics, culture, and people" has led some
Canadians "to draw upon nostalgic visions of an often-mythical
past." Indeed, "it is at such times that romanticized interpretations
of the place of ice hockey … are likely to be reproduced as a means
of forging a dominant form of white, masculine, heterosexist, anglophone, national identity" (Jackson and Ponic 2001, 59).

Beyond suggesting hockey's definitive and consolidating role in a
period of perceived instability, Dowbiggin associates the lack of
cohesiveness and unified vision that he bemoans in contemporary
Canada with a corresponding lack of vision in recent English-
Canadian art. According to Dowbiggin, while

> a linguistically confident Quebec has set one great movie after
> another, one great novel after another, against a canvass of mutu-
> al assumptions and purpose, the ROC [Rest of Canada] has large-
> ly had no compelling backdrop since Paul Henderson's goal
> against which to frame its identity or art … Predominantly,
> English-speaking Canadian authors and directors either reflect
> the immigrant experience (Mordecai Richler, Michael Ondaatje,
> Austin Clarke) or are *auteurs* serving an international market
> (David Cronenberg, Atom Egoyan). What emanates from the
> most celebrated native writers such as Alice Munro, Margaret

Laurence, or Alistair MacLeod is more the internal personal dia-
logue, divorced from mainstream culture. Their Canadian experience is framed less by the ROC than by an isolated sense of self or
landscape ... How can there be a great Canadian novel without a
great Canadian narrative to support it? And how can there be a
narrative without a set of mutual agreements about who we are
or why we exist apart from the United States? (2008, 71–2)

The point of quoting Dowbiggin's argument here isn't so much to
refute his claims as to illustrate one of hockey's significations in
Canada; indeed, much could be said about Dowbiggin's assessment
of English-Canadian art, which is at the very least a problematic
generalization. Like Dowbiggin, many Canadians appear to see
hockey as the last remaining "mutual agreement about who we are"
and believe that this "great Canadian narrative" offers a compelling
reason why Canada should "exist apart from the United States."
Contra authors whose sole concerns are (as Dowbiggin sees it) to
articulate the immigrant experience, indulge in artistic experimentation, or remain mired in their own sense of isolation, hockey purports to be the voice of "mainstream culture" and the "Rest of
Canada" – by which Dowbiggin surely means the white anglophone
lower and middle classes. Hockey novelists, then, appear to speak
for this neglected "mainstream" in their willingness to take up the
important cultural work of unifying and articulating the nation that
other artists – the out-of-touch elites and intellectuals – have shunned
and neglected. Of course hockey's purported ability to speak for
average, everyday Canadians depends in large part the game's supposed working-class origins, an idea in which the hockey myth
remains considerably invested. But to maintain the game as a rightful
domain of the working class obscures the reality that the high costs
of ice time, equipment, and tickets to professional games actually
prevent many Canadians from experiencing hockey directly. While
Blake is correct to suggest that in modern Canada "hockey is not a
social or class statement in the way that golf or skiing is" (2010,
147), first-hand involvement does remain limited to those who can
afford it.

Another way of saying all this is that hockey novels conceive of
themselves as popular novels with populist aims. According to cultural critic John Cawelti, popular fiction tends to "affirm existing
interests and attitudes by presenting an imaginary world that is

aligned with these interests and attitudes" (1976, 35). Popular fiction, then, is inherently conservative, confirming (rather than challenging) prevalent opinion and visiting pertinent themes in comfortable and non-disturbing ways. As such, it is hardly surprising that Canadian hockey novels tend to address cultural anxieties about the loss of a centralized and homogenous national identity by suggesting that in fact these things are still benignly in place in at least one sector of culture: the hockey rink. Several hockey novels play on this sentiment more directly than others in their objections to destabilizing processes and their consequences, especially insofar as these processes appear to diminish the inherent "Canadianness" of hockey. Broadly speaking, then, the conventions of popular fiction help to account for the findings of this study. This is not to say, of course, that conservative form necessarily translates into conservative ideology; again, several of the novels discussed in this study do offer possibilities for resistance or problematize the inherited assumptions of the myth to some degree.

A similar conservatism to that of the genre's perspective on national identity appears to manifest itself in the work of hockey novels to referee gender, in that violent and confrontational sports are one of the few areas of culture that still celebrate the traditional connection between masculinity and toughness. As Hanna Rosin suggests in an article entitled "The End of Men," "man has been the dominant sex since, well, the dawn of mankind. But for the first time in human history, that is changing – and with shocking speed." According to Rosin, we have reached a moment in which "the balance of the workforce [has] tipped toward women, who now hold the majority of the nation's jobs. The working class, which has long defined our notions of masculinity, is slowly turning into a matriarchy, with men increasingly absent from the home and women making all the decisions. Women dominate today's colleges and professional schools – for every two men who will receive a BA this year, three women will do the same. Of the 15 job categories projected to grow the most in the next decade ... all but two are occupied primarily by women."[15] Because "the postindustrial economy is indifferent to men's size and strength" (Rosin 2010), traditional masculinity has appeared less and less applicable in the last thirty or so years. Although it could be argued that every generation experiences its own crisis of masculinity – for instance, modern sport developed in part as a response to the late nineteenth-century perception that men were becoming weak and effeminate – we have entered a period in which the social, cultural, and demographic changes outlined above have combined to make traditional masculinity appear more suspect and less relevant than at any other time.

Masculine identity has often been linked to national identity by way of military service and productive physical labour. Dowbiggin illustrates this thematic marriage in his claim that "outside of hockey" the "ROC" "is now a place largely without a narrative": "the men who perished at the Somme or Cortona or Korea must now be seen as earnest – but gullible – victims of the military–industrial complex. The civilizing effects of British law and custom are now trappings of an imperialist past. Moral equivalence is everything. The result, Mark Steyn writes, is that 'In the space of two generations, a bunch of tough *hombres* were transformed into a thoroughly feminized culture that prioritizes the secondary impulses of society – rights and entitlement from cradle to grave – over all the primary ones'" (2008, 71). According to Dowbiggin and Steyn, the absence of a cohesive and coherent national identity, represented here by Canada's military involvements and historical Britishness, also works to divest men of their ambition, work ethic, and civic duty. Hockey, then, hearkens back to an apparently more stable time in which national identity was clear, decent, and "civilized," morality straightforward, and men were hard-working, tough, and willing to fight to preserve justice at home and abroad.

One final factor should be noted from the outset in explaining the general unwillingness of hockey novels to challenge the terms of the myth. Robert Hollands has suggested that the first wave of juvenile hockey novels tend to reinforce the game's existing attitudes and assumptions in part because many are written by authors who are also hockey journalists. Hockey culture is highly coercive and disciplinary when it comes to policing and reproducing the game's status quo, and one of the ways this plays out is in the efforts of professional owners and management to control the output of hockey journalists through threats of diminished access to players, ostracism within the game's social networks, and even, in some extreme cases, the possibility of being fired. According to Hollands, when hockey journalists try their hand at the writing of hockey novels "elements of this hegemonical process (ranging from editing practices to self-imposed limitations regarding the type of literary devices used) are carried over" (1988, 218). Although this phenomenon doesn't account for the tendencies of the genre as a whole, adult-oriented hockey novelists such as Roy MacGregor, Eric Zweig, Michael McKinley, Adrian Brijbassi, Frank Orr, and Jack Falla are also journalists who cover or have covered the game professionally.

BEER COMMERCIAL NATIONALISM, OR, STRUCTURE VERSUS AGENCY

The central claim of this study is that Canadian hockey novels work to inculcate and enforce the ideas of hockey-as-nation and masculinity-as-toughness. This is accomplished largely through repetitive and exemplary rehearsal of these identities, as well as through arbitrative refereeing of their terms. Nothing particularly complex or theoretical is meant by the word "refereeing." Hockey novels work to adjudicate identity in much the same way as actual referees officiate a game: subjectively, and on the basis of pre-existing rules, assumptions, and norms. Referees deem certain behaviours acceptable while deeming others unacceptable, and hockey novels perform largely the same function in regards to gender and national identities. Although this study rarely refers directly to the following theorists, its understanding of identity formation arises loosely from Althusser, Michel Foucault, and Judith Butler. Althusser sees individuals as interpellated by various ideological forces that contribute to their preferences, opinions, reactions, presuppositions, and so forth, often without their own recognition or intellectual sanction. In other words, if subjects are constantly exposed to certain positions and assumptions, they will eventually come to occupy them. Foucault has similarly suggested that "the individual is carefully fabricated in ... a whole technique of [cultural] forces and bodies" (1979, 217). For Foucault, contemporary society is "disciplinary" in nature in that it regulates compulsory norms, values, and identities by producing cultural subjects who willingly assent to them. Butler has similarly suggested the "coercive and regulatory consequences of representation" (1990, 4). For Butler, categories of identity, especially gender, are inevitably produced and normalized by socially sanctioned roles and expectations. In this framework, the power of representation is such that it *creates* identity through constant and compulsory repetition. Because this repetition is "at once a reenactment and reexperiencing of a set of meanings already socially established" (178), it is important to see the identity performances enacted by these novels as signifying within a network of pre-existing cultural meaning. At the crux of this study's argument, then, is a theoretical intersection between the "coercive representation" proposed by Butler, Althusser, and Foucault and the complex matrices of cultural meaning in which Barthes understands the function of myth.

The suggestion that cultural representations contribute to identity formation brings up an important distinction arising from Anderson's discussion of the novel. For Anderson, it was the ability of the novel to render a convincing simultaneity of events, characters, and geography that initially created the condition of possibility for thinking about nations. Because of its power to enfold "readers ... in the embrace of its omniscient narrative," Anderson suggests that the novel provided a conceptual map which enabled individuals to "'see' or represent their surroundings as part of the larger proto-national or national community to which they belong[ed] as members" (cited in Cheah 2003, 7). In other words, Anderson is more interested in the form of the novel as an analogue for national imagining than in the ways in which the content of the novel contributes to the character of this national imagining. Culler has objected to the way in which "critics, who are interested in the plots, themes, and imaginative worlds of particular novels, have tended to transform [Anderson's] thesis into a claim about the way some novels, by their contents, help to encourage, shape, justify, or legitimate the nation" (48). For Culler, it is important to distinguish between "the novel as a condition of possibility of imagining the nation and the novel as a force in shaping or legitimating the nation" because to elide these categories is potentially to represent the nation as made through novels rather than enabled by them (48).

The root of Culler's argument is that by misreading (or misrepresenting) Anderson, critics have afforded too much power to the ability of novelistic representations to affect the character of the imagined nation. Because this concern is legitimate, it should be clearly stated – following Culler's categories – that the purpose of this study is to expose and illuminate some of the ways in which hockey novels, "by their contents, help to encourage, shape, justify, or legitimate" certain national and gender identities. Although this study suggests the power of representation to rehearse and referee identity, the efficacy of these novels at replicating their assumptions in the real world is difficult to gauge and remains a relatively open-ended question. In other words, this study argues that hockey novels attempt to contribute to cultural attitudes but makes no claims about how successful they are at doing so. It must be remembered from the outset that hockey novels are cultural products as much as they are producers, which is why they must be situated in relation to the larger cultural networks in which they derive their meanings.

All of this leads to the question of subjective agency, which can be addressed by way of example. One of the most frequently aired television advertisements around the time of the 2002 Olympics was a Labatt's Blue beer commercial which featured an impromptu game of road hockey erupting on a busy Canadian street. In the wave of celebrations that swept the nation after Team Canada's gold medal win, the scene from the Labatt's ad actually replicated itself at Winnipeg's most famous intersection, Portage and Main. In response, Sheppard suggested that "it doesn't get more Canadian than that: life imitating a beer commercial" (2002, 27). In one reading, Sheppard is absolutely right. Theodor Adorno and others of the Frankfurt School have tended to see culture as a top–down imposition, functioning to meet various "false needs" (which in this case might be seen as the desire for nationhood, unity, and identity belonging). It certainly wouldn't be difficult to see the beer-commercial facsimile that played out at Portage and Main through the lens of the Frankfurt School: both the content of the impromptu road hockey game and the appropriateness of the game as a response to Team Canada's victory appear drawn directly from the implied nation–hockey–beer triumvirate of the Labatt's ad. If culture is to be seen as a top–down imposition that is passively absorbed by individual consumers, it should hardly be surprising that an actual expression of Canadian popular nationalism would look a great deal like a beer commercial.

The problem with this reading, however, is that it robs the participants in the Portage and Main road hockey game of an important degree of agency. Cultural texts such as the Labatt's commercial are, in the words of cultural theorist John Fiske, "never self-sufficient structures of meanings" so much as they are "provokers of meanings and pleasure … completed only when taken up by people and inserted into their everyday culture" (1989, 6). In this reading, the form of the road hockey game may have been supplied by Labatt's, but the content and signification (to use terms drawn from Barthes' discussion of myth) were supplied by the brazen individuals who actually stopped traffic in one of Canada's busiest intersections for a game of road hockey, no doubt sharing a wildly fun and memorable afternoon. The trajectory of Fiske's argument follows those made by

Raymond Williams and others of the Birmingham School, who see culture as a bottom–up development and theorize the possibility that lived experience can trump external ideological impositions. In this interpretation people actively negotiate the various meanings and representations which culture offers them, accepting these in their entirety or modifying them to create new or partial meanings of their own.

Certainly the most sensible model of identity construction combines the top–down and bottom–up frameworks to meet somewhere in the middle. While it would be a mistake to deny the power of ideology and coercive representation, it would be equally imprudent to suggest that individuals don't play an active role in shaping their own identities. This study, then, works from the premise that an abundance of cultural representations that reinforce the ideas of hockey nationalism and traditional masculinity do not make these things either natural or inevitable. By illuminating some of the ways in which prevailing assumptions about hockey derive their power through cultural networks of representation and signification, the hope is to encourage more inclusive renderings of national identity and to challenge masculine identities that have consistently proven harmful.

"THE SEDUCTIVE PLEASURE OF BELONGING": LIMITATIONS AND APPEAL OF THE HOCKEY MYTH

It is probably evident from my reaction to Canada's 2002 Olympic gold medal win that I have a strong personal sense of the hockey myth's appeal. Having dedicated a great deal of energy to exploring the ways in which the myth attempts to naturalize and normalize certain emotions and opinions that are neither natural, historical, nor ultimately tenable, I'm often surprised by how easily I can slip back into the feeling that my identity as a Canadian is somehow determined by hockey. In this regard, the hockey myth certainly reflects what Rosemary Marangoly George has referred to as the "seductive pleasure of belonging ... in nations" (1996, 200). This study is offered, then, in a spirit of critique which I hope will embody Barthes' notion that in order to be an insightful critic one must first be a fan. I love the beauty and intricacy of the game, as well as the feeling of common ground it can mysteriously create where none seemed otherwise possible. I once spent two full hours of a train ride from Berlin to Amsterdam talking hockey with a woman at least thirty years my senior. She had left Canada as a teenager, and had never been back for any significant amount of time, yet when she saw the Canadian flag on my backpack she assumed we had the game – if nothing else – in common. When I first tell new acquaintances that I'm writing a book about hockey, the reaction is almost invariably excitement. "That's great," they often reply, "are you going to write about such and such a player, or such and such a moment?" Hockey undeniably provides a powerful point of connection for many Canadians, and as such, remains "one of this country's most significant collective representations – a story that Canadians tell themselves about what it means to be Canadian" (Gruneau and Whitson 1993, 13).

But the operative word here is "many." Hockey provides a powerful point of connection for many, not all. It is the tension between unity and division that most frequently informs and underwrites this study's ambivalence about hockey novels and the hockey myth itself. Hockey often works to unite, but we need to recognize that it also works to divide. By appealing to a monolithic cultural whole and purporting to homogenize, the hockey myth inevitably either excludes outright or sets up various hierarchies and gradations of belonging. This is certainly the case with an equation drawn by Kennedy, who is also the editor of two anthologies of hockey poetry and prose, in a short piece entitled "I Am Hockey": "Logic? The logic is there, of course, as any real Canadian would know. Hockey is Canada. I am Canadian. Therefore it is crystal clear ... I am Hockey!" (2005, 22). Kennedy's tautological definition poses hockey not only as the substance of Canadianness, but as a sort of litmus test for determining how real or authentic a Canadian might be. What would a false Canadian or a lesser Canadian look like? In Kennedy's framework, it would be someone who doesn't like hockey. This study shares in the concern that globalizing processes are effacing any significant sense of the Canadian "local," an anxiety which, again, also informs many hockey novels. But while this study agrees with D.M.R. Bentley's conviction that "a tolerant and protective nationalism, a nationalism rooted in local pride and responsibility, can provide the wherewithal to counter a multi- and supra-national capitalism that knows no loyalty to particular places and their inhabitants" (1992, 7), it doesn't accept the myth's insistence that hockey provides the substance of such a nationalism. Hockey, then, may well be seen as a constitutive part of the subjective Canadian experience, but shouldn't be rendered as compulsory or as a marker of legitimacy.

As with the issue of national identity, the hockey myth's appeal in terms of gender should be recognized from the outset. As a

fast-paced and highly physical game, hockey has often been associated with a version of masculinity that depends on aggression,
determination, endurance, and strength. Hockey's toughness is part
of what makes the game so compelling, but it also leads to excessive
roughness and harmful attitudes and behaviour. Alison Pryer
describes her intermingled sense of "horror and excitement, shame
and ... passion and aliveness" (2002, 73) upon watching a hockey
fight, articulating a complex and ambiguous tangle of emotions that
many fans and casual watchers of the game have likely experienced.
Pryer understands her mixed emotions about the fight by asserting
the ability of spectators to "desire certain gender performances and
derive pleasure from them even while they perpetuate social and
psychic violence" (74). Following Pryer, then, part of this study's
purpose is to explore "the ways in which" people can be "constituted by precisely those discourses and practices that [they] seek to
oppose" (76). Unlike many critical accounts of hockey violence,
however, this study doesn't object to violence itself but to the gender
performance such violence is often seen to represent.

   Sport sociologists often use a typology devised by Michael Smith
in *Violence and Sport* (1983) to classify athletic violence. Smith separates in-game violence into four distinct categories: brutal body
contact (physical contact within the game's accepted rules and culture), borderline violence (practices that violate the rules but are
nevertheless present – and even encouraged – within the culture of
the game), quasi-criminal violence (violence that violates the formal
rules or informal norms of the game), and criminal violence (violence that transgresses criminal law; this is the rarest form of athletic
violence and is for the most part universally condemned). In his philosophical treatise *In Praise of Athletic Beauty*, Hans Ulrich
Gumbrecht makes the case that brutal body contact – the act of
"occupying or blocking space with bodies ... against the resistance
of other bodies" (2006, 64) – is essential to most team sports.
According to Gumbrecht, without body contact or the threat thereof, athletic grace and beauty could not exist. Indeed, the "elegance of
the greatest players in basketball or soccer [and we may well add
hockey to this list] also depends on adeptly evading or bypassing the
violence of those who want to stop them" (64). Part of the appeal of
violent sport, then, objectively speaking, necessarily consists in the
dramatic and aesthetic possibilities that Smith's most basic level of
violence represents. In this framework it is entirely possible to view
hockey violence in gender-neutral terms. This study's conclusion

about gender, then, is not to deny the appeal of toughness or to argue that all levels of violence should be removed from the game, but to disrupt the idea that these things are contingent on or constitutive of masculinity.

One further clarification is necessary on this issue. This study parts ways from Butler in the conviction that gender is far more socially determined than sex. Butler leaves room for the idea that identity is determined by sex as well as by gender, but sees sex as similarly constituted by discourse to the point of questioning "the immutable character of sex" and speculating that "perhaps this construct called 'sex' is as culturally constructed as gender; indeed, perhaps it was always already gender, with the consequence that the distinction between sex and gender turns out to be no distinction at all" (1990, 10–11). Simply put, this seems to be a naive denial of the biological differences between men and women. To borrow again from Bentley, this study assumes "that men and women are what they are because of biology (male, female) and social construction (masculine, feminine)" and that "in different proportions, we are each given and make our identity, our character, and the way in which we are perceived" (1992, 6). Gender theorist and literary critic Susan Gubar articulates this principle more specifically for the context of university sports: "most people are driven by female and male hormones that explain why separate but equal sporting events continue to be funded by ... members of the university athletic committee who understand that all but a few (highly unusual) women cannot possibly compete with men in integrated tennis matches, soccer leagues, and hockey tournaments" (Gubar 2006, 61). In the sporting context, then, according to Gubar, "it would be sexist to ignore [the] biological differences between men and women" (61). It is difficult to deny that men tend to be physically bigger and stronger than women. Where we often go wrong, socially and culturally, is to see men as "better" or "more athletic" on the basis of this fact. To summarize, then, by way of conclusion, the hockey myth is problematic both as a totalizing gesture towards national identity and as a normalizing gesture towards traditional masculinity. The deeper I've gotten into this study, the more I've been surprised by my capacity to be troubled by the myth's exclusions, elisions, and transgressions, while remaining captivated and delighted by the game itself. In the words of Don Gillmor, myth can "be the distillation of a sacred truth or simply a lie repeated often enough. Hockey is a bit of both" (2005, 93).

1

Hockey and Canadian Identity

Steve Lundin's *When She's Gone* (2004) is the story of two hockey-loving brothers from Winnipeg, Mark and Jack, who embark on a canoe trip across Britain to deliver Mark to a tryout for a professional team in Cardiff.[1] Along the way the family's history unfolds, as well as the brothers' various philosophies on life, love, history, and hockey. Much of this involves Mark and Jack trying to come to terms with the relocation of their beloved NHL team, the Winnipeg Jets, to Phoenix, Arizona and their sense of the underlying selfishness and greed that they perceive to be destroying Canadian hockey. Interspersed throughout the narrative are several fantasy sequences that retell Canadian history *as* hockey and invent various hockey creation myths (the origins of skating, sticks, etc.) that attempt to recuperate a lost or inaccessible "pure" essence of the game. This "Platonic form" of hockey (as the narrative characterizes it) is described most fully in the novel's final fantasy sequence:

> Somewhere in the Canadian bush, on a frozen pond surrounded by trees where the mist hangs knee-deep, a kid plays hockey. He plays the game against the forces of nature, turning the laws of physics into poems.
>
> Occasionally some passer-by stumbles into view, and watches in reverence, the slow realization that the kid is more than just a kid, the game more than just a game, the love more than just love. The witness sees sport without a coin to its name.

The passer-by moves on after a time, because like staring into the burning bush you shouldn't look too long, and never tell anyone anything, ever. But the rest of that person's day is measured from that single point, and it's there in the eyes of the chosen at every game, in every arena, every stadium, a shimmering glimmer of sadness. (189)

Several features emerge in this passage that will become abundantly familiar over the course of this chapter. First, the pure essence of the game is rendered as Canadian, notably taking place in the "Canadian bush." Second, it occurs on a frozen pond in an intimate natural setting and appears as a natural extension of this setting. Finally, it is associated with childhood and innocence, and, as such, is "without a coin to its name." Taken together, these features – Canadianness, northernness, and innocence – comprise the national identity component of the hockey myth as it is enacted in Canadian hockey novels, and are often intimately linked.

In the fantasy sequence quoted above, Mark, the narrator of *When She's Gone*, ascribes religious significance to hockey, both through his allusion to the burning bush in Exodus 3 and through his hint at a form of predestination that governs which "chosen few" will glimpse or perceive the game's mythic essence. It is certainly no coincidence that hockey has often been referred to as Canada's national religion.[2] As Kidd and Macfarlane put it, "to speak of a national religion ... is to grope for a national identity" (1972, 4). According to Anderson, "nationalist imaging ... suggests a strong affinity with religious imagining" because it attempts to accommodate "the overwhelming burden of human suffering" and "responds to obscure intimations of immortality" (10–11). Hockey novels often propose the game as an answer to these specific spiritual dilemmas, and reinforce the religious tenor of such characterizations, by seeing the game as ontologically inevitable and spiritually meaningful. By ascribing religious significance to the game, hockey novels work in the service of cultural nationalism by casting hockey as a central element of Canadian identity. Furthermore, the hockey myth is simultaneously at its most compelling and unobtrusive in its religious aspects, the cultural work of such representations being in part to efface the fact that cultural work is indeed being accomplished.

On a readily apparent level, hockey novels address the issue of immortality through their veneration of tradition. In the framework of the hockey novel, former players are invariably preserved beyond their physical passing by statistics and memorable achievements. Heaven, in this configuration, is figuratively the Hockey Hall of Fame, which is also a "place of worship" of the game's anointed heroes. More complicated, however, is the tendency of hockey novels to create a fictional reality in which it is ontologically inevitable for Canadians to play, practice, and/or venerate hockey, simply because it is natural that they should do so. *When She's Gone* begins with the apparently uncomplicated suggestion that "being Canadian I'm thinking about hockey" (9). Why think about hockey? Because I am Canadian. The connection appears to be both natural and obvious. Canadians think about hockey simply because that is what Canadians think about. Hockey novels tend to hold this "truth" as self-evident, an inalienable first principle that doesn't need to be substantiated or justified. In the words of Whitson and Gruneau, cultural myths often appear true simply "because 'everybody' knows [them] to be true as a matter of belief or common sense" (2006, 4). Hockey novels tend to see the game as "more than just a game" (as Lundin puts it in the passage quoted above), ascribing spiritual significance to what is – objectively speaking – an ostensibly material practice. For Lundin's narrator, the Canadian love of hockey is animated by transcendental yearning and loss, the desire to capture an ultimately unattainable and otherworldly perfection. While this may be dismissed as simply a complicated and quasi-mystical form of nostalgia, the essentially religious supposition of a transcendental order effectively performs what Anderson calls "the magic of nationalism" in turning "chance into destiny" (1991, 12). By suggesting this vision of Canadian pond-hockey purity as the perfect spiritual form of a flawed material reality, Lundin sets forth a world in which hockey and Canadianness are ontologically synonymous, or, at the very least, intended as such by the divinity that shapes our ends. The fictional reality of *When She's Gone*, then, is one in which Canadians are drawn to hockey by either divine predetermination or natural design. The seemingly organic inevitability of this connection appears as a matter of truth, when in fact it is a matter of belief: because the "truth" of hockey's ontological inevitability remains ultimately unverifiable, the "reality" presented by the novel must be accepted on faith. By presenting the connection between hockey and Canadianness as an effect of nature rather than culture, Lundin's narrator "abolishes the complexity of human acts ... gives them the simplicity of essences ... [and] organizes a world which is without contradictions because it is without depth, a world wide open and wallowing in the evident," as Barthes describes the myth-making process (1972, 143). By effacing the cultural processes that have in reality come to determine hockey's association with Canadian identity, *When She's Gone* suggests a fictional reality in which these things appear naturally – and, as such, inevitably – connected.

By representing hockey as ontologically Canadian, hockey novels also purport to answer the existential problem of suffering by accounting for human teleology and proposing examples of the "good" or "meaningful" life. Ray Robertson's *Heroes* (2000) is particularly interesting in this regard. *Heroes* is narrated by Peter Bayle, a doctoral candidate in Hellenistic philosophy who is undergoing a massive existential crisis and trying to come to terms with the suicide of his sister Patty (the entire narrative is an imagined monologue in which Bayle addresses Patty, although the fact of her death isn't revealed until near the end). In an attempt to shake Bayle out of his existential rut, his girlfriend, Jane, the editor of a prominent Canadian magazine, decides to send him to "an American prairie state" to "[write] an article on the minor-league hockey boom in the mid-western and lower United States" (21). Bayle makes it clear that he isn't qualified to undertake the assignment, but Jane insists, establishing his credentials as follows: "you're a Canadian male between the ages of 7 and 84 so you obviously know the game" (24). Jane's argument here is rhetorical and obviously sarcastic, but her logic prevails; Bayle is sent off on an assignment he doesn't feel qualified to undertake, but eventually rediscovers his love for the game and realizes that hockey is the one teleological imperative that can give his life meaning.

The major philosophical and theological concerns of *Heroes* are the existential problems arising from human suffering and banality. What makes life meaningful? What gives humanity purpose? How can continued existence be reconciled to the reality of suffering? Bayle's provisional answer at the beginning of the novel relies on the stoicism of the third-century sceptic, Sextus Empiricus, who advocated the suspension of emotion and judgment as a means of achieving existential equilibrium. At one point in the story Bayle's doctoral supervisor tells him "you're either the coolest, most cocksure sonofabitch I've ever met who just might be Empiricus incarnate, or you really just don't care" (288). The events of the plot, however, show that neither of these assessments is ultimately true; as Bayle travels to the unnamed American town to write his hockey article, he quickly becomes involved in a complex web of character relationships that expose his inability to either remain apathetic or suspend emotion indefinitely. As Bayle is forced to grapple with the failure of his own philosophy, he begins to contemplate two alternative existential answers embodied by his sister Patty and his father Walter.

Patty tries to find meaning in life by passionately dedicating herself to a series of successive interests: "the Kennedy Conspiracy Thing," "the Punk Thing," "the Ecology Thing," "the British Thing," and finally "the Catholic Thing" (14, 15). The problem for Patty, however, is that the all-consuming passion that underwrites her successive interests can't sustain itself for very long before depression and despair inevitably creep back in. During the eventual aftermath of her "Catholic Thing," Patty procures a collection of art supplies (portending the onset of an "Art Thing") only to have them stolen from her on the subway. When she arrives home, she barricades herself in her room and eventually commits suicide. The existential philosophy embraced by Bayle's father is similar to the one that ultimately fails Patty, but with the all-important difference that Walter has discovered the one "Thing" that is ultimately able to make his life meaningful: "For thirty-two years Walter Bayle put in his forty hours a week at Ontario Hydro because it paid the bills. End of story. What he lived for, though, were his Maple Leafs, Bayle's father's love of Toronto's home-town team making its way into nearly every life lesson the old man sent Bayle's way" (40). When Walter is diagnosed with prostate cancer and forced to come to terms with "partial incontinence and impotence," Bayle is struck by his father's resilience in cheering the Leafs through a playoff push: "even with a three-inch plastic catheter inserted inside his penis and a urine bag taped to his thigh, Bayle's father had never seemed to his son more alive" (167). When Walter Bayle eventually dies, it is while recuperating from an operation during the summer months when he doesn't have "the Leafs to wake up to every day to help keep his mind off a future filled with not knowing whether a can of cold beer on a hot summer day after cutting the grass was going to soil his pants or whether or not he was ever going to be able to make love to his wife again" (171). For Bayle's father, then, hockey provides passion and purpose, or, at the very least, a necessary distraction from the heartache and thousand natural shocks of human existence.

By the end of the story this has become true for Bayle as well.
When Bayle returns home to Canada he is promptly hospitalized for
complications stemming from a bout of pneumonia. After a three-
week hospital stay he returns home to his mother's house to recover,
and begins watching hockey again: "Bayle had become a fan again
... the empty expression stuck to his face since he'd gotten out of the
hospital seemed to say that he watched hockey with no more interest
than he did MuchMusic and the black-and-white late-night double
features on CBC. But his mother could see the slow signs of change in
her son as the days began to get longer outside and the Leafs briefly
flirted with the last Western Conference playoff spot" (312–13).
Eventually the transition is complete, and Bayle's mother tells her
son that his reaction to Leafs games has become the same as his
father's: "he [Walter] *would* look so happy. Just like a happy little
boy. Just the way you looked now" (313; italics in original).

By the end of the novel, then, Bayle has learned the existential
necessity of being a fan. According to *Heroes*, the power of hockey
is such that it can capture interest, animate existence, and supply a
sufficient measure of happiness and joy as to make life worth living.
But Bayle has also learned the lesson his sister could not, that when
this happiness seems to evaporate you need to "be like a smart goal
scorer in a ten-game scoring slump: keep skating hard, keep going to
the net, keep your stick on the ice ... [because] sooner or later the
puck's going to go in the net and the red light is going to come on
and the crowd is going to rise to their feet and all of a sudden your
arms and stick will be raised in the air over your head in celebration
just when thirty seconds before you wondered – you really, really
wondered – if you'd ever feel this good again" (346). In other words,
Bayle has realized that when life seems joyless and bleak people
need to keep on living, working, trying, hoping, and, most importantly in the framework of the novel, watching hockey. Hockey is the
crucial piece of the existential puzzle in *Heroes* because it fulfills an
unstated teleological imperative for both Bayle and his father.
Although *Heroes* doesn't explicitly rule out the possibility of soteri-
ological schemas other than hockey, the game is certainly privileged
as the only "Thing" that actually succeeds in making life worth living. W.H. Auden has famously suggested that "we must love one
another or die" ("September 1, 1939"; [1940] 1996, 106). In simplest terms, *Heroes* can be said to rephrase Auden's maxim for the
Canadian context: "we must love to watch hockey or die." The

religious tenor of this "imagining" is such that it attempts to account for the very nature of reality, and, in doing so, purports to provide humanity (in this case specifically Canadians) with a sense of teleological purpose.

While *Heroes* is both an obvious and extreme example, the idea that Canadians are somehow teleologically intended for hockey (and vice versa) underlies many of the novels to be discussed in this study. This idea remains surprisingly evident in the larger discourse of Canadian hockey as well. For instance, before the men's gold medal game of the 2010 Vancouver Olympics an ordained Protestant minister, John Van Sloten, wrote in the *Vancouver Sun* that "hockey is a unique product of Canada's divine cultural calling (one of its best). This game is part of what God created us for, a cultural gift that we made, mastered, and now share with the world. It's a gift that gives us life" (2010). One of the problems with this way of thinking is that it elevates hockey beyond any reasonable expectation of what the game might actually hope to accomplish. A less optimistic reading of *Heroes* would be that hockey doesn't give us meaning so much as distract us from the existential fear that there is no ultimate meaning or that life is little more than an unrelenting succession of pain, injustice, and unfulfilling work. At best, then, hockey is a pleasant distraction, while at worst it amounts to a false god. Because while hockey may animate and enhance our time on earth, it doesn't "give us life" as Van Sloten suggests. Furthermore, to depict hockey as "one of the best" products of "Canada's divine cultural calling" sets the bar fairly low in terms of both national ambition and divine expectation. If hockey truly is the most brilliant outgrowth of our collective imagining, our major source of national pride, and the primary way in which we distinguish ourselves from other nations, Canada doesn't seem to have much hope of solving climate change, asserting sovereignty in the artic, creating a viable high-speed rail network, or qualifying for the FIFA World Cup of soccer (to name just a few of the challenges that currently confront Canadians, some admittedly less important than others).[3] By proposing hockey as a natural and inevitable apex of Canadian purpose and achievement, the religious aspects of the myth distract from the possibilities of actual political action and a more meaningful vision of what the Canadian polity might hope to be and achieve.

Another limitation of the myth's religious aspects is that the teleological imperative toward hockey applies specifically to men. Given the ontological maleness of Canadian hockey as Jane defines it at the beginning of *Heroes*, it is hardly surprising that the game doesn't validate Patty's existence in the same way it does her father and brother's. One is left wondering, in fact, what *Heroes* supposes the *telos* of Canadian women might be, or, in existential terms, what "Thing" – if any – would have given Patty purpose? As Jane's comment delineates, the fictional reality presented by Canadian hockey novels sees the game as an exclusively male domain. Masculinity has historically been tied to the discourse of hockey nationalism in Canada, and with only three exceptions – Alguire's *Iced*, Cara Hedley's *Twenty Miles* (2007), and Susan Zettell's *The Checkout Girl* (2008) – the adult-oriented hockey novels discussed in this study are written by men and (seemingly) for a male audience. Lynn Coady's *Saints of Big Harbour* (2002) criticizes the connection between hockey and masculinity but isn't a hockey novel in the sense outlined earlier (21), because the game only factors prominently into two chapters.[4] Furthermore, despite billing itself as "an intimate memoir by the first woman ever to play in the National Hockey League," DeLillo's *Amazons* is surprisingly uninterested in exploring the gender politics occasioned by this premise.

Of the female-authored Canadian hockey novels mentioned above, *Twenty Miles* most explicitly recognizes the exclusionary consequences of seeing the game as a religion: at one point in the story Hedley's narrator, Isabel Norris, a first-year student playing for the fictional Winnipeg University Scarlets, exclaims that "I've always known about hockey being the Religion of Canadians. But what about the other side: the hockey atheists, the disbelievers, the half-believers?" (116). Hockey novels leave this question largely unanswered, or, in other words, appear to preach primarily to the converted. F.G. Paci's *Icelands* (1999), for example, corroborates Jane's assessment in *Heroes* of the male inevitability of hockey by identifying a fixed-pattern in the development of Canadian boys: "you learned to talk, you learned to walk, you learned to skate" (212-3). When one of the characters in *Icelands*, Steven Farelli, recalls skating without help for the first time, the focalized narrative explains that he was taking part in "the initiation rite of almost every boy in the country" (212). The taken-for-granted male universality of the Canadian hockey experience in *Icelands* doesn't end with adolescence, however, as Steven suggests that "many would never leave the game, playing in adult leagues until their sticks would be more like canes" (213). As with *When She's Gone* and *Heroes, Icelands* represents hockey as both naturally and inevitably accompanying Canadian men from the cradle to the grave. In fact, it is the lot of the female characters in *Icelands* to accept this seemingly unchangeable reality or grow bitter and joyless in their inability to do so.

"HOCKEY HAS CREATED OUR HISTORY"

Because the ontological connection between hockey and Canadian-ness can't be tested or proved, it is often assumed, illustrated, or accepted simply as a matter of belief. Several hockey novels, however, work to represent the game as inherently Canadian by positioning it alongside formative historical events. Because history is a product of culture rather than nature, the logic of this claim must initially appear counterintuitive. According to Barthes, however, the work of myth is to give "historical intention a natural justification" (1972, 142). For Barthes, the movement from "history to nature ... does not deny things" but rather "makes them innocent ... [and] gives them a clarity which is not that of an explanation but that of a statement of fact." To paraphrase Barthes, then, if I *state the fact* that hockey is synonymous with Canadian history without explaining it, I am very near to finding that it is natural and *goes without saying* (143). By representing hockey *as* history without belabouring the artifice of this representation, hockey novels give the impression of an indubitable march of almost predetermined events that have somehow organically constituted hockey as integral to Canadian identity.

Several of the fantasy sequences in *When She's Gone* attempt to do just this by literally conflating hockey with history. Take, for instance, the following retelling of the Riel Rebellions as a competition between two rival hockey leagues: "Those first leagues were vicious. There were two major ones, the Northwest League and the Hudson's Bay League. Serious rivals and it all came to a head when Louis Riel, left-wing for the Voyageurs, jumped leagues and signed with the Metis Traders right there at the corner of Portage and Main, posing with a buffalo hide signing bonus. The whole territory went up in flames – the Riel Rebellion – culminating in the slaughter of nineteen Selkirk fans. Redcoats came from the east and refereed the mob that strung Riel up and hung him until dead. The Northwest League got merged into the Hudson's Bay League shortly afterward and a troubled peace came to the land" (7). The basis for Lundin's

rewriting of the Riel Rebellions is the competition between the now
defunct WHA (World Hockey Association) and the NHL. To legitimate its existence, the WHA tried to lure high-profile players away
from the NHL with big contracts. The largest such signing was that
of Bobby Hull, who joined the Winnipeg Jets for hockey's first
million-dollar payout (which he accepted on the corner of Portage
and Main). When the WHA eventually folded, several of its teams
(including the Winnipeg Jets) were absorbed into the NHL, signalling
the "troubled peace" mentioned above. What is most striking about
this passage is its ultimate incoherence. The competition between the
WHA and NHL doesn't seem to function as a gloss on the historical
events of the Riel Rebellions or vice versa, nor do these events seem
remotely analogous or engaged in any sort of commentary on each
other. It appears, then, that the "meaning" of this hockey/history
fantasy doesn't result so much from what it *says* as from what it
does. By mapping the story of Bobby Hull and the Winnipeg Jets
onto the Riel Rebellions, Lundin's retellings of history as hockey
don't merely assert the interconnectedness of the two. Rather, they
suggest that Canadian history and hockey are one and the same, or
perhaps, following Beardsley (1987, 36), that "hockey has created
our history."

The same effect is accomplished by several other hockey/history
fantasy sequences in *When She's Gone*, but also by the novel's cover
art. The cover of *When She's Gone* is an original collage by Patrick
Carroll entitled *The Deth of Wulf*, which imitates *The Death of
General Wolfe* (1770) by Benjamin West, a prominent possession of
the National Gallery of Canada. *The Deth of Wulf* depicts Lundin
himself as the slain British General, clothed in a Winnipeg Jets jersey
and clutching an oversized Stanley Cup. Lundin's ersatz Wolfe is surrounded by a hockey referee (who appears to be signalling a "spear-
ing" call), two linesmen, and several prominent Canadian hockey
players and personalities, including Foster Hewitt, Ken Dryden, Mark
Messier, and Guy Lafleur. Other onlookers include a rosy-cheeked
boy on skates (lifted from one of the photos in Dryden and
MacGregor's *Home Game*) and a Native man who also appears in
The Death of General Wolfe, though in Carroll's version he is wearing full hockey gear from the neck down and carries a lacrosse stick
as a gesture to that game's symbolic connection with hockey. In the
background, an American flag is being run up a flagpole in place of a
Canadian flag that seems to be fading into oblivion. Aside from

pointing to one of the main themes of *When She's Gone* – that "American" capitalism is killing Canada's game and that the fans, represented by Lundin himself, are the victims of this atrocity – *The Deth of Wulf* again suggests the essential sameness and simultaneity of Canadian history and hockey. As with the retelling of the Riel Rebellions by way of the NHL/WHA conflict, *The Deth of Wulf* doesn't offer analogical comparison or discernible commentary on either *The Death of Wolfe* or the historical moment on which it is based. Context is important to this interpretation, however, as Carroll's collage consciously mimics the myth-making strategies of Lundin's novel. If one were to encounter *The Deth of Wulf* in a gallery space, for instance, rather than as the cover for *When She's Gone*, the piece could easily be seen as questioning the Canadian deification of hockey.[5]

Although *When She's Gone* is uniquely explicit in its efforts to combine hockey and history in the creation of myth, other hockey novels also work to naturalize the connection between hockey and national identity by representing the game in association with formative Canadian events. Especially noteworthy in this regard are Zweig's *Hockey Night in the Dominion of Canada* and Reddick's *Dawson City Seven*, both of which are historical novels set around the beginning of the twentieth century, a time in which events such as the Boer War and the First World War were raising public debates about Canada's status as a distinctive nation within the British Empire. While many English Canadians wanted their nation to be active in the British Empire and supportive in Imperial conflicts and defence, many French Canadians opposed these ideas and argued for a nationalism based on independence and self-interest. *Hockey Night in the Dominion of Canada* revolves around the four star players of the famous Renfrew Creamery Kings (aka Millionaires) of the pre-First World War era of professional hockey, Frank and Lester Patrick, Cyclone Taylor, and Newsy Lalonde. The novel is mainly concerned with the lives and development of these players, as well as with multimillionaire financier Ambrose O'Brien's formation of the National Hockey Association (the precursor of the NHL). To the historical skeleton of Renfrew's bid for a Stanley Cup challenge in 1909–10, Zweig appends a fictional plot to assassinate the Canadian prime minister, Sir Wilfrid Laurier, which the Renfrew players discover and foil using their hockey skills (Newsy Lalonde actually cross-checks the would-be assassin). This fictional intervention of hockey in history appears to signify the cultural relevance of hockey in the process of Canadian

nation-building; in Zweig's characterization, it is hockey players acting on their hockey skills that are able to determine the national
course by saving a prime minister who, in the framework of the
novel, is able to effect a golden age of national consensus. With its
clear reference to *Hockey Night in Canada*, Zweig's title emphasizes
the transitional status between Dominion within the British Empire
and independent nation that the novel explores.

Hockey Night in the Dominion of Canada represents the turn of
the twentieth century as a time of great hope for Canada. Each chapter opens with an epigraph from a politician, journalist, or theorist
of the day, most of which are taken from Laurier and Borden's
exchanges in the House of Commons over the Naval Debate (the
debate over whether Canada should build a navy to support Great
Britain or whether such a navy should be used at Canadian discretion). The epigraph to Chapter 10 is Laurier's famous declaration
that "as the nineteenth century was that of the United States, so I
think the twentieth century shall be filled by Canada." Laurier characterizes his expectation as applying to a "United Canada cherishing
an abundant hope for the future" (quoted on 87). *Hockey Night in
the Dominion of Canada*, then, invests in the nationalist project of
creating a usable history and tradition. Zweig is particularly interested in canonizing certain events as touchstones of Canadian identity (the Boer War, the building of the railroad, western expansion,
the naval debate, etc.), and in linking these events ultimately back to
that overarching signifier of Canadianness, hockey.

Zweig's desire to inscribe a myth of national progress through history is particularly evident in the novel's postscript, "Postgame":
"During Laurier's fifteen years as prime minister, 'The Dominion
from sea to sea' ceased to be a mere geographic or political expression. It became a reality with the construction of two new trans-
continental railway lines. It became a reality with the admission of
Saskatchewan and Alberta to Confederation. It became a reality
with waves of new citizens settling in the West, establishing population centres that rivalled those of the East" (338). While *Hockey
Night in the Dominion of Canada* shows this sort of optimism to be
naive by juxtaposing it with the racism, injustice, poverty, and squal-
or associated with the lower-class and recent immigrant experience
in Winnipeg (which transforms an earnest young immigrant character, Anton Petrovic, into a would-be assassin), the fact that the narrator largely fails to reflect on this contrast testifies to the novel's

foundational investment in myth-making. While the assassination subplot at least provides a tacit criticism of Laurier's "Golden Years," its critical sentiments are effectively whitewashed in the postscript. To conclude, the narrator reflects on the First World War as a sort of national loss of innocence, lamenting the passing of "the carefree days of a more optimistic era, an era when small towns like Renfrew could capture the hearts of a nation in their quest for hockey's most prized trophy, the Stanley Cup" (339). While this passage suggests two categories that will be further developed later, the idea of hockey as small town and nostalgia for the pastoral, it also elides the incongruity between the Petrovic subplot and the concluding characterization of the Laurier years as a golden era. In the end, the righteous indignation of Petrovic against the poverty and discrimination he faces appears to be nullified by *Hockey Night in the Dominion of Canada*'s resoundingly positive attitude toward nation-building, the Laurier era, and the important role of the "great Canadian game" in these events (120).

Dawson City Seven is similar to *Hockey Night in the Dominion of Canada* in that it associates hockey with several formative Canadian identity events, and in its setting at an idealized pre-First World War historical moment. Set against the historical backdrop of the Dawson Nuggets' 1904–5 Stanley Cup bid against the Ottawa Silver Seven, *Dawson City Seven* is the story of Boston Mason, a fictional American character who comes to Canada to seek his fortune in the Yukon gold rush only to end up learning hockey and becoming skilled enough to join the Nuggets' Stanley Cup team. Reddick's use of an immigrant narrator allows him to explore several emerging Canadian myths – or myths of an emerging Canada – from around the turn of the twentieth century. As Mason journeys across Canada by train (a significant gesture in and of itself), he encounters characters who inform him about the importance of the Riel Rebellions, the Yukon Gold Rush, and the Canadian Pacific Railway. Reddick also brings Mason into direct contact with what Mackey has called the myth of the "benevolent Mountie" (34), when upon seeing his first Mounted Police officer Mason reflects that "this was momentous for me, for the Mounties were famous throughout all of North America as disciplined and honest men. This, I was to learn soon, was even more impressive considering the world that swirled around them and the opportunities it created for men in power" (65). *Dawson City Seven* positions hockey alongside these familiar

Canadian icons as an all-consuming cultural passion: "the summer brought an end to hockey in Dawson, but hardly an end to hockey talk. I was amazed at the intense interest it held over the Canadian community, and then amazed at how quickly my own interest developed" (183). The Stanley Cup is seen as a marker of Canadian identity on the same level as the railway or gold rush, inasmuch as it has become "the passion of Canada, already dreamed of by young boys, already fought over by grown men with a ferociousness and desire unknown in baseball or ... football, as popular as they were at the time" (258).

Dawson City Seven also attempts to canonize the Nuggets' journey to Ottawa as a formative national event, although Reddick appears to take slight liberties with the actual route taken by the team.[6] As the Nuggets journey closer and closer to the capital, they find themselves increasingly recognized and welcomed in the small towns along the way. When they reach Kamloops, British Columbia, Mason realizes that "we were heroes on a national scale, all the people in every one horse town across all of Canada rooting for us to beat them damn Silver Sevens" (242). The magnitude of the Nuggets' journey and Stanley Cup challenge is again underscored when Mason learns that the Governor General, Lord Grey, will be in attendance at the challenge matches: "It now was beyond doubt – and comprehension – that our challenge for the Stanley Cup was a national event of epic proportions. The Cup series was already vastly popular, but for some reason this team from the Yukon, the Dawson Nuggets, was making it wilder this time" (247). As if to reinforce Mason's characterization of the Nuggets' Cup challenge as "epic," Reddick's narrative embodies several conventions of the literary epic itself: the treatment of a team of heroes who assume national importance, the national scope of the setting, the metaphor of the game as battle, the arduous journey in pursuit of a "cup," and the gesture toward the power of oral discourse – "hockey talk" – in sustaining the heroic narrative. These epic conventions work to mythologize both the journey and the sport itself; if the epic is, in the words of Ezra Pound, "the tale of the tribe" (1952, 194), *Dawson City Seven* portrays the formative years of the Canadian "tribe" as defined in large part by hockey.

As with the religious aspects of the myth, representations of hockey that attempt to naturalize the game's connection with Canadian history are problematic because they create "a kind of cultural amnesia about the social struggles and vested interests – between men and women, social classes, regions, races, and ethnic groups – that have always been part of hockey's history" (Gruneau and Whitson 1993, 132). The histories of hockey and Canada are not inextricable, nor have they been the steady, progressive, unified, and coherent developments that hockey novels portray. By belying the complicated (and often conflicted) cultural processes by which the game and the nation came to be the way they are, such representations encourage readers to accept the game's status quo and invest in a potentially exclusionary and overly simplistic sense of patriotism. Not all hockey novels, however, attempt to naturalize the game as an element of national identity by associating it with familiar iconography and formative historical events. Frank Orr's *Puck Is a Four Letter Word* (1982), for instance, offers an interesting counterpoint to the specific conflation of hockey and history enacted by *The Deth of Wulf*. When the narrator of *Puck Is a Four Letter Word*, Willie Mulligan, arrives in Quebec City to play against the (now defunct) Nordiques, he notes that "Quebec is a beautiful, historic old spot, a town that has built the new and modern and retained the old in fine coexistence. To Canadian school kids, the place is vivid from the history books from the Wolfe-Montcalm battle on the Plains of Abraham, though Americans never heard of the place" (204). After acknowledging the importance of Quebec to the official versions of Canadian history and tradition that are disseminated in schools – the message of which, that history constitutes "who we are" as Canadians, is earnestly repeated in MacGregor's *The Quebec City Crisis* (1998) when the Screech Owls visit the Plains of Abraham (34) – Willie deflates the seriousness of the myth with a rather crude joke: "Quebec City is regarded as the best 'wool market' in the NHL ... it's appropriate because Quebec was once the center of the fur trade in North America, specializing in beaver. It's nice to know old traditions still exist" (204). In Willie's configuration, the old tradition of the fur trade – another recognizable piece of Canadian iconography – has been replaced with the opportunity to meet enthusiastic groupies, "wool" and "beaver" both serving as off-colour slang for the female genitalia. Not to belabour the obvious, the joke trades on the double meaning of the word "beaver" as it signifies in the historical fur trade and in the context of modern sexual slang. Willie's wry suggestion that "old traditions still exist" puts the two into juxtaposition, implicitly making light of the historical myth-making effected in other hockey novels. While *When She's Gone*, *Hockey Night in the Dominion of Canada*, and *Dawson City Seven* earnestly attempt to characterize the game as Canadian by associating it with Canadian history, *Puck Is a Four Letter Word* reduces the historical myth-making impulse to an off-colour joke. It is also worth noting that this passage reduces the role of women in hockey to that of sexual object, a representation that is certainly in keeping with *Puck Is a Four Letter Word*'s general portrayal of women and an issue I will return to later.[7]

"HOCKEY EQUALS FROZEN RIVERS, WIND AND LAUGHTER"

Another way in which hockey novels work to represent the game as both naturally and inherently Canadian is by casting hockey as a symbolic extension of landscape and northernness. Many commentators have seen setting and geography as major determinants of Canadian identity. Probably the most famous articulation of this principle has been Northrop Frye's (1971) suggestion that the Canadian sensibility "is less perplexed by the question 'Who am I?' than by some such riddle as 'Where is here?'" (220). In the framework of the Canadian hockey novel, the Canadian "here" is the frozen pond, river, lake, or homemade rink. The idea that hockey is a natural extension of the Canadian landscape is one of the central tenets of the hockey myth. As popular historian Daniel Francis puts it, "hockey is our game not just because we hold the patent on it but because it embodies the northern landscape. Whether it is played on frozen ponds or indoor arenas, it speaks to us of winter, Canada's season. The blank expanse of ice represents the vast, frigid, dispassionate wilderness, or so the metaphorically-inclined tell us, and every game dramatizes the struggle for survival in such a difficult land" (1997, 167). Indeed, Canadian hockey "has been widely understood as connoting a kind of happy naturalism, a direct expression of our ability to survive, indeed to thrive, in an inhospitable land of ice and snow, long winters, and vast open spaces" (Whitson and Gruneau 2006, 1). Whitson and Gruneau attribute this to "innumerable images of apple-cheeked boys on frozen ponds, and ... a host of literary references to hockey's roots in the Canadian climate and landscape" (1). Although the description of "apple-cheeked boys on frozen ponds" is a rhetorical exaggeration, the characterization remains applicable to the many hockey novels that cast the game as a natural extension of Canada's northern climate, a continuation of geography by other means.

In effect, such scenes offer a kind of winter pastoral vision. Certainly the pastoral is central to Frye's mythic understanding of Canadian sensibility. In *The Bush Garden*, Frye suggests that "what may be called ... a pastoral myth, the vision of the social ideal" lies "at the heart of all social mythology": "The pastoral myth in its most common form is associated with childhood, or with some earlier social condition – pioneer life, the small town, the *habitant* rooted to his land – that can be identified with childhood. The nostalgia for a world of peace and protection, with a spontaneous response to the nature around it, with a leisure and composure not to be found today, is particularly strong in Canada" (1971, 239). Two features of Frye's description are especially apparent in Canadian hockey novels. First, hockey is often characterized as a "spontaneous response to nature" inasmuch as it exists at its "purest," most "natural" form when played outdoors on the lake, pond, river, or homemade rink. Second, this "pure" state of hockey is often associated with childhood and the innocent joy of play.

In Paul Quarrington's *Logan in Overtime* (1990), the hockey-playing title character, Logan, encounters an absurdly intellectual eleven-year old, Anthony O'Toole, who analyzes hockey in terms of mathematical theorems. Logan tries to teach Anthony to experience the elemental joy of hockey by imagining a frozen-river scene with the current NHL leading scorer, playing the game as a young boy. Anthony's thought experiment works, and when he watches Logan play later in the story Anthony realizes "sudden insight into this equation: hockey equals frozen rivers, wind and laughter" (169). It is by evoking hockey's proximity to nature that Logan helps Anthony understand hockey as it is meant to be experienced: as a feeling or sensation, a natural occurrence more primordial than reason. In other words, Anthony learns that it is "unnatural" to analyze the game with calculations and statistics, or that, as Richards puts it, hockey "is the non-intellectual impulse for life" ([1996] 2001, 73).

The general applicability of Anthony's "equation" to Canadian hockey fiction is striking. Pond hockey is repeatedly represented as, to reiterate Frye, "a spontaneous response to ... nature" and a "world of peace and protection" in which childhood (and childlike) innocence can be realized and celebrated. The first known reference to hockey in Canadian literature – which occurs in Thomas Chandler Haliburton's *The Attaché; or, Sam Slick in England* (1843) – describes boys "hollerin' and whoopin'" as they play "hurley on the long pond on the ice" (305). Many of the first wave children's hockey novels produced throughout the 1950s, 60s, and 70s echo this characterization of pastoral purity, although they tend to see pond hockey as the earliest stage in a player's development on the way to the ultimate achievement of becoming a professional. Foster Hewitt's *"He Shoots, He Scores!"* (1949), for instance, depicts the outdoor rink as a magical place where young players can "dream hockey, then work [their] hardest to make these dreams come true" (43). While adult hockey novels tend to be less optimistic about professional and organized games, they depict the outdoor rink as a place of natural purity, childhood (or childlike) innocence, and good-hearted fun. The unnamed narrator of Pete McCormack's *Understanding Ken* (1998), for instance, contrasts his stressful experience playing organized minor hockey with his love for "skating at night with the sky above me as black as a puck with sparkles on it" (118). *Dawson City Seven* notes the "lovely, lovely feeling" of skating outdoors and "the perfect joy this game gave us" (129). *When She's Gone* imagines "some quiet kid with the dream he'd make real skating alone under stars diamond sharp in brittle plastic shattering cold and a few years later he steps out onto the ice at Maple Leaf Gardens in Toronto or the Forum in Montreal and it's for real, but those cold nights under the stars stay inside him, joy-filled, the memory of paradise and unsoured dreams" (22). Paci's *Black Madonna* (1982) depicts its protagonist, Joey Barone, dreaming of skating on the "limitless expanse of a lake as huge as Superior" on which he "[moves] in hard sure strides against the Northern expanse," feels "invincible," and enjoys the "incredible beauty" of the ice (57). Later in the story the boundless feeling of skating in this dream is contrasted with the constraints of the indoor rink: "The clean smell of the ice. The sound of his blades cutting the surface. The smoothness under his feet that could lead him anywhere he wanted to go. Only the boards could restrain him. And when he unexpectedly found himself crashing into the wood he felt cheated that there wasn't so much room as in his dream" (87). A similar preference for the outdoors occurs in Paci's *Icelands*, when one of the characters, Mike Horseford, plays shinny "at night, with the black sky beyond the lights, and a soft snow falling" (51) at the "outdoor rink ... where he felt most alive" (88): "He just never got the same feeling indoors as he did at the Mimico out-door rink, where he played under the stars. There it was just the clean smell of the ice that he liked so much. Sometimes he thought he had ice in his veins. There was something about the feel of the ice under his skates and under his stick. It was a different world. A place where he was more powerful, more joyous. A place where he could get bigger and bigger and still be a kid playing at a kid's game" (147–8). Such passages continually rehearse the idea that hockey is, at heart, a childhood expression of energy, exuberance, and fun, and that the fullest experience of these values can only occur in an out-door and natural setting. For characters like Mike Horseford and the unnamed narrator of *Understanding Ken*, the outdoor rink is a place to play without pressure or concern, mindful only of the joy of physical exhilaration. As Blake suggests in his description of Horseford, "when not playing organized hockey, Mike can act like the child he is" (2010, 68). In this sense, the rink becomes a "world of peace and protection" where characters can escape from or deal with "real-life" concerns such as an absent father and alcoholic mother (in the case of Mike Horseford) or an increasingly nasty parental divorce (the narrator of *Understanding Ken*).

Narrative reminiscences and re-enactments of pond hockey purity also frequently connect adult characters to the "true spirit" of the game. In *Puck Is a Four Letter Word*, Willie Mulligan is told by one of his NHL teammates that "you always look like you're ten years old and out on the frog pond for shinny with the farmers" (87). The nar-rator of Bill Gaston's *The Good Body*, an aging minor-league profes-sional player who refuses to admit he has been diagnosed with multiple sclerosis, reflects that "the pond gives you magical speed, and the faster you go the bigger the thrill" (190). In *Dawson City Seven*, Boston Mason suggests that "the sport captures your mind and soul … because of the sheer joy of playing" (183). For the pro-tagonist of Zettell's *The Checkout Girl*, a twenty-year-old woman trying to sort out her complicated vocational and romantic situa-tions, skating is a place where "uncertainty and sadness evaporate. There are no tears on the ice, only movement, only this foot and this foot and this" (210). Steven Farelli opines in *Icelands* that "the coun-try's psyche was formed by hockey … there was something in the game that made the blood race, that made the knees shake – even if you were just watching it" (217). At another point in *Icelands*, Steven's father, Vince, remembers hockey as a childhood "way of life": "It was a love for the game. It was the endless hours at the outdoor rinks playing shinny. It was going into the shack afterwards with his buddies and shooting the breeze while their noses thawed and the pot-bellied stove glowed red with heat" (9). This sort of pastoral nostalgia is not unique to Canadian hockey novels, however, as Falla's *Saved* illustrates when its hockey-playing narrator, Jean Pierre Savard, violates his NHL contract with the Boston Bruins to risk injury by playing on the pond: "I didn't care. I was having too much fun, the kind of spontaneous good time that's become a foreign concept to most NHL players, including me. If there's a better game than pond hockey on black ice I've never played it" (113). Some children's hockey novels even participate in the idea that hockey allows adults to experience or recapture childlike innocence and fun. For instance, when the fictional Toronto Redshirts win the championship in McFarlane's *The Dynamite Flynns* (1975) the narrator notes that "there was wild hilarity in the dressing room ... They behaved like kids let loose from school" (125). Again, hockey allows these grown-up professional players a childlike moment of exuberance and fun.

All of these examples rehearse and reinforce the pastoral hockey myth by connecting adult characters back to the "pure essence" of the game through nostalgic reminiscences of childhood or expressions of childlike innocence. Another such moment in Alguire's *Iced* is particularly interesting for its self-reflexivity. *Iced* begins with an introductory prologue in which the narrator, Alison Guthrie, informs her reader that many women play hockey because "somewhere on an icy patch of farmer's field or on an outdoor rink we learned how good it felt to move like the wind, to stop on a dime with a spray of clean white powder off shiny silver blades or release a shot that lifted the puck off the ice like magic and made the net bulge" (1995, 2). Guthrie's pastoral nostalgia is somewhat surprising given that only a page earlier she had specified that "sometimes [hockey] is played on the river or frozen lake but then it becomes a metaphor for our history as a people and I don't want to get into that right now" (1). As a narrator, Guthrie is clearly aware of the larger cultural significations of Canadian hockey, and is particularly concerned with overturning at least a few of them. Such a self-conscious and culturally conscious narrator is a rarity among hockey novels, which makes Guthrie's momentary lapse into myth-making especially informative about the seductive nature of myth.

What Beardsley calls "the pure joy of shinny" (1987, 39) is especially important to *Logan in Overtime*. Logan's credentials for guiding Anthony O'Toole to the insight that "hockey equals frozen rivers, wind and laughter" are established later in the novel by a flashback episode from his own youth: "Once, when they were young with hearts that were whole, Logan and Lindy played shinny on the Rounder. It was Christmas Eve ... they had gone to the river, on a clear and star-filled night ... The river was wide there, as wide as their hearts ... And on the Rounder they played shinny, a long time ago" (209). This flashback anticipates a coming reconciliation for Logan and Lindy, who have since fallen out, been damaged by the world (Logan's heart is said to have "a hole in it, about the size of a hockey puck" [12]), and are now playing as rivals on opposing teams. The main plot event in *Logan in Overtime* is an old-timers professional league game that goes into overtime and simply won't end. After playing a seemingly interminable series of overtimes on several successive nights without either team managing to score the winning goal, the combatants finally decide to settle the matter with an old-fashioned game of outdoor shinny. The frozen river, then, resolves two of the plot's running themes, the tension between Logan and Lindy and the increasingly bitter overtime challenge. In *Logan in Overtime,* playing on the river is a way of symbolically getting back to what was simple and pure about hockey, an antidote to the problem Logan identifies with adult life in general: that "everything [is] too serious" (152).

Beyond representing a nostalgic world of childhood or childlike innocence, the pastoral myth also suggests a "natural" relationship between hockey and winter. In Steven Galloway's *Finnie Walsh*, for instance, when the narrator, Paul Woodward, and his friend Finnie Walsh are discussing the Edmonton Oilers' decision to trade Wayne Gretzky to the Los Angeles Kings, Finnie objects on the basis that "they don't even have *ice* in Los Angeles" (107; italics in original). When Paul retorts that Los Angeles has "ice in the arena," Finnie insists that "[it's] not the same thing" (108). It soon becomes apparent that Finnie – the novel's voice of moral and insightful clarity – sees hockey as necessarily linked to winter: "How can you love hockey if you've never played it? How can you play it if there's no winter? If there's no ice?" (108). Finnie, of course, doesn't explain *why* hockey's authenticity depends on winter and natural ice; like the frequently assumed connection between hockey and Canadianness,

the link between hockey and winter is ultimately posited as a matter
of belief. *When She's Gone* poses a similar complaint to Finnie's
invective against the Gretzky trade in that when "small-town prairie
boys from Saskatchewan" make it in the NHL and "head south," they
"become multimillionaires" and "have kids now living in some
desert city … [who] don't grow up on wind-swept rinks, … don't
ever realize the game is a country where the dream started out pure
and true" (74). Notice the characterization of Canada *as* hockey;
again, the game and the nation are seen as ontologically the same. It
should also be noted here that both *Finnie Walsh* and *When She's
Gone* suggest the connection between hockey and winter as part of
a Canada–United States binary that will be returned to later.

Putting aside, however, the national distinctions drawn by these
statements, the logic in play is that hockey can only be "pure and
true" in a place that has naturally occurring ice. In Canadian hockey
novels, then, Beardsley's suggestions that "winter is vitality and energy to [Canadians]" and that "hockey and shinny are natural winter
ways to use that energy" (1987, 31–2) certainly appear to be true.
When She's Gone offers a summary, of sorts, on the importance of
ice in Canadian society: "Ice rinks lived in their thousands every winter, in every neighbourhood, outside every school and in every park
at community centres and on the river's ice. Wind-chills that froze
sled-dogs into solid lumps couldn't stop a kid stepping onto the ice,
couldn't stop the shinny games, the industrial league games, the
double-A-games, the sponge hockey, the Midget League Triple-A
Junior Senior Old-Timers, the Native League games. We were red-
faced ice-dwellers who'd be content with an ice age ten thousand
years long" (21). The hyperbole of this statement hardly needs to be
pointed out, but it is perhaps only slightly more glaring than that of
the prominence given to the symbolic resonances of ice, snow, and
outdoor rinks in Canadian hockey fiction in general.

Already in 1983, well before the majority of novels discussed in
this study had been published, Dryden recognized the separation of
Canadian hockey from the outdoor rink: "a game we once played on
rivers and ponds, later on streets and driveways and in backyards,
we now play in arenas, in full team uniform, with coaches and referees, or to an ever-increasing extent we don't play at all" ([1983]
1984, 134). While Canadian hockey "is flourishing both as a form of
recreation and community entertainment, the game simply does not
have the same claim on the time of Canadian children that it had for

the generations of boys who grew up between the 1940s and 1980s" (Gruneau and Whitson 1993, 283). By propounding the cultural prominence of the outdoor rink and reinforcing the larger myth of identity as northernness, many Canadian hockey novels come dangerously close to what Gruneau and Whitson call "the marketing of nostalgia" (283). This hockey nostalgia is "dangerous" because when readers submit themselves to it they are longing for a purportedly simpler time in which the game was "innocent" and "pure" (i.e., untainted by capitalism or institutional structures), masculine identities more firmly linked with physical toughness, and national identity comfortably associated with northernness and racial homogeneity (or at least untroubled by the social and cultural differences that complicate a diverse and multicultural society). While participation in such nostalgia could conceivably, as Hughes-Fuller (2002) suggests, allow us the possibility of imagining "better worlds," the fictional realities envisioned by hockey novels frequently re-enact the harmful and exclusive identity assumptions that have attended Canadian hockey and diminish the game's albeit imperfect present at the expense of a factitious and idealized past.

To imbricate hockey with Canada's myth of the north also significantly limits the game's potential and appeal. As Dryden suggests, hockey is now a predominantly indoor game, both in Canada and around the world. What hockey novels generally fail to acknowledge is that the experience of playing on natural ice is simply unavailable to most Canadians, approximately 80 per cent of whom live in urban centres where the space required to build an outdoor rink isn't readily available. This fact also makes outdoor hockey disproportionately unavailable to recent immigrants and people of colour, demographic groups who are largely located in Canada's cities. Even those Canadians fortunate enough to find space for an outdoor rink or to be located in close proximity to a pond or river can no longer rely on winter to do the work of ice-making for them. Especially in the southern border region where many Canadians live, midwinter thaws are becoming increasingly common and make it very difficult to maintain a homemade rink and potentially unsafe to skate on frozen ponds and rivers. To say that hockey is less authentic when played indoors, then, is to undermine the actual participation of most Canadians who play the game and, less explicitly, to perpetuate outdated assumptions about the game's racial boundaries. Furthermore, the suggestion that hockey is less authentic on artificial ice dismisses the actual experience of players and fans in non-northern places who have become passionate about the game. For instance, Richard Harrison's "African Hockey Poem #1" was written upon the poet's discovery of a yearly hockey tournament staged by hotel employees in Côte d'Ivoire at a rink built for Scandinavian tourists in the 1950s, and captures the joy that hockey can bring in even this most unlikely of places. Harrison describes the feeling of skating on African ice, "way / ahead of schedule and nature; I will tell you / I touched the ice and I could be any boy in love." As Harrison rightly recognizes and celebrates, hockey's elemental character and the excitement the game occasions aren't any less authentic or enjoyable when played indoors.

Two noteworthy exceptions to the genre's tendency to mythologize the connection between hockey and winter are Rob Ritchie's *Orphans of Winter* (2006) and Delillo's *Amazons*. *Orphans of Winter* is the story of Stephen Gillis, a scout for the fictional Toronto Centennials (a thinly veiled clone of the Maple Leafs) who finds himself unexpectedly in charge of the club's entry draft proceedings. After an encounter with an old man who could be best described as a hockey mystic, Gillis uses the Centennials' first overall pick to draft an obscure minor league fourth-liner, Casey Bruford, who hasn't been ranked by any other scouts or hailed as even remotely draft worthy. As Bruford miraculously becomes the Centennials' star player, Gillis becomes involved with a consortium of spiritual searchers who try to make esoteric connections between a series of seemingly random events. Blake refers to *Orphans of Winter* as "an unusual sort of quest novel that connects hockey with various types of spiritual traditions" (2010, 181), which range from Christianity to Native spirituality to New Age beliefs about cosmic energies and geospatial connectivity. Among the main themes to emerge in Gillis' explorations of these beliefs – which constitute almost the entire novel – are the ideas that sports are a form of religious activity and that hockey uniquely embodies and expresses the spirit of winter. What makes *Orphans of Winter* so unusual as a quest novel, to go back to Blake's description, is that after its lengthy conflation of hockey, nature, and spirituality, Ritchie ultimately ends up rejecting the ideas his novel appears to put forward. In the final pages of *Orphans of Winter*, Gillis comes to the realization that "for all its window dressing – for all the attempts to mythologize itself as something more than a pastime, and for its attempts at self-exaltation as a teacher of values and dispensary of life lessons – the reality was that skaters like himself, from pee-wee to pro, played the game under the ruling auspices of the humourless discerning eyes that watched from their perch in the arena rafters; cheering the game with stone-faced nods and lording over the skaters the sport's real prize ... [which is] nothing more than the elusive word and gesture of approval from somewhere behind those serious, lifeless eyes. No, hockey wasn't *winter*. Not for Stephen Gillis. Hockey was but fathers and sons. And Stephen Gillis, now floating and weightless ... was finally free" (italics in original; 240). The fulfillment of Gillis' quest, then, is the realization that hockey isn't an abstruse spiritual exercise but a social mechanism by which relationships are formed and negotiated, in this case between father and son. In the end, *Orphans of Winter* turns out to have been the story of several orphaned characters (Gillis first and foremost among them) whose exploration of the strange and seemingly spiritual connections between them unexpectedly allows them to come to terms with their unresolved feelings of familial loss. Rather than endorsing the mythology it so thoroughly explores, *Orphans of Winter* ultimately depicts the game straightforwardly as a social and material practice that can be harmful as easily as it can be wholesome.

DeLillo's *Amazons* reaches a similar conclusion about the pastoral myth as *Orphans of Winter* but with a very different tone. *Amazons* is a comic novel that doesn't take much seriously, and, as such, DeLillo is far more interested in making fun of hockey's myths than contributing to them. At one point in the story Cleo Birdwell (DeLillo's narrator and "first woman ever to play in the NHL") suggests that airplane "window seats may be the only way that remains for adults to stay in direct touch with their own childhoods" (188). Although this comment appears relatively unobtrusive, it actually represents a major affront to the hockey myth's idea that hockey is what connects adults back to childhood innocence. Rather than hockey, a game she plays as a career, it is sitting in the window seat of an airplane that allows Birdwell to nostalgically revisit what it was like to be a child. DeLillo makes fun of the pastoral myth more explicitly elsewhere in *Amazons* in an advertisement for which "the set was a frozen pond, strictly man-made of course, and it was located in a weedy lot at the edge of a trailer camp, in the blazing sun" (313). As part of the ad, Birdwell is supposed to skate around the fake pond and talk about how good it is to "come home to, the good, the simple things ... mention life in the big city, life on the road, a woman playing a man's game" and eventually extol the benefits of the product, a new line of snack food aimed particularly at women (314–15). The message that pastoral nostalgia is artificial, quaint, and demeaning to the actualities of Birdwell's life is made abundantly clear, and Birdwell eventually refuses to do the shoot.

The exceptions of *Amazons* and *Orphans of Winter* aside, it should be noted that the representations of pond-hockey purity discussed in this section seldom explicitly associate the pastoral myth with Canadianness or national identity. As with the connection between history and hockey, this association is supplied by the working of the myth system itself, specifically in the interplay between form and content. Barthes suggests that "the form does not suppress the meaning," but rather "impoverishes it ... puts it at a distance ... holds it at one's disposal" (1972, 118). In Barthesian terms, novelistic representations of pond-hockey purity are not in themselves symbols of national identity: "[They] have too much presence, appear as a rich, fully experienced, spontaneous, innocent, *indisputable* image. But at the same time this presence is tamed, put at a distance, made almost transparent; it recedes a little, it becomes the accomplice of a concept which comes to it fully armed, [the idea of identity-as-northernness]: once made use of, it becomes artificial" (118; italics in original). In the working of the myth system, the specific images of pastoral purity in hockey novels become associated with the larger and more general idea that Canadian identity is determined by setting, a concept that extends beyond any one particular image to a wide-ranging history of discourse and opinion. The signification of the pastoral myth, then, infuses these individual representations of pond-hockey purity with pre-existing cultural ideas about identity and northernness. As with the other categories of representation discussed above, the pastoral myth conceals the work of cultural processes that have in reality contributed to the game's development, conveying instead the appearance of organic certainty. By suggesting that hockey arose as a geographic inevitability or a "natural" response to Canada's northern climate, hockey novels implicitly assert the game's authentic and indisputable Canadianness.

The work of the myth to Canadianize hockey's pastoral origins distinguishes hockey novels from others that similarly mobilize the pastoral in their depictions of sport. Probably the most famous Canadian sports novel, W.P. Kinsella's *Shoeless Joe* (1982), puts forward a very American pastoral and premodern myth about baseball which has been articulated by Cordelia Candelaria (1989), Michael Mandelbaum (2004), Christopher Evans and William Herzog II (2002), and others. Like the hockey myth's yearning for the game's origins on the pond, *Shoeless Joe* is intensely nostalgic for a "purer" time in which baseball was played for fun, unfettered by capitalism, and more closely connected with nature. But unlike hockey novels, *Shoeless Joe* isn't invested in defining or preserving a distinctive Canadian identity. Although Kinsella is a Canadian author, *Shoeless Joe* takes place in the United States and (in the words of one of the book-jacket reviews) deals with the "quintessentially American." Kinsella's *The Iowa Baseball Confederacy* (1986) also explores the place of baseball in American society, celebrating that game's pastoral myth in ways similar to *Shoeless Joe* but going further to suggest baseball as a mystical or magical experience.

A more kindred spirit to the hockey novel genre than Kinsella's baseball fiction is W.O. Mitchell's *The Black Bonspiel of Willie MacCrimmon* (1993). In addition to suggesting curling as an extension of the natural world that is positioned alongside hockey in its elemental connection to ice and snow ("they devoted equal time to hockey and curling on the Spray River" [3]), *The Black Bonspiel of Willie MacCrimmon* mythologizes the history of curling, positions the game alongside important Canadian events such as the battle on the Plains of Abraham, and exaggerates the importance of curling in Canadian society to the point that the story's protagonist, Willie MacCrimmon, is willing to make the Faustian deal with the Devil for a chance to win Canada's national curling championship, the Brier. Despite these striking similarities to some of the ways in which hockey novels attempt to mythologize their game, Mitchell's novel remains different in at least two important respects. As the story of Willie MacCrimmon's curling rink entering into a match against the Devil and his rink (which includes Judas, Macbeth, and Guy Fawkes), *The Black Bonspiel of Willie MacCrimmon* is clearly more fantastic than real. In this respect, Mitchell's novel has more in common with Kinsella's baseball fiction than with the majority of hockey novels. Although realist novels can certainly take critical perspectives toward the subjects they depict, their attempts toward accuracy and verisimilitude make it easier for readers to confuse fiction and fact. In other words, readers are more likely to accept the apparently realistic ideas being put forward in hockey novels at face value than to straightforwardly believe Mitchell's depiction of curling, because of the story's obviously fantastical elements. Despite their mutual investment in the pastoral myth, the other major difference that distinguishes *The Black Bonspiel of Willie MacCrimmon* from the hockey novel genre is the former's depiction of an immigrant game. Mitchell repeatedly emphasizes the Scottish origins of curling and configures the game as particularly Scots-Canadian. While curling may be a significant cultural institution in Canada, *The Black Bonspiel of Willie MacCrimmon* makes clear that it isn't a home-grown game like hockey and is therefore more difficult to saddle with the same nationalist freight.

"WITHOUT THE RINK, AND ALL THAT WENT ON SURROUNDING IT"

The preceding sections deal with several ways in which hockey novels represent the game as both naturally and inevitably Canadian. While myth often functions to efface the cultural processes by which the game has come to be associated with Canadianness, it also works in more direct and representational terms to rehearse and enforce the idea of hockey-as-national-identity. To say this another way, hockey novels ultimately see the Canadianness of the game as a function of both nature and culture, and the convergence of the two is nowhere more evident than at the rink. One of the major tenets of the hockey myth is the idea of unity by common experience, and hockey novels see the rink as providing this for Canadians by connecting them to the "Canadian universal" of snow, ice, and winter (i.e., nature) while at the same time connecting them to each other in fellowship, ritual, and proximity (i.e., culture). This is certainly the case in *Finnie Walsh*, in which Finnie and Paul spend a great deal of time building, maintaining, and playing on their own outdoor rink. The rink provides a central place of action in the novel, to the point where Paul suggests that "without the rink, and all that went on surrounding it, I honestly don't believe things would have turned out the way they did" (*Finnie Walsh*, 64). In plot terms, Paul's assessment proves true: the rink facilitates the skills development that eventually gives both boys a chance to play in the NHL (although an accident at the rink might also be said to contribute to the frame of mind that leads to Finnie's downfall). For Finnie and Paul, the rink allows for the cultivation of a strong friendship based on hockey, and, as such, appears as a place of human culture and interaction. But the rink is also a natural domain of geography, weather, and the body in *Finnie Walsh*. Beyond allowing the boys to hone their hockey skills, the rink provides a sometimes necessary place of retreat from the pressures of school and family. Built in an abandoned reservoir in the woods behind the sawmill owned by Finnie's father, the rink is isolated enough to afford privacy and pastoral enough to allow for communion with nature.

The outdoor rink plays a similar role in Robert Sedlack's *The Horn of a Lamb* (2004). Sedlack's protagonist is Fred Pickle, a thirty-eight-year-old man who had suffered a brain injury during a hockey accident when he was nineteen. Fred has two all-consuming passions in life, his season tickets for the local NHL team and the building of his own outdoor rink every winter for the whole neighbourhood to skate on, a fact which prompts Blake to propose the possibility of unintended irony in the "suggestion that such devotion to hockey is tantamount to intellectual limitations" (2010, 162). Each winter when Fred has completed his rink, he takes down the Canadian flag at his uncle's farm and runs up a homemade replacement announcing the good news to the community. For the surrounding farms, the omniscient narrator explains, "[Fred's] flag was a community reveille. It was a call to arms" (22). Things soon get so busy that Taillon, the guard dog, has to "get used to the daily disturbances from vehicles and visitors to Fred's rink" (104): "There was a seniors group on Tuesdays and Thursdays. There were shinny games almost every day after school and always after supper. Weekends were busiest, with a non-stop parade of skaters from Eddie Shack [the shack in which people sit to lace up their skates] to the ice and back again" (104).[8] In *The Horn of a Lamb*, then, the rink is a place where members of the community experience fellowship and play together. But despite being a nexus of human contact and interaction (i.e., culture), the rink also remains closely associated with the natural world. Throughout the process of rink-building, Fred appreciates "the snow ... working its magic" (17) and the fact that "he could water for an hour and Mother Nature would do the rest" (73). When it comes to hockey, Fred sees the game as most ideal when enacted under "natural" conditions: "You have not lived until you've played hockey at midnight on a fresh sheet of ice. You get to skate without a helmet and pretend you're Guy Lafleur" (123). Indeed, outdoor ice connotes a sense of magic and wonder in

Canadian hockey novels that attaches to the pastoral myth's larger vision of childhood innocence. In a scene reminiscent of Lindy and Logan playing shinny on the Rounder in *Logan in Overtime*, Fred and his uncle Jack go for a Christmas Eve skate, "passing the puck lazily back and forth under the raven-black sky. The air was still and the sound of their blades carving the ice echoed across the darkened pasture" (116). The "magic" of the outdoor rink, then, is such that it brings people into communion with both nature and each other.

The congruence of nature and culture at the outdoor rink is also an important element of Quarrington's *King Leary*, in which an elderly former NHL superstar, Percival "King" Leary, reflects on his youth and fading greatness.[9] Quarrington himself has specified the novel as being first and foremost about winter: "hockey … is merely the – I don't mean to make a pun here, but I can't avoid it – arena in which the story is set. No, *King Leary* is ultimately about winter, the thing that defines us most eloquently as Canadians" (Quarrington 2007). In addition to illustrating the frequent reluctance among novelists and commentators to acknowledge hockey novels as actually being "about" hockey, Quarrington's comment suggests a conscious effort to establish hockey's place in Canada's myth of the north, again forwarding what Leon Surette has called a "topocentric" version of Canadian identity, an identity based on the "physical environment – climate, soil, and topography" (1982, 49). Morrow's reading of *King Leary* and *Logan in Overtime* similarly recognizes the winter aspects of these novels, suggesting that they "take the giant-ness of the land that is Canada, its snow and darkness and compresses them into 'winter tales' of a needed literature of near-legends, legendary memories and heroes of eccentricity and humour" (2002, 115). Morrow, then, sees Quarrington as consciously feeding into the myth of the north and responding to winter's afflictions with humour and levity. Because these devices are "absent in most competitive sport," Morrow also acknowledges Quarrington's humour as a way of "de-mystif[ying] the heroic in hockey" (114, 113).

Because *King Leary* does work in some ways to "de-mystify" the hockey myth, it is worth emphasizing Quarrington's apparent earnestness about the centrality of winter in the novel and the connection between hockey and nature that it proposes. Early in the story, Quarrington's title character and narrator suggests a moment of communion with nature by reminiscing about skating on the frozen canal as a young man: "A few nights of the right weather, and I'm talking thirty below, teeth-aching and nose-falling-off type weather, and the canal would grow about a foot of ice. Hard as marble, and just as smooth. Strong and true. It gives me goose bumps just thinking about it" (7). Leary later tells of his time in a reform school run by hockey-playing monks, which, as Dopp suggests, "becomes an extended satire on the strain of muscular Christianity linked to hockey through figures like Father David Bauer, a key developer and coach of the Canadian national team" (2009, 85). But while Quarrington makes fun of the idea that hockey builds moral character (a long-standing trope in Canadian hockey literature that will be discussed more fully in chapter 4), he does allow that hockey can be a sort of mystical or spiritual experience when played in an outdoor setting. Leary reminisces in particular about one moonlit night when the monks constructed an outdoor rink: "On Christmas Eve the temperature fell about forty degrees. The brothers rushed out with buckets and hoses. They stayed out there all night, and to keep themselves amused they sang. They sang strange songs with words I didn't understand. All night long the monks watered the world, and the winter air turned the water to ice. Blue-silver ice, hard as marble. On Christmas morning the rink was ready" (37). With their "strange songs" and ritualistic behaviour, it is as if the monks attach sacramental importance to the work of ice-making. In other words, the outdoor rink appears to be an intersection between the spiritual and the material worlds in *King Leary*, a fact that is further suggested by its association with Christian spirituality in the context of Christmas. The rink is certainly the central focus of life at the reform school, as well as the core element of its rehabilitation program; a sign at the entrance informs newcomers that "TO KEEP A BOY OUT OF HOT WATER, PUT HIM ON ICE" (34). Again, readers are supposed to take the message that hockey builds moral character with a grain of salt, but the lessons Leary learns playing pickup under the tutelage of the monks do help shape him into the NHL star he will become. In the same way that the rink helps facilitate Finnie and Paul's friendship in *Finnie Walsh*, playing on the reformatory rink also cements Leary's lifelong friendship with his future teammate Manfred Ozikean. Again, the outdoor rink in *King Leary* suggests an intersection between the natural world of landscape, physicality, and weather and the human world of culture, ritual, and community.

Beyond illustrating the prevalence of such representations, these examples form the groundwork for a larger claim about the general importance of the rink to Canadian hockey novels. In the same way that Anderson cites the novel as a condition of possibility for national imagining, the rink might be seen as providing a conceptual model for the cultural work of hockey novels in regards to national identity. For Anderson (1991), the imaginative and empathetic multiplicities of the novel supplied a *way of thinking* by which the abstract identifications required by nationalism were initially made possible. Similarly, the *idea* of the rink might be said to provide an intellectual blueprint for the cultural work of hockey novels. So far this study has treated myth in a largely Barthesian sense, in which it functions as an inconspicuous vehicle for ideology. But as noted earlier in this chapter, hockey novels also enforce the myth in direct and representational terms. Working by way of performative rehearsal and repetitive re-enforcement, this mode of identity transmission appears as a function of culture. In other words, hockey novels affect the appearance of naturalness by way of complex semiotic systems while simultaneously enforcing existing cultural ideas about the game through directness and apparent verisimilitude. The outdoor rink most fully exemplifies this two-pronged strategy of representation because it poses an intersection between nature and culture.[10] In the same way that hockey novels combine these forces in the project of linking hockey with identity, the rink appears to combine them in the framework of the novels themselves. Just as the rink provides the material condition of possibility for the actual exercise of hockey, it is the *idea* of the rink that might be said to make possible the cultural work of hockey novels regarding national identity.

"KILDARE HAD HOCKEY": THE GAME AS SMALL TOWN

Underwriting the pastoral myth are several generally recognizable Romantic binaries: the privileging of nature over human society, childhood innocence over adult experience, and small-town community over big-city impersonality. Canadian identity has traditionally been closely identified with at least one of these binaries, the relationship between nature and human society (which has often been characterized as antagonistic). Part of the work of the rink in Canadian hockey novels seems to be the resolution of this binary; by bringing nature and culture into a relatively harmonious coexistence in the service of identity, hockey novels implicitly respond to the versions of cultural nationalism disseminated by Frye and his disciples.

Hockey often serves as a vehicle by which the gulf between child-hood innocence and adult experience can be mediated, and in this reading the rink represents a proving ground in which children and adolescents hone their hockey skills while older characters remember or revisit the purity and innocence of youth. In fact, it is the distance between child- and adulthood that most consistently defines the plot trajectories of Canadian hockey novels, the two most frequent storylines being the *Bildungsroman* (the coming-of-age story) and the "aging" or retirement narrative.

The one Romantic tension that the rink doesn't propose to solve is the privileging of small-town or rural community over big-city impersonality. Already in the first wave of children's hockey novels, the small town is valorized as the locus of Canadian hockey and the guarantor of its authenticity. The narrator of Leslie McFarlane's "They Didn't Know Hockey," for instance, suggests that "sports followers who think that a packed house at Madison Square Garden, or the Montreal Forum, represents the ultimate in hockey fever have never seen a real, bang-up, small-town, amateur clash between teams that have been bitter rivals from way back when" (*Leslie McFarlane's Hockey Stories*, 117). Similarly, McFarlane's "Montville Boy Makes Good" tells the story of an entire town that travels to Montreal to watch a local boy play his first game for the Canadiens: "pushing and scrambling, laughing and chattering, with smiles on their faces and expectation in their eyes, they left Montville as if this departure was the most joyous occasion of their lives" (*Leslie McFarlane's Hockey Stories*, 16). This hockey-as-small-town ethos is especially evident in Hewitt's *Hello, Canada and Hockey Fans in the United States*, in which the fictional small town of Gloster, Ontario appears to "save the country" (14) by committing its team to resist the monetary lure of the professional leagues and stay amateur in order to win Olympic hockey gold. Written in 1950, the central premise of *Hello, Canada and Hockey Fans in the United States* is that Canada will soon cease to be competitive in international amateur events such as the Olympics because all the best players are absorbed into the professional game. Hewitt repeatedly argues for the importance of international competitiveness as a source of national pride and international prestige, and the team from Gloster appears to secure these things when they win hockey gold at the 1952 Olympics. Although Hewitt's version is fictionalized and written two years before the actual event, his story turned out to be remarkably prescient: a team from Canada, the Edmonton Mercurys, did win Olympic gold in 1952, and Canada didn't win another Olympic gold medal in men's hockey for fifty years until after the rules were changed to allow professional players. Beyond the promotion of national pride and assertion of Canadian ownership of the game in *Hello, Canada and Hockey Fans in the United States* (1950), Hewitt gives local reasons for keeping high-level hockey in the small town as well: "it will give us a common local interest. It will give our young people a healthy topic of conversation and a rallying point for their Saturday night fun. The success of a big team will also encourage young gaffers to get out on the ponds and the canal and emulate their heroes" (17). *Hello, Canada and Hockey Fans in the United States*, then, sees small-town hockey as an important local institution that in turn helps secure and preserve the larger national well-being.

Quite similarly, Young's *That Old Gang of Mine* (1982) – which continues the story of several characters from his juvenile hockey trilogy but injects a more adult-appropriate dose of booze, sex, and profanity – involves a group of amateur players coming together to win Olympic hockey gold for Canada. When a tragic plane crash kills Canada's entire national hockey team en route to a fictionalized version of the Winter Olympics in Moscow, Peter Gordon and Bill Spunska round up their old high-school hockey team and a few others to compete for Canada instead. Although not all of the team members are drawn from small-town and working-class Canada, Young's narrator belabours the description of several who are in order to signify the team's amateur ethos: "one came off a tractor with a snow-blower that was out clearing the streets of a prairie town. One was a call-back when a freight train stopped long enough for the crew to pick up a phone message for the brakeman" (25). Regardless of their provenance, however, it is made clear that at least on some level each player is "do[ing] this for Canada" (28). Although Young suggests that Canada's on-ice tactics aren't always honourable, *That Old Gang of Mine* attempts to define and preserve national identity by safeguarding Canadian possession of the game through international success. Furthermore, *That Old Gang of Mine*'s complaint about the professional leagues "grabbing off good Canadian kids before they had a chance to play for their country" (12) exemplifies the general fear among hockey novels that money is detracting from the purity and Canadianness of the game, an issue which will be explored more fully in the following chapter.[11]

Like *Hello, Canada and Hockey Fans in the United States* and to a lesser extent *That Old Gang of Mine*, several adult-oriented hockey novels see the ability of the local rink to affect community spirit and fraternity as a characteristically small-town phenomenon. In *Puck Is a Four Letter Word*, for instance, Willie Mulligan suggests that "not even a Stanley Cup in Montreal where the Canadiens are a religion matches what happens in a small Canadian community with a good hockey team" (17; note once again the characterization of hockey as religion). Similarly, the narrator of Larry O'Connor's *The Penalty Box* (2007) suggests of the small Ontario town where he grew up that "ice hockey is all in Keppel. Like the sea in a Caribbean village" (15). Adrian Brijbassi's *50 Mission Cap* (2001) illustrates these sentiments further when the fictional town of Kildare, Ontario celebrates the championship victory of its Junior A team, the Kougars: "Folks ate and drank and applauded their Kougars ... they walked with smiles wherever they went and shook each other's hands exuberantly upon passing on the street. They, again, felt a part of something real and vital. Ottawa had the builders of the nation and Toronto had the employers of it, but Kildare had its team, not a bunch of overpriced millionaires who lived in the States and jumped from squad to squad every couple of years. No, Kildare had hockey. It owned it. As sure as the sweetness of sugar and cinnamon on a beavertail, Kildare had the essence of this country: Its game. In our group of immature and sometimes arrogant boys, most of whom found our selves in Kildare, the town lived. It saw itself a winner" (280).

Several features of this passage are especially noteworthy. First, hockey success in the small town is seen as a matter of civic pride, enabling the town to perceive itself as a "winner." Second, Kildare's possession of the game is posited as an antagonism of small town versus big city. Toronto and Ottawa may have the nation's power, but Kildare has its symbolic "essence." Third, the passage portrays hockey as facilitating community interaction: after the team wins, people eat together to celebrate and walk around shaking hands. Finally, Kildare's hockey team is seen as "authentic" (evoking the pastoral myth) in contrast to the big-city professional teams who play for money. What isn't mentioned, of course, is the fact that half the team's players are from out of town, or that most of the players see junior hockey as a stepping stone either to the NHL or a university scholarship. In other words, the hockey team is neither organically arisen from the town or authentically pure in its not-for-profit ethos. These inconsistencies are never recognized within the novel, however, and readers are left to participate in the naivety of Brijbassi's young narrator, Scott MacGregor, an eighteen-year-old who himself has left his home in Ottawa to be billeted with a family in Kildare so he can play for the Kougars. Despite containing these moments of slippage, then, *50 Mission Cap* participates uncritically in the "small-town" aspect of the myth.

Several of the features that characterize Scott's description of small-town hockey in *50 Mission Cap* are also evident in Don Gutteridge's *Bus Ride* (1974). Set in 1939 in the village of "the Point" (likely based on Point Edward, Ontario, where Gutteridge grew up), *Bus Ride* opens with an inter-village game on an outdoor rink. The narrator underscores the importance of hockey to the town by taking a sort of attendance roll call at the game: "the grocer, butcher, druggist, policeman (the day one), housewives, young-wives, dock-workers, day-labourers from the pool room, a foreman from the Refinery, the Reeve and those who voted for him, and some who didn't – young or old, wet or dry, you could not find a larger single gathering of villagers anywhere except at Church on a Sunday morning, and since there were three houses where God dwelt (or visited on Sabbath) it was not nearly as unanimous a conclave as Friday night at the hockey rink" (8). It is further noted that the whole town has arrived despite adverse weather conditions, "the village besieged by snow, windows buried, the very doors blocked" (8). Although these passages suggest hockey as bridging differences (both vocational and religious) to form community, it is soon made abundantly clear that the game does more than simply bring the villagers to the same place at the same time. When the local star, Bill Underhill, scores his third goal of the night, the narrator explains that "it is not exaggerating to say that during the two-minute standing ovation ... accorded to their hero, the people of the Point came alive – individually and collectively – as they did on few other occasions" (9). The narrator insists on the unifying power of the moment: "the victory was to be shared, the triumph communal. And in the sharing and the spontaneous approbation of their applause, all the petty human divisiveness, the pain of ordinary days, the long dream-distorted nights, the memories of Wars on far-away ground, the half-healed scars – all that divides us from each other and ourselves faded with the blending voice, the harmony of the universal cheer" (9). In the powerful spirit of community occasioned by the "universal cheer," the persistent human problems of pain, suffering, and banality appear to fall away. By bringing people together and uniting them on an almost spiritual level (the rink is seen as a more "unanimous conclave" than the village churches), hockey offers the people in *Bus Ride* a communal version of Bayle's existential conclusion in *Heroes*.

The idea that the small-town rink brings about fraternity and fellowship in ways that the big-city rink can't is particularly evident in *Icelands*. *Icelands* explores the culture of minor hockey in Toronto as enacted in one particular arena, Iceland, one of almost one hundred such facilities in the area – "and even that number wasn't enough for the hockey-mad city that had the largest minor hockey program in the world. There were 400 teams and over 20,000 games a year" (6). The Iceland rink does manage to facilitate some sense of community among the parents who faithfully attend their children's games, but the atmosphere of this community is hardly the one of fraternity embodied in "the universal cheer." Instead, the Iceland rink is a place of gossip, hostility, unhealthy competition, illicit affairs, and political jockeying among parents for increased ice-time for their child and a spot on next year's team. The negative culture of the Iceland rink is juxtaposed by several adult characters who reminisce about their small-town hockey experiences as children. In addition to Vince's fond memories of the pot-bellied stove after childhood games of outdoor shinny, Andrew's father specifically remembers being "brought up on the game in his hometown where everyone flocked to the arena on cold winter nights (216–17). By positing these prelapsarian visions of small-town hockey, *Icelands* tacitly condemns the competitive and unfriendly hockey culture that arises in the "big city."

In this sense, *Icelands* is similar to McFarlane's *The Dynamite Flynns*, which tells the story of two small-town cousins, Dan and Jerry Flynn, who make it to the NHL but succumb to the corrupting influence of the big city when Dan becomes involved in a gambling racket and other unlawful intrigues. As the team's coach describes Dan's situation, "I've seen plenty of promising hockey players go all to pieces when they hit the bright lights" (53–4). The trope of small-town innocence corrupted by big-city experience appears in *King Leary* as well, when Leary explains the rowdiness of the New York City Americans: "back then [in the early days of professional hockey] players were young Canucks from small towns, if they happened to be from towns at all. Many of the lads came from farmhouses so isolated that the cows had to ask for directions home. Howie Morenz, for instance, was from Swastika, Ontario. Pleasant-sounding place, eh? Bullet Joey Broun was from East Braintree, Manitoba. Jacques La Rivière was from St Louis-de-Ha!-Ha! ... Anyway, the point is that the Amerks were young boys from small Canadian towns and outposts, plunked down amidst the bright lights of New York City. This is why they went how they went. Which is hog-wild" (154–5). Again, the harmful influence of the big city is seen to corrupt small-town innocence and naivety. But as Dopp has noticed of this passage, "the names of the towns ('Swastika' especially) hint that small towns already have a dark underbelly that has nothing to do with being corrupted by the big city" (89). *King Leary*, then, is ironic in its suggestion of small-town innocence and subtly mocks the more earnest investment of novels like *Icelands* and *The Dynamite Flynns* in this aspect of the myth.

The specific problem that many hockey novels have with the big-city game is its tendency to see hockey as competition rather than amusement, commodity rather than sacrament, and spectacle rather than sport (this is why Steven eventually decides to leave the organized game in *Icelands*). Canadian hockey novels also frequently configure the antagonism of small town versus big city along national lines between Canada and America. In this characterization, Canadian hockey is on a national level ascribed with the small-town hockey virtues of innocence, purity, and authenticity. In other words, Canada itself becomes the symbolic small-town that possesses the "true essence" of hockey against the putatively American big-city values of falsity and greed. In a way, then, Canadian hockey novels see small towns and local communities as metonymic for the imagining of larger national community. Just as local communities are seen to derive their unity and togetherness from hockey and the rink, hockey novels suggest that the nation itself is symbolically united by our game and our "national icescape" (Beardsley's term). This device, of course, both conveys an idealized, nostalgic, and uniform view of small-town living and absorbs the differences between urban and rural living within its homogenizing account of Canadian identity. Such characterizations are central to the ways in which hockey novels react against the perceived threat of Americanization, not only in the specific arena of "Canada's game" but in the nation's larger sense of itself as a distinct cultural and political entity.

2

The Myth in Crisis

For the small town to function as a representative subset of the larger national community, it must have some way to appear connected. Given the Canadian context of vast open spaces and often-imposing distance between even the nearest settlements, communications technologies have always played an important role in the imagining of national community. According to Francis (1997), the ability of hockey broadcasting to bring about unity is a central tenet of the hockey myth: "Hockey would not be Canadian if it ... was not expected to make a contribution to national unity. A passion for the game is considered to be one of the rare things that brings Canadians together. He Shoots, He Scores becomes the national motto, rather than From Sea to Sea. In this reading, 'Hockey Night in Canada,' the most popular radio, then television, show in Canadian history, is much more than entertainment; it is a weekly reconciliation of our differences, be they regional, linguistic, ethnic or class" (168).

Maurice Charland has suggested that the rhetoric of Canadian nationalism has been technological more often than cultural in that it "ties Canadian identity, not to its people, but to their mediation through technology" (1986, 197). For Charland, it was first the railroad and then the radio that enabled Canada to "[imagine] itself into existence" (196). Much of hockey's growing reputation as Canada's national game around the turn of the twentieth century can be attributed to these same "new" technologies. The completion of the Canadian Pacific Railroad in 1885 made it possible for teams

from all across the nation to challenge for the Stanley Cup, and as
early as 1896 a rudimentary form of play-by-play was being used to
transmit games across the country.[1] In general terms, the development of wireless radio had an enormous impact on the ability of
Canadians to envision a cultural identity. When Prime Minister
Mackenzie King made one of the first live broadcasts from Ottawa
on the sixtieth anniversary of Confederation in 1927, he told the
nation that "henceforth all Canadians will stand within ... hearing
of the speakers on Parliament Hill" and that because of this new
technology "there will be aroused a more general interest in public
affairs, and an increased devotion of the individual citizen to the
commonweal" (quoted in Charland 1986, 204). In other words,
radio would have the power to bring Canadians together by over-
coming the realities of a geographically dispersed population and
"[reducing] Canada to a community or small city which does not
suffer from the isolating effects of distance, regionalism, or cultural
diversity" (Charland 1986, 204). Perhaps King would be surprised
to learn that the potential of radio to unify the nation was made
most fully manifest by hockey rather than politics.

Foster Hewitt broadcast the first game from Maple Leaf Gardens
on 12 November 1931, and, in the words of historian J.M. Bumsted,
for the next thirty years "[Hewitt's] high-pitched voice – and his
excited refrain, 'He Shoots! He Scores!' – was hockey for most
Canadians." According to Bumsted, "'Hockey Night in Canada' was
the one and only Canadian-produced radio program ... that consistently outdrew American offerings with the Canadian listeners"
(Bumstead 1998, 294). Although Hewitt authored two of the first
Canadian hockey novels, his most lasting impact is "almost single-
handedly ... immortalizing the game of hockey, its heroes, and the
[Maple Leaf] Gardens in the minds of Canadians" (Simpson 1989,
205). Similarly, Neil Earle has suggested that Hewitt's broadcast of
the 1972 Summit Series allowed for the "intensification and celebration of [this] collective myth," as well as for the "[unprecedented]
national fervour unleashed across the country" upon Henderson's
series winning goal (1972, 119). It is hardly surprising, then, that
Hewitt floats in and out of Canadian hockey novels as "a voice without a face but more familiar" (*Bus Ride*, 42).[2] Hewitt's voice functions as a totalizing gesture, an insistent reminder that the small
towns and individual characters in hockey novels make up a national whole that is defined by, or at least identified with, hockey. Steven

Farelli suggests as much in *Icelands* when he claims that radio enables "people as far apart as Newfoundland and British Columbia, with Quebec in between, [to] be joined in a hairbreadth's moment by the artistry of a beautiful goal" (*Icelands*, 217). Elsewhere in *Icelands*, Vince remembers being "five years old ... when he was fiddling with the dials of his uncle's old console radio one Saturday night and this mesmerizing voice came on. 'Hello Canada and hockey fans in the United States and Newfoundland'" (17). Hewitt's trademark greeting hints at the cultural unity that his broadcast seeks to accomplish. According to Charland, "the rhetoric of technological nationalism ... is the dominant discourse of the official ideology of nation-building through state-supported broadcasting, and has been a significant (but not exclusive) determinant of the form of Canada's broadcasting system." Media technology, then, facilitates an imaginary connection between citizens separated by race, class, religion, and geography, but also works to inculcate and naturalize the very idea that this is possible. In other words, the ideology of state-sanctioned broadcasting works to reinforce the main assumption of technological nationalism, that technology gives us "the capacity to create a nation by enhancing communication" (Charland 1989, 197). By addressing his broadcast to *all* Canadians but only to *hockey fans* in the United States and Newfoundland, Hewitt collapses the distance between "hockey" and "Canadian." The assumption in play is that the entire nation is listening, and the significance of this unity can hardly be separated from the mode of its conveyance, radio.

Beyond simply reflecting the reality that radio, and later television, have been instrumental in facilitating the imagining of national community through hockey, the novels addressed in this study work to canonize *Hockey Night in Canada* as an important cultural institution. This is especially apparent in MacGregor's *The Last Season*, when the narrator, Felix Batterinksi, describes the night of his grandfather's death: "I was upstairs crying about Jaja [Felix's grandfather] ... when [Uncle Jan] came up and scooped me up and took me out to where he already had the Meteor warming up. On the front seat were a couple of Cokes for me and some beer for himself, and ... we sat out and listened to the Detroit–Leaf playoff game fading in and out from Toronto, Foster Hewitt in the gondola, which was to me even holier than the heaven I knew Jaja was off to" (27). While the "holiness" of the broadcast should be seen in the context of young

Batterinski's all-consuming passion for hockey, as well as, perhaps, that of the general inability of youth to fully grasp human mortality, the consecrating impulse is certainly evident. Indeed, the aspiration of every small-town player in Canadian hockey novels – including Felix Batterinski – is to make it big in the NHL, and more often than not the ultimate measure of this success is to be broadcast on *Hockey Night in Canada*. In *Bus Ride*, for instance, Bill Underhill dreams of playing in "a real arena where every shift, every glistening shot, was rewarded with cheers, was recorded and sent-winging on air-waves over all the snows of this country's towns and hamlets" (13). The idea of appearing on *Hockey Night in Canada* is so appealing that it even captivates spectators, hence Bayle's reminiscing in *Heroes* about going to a Leafs game as a child with his father: "One more stop and this is it, Peter, the Gardens, and pretty soon all of Canada's going to be watching *us* on TV tonight, son, because *we're* going to be on 'Hockey Night in Canada'" (31; italics in original). Rather than anticipating the game they are about to watch, Bayle's father looks forward to being included in some way – even simply as a spectator – in the national ritual of *Hockey Night in Canada*. In a way, this also evokes the participatory pleasure of hockey novels themselves, the readerly feeling of partaking in "Canada's game" and thus being included in the sense of unity and belonging it appears to deliver.[3]

When small-town players "make it" in the NHL, they are seen as having symbolically brought the small town with them. Such players are seen as sources of community pride, symbolic assertions of the town's viability and ability to contribute productively to the larger national whole. When reflecting on the Falconbridge Falcons' various shortcomings, the narrator of *Logan in Overtime* suggests that "in the final analysis … the Falcons' greatest failure was in not putting Falconbridge on the sporting map. All the other towns had contributed players to the National Hockey League, with the result that all the other towns were getting their names on 'Hockey Night in Canada'" (25–6). To get your town's name on *Hockey Night in Canada* is to be recognized nationally as an important local component of the larger hockey-playing whole. (This goal is eventually realized in *Logan in Overtime* when the CBC shows up to cover the Falcons' overtime game that refuses to end.) A similar, though less comic, moment occurs in the fictional Ontario town of Huron Falls in Richard B. Wright's *The Age of Longing* (1995), when local hockey hero Buddy Wheeler gets called up to play for the Montreal

Maroons in a game against the Toronto Maple Leafs: "Thursday's edition of the *Huron Falls Times* carried a feature on Buddy Wheeler ... entitled 'Local Hockey Star on Radio Saturday'" (161). Wheeler's accomplishment brings the town together in that "even Leaf fans ... were pulling for Buddy Wheeler; after all, he was one of them and he had made it to the National Hockey League" (161). On the evening of the game the townspeople gather together to listen, but are thoroughly dismayed when Buddy Wheeler only gets to play one shift. Although the narrator of *The Age of Longing*, Buddy Wheeler's son, is ultimately critical of the small-town impulse to "make it big" in hockey (or anything else for that matter), it is evident to him that the broadcast caused genuine excitement in Huron Falls and offered a brief moment of community unity. The role of *Hockey Night in Canada* in Canadian hockey novels, then, is three-fold: 1) it validates the existence of the small town as a representative component or subset of the nation, 2) offers a means by which the small town can "plug in" to the national pulse and participate in the process of national imagining, and 3) venerates the cultural importance of hockey broadcasting to Canadian society.

CANADA'S NATIONAL SMALL TOWN; OR, THE "UGLY AMERICAN" GOES TO THE RINK

Whether by suggesting the ontological Canadianness of the game, the "natural" connection of hockey to Canadian history and geography, the cultural work of both rink and radio in facilitating national imagining, or the metonymic importance of the "small town" to the larger national whole, hockey novels see the game as a primary marker of Canadian cultural identity. Underlying these representations is the perceived need to distinguish Canadian culture from that of the United States. In this regard, hockey novels align with the literary nationalism that Szeman identifies in Canadian criticism since the Second World War, which is generally "directed toward an identification of the unique national characteristics of the Canadian nation either in opposition to the values of the United States or to what the United States represents: the embodiment of the values of modernity in national form" (Szeman 2003, 161). The purpose of myth-making in Canadian hockey novels, then, is first to suggest the continued viability of the nation by defining hockey *as* identity, and, second, to resolve the symbolic crisis proposed by American intervention in the game. Hockey novels tend to accomplish the later by extending the Romantic antagonism they propose between small towns and big cities to the international relationship between the Canadian and American nations. In this configuration, Canada is seen as embodying the "small-town" values of innocence, natural-ness, authenticity, and community, while America is inscribed with the corruption, impersonality, greed, and artificiality of the "big city."

Hockey novels often go out of their way to enforce this character-ization through familiar cultural stereotypes that cast Canada as a kinder, gentler, more collectively focused society than its southern neighbour. In *The Good Body*, for instance, Bobby Bonaduce reads a Fredericton newspaper upon his return to Canada and is surprised to find "letters to the editor, half of which quoted the Bible while railing against a gay group's attempt to hold a Pride parade. Where was he, Montana?" (41). The implicit suggestion is that Canada is supposed to be a place of pluralistic tolerance in which all members of society can experience equal treatment and acceptance, contrary to the putatively American tendencies toward religious bigotry and mandatory homogeneity. Bonaduce later reflects that perhaps "on some deeper level he hadn't chosen Canada so much as he'd fled the medical bills of the United States" (100), this time implying the shortcomings of American individualism by intimating a Canadian sense of collective responsibility that is often seen as the basis for universal health care. A similar characterization occurs in *Heroes*, when Bayle recalls the feeling of going to United States as a child and "everything seemed slightly dangerous, unpredictable, *American*" (85; italics in original). He goes on to describe a sense of safety and familiarity upon returning to Canada and seeing one of the "Halloween-orange BREWER'S RETAIL sign[s] a mile or so on the northern side of the border. The state-sanctioned distribution and sale of all alcoholic beverages. Canada. Home" (85). Again, the idea of collective responsibility is underscored by highlighting the Canadian policy of governmentally controlled distribution of alco-hol (which, in actuality, varies from province to province; Bayle is in Ontario). Although this passage could be read as ironically conflat-ing "home" with the possibility for drunken escape, the thematic of Canada as a kinder, gentler, more progressive society is frequently reinforced throughout *Heroes* by various caricatures of American conservatism: an extremely conservative talk radio host named I.M. Wright (an obvious Rush Limbaugh parody), a radical right-wing militia known as the Concerned and Armed Citizens for the American Way who periodically blow things up throughout the story, a drug dealer who describes his line of work as "the only logical career choice for any energetic young American entrepreneur from the wrong side of the tracks" (65), and a character who keeps a framed copy of the US Constitution hanging on the wall beside "a framed movie still of a youthful Ronald Reagan horseback with guns ablazing" (54). While these elements are obvious exaggerations, the suggestion of America as dangerously conservative (and even criminal) is ultimately put forward and even contributes to Bayle's decision to return to Canada. Hockey novels also tend to see Canadians as more gentle and polite than Americans, sometimes even to a fault as in *When She's Gone*'s suggestion that Canadians are "too nice too quiet too modest too apathetic" (89).

The effacement of Canadian cultural distinction from its southern neighbour is emblematic of the general cultural anxieties against which hockey novels appear to be reacting: the growth of continental monoculture, increased globalization, and the loss of a centralized and homogenous Canadian identity. As one character puts it quite directly in *The Penalty Box*, "it's a global village now and everything changes" (77). Thus in *The Good Body* Bonaduce finds himself thinking that "he was everywhere on the continent at once. McDonald's had done this, and Ted Turner had done this too, hiring his unidentifiably clean Yankee voices. These Fredericton mall kids wearing Nike hats – shoe company conquers the planet's feet and now does the head. It was like something out of *Batman* – Sameness Drops diabolically added to the water supply" (17). For Bonaduce, the dominance of American culture (seen here in the products of media, fast-food, and clothing corporations) threatens to efface any significant sense of Canadian difference. This is how it is possible to be "everywhere on the continent at once" – the mall in Fredericton is ostensibly the same as the mall in Boston or New York or Los Angeles. As with the other trappings of culture suggested in Bonaduce's dystopian vision of continental sameness, hockey novels often see the game as threatened by American influence. One of the major complaints is that "Americans have hijacked 'our' game, brutalizing and commercializing it in order to attract an audience which is ignorant of its grace, subtlety, and history" (Francis 1997, 168–9).

Hockey novels often see American fans as unappreciative of the game's sophistication and artistry, and therefore unworthy of

possessing or controlling it. When Bayle travels to the unnamed
American prairie town in *Heroes*, one of the first people he meets is
a janitor who has worked at the local arena for years. When asked
about his interest in the game, the janitor confides that despite his
years of close proximity to hockey he "[has] the hardest time just
following that little puck around. Thing no bigger than a hamburger
and you're supposed to keep track of it while all these big fellas be
whippin' by, fallin' over each other?" (43). Later in *Heroes* a local
sports reporter shares an anecdote with Bayle about "the necessity
of educating the public in a non-traditional hockey market about the
very rudiments of the game itself" (144). The story goes that one
night a local player scored a hat trick and a fan responded by throwing his hat on the ice, proper spectator protocol under the circumstances. The arena security guards had been sternly instructed to nip
any boisterous behaviour – such as throwing things on the ice – in
the bud, and promptly arrested the hat-throwing fan. The club had
to offer an apology and free passes to the next five home games. The
incident, of course, works to expose American inscience of even
hockey's most rudimentary rituals, a device which simultaneously
suggests Canadian distinction and appears to dismiss Americans as
crass, uncultured, and ignorant.

Rather than the game's artistry or traditions, it is the potential for
violence that is most often seen to attract Americans. A fictional
article about Felix Batterinski's development as a player in *The Last
Season* unfolds as part of the novel's plot and explains this phenomenon along commercial lines: "The vast majority of expansion took
place in the United States (in the 1974–75 season fifteen of the NHL's
eighteen teams were American-based) where the customers were
too often hockey unsophisticates. ('How do they pump the air into
that li'l black thang?' a Houston fan asked Gordie Howe.) Hockey
had to be sold, and any ticket outlet knew wrestling outdrew the
symphony: the stage was set for a Schultz, a Kelly and, of course, a
Batterinski" (62).

In Mark Anthony Jarman's *Salvage King, Ya!*, the narrator,
Drinkwater, recalls the bloodthirsty American fans he encountered
while playing for a minor league team in Seattle: "They mouthed an
amazing noise when we scored but they had no appreciation for fine
plays, thought or dekes; they didn't know the rules, the niceties; they
simply desired hick farmboy minor league blood to fall from me like
syrup. They wanted dumb Canucks to hit each other with sticks"

(170). A similar moment occurs in *The Good Body*, when Bondaduce reflects on playing for a minor league team in Tusla, Oklahoma: "Strange to be the home team here, trying to beat the shit out of a busload of fellow Canadians while all the cowboys in the audience hollered. They didn't shout here, they hollered and sometimes they yipped. On the scoreboard the word HOME could tear your heart out" (125). All these illustrations see violence as underscoring the American attraction to hockey and improper fan behaviour as detracting from America's right to symbolically possess the game; clearly, in Bonaduce's mind, "hollering" and "yipping" aren't the way to cheer at a hockey game. Later in the *The Good Body* Bonaduce remembers one of his minor league teammates in Tulsa who was convicted of raping a teenaged girl, recalling that "the newspaper ... [published] blatantly disparaging remarks about hockey players and Canadians, and the fact that hardly anyone went to see these games anyway, as if the converse would somehow have excused the rape, as if the star quarterback from Oklahoma State would be above such charges" (138). The same faulty logic of implicating all Canadians in the actions of one, of course, also sees American Hockey fans as unappreciative of the game's artistry and finesse. Reddick's Boston Mason, a rare American character in Canadian hockey fiction who understands and excels at hockey, suggests that simply being an American is enough to incur disfavour in the Canadian hockey scene: "to this day there exists a distaste for any American involved with Canadian hockey ... I suffered for it" (157). Similarly, the small-town fans in *Bus Ride* hate a particular player simply on the basis of his nationality: "that he was American was condemnation enough" (9).

DeLillo's *Amazons*, an American hockey novel, takes a rather different perspective on the appeal of hockey violence in the United States. At one point in *Amazons* the president of Madison Square Garden, James Kinross, informs Cleo Birdwell that "[to] tell you the truth ... I hate hockey. It's a fuggin shit-ass game for my money. You don't have a black or Hispanic element. It doesn't reflect the urban reality. Who wants to see two white guys hit each other? The violence has no bite to it. It's not relevant. It doesn't reflect the streets, and I come from the streets" (10). Birdwell responds that hockey "reflects the Canadian streets. It's a Canadian game. It reflects ice and snow, that's what it reflects" (10). Although like most of *Amazons* this exchange is obviously meant to be comedic, it articulates several familiar aspects of Canada's hockey myth and recognizes the extent to which the game continues to function as a white male preserve. For Kinross, this is precisely what makes hockey unappealing: that its violence and pastoral mythology aren't applicable in the American big city. The exchange continues as Kinross responds "well and good. I understand that [hockey is a Canadian game]. But this is New York, New York. Where's the fuggin criminal element? Who do we root for? Escapist violence is alright in the movies. But this is live. Real people swinging sticks. Without any relevance, it's kind of disgusting. If it doesn't reflect the streets, you wonder what these guys are doing it for. What's the point?" (10). The intended humour of this passage, it would seem, is that Kinross rejects the idea that Americans love watching "dumb Canucks hit each other with sticks" (as *Salvage King, Ya!* puts it) not on the anticipated grounds that violence itself is distasteful, but on the racist assumption that real American violence occurs among blacks and Hispanics and that violence meant to be consumed for entertainment should reflect and explore this "reality."

One exceptional Canadian hockey novel that does see American fans as knowledgeable about the game is Michael McKinley's *The Penalty Killing* (2010). Although a character jokes at one point in *The Penalty Killing* that hockey should be able to "get a proper TV deal in the US of A" because "all those strapping white men, shedding their blood at the drop of a hockey glove" is "far more entertaining than the nightly highlight reel of our gift of democracy to Jihadville" (19), American fans generally aren't portrayed as ignorant of the game's finer points or disproportionately interested in its violence. The joke about America's "gift of democracy to Jihadville" is one of several moments in *The Penalty Killing* that criticize what McKinley sees as the paranoid, overbearing, and self-righteous culture of post-9/11 America, but this critique isn't ultimately related to hockey culture or used as a foil to depict Canada as a preferable alternative. At one point in the story McKinley's protagonist, Martin Carter, a Canadian former player living in New York and working for the fictional New York St Patricks professional team, clearly specifies that the American fans "knew their hockey" (297). Furthermore, this knowledge of hockey is connected directly to national pride by way of the singing of "The Star-Spangled Banner" before an important playoff game: "tonight's singers, a mixed chorus of eight graders from St Patrick's Old Cathedral School, touched the crowd as if the bombs were bursting in mid-air right here and now, and the rafters shook with patriotic pride and energy of expectation that tonight was going to be a victory, here, in the home of the brave" (293–4). Clearly McKinley's American fans see hockey as powerfully connected to American pride and belonging in the same way that many Canadians associate the game with Canadianness. *The Penalty Killing* is a detective novel which follows many conventions of that genre, and the idea of American hockey patriotism is again underscored as the mystery is solved. Part of Carter's sleuthing involves preventing the team from being sold to a group of investors who, despite a faithful and fervent local fan base, are planning to move the team to Russia. In this respect, *The Penalty Killing* participates in the general anxiety that hockey novels exhibit toward global capitalism and big business; as will be seen, the fear that financial considerations invariably trump local tradition, good hockey sense, and fan loyalty is a powerful trope in Canadian hockey novels. Again, however, *The Penalty Killing* draws different national distinctions on this issue. While most Canadian hockey novels see franchise relocation as representing the Americanization of Canada's game, McKinley uses this trope more broadly to suggest that the increasing globalization of professional hockey could work against established American fans as much as against Canadians.

Beyond representing hockey as legitimately American, *The Penalty Killing* also reconfigures the pastoral myth to transcend national boundaries. Speaking of professional teams in Vancouver and Los Angeles in the novel's fictional Continental Hockey League, McKinley's omniscient narrator suggests that "West Coast teams … were so seduced by la dolce vita that they forgot what it was like to suffer in winter. The desire for revenge came from misery of blizzards and ice storms and deep snow at your door. What fury fuelled these two Pacific teams? Having no snow to shovel and not having to drive to the rink through flat, ice bound industrial wastelands?" (148). This passage reconfigures the pastoral myth that hockey is naturally and inherently connected with winter in two noteworthy ways: 1) that winter provides the motivation to play rather than simply the means, and 2) that the "artificialness" of playing in a warm climate applies in the temperate Canadian locale of Vancouver as much as it does in sunny Los Angeles. Having made this judgment, however, McKinley's narrator immediately qualifies it by explaining that "tonight the [Vancouver and Los Angeles] teams offered the kind of hockey that Carter had played on outdoor rinks on endless weekend afternoons, before he knew there were rules and strategies, when instinct and imagination united with the energy that kids have, the force of creation flowing through them like light" (148–9). *The Penalty Killing* ultimately suggests, then, that the youthful purity of pond hockey play – which, in keeping with the genre as a whole, is idealized in this passage – can be available and applicable regardless of venue or national setting.

As hostile as many Canadian hockey novels are toward American ignorance, they are markedly more critical of American greed. Hockey novels typically see a putatively American capitalism as having ruined professional hockey by making it more about profit than play. As Bonaduce puts it in *The Good Body*, "in a brief time we have seen the game change to its corporate, crumbling state. The way owners buy winning teams, the way the players change teams" (122). *Heroes* makes the same point more subtly when Bayle meets the Warriors' play-by-play broadcasters, both of whom started their careers covering basketball. After going on air to thank a tediously long list of corporate sponsors, the broadcasters tell Bayle that "when you get right down to it, it's all really the same game, isn't it?" (123). The joke is that professional sport – be it basketball or hockey – is ultimately controlled by commercial interests, and that to work as a commentator one has to master the art of advertising rather than the intricacies of the game. To answer the concern that American greed is ruining Canada's game, hockey novels extend the representational antagonism between Canadian "small-town" purity and American "big-city" corruption to the difference between the amateur/ recreational and professional games. Generally speaking, these representations congeal around two specific events: the infamous Wayne Gretzky trade from the Edmonton Oilers to the Los Angeles Kings and the relocation of the Winnipeg Jets to Phoenix.

"THE DAY THE MUSIC DIED": THE GRETZKY TRADE

Perhaps the most talented player ever to shoot a puck has been Wayne Gretzky. The debate about Gretzky's relative merits versus those of other possible contenders for the mantle – Gordie Howe, Bobbie Orr, Mario Lemieux – rages on among avid fans and is accordingly enacted in several Canadian hockey novels. Certainly a reasonable case can be made for Gretzky: he amassed a breathtaking number of points and records over the course of his career, and led the Edmonton Oilers to four Stanley Cups throughout the 1980s. More important than any discussion of Gretzky's relative greatness, however, is what is at stake in the debate itself. During his time with the Oilers, Gretzky quickly became (and arguably remains) Canada's most recognizable hockey icon. Gretzky was seen by many as the face of an emerging reinvigoration of skill and finesse play over the clutch-and-grab physicality of the 1970s. Gzowksi's *The Game of Our Lives* casts this sea change as a vital reclamation of "Canadian" play, and in Gzowski's reading the early Gretzky years appear to be something of a golden age of Canadian hockey. Gretzky, then, provided symbolic validation for two important tenets of the hockey myth, the related ideas of Canadian pre-eminence and symbolic possession. Gretzky had become such a prominent public figure in Canada by the 1987–88 season that when the owner of the Oilers, Peter Pocklington, announced on 9 August 1988 that Gretzky had been traded to the Los Angeles Kings, Canadian hockey fans erupted in a fury of outrage and protest. "The Trade," as the deal soon became known, upset Canadian fans to the point where effigies of Pocklington were burned on public streets (Associated Press 2010), and the federal New Democrats actually demanded that the government intervene to keep Gretzky in Canada (Morrison 1988). In exchange for Gretzky, the Oilers received two journeyman players, three first-round draft picks, and, most notably, $15 million in cash. Many fans perceived the deal as the logical outcome of the recently finalized but not yet officially enacted free-trade agreement, and media coverage overwhelmingly portrayed the event as a national crisis that was indicative of the larger trend in Canadian society toward Americanization (S. Jackson 1994). For many Canadians, the significance of the trade seemed abundantly clear: America was buying Canada's game.[4]

In the introductory preamble to *Iced*, Alison Guthrie gives her opinion of the Gretzky trade: "in Canada [hockey] is geared toward producing players for the National Hockey League. This is where Wayne Gretzky plays. Wayne used to play in Edmonton, but now due to the profit-motivated machinations of the sports world, he plays in Los Angeles" (2). Guthrie's comment is exemplary of Canadian hockey novels in general, which tend to see the Gretzky trade as the ultimate betrayal, the heart and soul of Canadian hockey sold to the United States for a mere $15 million. In *Heroes*, Bayle's father bitterly watches Gretzky and the Kings defeat the Maple Leafs in the 1993 conference final. Bayle's father complains after Gretzky is spared from a penalty that should have ejected him from the game, only to score a hat trick and almost single-handedly defeat the Leafs: "I wouldn't put it past those American bastards in New York who are calling the shots in the NHL these days having something to do with this ... You think those pencil-heads weren't just dying to see Los Angeles in the Stanley Cup final? Think of the media coverage. Think of the TV markets they're going to get. Think of all the exposure. Now I'm not saying that *every* referee in the league is in the direct payment of those corporate whores down in New York, but that sonofabitch Kerry Fraser and a few of those linesmen, well ..." (169). Although Bayle's father isn't upset about the Trade per se, it is clear that in his mind Gretzky has come to symbolize everything wrong (read "American") with the NHL. The suggestion of a conspiracy theory by which Gretzky's Kings are privileged over the Leafs in a Stanley Cup run conveys both the "machinations" of big business (as Alguire puts it in *Iced*) and the artificiality of the professional game, in that it can be tampered with and externally controlled. What is most at stake in the complaint made by Bayle's father is the authenticity of the play: what should have happened didn't happen, for the simple reason that it was not profitable. The result, notably, is to detract from the implicit Canadianness of hockey; Bayle's father seems to assume that, as a Canadian team, the Leafs have a more natural right to play for the Stanley Cup than the Kings.[5]

Although neither *Salvage King, Ya!* nor *The Last Season* deal specifically with the Gretzky trade, both characterize Los Angeles as metonymic for American hockey culture in general, and, in doing so, reflect some of the sentiments that made the Trade so abhorrent to many Canadians. In *Salvage King, Ya!*, Drinkwater complains when "GMs horse-trade and I awake one summer day an indentured servant of the L.A. Kings, the league's famous burial grounds festooned with palms ... This is pre-Gretzky, pre-Cambrian. It's the bigs but it's not the bigs. They're always last place. Outsiders can never know what it feels like. Better money though than Seattle [the minor league professional team Drinkwater had been demoted to earlier]" (191). The idea of "indentured servitude" foregrounds the economic aspect of Drinkwater's complaint (i.e., American ability to buy the game), but his real objection to playing in Los Angeles is the lack of legitimacy and respectability: "it's the bigs but it's not the bigs." For Drinkwater, as for Felix Batterinski in *The Last Season*, a trade to

Los Angeles signals the decline of his ability to compete in the NHL. As the "league's famous burial grounds," Los Angeles is a place of high-salaried mediocrity. While Drinkwater doesn't object to his pay raise, he certainly seems to feel compromised or demeaned by what the salary requires of him. In this sense, Drinkwater is complicit in the "American" hockey enterprise in that he values his pocketbook more than his dignity.

Part of the particular indignity of playing in Los Angeles, of course, is enduring the "improper" conduct of fans and promoters who don't conform to typical hockey expectations. As Batterinski puts it, "the magic mountain in Disneyland was more real than a bunch of half-talented Canadians charging around on ice after a forty-five-cent piece of black rubber in a replica of the Forum in Rome, all for a mere $12.50 a seat. They even sold margaritas and tacos in the tuck shop at the Fabulous Forum [the Los Angeles arena]. No fat men with runny noses peering knowingly through the steam of their Styrofoam cups; in California there might be foam cups and heat but it began with cleavage and ended with skintight acrylic pants" (219). Batterinski's markers of artificiality are particularly interesting. The fact that the arena is a replica of the Roman Forum, coupled with the relatively low ticket prices, indicates the spectacle of the hockey event in Los Angeles: Batterinski seems to be suggesting that hockey is at best a curiosity in America and at worst a freak show. The complaint about margaritas and tacos in the tuck shop and the description of coffee cups reconfigured as bra cups suggest a more sinister grievance, that the knowledgeable (white) male culture of the rink is being Hispanicized, feminized, and glamorized, and thus somehow demeaned. For Batterinski, as for Drinkwater, Los Angeles represents an inauthentic, illegitimate, and indeed, abhorrent hockey experience, but, again, it is an experience in which Canadians are actively complicit. The Canadian players in Batterinksi's narrative, himself included, would rather endure the spectacle of hockey in Los Angeles than accept minor league demotion, or, worse still, the obsolescence of retirement.

While *Salvage King, Ya!* and *The Last Season* merely complain about the Americanization of hockey, *Finnie Walsh* attempts to suggest a solution to this "problem" using the Gretzky trade as its thematic center. Generally speaking, *Finnie Walsh* sees hockey as "pure" when played for fun and "impure" when played for money. When Finnie – the moral voice of the novel and a sort of hockey mystic with intuitive spiritual knowledge about the game – plays hockey, it is always for the "right" reasons; even when he makes it to the pros, Finnie tells Paul that he is fuelled by "something in the arenas, an excitement, almost a fever" (140) rather than by his hefty salary. When Finnie is approached by agents after his NHL debut, he rejects their advances without hesitation: "[Finnie] believed that agents were a big part of what was wrong with hockey and he preferred to manage his own interests, using his lawyer to check contracts for legal snags" (141). Throughout the story, Paul and Finnie follow Wayne Gretzky's career and, upon the Trade, Gretzky becomes emblematic of Finnie's hatred of hockey capitalism.

When Paul first hears the news he reflects that "[Peter Pocklington] sold Wayne Gretzky, the Great One, the most talented player in the history of the game. He sold him like a pair of shoes, a used car or a piece of furniture. I was shattered" (107). Finnie is equally devastated, referring to the Trade as "the day the music died" (107), a reference to Don McLean's song "American Pie," a musical eulogy for rock and roll pioneers Buddy Holly, Ritchie Valens, and J.P. "The Big Bopper" Richardson. Finnie goes on to explain that players are "just commodities. They may as well be impaled on rods and put into a foosball table. There's no magic anymore. You can't own magic. And when you buy it or sell it, it disappears … What's the point of being as good as [Gretzky] is if you can still be bought and sold? Is it just about the money?" (108). When Paul counters that perhaps the game *is* just about the money, Finnie insists instead that "hockey is about Georges Vezina and Bill Barilko and Peter Stastny and people playing a game because it's part of who they are" (108). Throughout the novel these players function as exemplars of hockey for the "right" reasons; unlike Gretzky, these players didn't sell-out or pander to profit and marketability.

When Finnie eventually makes it to the NHL himself, he is surprised to receive a generous amount of playing time. He soon, however, realizes why he has been so fortunate: "he'd been getting called up … to increase his marketability, a move that had been calculated by [the] team's management. They had been getting Finnie good press and letting him play so that he would be worth more on the trading block. It had little to do with their confidence in him or his skill as a goaltender" (142). This experience, of course, is incredibly disillusioning for Finnie, and causes Paul to reflect about his own career that "it had been a long time since hockey had been fun for me. I still enjoyed playing, but it was a job now; the game was not what it was when we were kids. We were being paid to play hockey. It's hard to complain about that. Besides, I wasn't very good at anything else. But I didn't love the game the way I used to" (143). The moral lesson of the story, which Finnie seems to know intuitively and Paul has to learn by the end of the novel, is that if you don't love the game you're part of what is ruining it.

In the end, it is a hockey card of Howie Morenz – another symbolic "anti-Gretzky" who, according to *Finnie Walsh*, loved the game so much that he died when he found out he wouldn't be able to play anymore – that helps Paul realize you have to love hockey in order to play it. Morenz is described as "the man who died for hockey" (155), which, by the end of the story has also become true of Finnie who dies choking on a whistle he is blowing in order to help Paul score the winning goal of the Stanley Cup final. After Finnie's death Paul finally realizes "the point [Finnie had] been trying to make with the Howie Morenz card. To stay in hockey, I would have had to love the game the way Finnie had loved it. I refused to be one of the people who was ruining the sport. If you don't love it, if you can exist without it, then you shouldn't be there" (163). Finnie Walsh, then, is ultimately configured as a sort of hockey Christ figure, in that by his death Paul manages to learn the spiritual "truth" about the game. The logic of substitutionary sacrifice is applied to Finnie throughout the novel in general: it is by attacking his own teammate in defence of Paul that Finnie's professional career ends, and earlier in the story Finnie begins playing hockey with almost religious fervour to atone for a specific "sin" he has committed (the emotional logic of this substitution is made clear in the narrative). Upon realizing that you need to love hockey in order to play it, Paul quits the professional game despite having scored the Stanley Cup-winning goal and having the potential for a "multimillion-dollar career" (163).

While Finnie dies so that Paul can learn this necessary lesson, it is the reader to whom the moral truism is ultimately directed. In a sense, then, Finnie dies to save hockey itself from the forces of greed and selfishness that the novel sees as having besieged it. Again, Paul characterizes this situation in specifically nationalist terms: "After the Gretzky trade, Finnie started to dislike the United States. It's true that almost all Canadians share an inherent mistrust of the neighbours to the south and I think that in most cases it's justified because,

let's face it, America is nearly always up to something. Finnie, however, was much more adamant about his anti-Americanism than the
rest of us. He once remarked that the Gretzky trade was either
the day the United States started to buy Canada, piece by piece, or
the day it completed the purchase" (108). While Paul dismisses
Finnie's anti-Americanism as simply a heightened version of the
Canadian cultural norm – a noteworthy characterization in and of
itself – it becomes clear by the end of the novel that Finnie's position
has been privileged as a sort of spiritual truth. While Finnie works as
a redeemer of the game, he is also a moral referee (he dies by choking
on a whistle) who adjudicates what is and is not acceptable in hockey terms. At the very extreme of the unacceptable is the fact that
American greed should be able to buy Wayne Gretzky, and by proxy
Canada's symbolic possession of hockey, and, as such, *Finnie Walsh*
signifies in the representational binary in which Canadian hockey is
good, pure, and played for the love of the game while American
hockey is about profit motive and commerce. Unlike *Salvage King,
Ya!* and *The Last Season*, however, which complain about America's
theft of hockey but don't really object to Canadian complicity in it,
Finnie Walsh urges Canadians to take the drastic action of simply
refusing to play if not for the "right" reasons.

"SAVE OUR TEAM, SAVE OUR GAME"

The other event that Canadian hockey novels see as emblematic of
American capitalism ruining Canada's game is the relocation of the
Winnipeg Jets to Phoenix, Arizona.[6] In *Heroes*, Bayle suggests that it
is "slightly depressing to learn that the number of Canadian professional hockey franchises [is] steadily diminishing each year and that
every day new teams [seem] to be popping up in unlikely American
cities like Memphis, Nashville, and Atlanta" (66). Bayle tries to suppress his dismay about hockey's southward migration by appealing
to his philosophical hero, Sextus Empiricus: "Empiricus dictum
number one: Freedom from disturbance means suspension of judgment. If, like clean water, raw timber, and maple syrup, Canada's
game was becoming just one more Canadian export steadily seeping
south, well, then, Empiricus dictum number one" (66). Although
Bayle's suspension of emotion ultimately doesn't hold, he is a rarity
among fans for even attempting to be stoic about the loss of Canadian
teams. When the NHL hired its first commissioner, Gary Bettman, in

1992, it did so specifically with the idea of expanding its presence in the American market. To this end, Bettman's "first years in office saw new expansion franchises and relocations of existing teams, as well as new television contracts and merchandising initiatives" (Mason 2006, 181). As Bettman and the NHL pushed to attract high-profile buyers for new markets such as Miami and Anaheim, existing small-market teams in Quebec City and Winnipeg were struggling. Quebec and Winnipeg's troubles stemmed from their inability to tap into the NHL's expanding media efforts, the lack of a league-wide revenue-sharing plan at the time, and from their outdated arena facilities. Despite massive public outcries and grassroots fundraising campaigns both teams eventually relocated south.[7] The Quebec Nordiques moved to Colorado and became the Avalanche in time for the 1995–96 NHL season (in which they won the Stanley Cup), while Winnipeg held out one year longer before moving to Phoenix and becoming the Coyotes. After the loss of Quebec and Winnipeg, teams such as Calgary, Edmonton, and Ottawa also struggled to survive in the economic climate created by the NHL's drive for American expansion. One hockey novel, O'Connor's *The Penalty Box*, responds to this situation by proposing the creation of a new professional hockey league predicated on northernness and the prospect of repatriating "Canada's game." As one character puts it, "we owe it to our history to bring the game back" (203). Another, Fred Stenson's *Teeth* (1994) suggests the attitude of league governors toward an unnamed "Western Canadian prairie city" that wants to acquire an NHL team: "[the city] was certainly hockey-mad enough, but every attempt in that direction had been foiled – you could even say 'scorned' – by the league's governors and team owners. The city … was seen as simply too rustic for the 'Bigs,' a backwater with zero television appeal in Eastern Canada and south of the border" (16).[8] Of course, it should be noted that "little work has been done to incorporate the American hockey fan's perspective into the larger debate about the United States' aggressive takeover of Canada's national pastime," and that – as Craig Hyatt and Julie Stevens point out – "Canadian hockey capital serves its own interest just as much as does American hockey capital. In fact, the negative impact of Canadian businesspeople upon hockey may be more pronounced than that of American businesspeople given that, over time, the former have made many of the key decisions related to the commercialization of men's hockey. Quite simply, Canadian capitalists

allowed several decisions about the development of hockey in
Canada, and abroad, to be left to the marketplace, where hockey
was just another commodity" (Hyatt and Stevens 2009, 26–7, 40).

The issue of American expansion throughout the 1990s and the
threat to Canada's game that it allegedly represents goes a long way
toward explaining the profusion of Canadian hockey novels in
recent years. Coupled with the relocation of Canadian franchises
and the financial worries of others, the proliferation of new American teams throughout the 1990s and early 2000s brought about the
feeling among many Canadian fans that "our game" was being sys-
tematically dismantled and shipped south. These fears, of course,
were part and parcel with more general concerns over growing
Americanization, the cultural consequences of free trade, and the
seeming instability of the Canadian state (which was arguably being
called into question by the ongoing constitutional debates during
this time). Because hockey has often been seen as a guarantor of
Canadian cultural distinction, the NHL's program of American
expansion and the resulting uncertainty surrounding Canadian
small-market teams appeared for many to confirm Canada's economic dependency on the United States and to symbolize the effacement of Canadian difference in favour of continental monoculture.
The NHL's American expansion, then, coupled with general anxieties
over Canadian cultural and economic distinction to effectively create a widespread desire for the kind of nostalgic, idealized, and distinctively Canadian vision of the game that is central to many of the
novels discussed in this study.

The scepticism Canadian hockey novels express toward the North
American professional game's growing penchant for southern locales
and big-money contracts illustrates the extent to which these novels
are reacting against the specific cultural and historical moment
described above. Rather than anticipating the critical posture of
adult hockey novels toward the professional game, many first-wave
children's hockey novels view professionalism as a worthy goal and
a viable means of making a living. In McFarlane's *The Dynamite
Flynns*, for instance, the Flynn cousins opt for hockey instead of college because they need to earn money for the family after their uncle
suffers a stroke. In some first-wave children's hockey novels going
pro is glorified as the means to a better life, such as Young's Bill
Spunska novels (*Boy on Defence* [1953] and *A Boy at the Leafs'
Camp* [1963]) and McFarlane's *Breakaway* (1976), which tells the

story a young hockey player who escapes from the "hard, hopeless, unrewarded work" of his uncle's farm by making a career in professional hockey (32). Beyond offering the possibility of a good wage, the professional game appears in these novels to let men fulfill the expectations of the breadwinner role on which masculinity has often been predicated. This is made abundantly clear, for instance, in McFarlane's "They Didn't Know Hockey" when a young player's girlfriend objects to him "working in a small-town tannery for eighteen dollars a week when [he] could be making hundreds of dollars for playing hockey" (*Leslie McFarlane's Hockey Stories*, 115). Indeed, the vast majority of first-wave children's hockey novels follow the rise a talented young player who through determination and positive attitude progresses from informal pond hockey or lower-level organized play to the professional leagues. Consequently, these novels often address the ins and outs of hockey professionalism in matter-of-fact detail by depicting business dealings with coaches, management, and scouts, and by devoting significant time to the ways in which young players negotiate the business aspects of the game. Rather than being critical, these depictions characterize the off-ice powers that govern professional hockey as supportive and paternal authorities who care about players' best interests and – despite having to make tough decisions about salaries, rosters, ice time, etc. – always deal honestly and openly with players. These optimistic accounts, of course, gloss over the NHL's troubled history of labour–management relations and outright exploitation of players, which has been well-documented in Cruise and Griffiths' (1991) *Net Worth*, Dowbiggin's (2006) *Money Players*, and elsewhere.

It should be noted, however, that not all first-wave children's hockey novels represent the professional game uncritically. Probably the best example of this is McFarlane's *McGonigle Scores!* (1966). *McGonigle Scores!* is the story of Skates McGonigle, a former professional player who since retiring has worked as a hockey scout. McGonigle travels to the remote Northern Ontario mining town of Snowshoe Lake in the interests of getting a star prospect, Tim Beckett, to sign a "c-form," the legally binding document which makes him property of McGonigle's professional club. Although McGonigle comes off more favourably than his rival, a scout for another professional team named Blackjack Snead who makes it sound as though "the NHL was a benevolent organization devoted to developing sound minds in the sound bodies of Canadian youth"

(166), it is clear that the process of getting young prospects and their parents to sign the c-form frequently involves misrepresentation. At one point in the story readers are even told that McGonigle has successfully "conned dozens of kids and their parents into signing c-forms" (249). But while McGonigle initially attempts to convince Beckett's mother that professional sports aren't about "trad[ing] and sell[ing] human beings like ... cattle" (125), a series of plot events persuades him that he is actually in the wrong. One of these involves McGonigle joining the local oldtimers team, a device which appears to reconnect him with the purity of play and love of the game that hockey novels consistently see as antithetical to economic motivations. In the end McGonigle makes the signing, but does so with a good-faith handshake rather than a legally binding contract. Perhaps because it is critical of the professional game and therefore more in line with the beliefs expressed in recent adult-oriented hockey writing, *McGonigle Scores!* is the only one of McFarlane's hockey novels to have been re-released in a contemporary edition.[9]

Several first-wave hockey novels aimed at a more adolescent audience are also critical of hockey professionalism. Unlike the complaint of adult-oriented hockey novels that professionalism results in Americanization, however, these novels see professionalism as making players vulnerable to exploitation and converting the game from a sacred institution to a media spectacle. Scott Young and George Robertson's *Face-Off* (1971), for instance, follows the hockey career of Billy Duke, "the third in a line of Canadian Golden Boys" that also includes Bobby Hull and Bobby Orr (2).[10] Although *Face-Off* stops short of seeing professional hockey as a "system that makes a hockey player a chattel, powerless to control his destiny" (245), it acknowledges the burden that hockey capitalism places on players and ultimately blames this pressure for the chain of events that lead to the novel's final crisis moment, the death of Duke's girlfriend Sherri Nelson. As he attempts to make sense of Nelson's death, Duke ponders his professional requirements to "feed [the] crowd what it wanted: the blood-bath in Los Angeles, the big wind-up behind the net, and the burgeoning roar as I pushed the puck along and slipped off the checks and watched for the right pass; the image of Canadian Boy, ruggedly playing a man's game, smiling for the cameras, signing autographs, visiting hospitals, knocking out teeth" (248). The "blood-bath in Los Angeles" refers to an earlier episode in which Duke gets in several fights and comes "as close as I had ever been to being beserk" (108). Duke concludes, then, that the expectations of having to play well (i.e., to put on a good show for the spectators), play tough, and keep up the image of the all-Canadian Golden Boy put too much pressure on him and strain on his relationship with Nelson, ultimately causing him to be "gone at the time she needed me most" (249).

After blaming hockey culture for Nelson's death and his own world-weariness, however, Duke ends his narrative by returning to the emotionally and psychologically draining obligations of his career. Having fallen asleep while mulling over his thoughts and grief, Duke wakes up and realizes he is late for a game. His response is instinctive and immediate: "I never once stopped to ask myself what I was doing. I only knew I had committed the unpardonable sin of being late for a game. I pulled on my skates and laced them, took one of my sticks from the rack, and was running on my skates for the door when I thought of her. 'Sherri, forgive me,' I said. Then I went out into the corridor [toward the ice]" (250). In the end, then, despite acknowledging the high personal cost of being a professional hockey player, *Face-Off* ultimately suggests that these sacrifices are worthwhile or at least bearable. As Duke arrives at the ice and the novel ends, his final comment to the reader makes clear that he remains firmly ensnared within professional hockey's vicious circle of affirmation and obligation: "the crowd had seen me and was on its feet, screaming" (250). In the words of Hollands, "while Billy Duke appears to bend all the rules and authoritative conventions of professional hockey, in the end he chooses to return to the very structures that oppressed all of his personal relationships" (224).

A similar thematic of defiance resolved into eventual affirmation of the professional game's culture and expectations occurs in John Craig's *The Pro* (1968), in which a fictional NHL team called the Falcons suspends their captain and best player, Les Burton, as a public relations move when he is unjustly blamed for the attempted suicide of a glamorous television star. The Falcons recognize that the decision is more about good publicity and keeping sponsors happy than justice, and, even worse, that it makes no hockey sense. When eight of the team's players refuse to take the ice, in solidarity with Burton's suspension, they are said to be taking a stand not only against the team's owners and management but also "against the league and its president and its statistics and its PR staffs. Against the whole medieval structure, the feudalism, the indentured military service of the NHL and its neatly codified laws" (253). When it becomes clear that neither the rebellious players nor the owners are willing to back down, the team's coach – after recalling his own bucolic hockey origins on the pond with "dozens and dozens of kids chasing a frozen horsebun over the rough ice" (280) – takes matters into his own hands and does the right thing within the framework of the story by sending Burton out to play. As in *McGonigle Scores!*, it is nostalgic recollection of pond-hockey purity that appears to connect the coach with the true essence of the game. The novel concludes, then, with the rebel players' integrity preserved and Burton's symbolic reinstatement into the game when he declares his intent to "go on playing hockey – as well as I can, for as long as I can" (302).

The degree of success that Billy Duke and Les Burton achieve in pushing back against managerial control is made possible in large part by their status as star players. The same is true of Joe Johannsson in R.J. Childerhose's *Winter Racehorse* (1968). *Winter Racehorse* follows Johannsson's rise through junior hockey to winning the NHL scoring title in his rookie season, a fact which he feels should give him considerable leverage with management. Throughout the novel, however, Johannsson becomes increasingly disillusioned with the ways in which management treats him as a "personality" rather than as a "player" (333). The issue comes to a head during an episode in which the team's owner, Forbes Fordham, plans to manage Johannsson's image in order to create publicity: "[Johannsson] wanted to cross the room and mash Fordham's aristocratic nose all over his face. He wanted to get the hell away from Toronto. From the NHL. From contrived publicity and people like Fordham" (333). Another aspect of Johannsson's disillusionment with professional hockey is the way in which the league tolerates borderline and quasi-criminal violence in order to attract fans. As the focalized narrator notes, "the commissioner of the NHL could stop the violence overnight. But [he] was paid by the owners, men like Forbes Fordham, who considered hockey a spectacle. Fighting and brawling a spectacle" (337). It is worth noting here that this position on hockey violence fits into a general trend among hockey novels that will be returned to later in chapter 4, in which excessive violence is rejected but the importance of toughness and physical play maintained. Indeed, *Winter Racehorse* requires players to be tough and doesn't object to "clean" hits. But the main complaint of this passage is that the purity of hockey has been compromised in order to make the

game a "spectacle." By neglecting the players' best interests in order
to attract fans, the commissioner reveals what Johannsson believes to
be wrong-headed and profit-driven priorities. Eventually Johannsson's
surliness toward the game's business aspects and unwillingness to be
manipulated by the team's governors gain him the reputation of
being a "sorehead" (400), but he nonetheless remains adamant
about conducting himself and managing his career on his own terms.
Near the novel's end, Johannsson's younger brother Arne (who looks
up to Joe and hopes to emulate his brother's NHL success), is seriously injured while playing junior hockey. Despite the fact that his
team is currently involved in a playoff semifinal series, Johannsson
requests permission from Fordham to take time off so he can visit
Arne in the hospital. When Fordham denies this request it becomes
ultimately clear to Johannsson that "to men like Forbes Fordham ...
hockey players weren't people" (418). Johannsson launches into a
long tirade against Fordham and hockey professionalism in general,
before eventually quitting the team despite the prospect of a huge
contract for the coming season. As the novel ends, Johannsson tells
his father that he will go to university and that he will try to convince Arne to give up on professional hockey as well. Like *Finnie
Walsh*, then, *Winter Racehorse* ultimately suggests that the only way
to deal with a culture that sees players as assets rather than individuals, and compromises the purity of the game through slavish devotion to profit, is to walk away.

Rather than depicting the damaging effects that professionalism
can have on individual players, adult-oriented hockey novels tend to
be concerned with what they see to be the cultural consequences of
hockey capitalism: the Americanization of the game. Although several hockey novels react explicitly against the NHL's program of
American expansion, it will be useful to begin with two that address
this issue implicitly, *Hockey Night in the Dominion of Canada* and
Dawson City Seven. Both of these novels were written in the early
1990s, a time in which the future of small-market Canadian teams
appeared to be in jeopardy as never before, and both, significantly,
are historical novels. Historical novels tend to be underwritten by
the assumption that the past can speak powerfully and relevantly
to the preoccupations and concerns of the present. The setting of
an historical novel, then, is not merely a backdrop; rather, it is
a carefully chosen context that attempts to address the cultural
moment in which the novel itself is produced. Both *Hockey Night in*

the Dominion of Canada and *Dawson City Seven* suggest historical moments of conflict between the small town and the big city for literal and symbolic possession of hockey. Since Canadian hockey novels see the small town as a representative subset of the larger national whole and as metonymic of the authenticity, naturalness, and pastoral purity of the Canadian game in general, it isn't unreasonable to see the struggle of small towns in these novels to preserve their stake in hockey as symbolically aligning with that of the Canadian "small town" against the capitalistic and commodifying impulses of the American "big city."

By the turn of the twentieth century, hockey had become an "important institution" in many Canadian towns "where citizens quite rightly saw themselves as contributing vitally to the nation's economy by harvesting the natural resources of the region" (Simpson 1989, 184–5). Many of these towns formed hockey teams as a source of recreation for the men employed in local industry, and competitive and regional play soon became a source of community connection and civic pride. In a sense, then, hockey came of age in small Canadian towns as much as – if not more so than – in the nation's major urban centers. From 1901 to 1911, however, Canada's population increased by 43 per cent, of which "fully 70 per cent joined the labour force in industry and transportation ... [and] much of this industrial workforce ended up in Canada's cities" (Bumsted 1998, 225). As the major cities burgeoned in size, various investors, organizers, and owners began to realize the potential profits to be had from professional hockey. Although it was arguably Ambrose O'Brien's indiscriminate spending to assemble the Renfrew Millionaires that accelerated the hockey bidding wars past the point of no return, the growing acceptance of professionalism and a series of league reorganizations throughout the 1910s and 20s eventually lured the majority of competitive teams and elite players away from small Canadian towns.

One of the main reasons that O'Brien initially decided to spare no expense in stocking his Renfrew Millionaires with the preeminent stars of the day – both historically and in the fictional rendering of *Hockey Night in the Dominion of Canada* – was that the team had been rejected for a Stanley Cup bid in 1907. *Hockey Night in the Dominion of Canada* portrays this rejection as stemming from the perceived illegitimacy of small-town hockey: "'And now Renfrew talks of challenging for the Stanley Cup,' a Toronto newspaper mocked in the spring of 1907. 'All because they have won a fence-corner league.' The paper went further, sarcastically advising its readers not to laugh at the Renfrew challenge: 'If you never lived in a country town you don't know how seriously these people take themselves'" (52). To be taken seriously, and eventually to bring the Stanley Cup to Renfrew, O'Brien believed he would have to obtain the best players money could buy. After several bouts of inter-league politicking in which O'Brien's National Hockey Association (NHA) eventually broke the back of its rival Canadian Hockey Association, it was finally arranged that the Millionaires would have a chance at their Stanley Cup challenge if they could finish first in the NHA regular season. In the push to mount this Cup bid against the reigning champions, the Ottawa Silver Seven, *Hockey Night in the Dominion of Canada* sees "all the small towns" as being "for Renfrew in the struggle ... their victory would be a victory for all the towns whose teams had struggled for years in the shadow of the great hockey clubs from the capital city" (257). Although Renfrew ultimately failed to win the league title and secure the Stanley Cup challenge, *Hockey Night in the Dominion of Canada* represents the players as working hard to beat Ottawa in a remaining league game because "[they] knew a win over the big-city team would be almost as sweet to residents of the small town as a championship trophy" (335).

Dawson City Seven is similar in its characterization of the small town. When Boston Mason first begins his tale, he fondly recalls "the people in all the towns spread out across Canada, all cheering and crying for us to beat them Silver Sevens" (9), and, as noted in chapter 1, later comes to the realization that "we were heroes on a national scale, all the people in every one horse town across all of Canada rooting for us to beat them damn Silver Sevens" (242). Both *Dawson City Seven* and *Hockey Night in the Dominion of Canada*, then, recall an historical moment when increased commodification was taking the professional game away from small Canadian towns, and, by doing so, implicitly speak to contemporary fears about small-market Canadian NHL teams being unable to compete in the North American hockey market (as well as to the larger cultural concerns in which these fears participate). By characterizing the game as a small-town possession (or at least privileging the small towns in their battles against the big city), these novels suggest that the "Canadianness" of hockey rests in pastoral innocence rather than in big city selfishness and greed.[11] The same is thematically true of *The Horn of a Lamb* and *When She's Gone*, both of which were written after the Winnipeg Jets' relocation and explicitly respond to this event.

One of Fred Pickle's all-consuming passions in *The Horn of a Lamb* is to watch the local NHL team play. Although the "local team" is never mentioned by name, they are clearly meant to resemble the Winnipeg Jets. *The Horn of a Lamb* addresses a hockey climate in which conversation at the arena focuses on "dwindling attendance, high taxes on the team, the Canadian dollar, [and] the possibility that the team might move. Nobody ever talked much about the game itself any more. They talked about small markets and exchange rates" (40). Fred becomes worried about the fate of the team when he hears rumours that Andrew T. Madison, the team's American owner, is thinking about "moving the team south after the season" (14). For Fred, the conflict is framed in markedly nationalistic, ideological, and economic terms: "[Andrew Madison] had been quoted in a newspaper as having called Canada a socialist country. In another interview he had called Canada the fifty-first state. He had brought in a larger American flag to fly beside the now-smaller Canadian flag at the arena. After enough fans complained, he said it had been an honest mistake and replaced it ... Fred had been told of some words of wisdom that Madison kept framed in his office: *The American system of ours, call it Americanism, call it capitalism, call it what you like, gives each and every one of us a great opportunity if we only seize it with both hands and make the most of it.* The name below the quote was Al Capone" (48; italics in original). The identification of American capitalism with the gangster values of Al Capone is certainly no compliment.

When rumours about the team's possible relocation become a frequent topic of conversation at the rink, Fred's friend Badger, an aging lawyer and political activist, makes an impassioned speech about the threat of American cultural imperialism: "Today it's the hockey team. Next week it's the airlines, the railroads. And then the trees and water. And a week after that we're walking around with American money jingling in our pockets, stuffing our faces with Big Macs and singing the 'Star Spangled Banner'" (87). Badger fears that the loss of the hockey team is merely the first step toward the wholesale Americanization of Canada. The gradations of the conquest, as Badger outlines them, begin with hockey as a marker of cultural distinction but move quickly to the appropriation of actual binding forces such as infrastructure (airlines and railroads) and natural resources (trees and water). The loss of these facilitators of Canadian union, as Badger tells it, would lead to a total dissolution of Canadian culture (Big Macs as marker of US imperialism), economic union (the loss of national currency), and, indeed, the collapse of the Canadian polity itself (the loss of the national anthem). For Badger, hockey is the first domino in this long chain reaction: knock over hockey, and the nation itself will fall. Badger's speech goes on for almost a full page and is intended to be taken at face value (i.e., Badger isn't offered as a caricature or satire), and lays the groundwork for what will later become a campaign to save the team.

When the news that the team will be sold is made public, Fred and Badger begin their campaign in earnest. Badger makes another impassioned public speech against the American attempt to "buy" Canadian identity and difference: "You didn't come here to save your hockey team. You came here to save your country ... A lousy hockey team has brought us together in this cold parking lot to mark a turning point in our destiny. This is a great day to be alive. The country is watching ... What is the price of a nation's soul? Is it one hundred million dollars? Is it five billion? Three trillion? Is everything for sale?" (159–60). To buy back "the nation's soul," as Badger puts it, the city will have to raise 18 million dollars in thirty days. To make matters worse, Andrew Madison has worked out a legal provision whereby he gets to keep 20 per cent of any failed bid. Nevertheless, the campaign begins in earnest. Money starts to flow in from all sectors of the community, including young children, but Fred is frustrated that big companies "couldn't dig as deep as most of the children were doing when they donated their life savings in their piggy banks" (167). Determined to do his part, Fred rides his bicycle from farm to farm outside the city to solicit contributions. As the money continues to roll in, hope flourishes. Fans hold up signs condemning Andrew Madison, and chant during games: "Save our team, save our game" (156). These events mirror the actual campaign to save the Winnipeg Jets, in which a public group that became known as the "Spirit of Manitoba" made a bid to purchase controlling partnership in the franchise that would keep it in Winnipeg. In the end, however, both campaigns failed, the fictional rendering of this event in *The Horn of a Lamb* falling short by a mere million dollars after the local newspaper "discredits" Badger by revealing his extremist past. Badger vows an ominous revenge on Andrew Madison, which he plans to enact during the team's last home game.

The nature of the plot is never revealed, and whatever Badger had in mind is foiled when Fred inadvertently lets slip that something is afoot. Badger does manage to grab the puck from the last game, however, and gives it to Fred with a note that says "the last puck for the last fan" (195).

As the story continues, Badger and Fred scheme about travelling to the team's new American city to enact their revenge on Andrew Madison. When Badger dies, Fred decides that despite his handicap he must make the trip alone. The narrative strategy surrounding Fred's plan is one of ambiguity and delay, resulting in a suspenseful climax where the reader has been led to believe that Fred is going to kill Andrew Madison. The revenge, however, turns out to be more benign: Fred hits Madison in the face with a boysenberry pie. The significance of this turn from expectation is to again enforce the stereotype that Canadian society is kinder and gentler than that of America; to kill Madison, *The Horn of a Lamb* seems to suggest, would not be the Canadian way. In other words, when "the beaver bites back" (to quote one recent examination of American popular culture in Canada), it does so quite harmlessly (Flaherty and Manning 1993). When Fred travels through America on his quest to get to Madison, his presuppositions about Americans are confirmed: "He encountered many Americans, Americans he thought would annoy and provoke him. But the only feeling that the worst of them instilled was pity. They seemed spoiled. And angry. Because deep in their hearts they knew it wasn't okay to be so spoiled … This was, after all, Babylon, where the snobby, money-hungry people lived" (338–9).

When Fred arrives at the team's new city, he plans to attend a game and try to confront Madison for an apology before enacting his revenge. Being a devoted fan, however, Fred can't help but watch some of the game first.

When Fred takes his seat he is shocked by the ignorance and indifference of the American fans: "He tried to explain what constituted an offside penalty, what a two-line pass was, why one play was tripping and another wasn't. But nobody listened" (344–5). After this Fred comes to the epiphanic realization that "[hockey] wasn't the game he remembered. In fact, it wasn't a game at all any more. It was a business. A business that had pulled his team out from under his nose because fans had stopped supporting mediocre hockey at prices they could no longer afford. A business that pulled players from one city to the next in search of bigger contracts and US dollars. A business that paid no attention to the time-honoured traditions of hockey: loyalty and respect. In fact, it was a business that now trampled those ideals. This was no longer a game Fred knew at all. This was garbage" (345). Motivated by his new perspective on the professional game, Fred manages to track down Andrew Madison. Madison, eager not to cause a scene, tries to placate Fred but eventually loses his patience and tells him that moving the team was "simple economics" and "if you don't understand that then you are as dumb as you look" (350). It becomes clear to Fred that Madison is beyond any hope of forgiveness or redemption, and after the game Fred arrives to deliver his boysenberry pie.

When Fred makes his way back to Canada after the pie incident he is greeted as a conquering hero. He is eventually hired by his old junior team, the Brandon Wheat Kings, and honoured with the opportunity to go for a warm-up skate with the team and to drop the puck in one of their games. When Fred is announced at the game, the crowd cheers and Canadian flags are waved. Several fans are dressed in costume to parody Andrew Madison and honour Fred's triumph over hockey capitalism. When Fred drops the puck for the ceremonial face off at center ice, he uses the "last puck" that Badger had salvaged for him from the professional team's last game: "nobody but Fred knew the significance of the puck. It said that no owners, no amount of money or greedy players were greater than the game itself" (385). This is the central thematic conclusion of *The Horn of a Lamb*: that the essence of Canada's game – the pondhockey purity and natural overtones of the homemade rink, the untainted passion that powers shinny games and junior hockey – can't be bought for any amount of money. Again, Canadian hockey is characterized by its small-town virtues in opposition to the American big-city values of selfishness and greed, and this binary is extended to encompass the divide between junior and recreational hockey and the professional game. As Fred becomes accustomed to life in Brandon, it takes him "no time at all to see that junior hockey was every bit as good as the professional game, minus the snobby, money-hungry players and owners" (392). As with *Hockey Night in the Dominion of Canada*, *Dawson City Seven*, and *Finnie Walsh*, *The Horn of a Lamb* sees amateur, junior, and recreational hockey as preserving the purity and Canadianness of the game. Because the love of the game can't be bought, these novels seem to say, the symbolic essence of Canadian hockey is ultimately safe.

Like *The Horn of a Lamb*, *When She's Gone* similarly addresses the issue of "franchise fees nauseating contracts bottom-line-team's-gotta-move bullshit, buying for the pennant, buying for the cup, the money frenzy the whole goddamn mess" (52). Like Fred Pickle in *The Horn of a Lamb*, Mark and Jack suggest that "loyalty and respect" should be the heart of the professional game. This point is driven home when the brothers' team is beaten by a team of Plains Cree: "That boys, was a lesson in loyalty. You're Cree you play for the Cree, you're Blackfoot you play for the Blackfoot ... Wearing the jersey means something, a goddamn second skin you guys understand me? These people should be pros with a TV deal coast to coast" (45). For Jack, the Cree players' loyalty to their team is an exemplary counterpoint to the culture of greed that inspires NHL players to jump from team to team in search of the highest salary. Hockey loyalty, in a way, is like tribal loyalty, and Jack sees the Cree players' dedication to their team as a model for the sort of fidelity that he thinks professional Canadian players should feel for Canadian teams. But the problem isn't the culture of greed itself; rather, Jack blames the society that allows it to exist: "I blame money and fans and owners and this whole fucking culture of ours for giving greed a halo, how many times we smile and say way-to-go boy earn your millions then bitch at the ticket prices and guys jumping teams on the fucking money trail, how many times eh and why doesn't it sink in we've fucking gone along with it, made our bed, laid in it and the leeches sucking on our love of the game keep sucking cause it never runs dry. But it does you'll see one day it does" (45–6).

Jack also complains that "we take the sacred blade and deliver our own cuts and everybody smiles and nods like it was the right thing to do, smiles and nods because some things are beyond even questioning, some prairie boy's got a chance to earn twenty-six million US over seven years and we say 'hey boy you've done it now go for it'" (40). For Jack, then, Canadians are complicit in the "American" culture of greed because they have allowed and even encouraged hockey to be profaned by it. During a discussion of English history Mark tells Jack that "rape is rape even if you take it with a smile" (20). Jack responds that Mark has "spoken like a true Canadian hockey fan" (20). The American assault on Canadian hockey, then, is characterized as a rape, and Canadian fans are seen as accepting it without struggle or resistance. According to Jack, Canadians have "made cowardice a national trait, getting stepped on a way of life"

(75). What is ultimately called for, then, is a sort of hockey revolution, a "night when cynicism's put aside and all things are possible. The fans say no more, you're killing us, you're killing our love you fucking vampires, here's your empty arenas the switched channels we've turned our backs" (52). In other words, Canadian fans have the power to reclaim their game by refusing to support the big-money professional game. In a way, this is the same conclusion that Fred Pickle arrives at in *The Horn of a Lamb* when he decides to eschew his interest in the NHL in favour of the "play for the right reasons" junior game.

The ultimate goal of *When She's Gone* is to access the perfect essence of hockey, the "memory that Plato talked about, the ghost world of perfection we all use as a reference" (189). Much of this work is diagnostic. Mark and Jack go on for pages and pages about what is wrong with hockey, much of which can be summarized simply by the word greed (which, of course, is closely identified with the putatively American commodification of the game). The culture of hockey greed is illustrated most pointedly in *When She's Gone* by the loss of the Winnipeg Jets. When it is revealed that the Jets will be leaving, Mark reflects that the "NHL was delivering Winnipeg its message: Winnipeg you're nothing in the scheme of hockey, nothing in the eyes of the NHL, your fans are a drop in the ocean, who gives a shit about your loss, who really gives a shit" (112). Worse than the loss of the team or the cruel indifference of the league, however, is the fact that "the south tugged at our myth" (112). Mark had noted earlier that "when greed became a right worth fighting for" and "television brought Hollywood into professional sports" the "core of [hockey's] worth got bought out, never stood a chance against money but the myths kept [it] alive for a long time, struggling against the tide but now even the myth's dead, the withered roots of a starved tree" (85). By again underscoring the importance of myth, Mark helps to explain the presence of the fantasy and creation myth sequences that pepper the novel as a way of getting back to the pure, "Platonic," and, notably, Canadian, essence of hockey: the pastoral northernness of the game and the innocence of playing purely for fun.

Although *When She's Gone* is uniquely explicit about its myth-making, it illuminates the cultural work of Canadian hockey novels in general as an attempt to "save our team, save our game." The answer of hockey novels to American capitalism, then, and to the larger cultural anxieties it represents (growing continental monoculture, increasing globalization, the purported loss of a centralized and homogenous Canadian identity), is to suggest that despite the "loss" of the professional game to American greed and selfishness, Canada retains the "pure essence" of the game – Canadianness, northernness, and innocence – by way of the play-for-the-right-reasons *ethos* of junior hockey and the pastoral purity of recreational pond hockey. Because hockey is seen to remain symbolically Canadian, the nation's cultural distinction appears ultimately intact despite the challenges, uncertainties, and instabilities presented by Americanization and globalization. Again, the logic in play here is to fight fire with fire: hockey novels seem to suggest that when Canadian culture is encroached on by homogenizing forces, Canada must articulate for itself an equally homogenous identity as a means of resistance. But hockey's totalizing vision is both limited and preferential, a fact that becomes particularly evident in light of two specific areas of omission and exclusion, French–English relations and the question of race.

3

Unity through Hockey?

"ROME'S CANADIENS VERSUS CANTERBURY'S MAPLE LEAFS"

One of the central claims of the "unity-by-hockey" component of the myth is that the game works in the service of cultural identity by unifying Canadians who may be otherwise separated by language, culture, religion, ethnic background, class, etc. Hockey purports to be a great leveller, a bringer of unity where none would exist otherwise, and this idea is conveyed in Canadian hockey novels primarily through the space of the rink and the technology of radio. What the representations of radio discussed earlier don't reveal, however, is the reality that broadcasting has been culturally divisive at least as often as it has worked in the service of national unity. This was especially true during the Original Six era of the NHL, when only two Canadian teams battled for their country's sympathies. Throughout the 1930s, 40s, 50s and 60s, Canada was divided into two large broadcast regions: those who received the Montreal Canadiens games and those who received the Toronto Maple Leafs. These broadcast zones were largely drawn along cultural and linguistic lines, and, as such, clashes between the Leafs and the Habs became symbolic enactments of the larger conflicts between the English and French – and Protestant and Catholic – elements of Canadian society. It should be no surprise, then, that French–English relations are an important aspect of the unity-by-hockey component of the myth. According to Francis, "hockey's special contribution [to Canadian society] is that it brings together French and English in a mutual recognition of something that unites rather than separates" (1997,

168). As MacGregor puts it in one of the *Screech Owls* novels through the perspective of the narrator, Travis Lindsay, "what a strange, wonderful country Canada was, he thought. People who can't even talk to each other have a game that does it for them. From coast to coast they skate and play hockey, from the time they learn to walk until they're older than Travis's own father" (*The Quebec City Crisis*, 18).

The *Screech Owl* novels, of course, are aimed at young children, and in several passages such as this are openly didactic about their nationalist myth-making. Generally speaking, however, adult-oriented hockey novels are significantly more invested in the hockey myth than their second-wave children's counterparts. It is perhaps surprising, then, that adult-oriented hockey novels are relatively disinterested in the question of French–English unity. Only two English-Canadian hockey novels address this issue on any significant level, *Hockey Night in the Dominion of Canada* and Johnston's *The Divine Ryans*. *The Divine Ryans* is the story of nine-year-old Draper Doyle Ryan, a member of a prominent St John's Catholic family, "the Divine Ryans," who are so known because many of them have been priests and nuns. Set in the 1960s, *The Divine Ryans* portrays hockey as a site of religious conflict that emblematizes the larger cultural tensions in Canadian society during that time: the Catholic Canadiens are pitted against the Protestant Maple Leafs. The Ryans have a strange ritual to accompany this rivalry. Every time a Leafs–Habs game is televised the whole family gathers to watch, even though the only characters who really care about hockey are Draper Doyle and his uncle Reginald. For the rest of the family it isn't the hockey that is important: "as far as they were concerned, God had created hockey for the sole purpose of allowing Catholics to humiliate Protestants on nationwide TV … When Montreal was playing Toronto at the Forum … it was not a hockey game, but a holy war, a crusade … Rome's Canadiens versus Canterbury's Maple Leafs, 'the Heathen Leafs against the Holy Habs,' as Uncle Reginald put it" (76, 77–8). If the Habs win the Ryans make a taunting phone call to a prominent Protestant family down the street (although the phone is simply allowed to ring; there is no trash talk involved, and no personal contact is made), while if the Leafs win the Ryans can expect to receive a phone call of their own. *The Divine Ryans*, then, defies the myth-making prescription of unity by depicting a national climate in which hockey expresses (rather than resolves) prevailing cultural and religious tensions. This reading is congruent with Cynthia Sugars' suggestion that "hockey in [*The Divine Ryans*] is not an emblem of national coherence but an embodiment of the intangibility of consolidating structures of origin, progression, and teleology" (153–4). Similarly, Méira Cook has suggested that *The Divine Ryans* poses hockey as "a somewhat overdetermined symbol by which a game – hockey, Canadian hockey, 'Catholic' hockey – comes to stand for the machinations and governance of an entire national, religious, and cultural body" (133).

Hockey Night in the Dominion of Canada similarly portrays the game as a site of French–English conflict. This cultural tension is personified through the characters of Cyclone Taylor (English) and Newsy Lalonde (French), although the French position, characterized here as nationalist, ultimately comes off better. Lalonde is the more affable of the two characters and – in contrast to Taylor's inherited and unconsidered opinions about French Canada – is open to critical thinking. Taylor eventually realizes that he has been wrong to mistrust the patriotism of French Canadians, and apologizes to Lalonde in a symbolic affirmation of Laurier's victory in the naval debate (which is seen in the novel as a victory for Canadian autonomy). Throughout the conflict between Taylor and Lalonde, Lester and Frank Patrick appear to exemplify the ideal Canadian character: they are good-natured, kind, reflective, intelligent, ethical, and moderate, although they are perfectly willing to play hockey aggressively. Furthermore, they are of true cross-cultural pedigree: they are of Irish extraction, raised in Quebec, fluent in French and English, and have lived in Quebec, Ontario, and the West. In *Hockey Night in the Dominion of Canada*, the game of hockey brings French and English into contact, eventually (in the case of Taylor and Lalonde) allowing them to overcome their differences. The idealism of this conclusion, however, is disrupted by an interesting moment of slippage earlier in the story when the newly created Canadiens come to Renfrew to play the Millionaires. As the game is about to begin, the narrator feels the need to explain that "there was no underlying feeling of prejudice beneath the loud booing directed at the French team" because "violent partisanship was the standard of the day" (192). This suggestion is soon undermined, however, when a few enthusiastic French fans begin singing the "Chant Nationale" ("Oh Canada") over top of "God Save the King." Some of the Renfrew fans are appalled at this, but "most of the fans simply shifted uneasily from one foot to the other, upset by what was going on around them and unsure of what to make of it" (193). *Hockey Night in the Dominion of Canada*, then, suggests the potential of hockey as a unifying cultural force while recognizing the fact that the game has often been a site for the expression of cross-cultural tensions. This ambivalence, combined with the forthright contrariness of *The Divine Ryans* and the prevailing lack of interest in French–English relations among hockey novels in general, represents a curious break from the tendency of these novels to propound, rehearse, and reinforce the hockey myth.

The appearance of the French–English-unity question in *Hockey Night in the Dominion of Canada* and *The Divine Ryans* could be attributed simply to the historical periods in which they are set, although – as suggested above – both have something deliberate to say about the issue. As for the relative absence of French–English themes from the majority of English-Canadian hockey novels, several possible explanations spring to mind. The first of these is that the French–English-unity component of the myth is perhaps more vulnerable than its other tenets to the complex realities of hockey and history in Canada. While allegations about ontological reality, for instance, can't really be disproved, it isn't difficult to marshal evidence against the claim that hockey has worked to unify French and English cultures in Canada. This is not to say that hockey *hasn't* brought the "two solitudes" together in actual and significant ways, but to expose the complex realities that the simplifying tendencies of myth typically work to elide. The potential problem with this theory is that it proposes a level of self-consciousness that most hockey novels don't actually possess toward their myth-making. In other words, it probably isn't plausible to suggest that the majority of hockey novelists purposefully neglected the area of French–English unity on the conscious basis that it is especially vulnerable to the debunking pressures of actuality.

Another possible explanation for the relative absence of French–English-unity myth-making among Canadian hockey novels is that many of the novels discussed in this study were written throughout the 1990s and 2000s, and, as such, potentially suffer from the general fatigue that seems to have followed the Constitutional debates of the early 1990s and the narrowly failed Quebec sovereignty Referendum of 1995. Admittedly, this answer proposes what is at best a paradox: if hockey novels respond to the national instability resulting from increased globalization by insisting on the actual stability of Canadian unity and identity through hockey, it would seem inconsistent not to extend this thematic consideration to the area of French–English relations as well. The 1990s context of failed constitutional negotiations and heightened linguistic tensions, however, perhaps does help to account for the depictions of French–English relations in *The Divine Ryans* and *Hockey Night in the Dominion of Canada*. Both these novels were produced in the early 1990s, and both potentially provide readers with the nostalgic reassurance of a "simpler time" in which cultural conflicts could be hashed out on the hockey rink instead of by the premiers. Finally, a third and very simple explanation is also worth considering: if, following Dowbiggin's claims about hockey in general, hockey novels attempt to provide the so-called Rest of Canada with a "great Canadian narrative" and "mutual agreement about who we are," it is possible that the invitation to participate in this narrative simply isn't extended to francophone Canadians. While francophones are unified by their language and (to a lesser extent) cultural traditions, anglophones appear to need hockey to bring them together. If this is the case, of course, hockey novels could be understood to perpetuate the idea of "two solitudes" rather than participating in the myth's insistence that hockey breaks these cultural barriers down.

Ken Dryden has noted about the myth of "unity by hockey" that real unity tends to be personal rather than abstractly cultural. In Dryden's own experience of playing for the Canadiens,[1] the social unity of the team invariably trumped the cultural and linguistic differences among the players: "we know there are differences, we just don't think they are that important" ([1983] 1984, 24). For Dryden, hockey brought players of French and English backgrounds into close proximity and presented them with a series of shared goals that inevitably led both to friendships and squabbles. Dryden realizes, however, that hockey unity rarely translates into larger Canadian cultural unity because "while language may not divide [the team], others – the public, the press – whose experience is different, who themselves are divided by language and who find tension and rivalry by language in their workplace, understand us and explain us in *their* way, and in doing so, sometimes cause division" (25). In a sense, this is the same distinction drawn by *Hockey Night in the Dominion of Canada* where hockey allows for a cross-cultural reconciliation based on personal interaction between Taylor and Lalonde but ultimately fails to bridge the cultural rift that results in the pre-game shouting match between "God Save the King" and the "Chante nationale." Although many Canadian hockey novels depict cross-cultural friendships between French and English players, none of these depictions appear to be presented as symbolic of larger national or cross-cultural unity. Hockey, then, does have the power to facilitate unity, but Canadian hockey novels see this as interpersonal rather than intercultural.

Perhaps surprisingly, the English-language hockey novel most directly interested in French-Canadian culture is American rather than Canadian. Falla's *Saved* is the story of Jean-Pierre Savard, a second-generation American of French-Canadian descent who plays for the Boston Bruins but eventually gets traded to the Montreal Canadiens. Somewhat like Reddick's use of an American narrator to explore Canadian history and culture in *Dawson City Seven*, this device allows Falla to engage in an unusual level of exposition about the game's history and cultural importance to Canada. Thus, Savard informs his fiancé Faith that *Hockey Night in Canada* is "the most popular television program in Canadian history" and "when the matchup is Montreal–Toronto the game takes on undertones people don't like to talk about. 'To be blunt ... Montreal versus Toronto is French versus English; Catholic versus Protestant; working class versus ruling class. That's oversimplified and is less true now than it was a generation ago. But it's still more true than false'" (204–5). Many similar moments occur throughout the story as Savard discusses Québécois history, culture, and the importance of hockey to French Canadians. For example, at one point Savard explains that "it's hard to grasp the importance of [Maurice] Richard to the French. 'He was our flag,' said my grandmother, who was born in Montreal and who, even after the family resettled in Maine, continued to follow the Canadiens. Richard was the only one she ever spoke of as if he were the fleur-de-lis made flesh" (90). *Saved* depicts hockey, then, along the same lines as *The Divine Ryans*: as an institution which exposes the cultural and linguistic rifts in Canadian society rather than a vehicle for unity. It is no coincidence that *Saved* is the only novel discussed in this study to depict a Québécois separatist, a player named Jean-Baptiste Desjardin who "thinks Quebec should separate from the rest of Canada and form a new French-speaking country" (44). Although Desjardin's separatism doesn't upset the fraternal unity of the team, which – consistent with the terms of the myth – appears to transcend cultural and linguistic differences, it does "irritate most of the English-Canadian guys on the team" and become an occasion for raillery among friends. One player, for instance, tells Desjardin that a sovereign Quebec will never work out because it's "hard to build a national economy on doughnut shops and chain-saw repair" (44). While *Saved* undoubtedly stops short of endorsing Desjardin's brand of separatism, it is clear that Falla has a great appreciation for Québécois culture and the welcome diversity it brings both to Canada and the American Northeast where French-Canadian traditions and influence continue to be somewhat felt.

Another hockey story that deals directly with French-English tensions is Canada's most well-known and well-loved piece of hockey fiction, Roch Carrier's "The Hockey Sweater."[2] Aside from enacting the pastoral myth par excellence, "The Hockey Sweater" explores the symbolic tensions of the Maple Leafs–Canadiens rivalry like no other hockey text. Set in a rural Quebec village in the 1940s, "The Hockey Sweater" focuses on a young boy who idolizes the Canadiens and their great hero, Maurice "the Rocket" Richard. When the boy's mother writes to "Monsieur Eaton" for a new hockey sweater, a terrible mistake is made: the sweater that arrives is that of the hated Maple Leafs rather than the beloved Canadiens. When the boy's mother forces him to wear the Leafs sweater, the captain of his team won't even let him on the ice. Finally there is an injury and the young narrator believes his time has come: he leaps into the play and is immediately assessed a penalty by the local priest (who is acting as referee). The priest tells the boy that "just because you're wearing a new Toronto Maple Leafs sweater unlike the others, it doesn't mean you're going to make the laws around here" (80–1). The boy is then sent to church to pray for forgiveness, where he prays instead that moths will consume his Maple Leafs sweater.

Anne Hiebert Alton has suggested "The Hockey Sweater" functions as "a symbol of Canadian identity" because it "exemplifies two defining ideas of Canadian culture – the French–English tensions and the passion for hockey" (2002, 5). Hiebert Alton sees "the love of hockey [as] one of the things that makes us Canadians ... something that crosses both language and cultural boundaries" (5). "The Hockey Sweater," then, in Hiebert Alton's reading, demonstrates that the Canadian "passion for hockey is something that transcends linguistic and cultural division, perhaps making us more truly a nation than we realize" (11). At the heart of this reading, of course, is the idea of hockey as a Canadian "universal" that works in the service of French–English unity. While it may be the case that "The Hockey Sweater" "demonstrates what it meant to be a Canadian child ... in the 1940s" (7) and that "it is not much of a stretch to imagine a similar sort of tale being spun about a young lad in small-town Ontario or Saskatchewan receiving the wrong team's sweater and responding in a similar manner" (10), it is hard not to see Hiebert Alton's characterization of Carrier's story as naive.

Hiebert Alton notes that Maurice Richard was the first Canadian hockey player to receive a state funeral, suggesting "the Rocket" as "a symbol who crossed barriers between east and west, local and national, adult and child, and – most significantly – French and English" (9). What she fails to mention, however, is that Richard was also a lightning rod for one of Canada's most prominent French–English clashes. When Richard assaulted a referee near the end of the 1955 NHL season, league president Clarence Campbell suspended him for the remaining games, including the playoffs. According to Simpson, "the showdown between Campbell and Richard took on the dimensions of an English–French conflict, as Campbell was seen by French Canadians simply as an enforcer of English-Canadian interests in the game" (1989, 206). When Richard's suspension was announced, protestors pelted Campbell with smoke bombs and rotten tomatoes and the ensuing riot "devastated" the "fifteen square blocks surrounding the [Montreal] Forum" (207). In the instance of the Richard Riots, hockey was clearly a site of cultural divisiveness rather than cultural unity. The complaint of the priest/referee against the young narrator of "The Hockey Sweater" – "just because you're wearing a new Toronto Maple Leafs sweater ... doesn't mean you're going to make the laws around here" – is that of Quebec against English Canada in general, and the prominence of Rocket Richard in "The Hockey Sweater" points to that divide. While "The Hockey Sweater" does work to defuse French–English tensions through humour and charm, the pathos occasioned by the young narrator's expulsion from the game must ultimately remind the reader that in reality hockey has served as a site of intercultural conflict at least as often as one of overarching unity.

Perhaps the most famous fictional exploration of Canada's French–English cultural divide is Hugh MacLennan's *Two Solitudes* (1945). Despite the fact that it is not a hockey novel in the sense outlined earlier, *Two Solitudes* is particularly interesting for its investment in the idea that hockey contributes to French–English unity. In this regard, *Two Solitudes* is twice-over an exception: first, it bucks the general refusal of mainstream Canadian literature to participate in the project of nation-building; and second, it is perhaps more invested in the unity-by-hockey aspect of the myth than any of the hockey novels discussed in this study. *Two Solitudes* is essentially a fictional blueprint for Canadian cultural unity, symbolized in the marriage of two French and English characters, Paul Tallard and Heather Methuen. Paul Tallard can be seen as MacLennan's prototype for a Canadian identity: he is athletic, intellectual, commonsensical, a "natural man," patriotic though not slavishly French or English, and full of potential for growth and a future. Hockey is seen as a staple ingredient in MacLennan's well-balanced recipe for Canadianness: Paul plays the game intermittently throughout the novel and at one point reflects that "some winters I felt as if I lived at the Forum" (318).

For Paul, hockey is an important cultural activity inasmuch as hockey players "are about the best artists this country ever turned out" (319). The connection between hockey and art is underscored when Paul turns his hand to writing his own Canadian-content novel, the basis of which is essentially a formula for *Two Solitudes*: "a Canadian book would have to take its place in the English and French traditions ... As Paul considered the matter, he realized that his readers' ignorance of the essential Canadian clashes and values presented him with a unique problem. The background would have to be created from scratch if his story was to become intelligible. He could afford to take nothing for granted. He would have to build the stage and props for his play, and then write the play itself" (365). This is how *Two Solitudes* itself works: through various plot and character events the particulars of Canadian society – the "background," as it were – are revealed as the novel unfolds. In *Two Solitudes*, hockey is a component piece of Canadian culture, a necessary inclusion for "setting the Canadian stage." Shortly after deciding on the framework of his novel, Paul reflects that "life by itself is formless wherever it is" and that therefore "art must give it a form" (365). If hockey players "are about the best artists this country ever turned out," an implicit message of *Two Solitudes* is that hockey gives form to Canadian life. Like the novel itself, hockey functions as a vehicle by which community can be formed and unity achieved; true to the myth, and following the prescription of his title, MacLennan configures this unity as essentially French–English. In other words, *Two Solitudes* puts into effect as part of its central project an area of hockey myth-making that most hockey novels either inadvertently neglect or wilfully refuse to undertake.[3]

"THEY DON'T LOOK OPPRESSED TO ME, JUST BIG AND MEAN": HOCKEY AND RACE

As with the question of French–English relations, hockey novels are conspicuously silent on the issue of race. Although hockey derives much of its symbolic power from First Nations cultures and was played by a diverse array of Canadian peoples from early in its history, the game "has ... contributed to a vision of Canadian culture that is resolutely masculine and white" (Gruneau and Whitson 1993, 215).[4] Canadian hockey novels reflect this "vision" abundantly; of the hockey novels discussed in this study, every single protagonist is white and all but three are male. Only two hockey novels address the issue of race in any significant way, *When She's Gone* and *Puck Is a Four Letter Word*. Both depict racism as a general societal problem that – while periodically rearing its ugly head in the game itself and among otherwise sensibly "tolerant" characters – is for the most part resolved by the rituals of hockey and the togetherness of the team. Hockey, then, is depicted as contributing to multicultural unity by facilitating relationships that transcend racial differences and, arguably, supplying distinctively Canadian content or character to these relationships. As with the issue of French–English relations, the racial unity achieved by hockey is presented as interpersonal rather than intercultural. Hockey does appear in *When She's Gone* and *Puck Is a Four Letter Word* as the "great leveller" it is seen as in the myth, but this is in immediate and personal terms rather than abstract and collective. To say this another way, hockey novels work to sublimate historical and material conflicts into personal ones. This pattern is typical of popular culture itself, which often attempts to resolve complicated societal issues at the level of personal narrative (this is evident in the area of French–English relations as well). This device offers readers a sense of satisfaction at seeing a conflict raised and then comfortably resolved.

When Mark and Jack's hockey team play against the team of Plains Cree in *When She's Gone*, Jack jokingly worries that "they'll take out on us the last two hundred years of history" which he proceeds to characterize as "oppression" (27). Mark responds that "they don't look oppressed to me, just big and mean" (27). In other words, Mark doesn't see the opposing team in terms of prejudice or assumption, but rather in their immediate human terms as daunting opponents. After the brothers' team is trounced by the Cree team, Mark and Jack go for beers with two of the opposing players, Frank and Lester, and quickly become friends. Frank and Lester are presented throughout the story in situations that act as an indictment of Canadian intolerance and racism: they are constantly being hassled by police, scrutinized by mall security, and bothered by authorities on the assumption that, as Natives, they will be causing trouble. In some ways, Frank and Lester appear calculated to defeat the insidious stereotypes of Native laziness and alcoholism: both are possessed of an excellent work ethic and rarely drink, although this fact doesn't prevent an RCMP officer from subjecting Lester to a Breathalyzer and then warning him not to drive "back to the reserve" (29).

At one point when Frank and Lester decide to see Mark and Jack off on their journey to England, a plainclothes customs agent at the airport challenges them, apparently because of their skin colour, occasioning the following observation from Mark: "Now I've got nothing against cops, how they behave just reflects how society behaves, so looking back at them is looking at ourselves and I've heard about South Africa and the treatment of non-whites there back when the whites were in power, and all I'll say is from what I've experienced, Canada is just a north version of the same thing, racism and segregation of the *indigenous peoples* ... but my point is there's no point in getting high and mighty about South Africa, not in Canada, not in the States, not in the UK, that kind of bullshit goes on everywhere and that's that" (183; italics in original). Mark is essentially positing a downmarket version of Mackey's ([1999] 2002) allegation in *The House of Difference* and Bannerji's (2000) in *The Dark Side of the Nation* that widespread racism and intolerance persist despite Canada's official policy of multiculturalism, which has in actuality often served as a strategy for managing difference and maintaining power in the hands of the dominant group. Mark indicts Canadian society for its pervasive racism and holds up the hockey rink as a model for intercultural harmony (or at least a space in which cultural difference doesn't result in inequality or injustice). The implicit question, of course, is "why can't life be more like hockey?" *When She's Gone* is at least partially interested in addressing the racism in society at large, as the scene in the airport departure lounge continues by symbolically reversing the history of European colonization through a speculative conversation about Frank and Lester canoeing across the Atlantic using a portrait of the Queen from the local rink as a sail and founding a colony called "New Creedonia" (183–4). More frequently in *When She's Gone*, however, the answer to societal racism is the simple "that's that" of Mark's statement above; especially for Frank and Lester, racism appears as an unchangeable reality that must be borne and endured rather than battled and overturned.

While *When She's Gone* implicitly suggests the hockey rink as an overarching model for interracial harmony in Canada, it is more invested in the game's potential to bring about interpersonal relationships that transcend race. It is hockey that facilitates Mark and Jack's friendship with Frank and Lester in the first place, and throughout the novel their relationship remains rooted primarily in the game, as well as in another recognizably Canadian iconic activity, canoeing (they go on canoe trips together). At one point the brothers participate in a ritual sweat lodge with Frank and Lester, and the four friends end up having what they half-seriously refer to as a "spiritual experience" simply by "talking hockey" (162). Mark and Jack respect Cree culture and want to learn more about it, and are characterized as generally tolerant and accepting in that they relate by observation and experience rather than assumption (the Cree team as "big and mean" rather than "oppressed"). But there are brief moments when Mark and Jack are implicated in the larger structures of Canadian intolerance and racism that Frank and Lester draw attention to throughout the novel. At one point Frank even goes so far as to remind Jack that "you shouldn't call any non-whites at this table liars, Jack, you don't know their truths, you don't know anything about their culture" (31). Jack promptly apologizes. *When She's Gone*, then, simultaneously suggests the complexity of racial identities and the continued pervasiveness of Canadian racism, while maintaining that hockey can facilitate interpersonal relationships that transcend racial differences and, as such, suggesting the game as a model for interracial harmony in society at large.

Puck Is a Four Letter Word similarly suggests the power of hockey to facilitate interracial friendships, but unlike *When She's Gone* sees this power as located in the unifying mechanism of the team rather than in the game itself. *Puck Is a Four Letter Word* is narrated by Willie Mulligan, a professional hockey player and farmer. Willie is one of the best players in the league and has won several Stanley

Cups with the Montreal Canadiens, but, along with his friend and fellow player Hartley Laidlaw, has greatly annoyed team owners by agitating on behalf of the players' union for better free agency rights.[5] As retribution, both Willie and Hartley are left unprotected in an expansion draft, and find themselves playing for a new team based in Cleveland called "the Big Green" (named for a trucking company that owns the team, another gesture toward the commercialization of professional sport). Although the Big Green have the NHL's only Chinese player and draft the first-ever Polish player, race enters the novel largely along black–white lines through the character of Brooker "Midnight" Duncan. Willie says of Brooker, a black player and new teammate, that "I got to know [him] as a player rep and he's the toughest man I've ever met. He still takes a bit of crap about his color, but only from fans. No player in his right mind does anything to get Brooker sore at him. Brooker jokes about his colour and people he knows can, too. But if he ever senses legitimate racism in the gags, somebody gets drilled" (77). Later in the story Brooker follows through on this reputation, putting an opposing player in the hospital for spouting racial slurs during the pre-game warm-up and cheap-shotting him later during the game.

Unlike in *When She's Gone*, the mediating power of hockey itself isn't enough to overcome racial intolerance in *Puck Is a Four Letter Word*. What does facilitate interracial unity is the unifying mechanism of the team: as the Big Green begins to gel as a team, the players grow to respect Brooker and eventually suggest he should be captain. When it becomes clear that the team's coach is incompetent, Brooker, along with Hartley and Willie, assume a mentor/teacher role with some of the younger players. Within the framework of the team it is only the ignorant and ineffectual coach, Andy Jackson, who consistently calls attention to issues of race and ethnicity (he frequently criticizes European players for being weak and at one point refers to Brooker as "that dumb coon we drafted" [81]). By characterizing Jackson as ignorant, ineffectual, and, indeed, an anachronism, *Puck Is a Four Letter Word* privileges the tolerance and unity enacted by the rest of the team. Furthermore, like Lester and Frank in *When She's Gone*, Brooker seems almost obsequiously intended to defeat a familiar stereotype about black male licentiousness: he is a model father and a caring husband, scrupulously faithful to his wife when most of the other players – Hartley and Willie included – show no regard for sexual fidelity whatsoever.

As with the question of French–English relations, it is difficult to account for the relative absence of minority characters and/or racial issues from Canadian hockey novels. Again, it could perhaps be argued that this topical departure from the totalizing unity-by-hockey impulse of the myth stems from its heightened vulnerability to the pressures of actuality. As with French–English unity, it is not difficult to muster evidence that hockey has worked against racial togetherness in Canada at least as often as it has contributed to it. Another explanation for the scarcity of minority voices is that Canadian hockey novels are simply not interested in issues of race. Several recent commentators have critiqued the "normopathetic tendency" to construct hockey in white, male, and heterosexual terms, suggesting the need to open hockey to "plurality and all creative combinations and applications of the game in the expanded field of culture" (Genosko 1999, 141). It is certainly fair to say that hockey novels, in general, do not participate in this project. Gamal Abdel Shehid especially has theorized what it might mean to read hockey from minority perspectives in an article entitled "Writing Hockey thru Race" (2000). Shehid suggests "remapping" (81) hockey through Dionne Brand's notion of the Canadian identity as an "absent presence," hoping to "write back" black and other minority hockey narratives as a way of "mark[ing] the wounds that many of us suffer as a result of nation-state practices that seek to racialize and, at the same time, homogenize" (83). Both Richard Wagamese's *Keeper'n Me* (1994) and Morley Callaghan's *The Loved and the Lost* (1951) attempt to do this in various ways, despite the fact that neither are specifically hockey novels in the sense in which this study defines the genre.

Keeper'n Me is narrated by Garnet Raven, an Ojibway boy who is taken from his reserve at the age of three and placed in a series of foster homes. By the age of twenty, Garnet ends up in jail for dealing cocaine. While in jail he receives a letter from one of his brothers asking him to return to the reserve and discover his roots. Garnet reluctantly agrees, and *Keeper'n Me* follows his quest to rediscover his family, heritage, and cultural traditions. Hockey plays a relatively small role in *Keeper'n Me*, but provides an important mechanism by which Garnet is accepted back into his family and culture. Although most of Garnet's family immediately welcome him home to the reserve, his older brother Jackie remains unfriendly and goes so far as to suggest that Garnet isn't even a legitimate "Indyun." When Garnet decides to join the reserve hockey team, Jackie tells the family "he's gonna get killed out there. This is Indyun hockey. Gotta be an Indyun to take it. Prob'ly spend mosta my time peelin' him offa the blueline" (104). "Indyun hockey," in other words, is configured as rougher than average: "you gotta be tough to play Indyun hockey ... not like them city leagues an' lot tougher'n your jail playin'" (103). Given the importance of symbolic male violence to lacrosse and early Canadian hockey, the suggestion of extraordinary toughness in contemporary "Indyun" hockey might be seen as a way of undoing white appropriation of this Native value or reasserting Native possession of the core essence of the game. Regardless of symbolic meaning, the toughness of hockey on the reserve is presented as a badge of honour, an opportunity for Garnet to prove his mettle as a real or authentic "Indyun."

As the story continues, Garnet and Jackie square off during an early morning practice session in which they are alone on the ice. The brothers begin by trading hockey-related insults, but as things heat up they begin to respect each other's skills more and more. Eventually Garnet describes an incident where "I was making my famous loop-de-loop at the blueline, [and Jackie] reached out and bear-hugged me to the ice. The force made us slide into the corner with our arms wrapped around each other, sticks sprawled at the blueline and the puck forgotten. We were laughing real hard and almost choking from lack of breathing. We lay on the ice for a long time like that, laughing and getting our wind back slowly. Pretty soon we started to notice that we were still bear-hugging each other and there got to be a kind of embarrassed feeling but we never let go" (106). Garnet's demonstration of physical toughness establishes his ability to play "Indyun hockey" and admits him by proxy to the larger cultural identity that Jackie had earlier denied him. This reconciliation is cemented by the moment above in which physical play spontaneously becomes physical affection. After their bear hug, the brothers reconcile their differences and resolve to behave like a family from now on. Garnet goes on to credit hockey with effecting this same sort of family togetherness among the remaining Raven men: "The White Dog Flyers became the best native hockey team in the area and we won our fair share of tournaments with the big line of Garnet, Jackie and Gilbert Raven the scourge of the league. Had Stanley'n my uncle Joe on the blueline with us, and in a way, playing hockey as a unit really helped us men come together as family too ... We played a lotta games, and by the time spring started to break through we'd melted away a lot of those lost years" (109). Although these men are already biologically related, it is the unifying power of hockey that brings them together as an actual family. Hockey, then, facilitates the absorption of Garnet back into his own culture and functions as a way of strengthening both family and community connections in *Keeper'n Me*. In a sense, Garnet's hockey experience can be read as a narrative of racial reconciliation: although he is Ojibway by birth, he has no knowledge of Native culture or traditions, and, as such, enters the community as an outsider needing to be integrated. By portraying hockey as the mechanism through which this is accomplished, *Keeper'n Me* essentially reaches the same conclusion as *When She's Gone* and *Puck Is a Four Letter Word*: that hockey can function as what Sheila Watson has called a "mediating ritual" that transcends or negotiates racial differences (1974–75, 183).

Although the novels discussed in this and the previous section suggest vulnerabilities in the totalizing project of the myth, they maintain the basic thematic trajectory toward unity through hockey. This is not true of *The Loved and the Lost*, which both literally and symbolically identifies the game with the racism of Montreal society in the 1950s. *The Loved and the Lost* is the story of Jim McAlpine, a University of Toronto professor who comes to Montreal at the request of a newspaper baron, Joseph Carver, who wants McAlpine to become a regular columnist for his paper. McAlpine soon begins dating Carver's daughter, Catherine, but is also intrigued by Peggy Sanderson, an educated and attractive white girl who defies cultural norms by going to Negro bars and welcoming many callers, both black and white, in her Montreal apartment. The novel is essentially about McAlpine's quest to gain Peggy's romantic affection and to lure her back to the realm of "respectable" conduct; at the same time, part of her allure to McAlpine remains her willingness and ability to transgress social expectations. The structures and strictures of respectable (white) society in the Montreal 50s are conveyed through three recurring metaphors in *The Loved and the Lost*: the cold white snow that is always falling in the background of the novel's action, the figurative "white horse" that for the bartender, Wolgast, symbolizes financial success and social status, and a particular hockey game which McAlpine and Catherine attend at the Forum.

By the moment of the hockey game McAlpine's confusion about his situation with Peggy has reached full boil. Much of this stems from the propriety of her behaviour: is Peggy wrong to defy the unofficial segregation that society expects of her, or are the prevailing cultural expectations surrounding race the actual problem? In other words, McAlpine is trying to determine why Peggy's "uncontrolled tenderness and goodness" seem to be at odds with "those who stand for law and order" (164). Upon arriving at the hockey game, McAlpine reflects on the faces in the crowd around him: "they were fairly prosperous people, for the very poor didn't have the money to go to hockey games" (161). These people represent the most powerful and prosperous in Montreal society, although McAlpine notes that "of course a few Negroes... would be in the cheap seats" (162). When the Canadiens manage to score a goal, Catherine remarks that the play had formed a "pretty pattern," and the narrative continues by describing the scene: "Everybody was filled with a fine laughing happiness. But McAlpine, staring at the ice in a dream, thought, 'Yes, Catherine's right. A beautiful pattern. Anything that breaks the pattern is bad. And Peggy breaks up the pattern'" (163). Along with the ordered rows of white, respectable, high-society faces, then, the "pattern" of the game itself is configured as a symbol of the ordered rigidity and outright racism of Montreal society in the 50s.

As the action continues, one of the players on the opposing team commits a flagrant slash against a Montreal player that initiates a brawl. When the referee goes about restoring order, the player who perpetrated the original slash pretends to be innocent and manages to avoid getting a penalty. When a chorus of taunts and boos proceeds from the spectators, the narrative (focalized here through McAlpine) describes the situation as follows: "The ice was now a small white space at the bottom of a great black pit where sacrificial figures writhed, and on the vast slopes of the pit a maniacal white-faced mob shrieked at the one with the innocent air who had broken the rules [the guilty player], and the one who tolerated the offence [the referee]" (165). The offending player comes to represent Peggy's "innocent" transgression of social norms, while the referee stands in for McAlpine's vision of himself as having tolerated Peggy's offence and, as a consequence, bearing the sanction of respectable society. The only difference, as McAlpine notes, is that the "player was guilty ... [while] I'm sure Peggy's innocent" (166). Before the situation is resolved, another incident pushes the chapter to its symbolic climax. Someone in the row behind Catherine and McAlpine grabs McAlpine's hat and throws it down toward the ice. McAlpine immediately turns to confront the hat thief, but Catherine intervenes: "'Jim, Jim, what's the matter with you?' Catherine cried, and she laughed. 'What's the matter with *me*?' he asked indignantly. 'Nobody's got anything against you, Jim. The way you're going on you'd think you were rooting for the visiting team. Aren't you with us?' 'What? Why do you say that?' 'Why quarrel with the home crowd?' (166; italics in original). This exchange sets the terms of McAlpine's decision: he must choose whether or not he is willing to "quarrel with the home crowd" in order to pursue his relationship with Peggy.

McAlpine decides that Peggy (and the ideals of tenderness, goodness, and innocence she represents) is worth pursuing at the cost of his good social standing, but by the end of the story Peggy has been raped and killed after an altercation in a Negro nightclub and McAlpine sees himself as responsible. When McAlpine is questioned by a detective about the events of Peggy's final night, the detective comes to the conclusion that perhaps "we all did it … the human condition" (230). This is, of course, the "truth" within the framework of the novel, but McAlpine is blank with grief and can't initially accept such a platitude. He soon realizes, however, that the detective had been right: "I remembered that I too had come to Montreal to ride a white horse [i.e., to pursue success and respectability]. Maybe that was why I was trying to change her. That was the sin. I couldn't accept her as she was" (232). McAlpine goes on to suggest that Peggy was the only character who didn't own a white horse; in fact, she had been trampled to death by all the white horses riding over her. But Peggy is not ultimately seen as a victim. On the whole, *The Loved and the Lost* glorifies Peggy's unwillingness to accept the strictures of Montreal society in the 1950s or to selfishly ride the "white horse" of personal success. Rather than a victim, then, Peggy is configured as a sort of martyr whose death disrupts these things or at least calls them into question. Indeed, as the novel ends McAlpine is walking the streets and the snow – symbolic of the icy respectability of (white-raced) Montreal high society – is beginning to melt, indicating an incipient loosening of the social strictures and entrenched racism, forms of prejudice that Peggy has opposed throughout the story.

Callaghan's rendering of hockey in *The Loved and the Lost* is particularly interesting in the context of his seeming endorsement of the unity-by-hockey myth almost ten years prior to the novel. In December 1942, Callaghan was walking to Maple Leaf Gardens for a game when he observed a group of boys playing street hockey. He would later recall the "Anglo-Saxon faces and Scandinavian faces and Italian and Slavic faces … though they were all one, they were just a collection of Canadian kids playing shinny. The game held them all together … And come to think of it, hockey does more for the racial unity of this country than all the speeches of all the politicians who ever pointed with pride at Ottawa … It laughs at the supremacy of any racial faction" (Callaghan [1942] 2003, 25). Although there are no black faces in Callaghan's hockey mosaic, this passage clearly affirms the unity-by-hockey myth. It may also offer another context in which to read the hockey content in *The Loved and the Lost*. Perhaps the divide between these seemingly incongruent renderings isn't an internal inconsistency or an authorial about-face so much as the difference between the professional and recreational games. In the above passage, Callaghan depicts the childhood innocence that hockey novels in general associate with the pastoral myth and with Canadian hockey itself. *The Loved and the Lost*, by contrast, depicts a professional game that already in 1951 had become an upper-class preserve and, as such, another extension of the racist society that the novel sets out to condemn. Greed and selfishness are often seen as threatening the inherent "Canadianness" of the game, and these flaws are certainly denounced in *The Loved and the Lost* as well: Peggy is cast as a casualty of other peoples' ambitions, trampled to death by the symbolic white horses of their pursuit of success. In the contrast between spontaneous recreational play (i.e., the pastoral myth) and the organized institution of professional hockey, Peggy clearly aligns with the former. In fact, overcome by the values of the latter, she could be seen as a tragic romantic hero. Perhaps *The Loved and the Lost*, then, can be said to participate in the distinction between recreational and professional hockey that is fundamental to the way in which hockey novels characterize Canadian symbolic possession of the game, and indeed, the myth of hockey itself.

WHY DUDDY KRAVITZ IS A BAD CANADIAN

It is tempting to embrace the totalizing vision presented by hockey novels as an answer to Canada's persistent identity debates. A country could certainly choose worse ways to imagine community into polity: hockey is surely less harmful than many of the catastrophic

nationalisms of the last century. But while hockey will probably never precipitate a holocaust or ethnic cleansing, it often does represent
the benign face of an exclusionary impulse that can take more sinis-
ter turns. What about those whom the game and its traditions work
to exclude? What is their place in this version of national identity?
One such character from Canadian fiction is the eponymous protagonist of Mordecai Richler's *The Apprenticeship of Duddy Kravitz*
(1959). In hockey terms, *Duddy Kravitz* can be read as a direct counterpoint to *Two Solitudes*; although both novels are set in Montreal
and the surrounding countryside, Richler's focus is very different
than MacLennan's. *Duddy Kravitz* departs from the French–English-
identity binary that underwrites *Two Solitudes*, in order to focus on
a series of marginal Canadian characters, most of whom are Jewish.
The reader gets the sense that Duddy is positioned as a minority in a
cultural, economic, and societal field, and that he must negotiate this
field as best he can in pursuit of his fiscal goals – play the cards he is
dealt, as it were, engage in street-level realpolitik. Part of this is nego-
tiating the anti-Semitism, both real and perceived, that he frequently
encounters in Canadian society. Hockey enters the novel twice
through characters associated with the larger structures of hegemonic white Canadian society: a disenchanted Scots-Canadian high-
school teacher who dreams about gathering former students in his
parlour to "lament the lost hockey games of twenty years ago" (7),
and a jet-set university hockey player who befriends Duddy's brother, Lennie, with the expectation that he can be convinced to perform
a back-alley abortion on the hockey player's girlfriend (Lennie later
realizes somewhat pathetically that "they were never my friends ...
they were out to exploit my racial inferiority complex" [292]).

Hockey is the domain of the dominant group in *Duddy Kravitz*,
and as such becomes one of the symbolic structures of exclusion that
foreground Duddy's alterity throughout the novel. In this regard,
Duddy Kravitz works to expose the exclusivity of the hockey myth
as a marker of national belonging. But the novel also illuminates
the ways in which this identity posture can establish hierarchies of
Canadianness. Duddy certainly doesn't seem to mind the fact that he
has no stake in Canada's game; in fact, his most visceral connection
to hockey occurs in a "hockey stick sideline" (56) scam wherein he
steals hockey sticks during Canadiens practices and sells them as
collector items. For Duddy, a character who falls outside the traditional French–English-identity gridiron, hockey becomes simply

another opportunity to negotiate the cultural field to his advantage. Duddy doesn't venerate the game or participate in its rituals, and, as such (following the terms of the myth) appears unnatural, ahistorical, and abundantly less Canadian. In fact, Duddy symbolically aligns himself with the capitalist greed that hockey novels see as detracting from the game: rather than appreciating the grace and talent of the players, Duddy steals their sticks to sell for profit. Through these brief references to the game, *The Apprenticeship of Duddy Kravitz* uses hockey to indicate Duddy's outsider status within Canadian culture and society. Indeed, it is because of Duddy's place as an outsider for whom the powerful cultural symbol of hockey is meaningless that he is able to exploit the arbitrary values that others attribute to it in the first place. Like *Two Solitudes*, then, *The Apprenticeship of Duddy Kravitz* suggests hockey as a sort of "background" marker of Canadian cultural identity. Unlike *Two Solitudes*, however, *Duddy Kravitz* sees hockey as refereeing the terms of this identity (i.e., who gets to be Canadian and who doesn't). Duddy is no avatar of Canadian identity in the spirit of Paul Tallard, and Richler's St Urbain Street setting is peopled with mobsters, shysters, liars, braggarts, and troublemakers rather than the ideologues and symbolic personifications of *Two Solitudes*.

Another novel in which Richler suggests that hockey establishes hierarchies of Canadianness by excluding certain people and groups is *The Incomparable Atuk* (1963). *The Incomparable Atuk* is a satire against facile Canadian nationalism and Canada's anxious cultural relationship with the United States, and, as such, hockey was almost certain to make an appearance. The novel tells the story of an Inuit poet named Atuk (although Richler uses the dated word Eskimo), who comes to Toronto as an overnight literary sensation. After arriving in the big city Atuk develops an acquisitive capitalist sensibility, and quickly branches out into profit-making schemes such as running a sweatshop in his basement to produce "authentic" Inuit art. Eventually Atuk ends up on a television quiz show called *Stick Your Neck Out*, which entices contestants with the prospect of a million-dollar payout but at considerable risk in that incorrect answers result in execution by guillotine. This is where hockey comes in. Atuk's first two questions are relatively easy pieces of hockey trivia, which he manages to answer correctly but only with the help of a self-interested corporate executive who flashes the answers on little cards. For the third and final question, however, the executive – who views Atuk as a liability and wants him out of the picture – provides no help, and Atuk fails on a considerably more difficult challenge: name "the total number of third period goals scored by Howie Morenz in regular season play and how many of these were slap-shots, how many rebounds, and how many were scored when the opposition was a man short" (177). Of course the deck has been stacked against Atuk, as this question would be impossible even for Morenz himself. But reading quite literally here, it is Atuk's igno-rance of hockey that brings about his death. Beyond having disas-trous personal consequences, this lack of knowledge marks Atuk as an outsider within Canadian society, a theme that Richler has particular fun with when hockey is announced as the day's trivia category and Atuk responds with the exclamation "*Gevalt!*" (177). "Gevalt" is a Yiddish expression that connotes surprise and con-sternation, and in this context represents a clever yoking of subal-tern sensibilities and perhaps subtly connects Atuk to Duddy Kravitz's outsider relationship with hockey. Both novels, then, are light-heartedly critical of hockey's function as an identity shibbo-leth, a test to determine who gets to be Canadian and who remains on the margins of national belonging.

Richler's inclusion of "intelligent, hockey-mad characters" (Blake 2010, 212) in other novels is somewhat more germane to the terms of the hockey myth, and tends to portray the game as, in Richler's own words, a "secret [Canadian] idiom" (quoted in Blake 2010, 212). For instance, the narrator of *Barney's Version* (1997), Barney Panofsky, who less than three pages into the novel lists his literary influences in one paragraph and follows with his hockey influences in the next, suggests both the importance of the game in Canada and its potential to cut across traditional class and cultural boundaries. As Blake points out, foreign reviews of *Barney's Version* found it unlikely that such a sophisticated and high-cultured character as Panofsky would be interested in hockey while Canadian reviews accepted this detail at face value. The implication, both of the char-acter and the reviews, is that hockey is a particular national inflec-tion and omnipresent Canadian institution. But while Richler may have seen hockey as a secret idiom that colours Canadian difference from other countries, his writing doesn't depict the game as a sacred cow. As Blake also notes, the international circulation and reception of Richler's fiction could just as well serve to remind Canadians that, for the most part, our hockey heroes "[mean] nothing to the rest of the world" (2010, 212). As one character puts it in *The Incomprarable Atuk*, "I'm world-famous ... all over Canada" (30). And again, as both *The Apprenticeship of Duddy Kravitz* and *The Incomparable Atuk* suggest, hockey's idiomatic omnipresence in Canadian society doesn't mean that all Canadians are in on the secret.

It is worth noting the extent to which this chapter has resorted to exceptions (i.e., "non-hockey novels" or works with a more literary predilection) in order to address novelistic considerations of non-white characters who participate in the culture of the game. Several others could have been discussed: Austin Clarke's *The Question* (1999), for instance, in which an immigrant character from an unnamed Caribbean island disapproves of his wife's interest in hockey fights and the way in which hockey comes to regulate their sex life, or Audrey Thomas' *Coming Down from Wa* (1995), in which one character stages a "Hockey Night in Africa" as a symbolic culmination of his character growth throughout the novel. Thomas King's *Green Grass, Running Water* (1993) contains a scene in which a white character accuses a Native character of not being a "real Indian ... [because] you drive cars, watch television, [and] go to hockey games" (141), while the narrator of Robert Kroetsch's *The Studhorse Man* (1969) waxes eloquent about the pleasure of listening to hockey games being "those sudden and glamorous [player] names" (142). Although Kroetsch's narrator's delight is mainly nostalgic and pastoral ("those forever youthful names ... those children of winter are my dream"), the actual catalogue of player names listed – Mikita, Laperriere, Kelly, Hull, Delvecchio, Sawchuk, Ullman, Giacomin, Van Impe, and Esposito, to name only a few – reveals a noteworthy range of ethnic difference (142–3).[6] Moving slightly beyond the parameters of this study for further examples, Tomson Highway's play *Dry Lips Oughta Move to Kapuskasing* (1989) uses hockey to probe the meanings of both Native and gender identities, while Grant Tracey's short story collection *Parallel Lines and the Hockey Universe* (2003) revolves around a Macedonian-Canadian boy, Matt Traicheff, who despite not "fit[ting] into the WASP valley" – in part because he "[can't] skate or fire a slapshot" – becomes a sports reporter for the local Junior A hockey team (27).

By way of further contrast, children's hockey novels tend to be more inclusive of racial and ethnic diversity than their adult-oriented counterparts. Although Young's *Boy on Defence* and *Boy at the Leafs Camp* are essentially about a Polish immigrant's assimilation into Canadian culture through hockey, they depict the team as a pluralist model of cross-cultural unity on which the nation itself might be patterned. This theme is especially evident in Young's *Scrubs on Skates* (1952), in which the team is a veritable cultural mosaic of racial and ethnic backgrounds and at one point their enforcer actually starts a fight with an opposing player for uttering racial slurs. Ann Walsh's *Shabash* (1994) tells the story of Rana, the first Sikh player to join the local hockey team in a small British Columbia town, focusing on the obstacles and race-related challenges he encounters along the way. Similarly, the team in MacGregor's *Screech Owl* series is described as "Team United Nations" because it has players "who had come from, or whose parents or grandparents had come from, Japan, Saudi Arabia, Russia, Lebanon, Jamaica, Italy, Great Britain, and Germany. And now this year Jesse Highboy, a Cree, had joined" (*Mystery at Lake Placid*, 14). Although this characterization was originally intended as a "tongue-in-cheek … spoof on being politically correct," MacGregor decided to run with the idea of a radically multicultural team in earnest after reflecting on his own experience coaching minor hockey: "I've got kids on my teams with names like Sareen and Faud. And there are girls and Blacks and Asians" (1998).

As part of their "Team United Nations" ethos children's hockey novels are often particularly interested in exploring Native culture, often through the experience of a white protagonist who comes into contact with Nativeness by way of a friend or particular plot event. MacGregor's *The Screech Owls' Northern Adventure* (1996), for instance, uses the occasion of a tournament in James Bay to suggest the game as a mediating ritual that helps the players develop an appreciation for Native culture. More direct about confronting racial difference is Sigmund Brouwer's *Thunderbird Spirit* (2008), which follows Mike Keats and his "Cree Indian friend," Dakota, as they deal with racism in the game. Despite the fact that Dakota is relatively sanguine about the racial injustice he endures, Mike gets upset on his friend's behalf and actually starts a fight with a fan who calls Dakota a "redskin" and taunts that he should be carrying a "bow and arrow" (2). The characters' differing perspectives on this incident foreshadow the plot's central crisis, in which Mike learns that Dakota has infiltrated a group of Native terrorists who are planning to blow up a dam and assassinate the premier of British Columbia. According to Dakota, these terrorists are "using this

whole race thing just to get a war started. They want to fight, just for
the sake of fighting" (141). Although Dakota hates the racism that
he and his people are often subjected to, he disagrees with the terrorists' methods and believes that contentious issues are best solved
"through give and take" and by "work[ing] things through with the
government" (141). The philosophy Dakota brings to hockey, then,
is that which he brings to life in general, and Mike ultimately learns
from his friend that violence isn't justified as a response to racial
injustice. As such, *Thunderbird Spirit* uses the issue of race to participate in the recurring hockey-novel thematic of becoming a man
through hockey violence (which will be discussed more fully in the
following chapter), in this case by depicting the need for appropriate
restraint. Moving somewhat away from the template of encountering Nativeness through the lens of whiteness, Jacqueline Guest's
Rookie Season (2000) depicts a Métis girl who partners with her
white classmates and several Native girls from a nearby Reserve to
form an all-girl hockey team, while – reversing the thematic trajectory of *The Screech Owls' Northern Adventure* – Gloria Miller's *The
Slapshot Star* (2001) uses hockey to represent a young Aboriginal
boy's distance from his cultural heritage.

Outside the hockey novel umbrella, depictions of sport in Canadian
novels tend not to be as enthusiastic about the possibilities of athletic activity to facilitate intercultural connections. While hockey
novels see the game as contributing to an albeit limited range of
multicultural unity, facilitating relationships that transcend racial
and ethnic differences, and, most importantly in the framework of
the myth, supplying distinctively Canadian content or character to
these relationships, depictions of sports in other Canadian novels are
equally likely to suggest division as they are unity. Furthermore, novels that depict sports other than hockey tend not to burden what
tentative unity they suggest with nationalist freight, and in some
cases even work against the possibility of a monolithic Canadian
nationalism or identity. A throwaway moment in Jeannette
Armstrong's *Slash* (1985), for instance, suggests that sport can illuminate cultural divisions and expose the fact that not all Canadians
have equal access to power and resources: "Somebody from Indian
Affairs had a bright idea, I guess. According to the Council, the
Agent decided that Indian kids needed recreation to help them live
better. So they spent lots of money levelling some land and black-
topping it, then putting sides on it. The roller rink was real nice;

everybody on the reserve said so. Only thing wrong was nobody had roller skates or even knew how to roller skate" (48–9). This attempt to encourage more physical activity – and thereby, as Armstrong somewhat sarcastically suggests, better living – among Native kids backfires, of course, because it is externally imposed and completely ignorant of the community's actual priorities and experience. In this instance, sport is just another paternalistic attempt to manage Native culture and attests to the larger problem of racism in Canadian society that the novel addresses.

Another Canadian novel that exposes the potential of sports to divide different cultural groups is Steven Hayward's *The Secret Mitzvah of Lucio Burke* (2005), which one reviewer has compared to Kinsella's *Shoeless Joe* in that – beyond both depicting baseball – these novels share "the same sense of magic and same possibility of miracles" (Thiessen 2005). Unlike *Shoeless Joe*, however, *The Secret Mitzvah of Lucio Burke* is set in Canada and explores ethnic and political tensions in 1930s Toronto. Occurring at a time when "the city is ninety percent British, and Protestant. The Loyal Orange Order can be seen marching twice a year down the middle of the city ... The Union Jack flag flies over City Hall. [And] schoolchildren sing 'God Save the King,'" *The Secret Mitzvah of Lucio Burke* expressly focuses on the lower class Italian and Jewish residents – "the wops and kikes, as they are mostly called by most of the city" – who inhabit Toronto's Ward neighbourhood (5). Baseball is a powerful point of class, ethnic, and ideological division in the novel, as the story ends with a fictionalized account of an actual historical clash between Fascists and Jews that began after the unveiling of a swastika flag at a baseball game at Toronto's Christie Pits in 1933. But while Hayward proposes the possibility of baseball to divide, he also recognizes the game's potential to foster positive relationships between diverse ethnic groups. In fact, Hayward confesses in the acknowledgments to portraying the Lizzies, the fictionalized team from the Ward that *The Secret Mitzvah of Lucio Burke* depicts, as "decidedly more ethnically diverse" than their historical model (383). Hayward's aim in "placing so many different kinds of new immigrant Canadians on the same team" was "to suggest the alliances that existed between them in a more direct manner than the historical record might allow" (384). Although this decision could be interpreted as championing the idea of Canadian multiculturalism or suggesting an embedded multicultural sensibility in the still-emerging nation, the fact that *The Secret Mitzvah of Lucio Burke* ends on the divisive note of the Christie Pits riot seems to trump this reading. While recognizing the complexity of sport as a mechanism for social interaction, then, Hayward doesn't put forward an overarching nationalism or attempt to model Canadian pluralism on whatever tentative unity sport can facilitate.

One final example of a novel that depicts sport as a facilitator of intercultural connection but makes clear that the resulting unity isn't the basis for an overarching nationalism is Dionne Brand's *What We All Long For* (2005). *What We All Long For* includes an episode in which several of the novel's young minority characters take to the streets of Toronto's Korea Town neighbourhood for an impromptu celebration after Korea's victory over Italy in the 2002 FIFA World Cup. Although these characters aren't interested in sport so much as the experience of "something tingling on the skin, something where their blood rushed to their heads and they felt alive" (205), Brand depicts the soccer celebrations as a joyous coming together of diverse cultural elements but in which the waving flags don't bear the Canadian Maple Leaf and the songs rising up in the streets conspicuously aren't "O Canada." Soccer, then, which has often been called the global game, appears to contribute to the urban, multicultural, and post-national ethos that *What We All Long For* puts forward in general. In fact, Brand's choice of soccer is particularly instructive of her purposes in the novel, as she could just as well have chosen to represent the other event that brought Canadians of various cultural and ethnic heritages to Toronto's streets in shared celebration in 2002: Team Canada's gold-medal hockey win at the Salt Lake City Olympics.

The point of calling attention to the relative absence of minority characters in adult-oriented Canadian hockey novels is to illustrate the extent to which these novels constitute a limited genre. While authors from minority cultures certainly do write about hockey, they don't appear to write "hockey novels" that invest in the hockey myth's insistence on associating the game with Canadianness. To further elucidate the limitations of the genre, this chapter will conclude with a discussion of two hockey novels that make manifest the hierarchical, exclusive, or compulsory outcomes of the myth, McCormack's *Understanding Ken* and John Degen's *The Uninvited Guest* (2006). The protagonist of *Understanding Ken* is a hockey-mad ten-year-old growing up in the 1970s, trying to come to terms

with the nasty divorce of his parents and the decline of his beloved
Montreal Canadiens after the retirement of their star goaltender, Ken
Dryden. *Understanding Ken* works to reinforce several familiar
tenets of the hockey myth; for instance, hockey is seen as ontologically Canadian. Early in the story the narrator describes his philosophy of hockey as "You play. Period" (16). Later when the boy's
mother asks him why he likes the game so much he remarks to himself that "it was a dumb question" before answering "Mom, it's
hockey. That's why" (73).[7] For the unnamed narrator of *Understanding
Ken*, hockey is its own justification, its own excuse for being. Much
of this relates to the game's "Canadian" normalcy in the boy's life;
Understanding Ken sees hockey as it was for many, a defining feature
of Canadian childhood in the 1970s. The young narrator clearly conceives of the game as an emblem of national identity, a fact which is
revealed circumspectly after a run-in with a schoolteacher whom the
narrator derides as "know[ing] less about hockey than my mom"
(107): "He got so mad. He said he was sick of hearing about hockey.
Then he lied and said lacrosse is Canada's national sport" (157) (note
the derisive feminization of those who don't participate in hockey
culture). Technically, the teacher is correct: *Understanding Ken* is set
in 1973–74, when hockey wasn't yet officially recognized as Canada's
national winter sport. In the mind of the narrator, however, hockey is
so naturally and inevitably Canadian that it must be the national
sport, a fact that he argues (with a child's impeccable logic) on the
basis that "there's no Skiing Night in Canada" (17). What there is, of
course, is *Hockey Night in Canada*, which (again following the terms
of the myth) is inscribed in markedly nationalistic terms: "the Hockey
Night in Canada theme song … is twice as good as O Canada. It
should be the national anthem" (219).

In addition to rehearsing the tenets of the hockey myth, however,
Understanding Ken also illustrates the myth's totalizing consequences for national identity. At one point in the story the narrator
gets angry about the Peter Puck cartoons that come on during
Hockey Night in Canada to explain rules such as offside and icing,
complaining that "everybody in Canada except English women
already know that stuff" (162). The English woman who occasions
this generalization is the narrator's mother, who is basically indifferent to hockey. In fact, the only characters in *Understanding Ken* who
don't understand or care about hockey are specifically identified as
nationally other: the narrator's English mother and his Scottish

teacher.[8] In addition to specifying their non-Canadianness, the narrator delineates these characters as linguistically different by noting that both speak with an accent. At the same time, the alterity of another character who is more visibly marked as different, the narrator's "Negro friend," is considerably diminished: "I didn't know my new friend was a Negro until ... someone called him that" (97). The narrator's failure to notice his Negro friend's difference presumably stems, at least in part, from the friend's participation in the "Canadian" activity of hockey. We are never told whether the Negro friend is, like the narrator himself, the son of an immigrant or whether he is, say, a tenth-generation Canadian. In the mind of the unnamed narrator, it would seem that this information is irrelevant: the Negro friend is Canadian by virtue of his participation in hockey, in the same way that the narrator's mother and schoolteacher are "un-Canadian" because of their indifference to hockey. Hockey, then, appears to referee the terms of Canadianness in *Understanding Ken*, to the point where the characters who don't play or appreciate the game are seen as markedly different, other, and even un-Canadian.

Another moment in which hockey adjudicates national identity occurs in Degen's *The Uninvited Guest*. One of the strands in *The Uninvited Guest* follows Nicolae Petrescu-Nicolae, a Romanian immigrant who makes his way to Canada to escape Communism. On the morning of their first day in Canada, Nicolae and his family receive an unlikely visitor at their Montreal YMCA room: the former Romanian Securitate agent who had been assigned to shadow Nicolae for several years prior to his departure. The agent, Alexandru Ionescu, has heard of Nicolae's arrival in Montreal and has come to offer an apology and make partial amends for his actions by way of three tickets to the Montreal Canadiens game that night. "It is no football match," Ionescu tells Nicolae, "but it is interesting, and more importantly, it is Canadian – from the new life" (209). Ionescu's gift again suggests the relationship between hockey and Canadian cultural identity. The logic of giving hockey tickets to a family of new arrivals follows Roy MacGregor's claim that "it is impossible to know a people until you know the game they play" (2006, ix). Indeed, the hockey game serves as a sort of cultural passport in *The Uninvited Guest*, immediately immersing the Petrescu-Nicolae in the regular workings of Canadian society. When they arrive at the Forum it initially seems "impossible that this thing, this hockey game, just a normal part of life in Montreal would be theirs for the evening"

(211), but Nicolae and his family soon find themselves at ease among the crowd and even begin to see the game as "beautiful" (212). Although this brief sketch is all we are told about the Petrescu-Nicolae's first days in Canada, their initial hockey experience turns out to be immensely formative: Nicolae's son, Dragos, grows up to become the first Romanian-born player to win the Stanley Cup. In the case of *The Uninvited Guest*, then, hockey works to assimilate the Petrescu-Nicolae by incorporating them in the workings of Canadian "normalcy"; in fact, the story seems to be offering a myth of immigrant assimilation somewhat along the lines of Young's Bill Spunska novels, which suggest that anyone can achieve success in Canada if they only work hard and accept Canadian values and cultural norms. Again, hockey is characterized as normative Canadian behaviour, a cultural given whose status and prominence are largely taken for granted.

The problem with seeing hockey as a totalizing and definitive feature of Canadian identity is that to do so invariably effaces the pluralism on which any "tolerant and protective nationalism" (Bentley 1992) must surely be based. How would the Petrescu-Nicolae have fared in Canada if they had not appreciated the hockey game? It is not difficult to imagine an alternative plot in which their indifference to hockey marks them as outsiders and, like Duddy Kravitz, symbolically separates them from any significant participation in Canadianness. The majority of hockey novelists would likely be reluctant to accept the argument that insistence on the hockey myth is incompatible with pluralism; in fact, the few instances where hockey novels actually depict intercultural relationships are rendered in the service of the multicultural pluralist ideal and posed against a persistent strain of societal racism and intolerance that is acknowledged as real. The story of the Petrescu-Nicolae – outsiders whose hockey tickets are really symbolic entrance tickets into Canadian society – is a relative anomaly among adult-oriented Canadian hockey novels.[9] Although hockey novels frequently suggest sport as a "mediating ritual" (to again borrow Watson's phrase), they rarely employ the trope of assimilation that Timothy Morris has identified as common to American baseball fiction, in which "immigrants to the United States are intrigued and, as it were, naturalized by baseball" (1997, 13). Again in this regard, hockey novels appear congruent with the pluralist ideal: hockey mediates while baseball assimilates. Hockey's mediation, of course, applies to a relatively limited range of cultural difference: hockey novels contain almost no references to African, Asian, South Asian, Middle Eastern, or South American cultures and/or players. But hockey also works to referee, as in *Understanding Ken*, the issue of who gets to be "Canadian."

If there is any philosophical truth to the depictions of Canada's "mosaic" and America's "melting pot" that many Canadians have internalized as a marker of cultural distinction, Canadian identity can't be in any way uniform, compulsory, or hierarchical. If the Canadian mentality toward foreigners and new arrivals is to be (as we are so fond of telling ourselves) functionally different from "the common nineteenth-century vision of an immigrant being miraculously transmogrified into a different being – an American, for example" (Saul 1997, 130), then Canadian identity must be seen as a fluid and malleable concept that doesn't hang on any central vision or tenet. In other words, if Canadians do want to conceive of themselves as a "country of minorities" it is clear that we will have to dispense with "the old nationalist certitudes" (131). Some will say that this simply substitutes one mythology for another, but a functionally pluralist identity is both desirable and achievable while a national identity rooted in any one particular concept or activity – even one so appealing as hockey – simply isn't. By posing hockey as an identity shibboleth, hockey novels actually embrace the assimilative mentality that is often understood to animate American negotiation of difference and to encourage readers toward an overly simplistic and exclusionary patriotism. By slipping into the "old nationalist certitude" of a definitive and homogenous identity, Canadian hockey novels inadvertently work to eradicate a good deal of the national difference that they ostensibly set out to preserve.

4

National Manhood

To be masculine in sport has traditionally meant being "competitive, successful, dominating, aggressive, stoical, goal-directed, and physically strong" (Messner and Sabo 1994, 38). More generally, masculinity has traditionally been connected to familial leadership, protection, and provision, roles that in Western culture became associated with wage-earning work throughout the industrial era of the nineteenth and twentieth centuries. By fulfilling the expectations of the wage-earner role, men, specifically white men, have often been encouraged to see themselves as contributing productively to the national well-being and greater public good. Literary critic Dana Nelson refers to this connection between masculine labour and patriotic duty as "national manhood," an ideology that works "to link a fraternal articulation of white manhood to civic identity" (1998, ix). In Nelson's framework, individual men are expected to contribute to "national unity" through their participation in the capitalist marketplace via wage-earning work, but are "promised relief from the anxieties of [this] economic competition in the warm emotional space of civic fraternal sameness" (x). In other words, national manhood encourages individual men to work productively for the good of the nation, promising fraternal and patriotic identification with other men as both rationale and reward for their efforts. Nelson makes it clear, however, that this "brotherly state of unity and wholeness" turns out to be little more than an "imagined fraternity" which is constantly short-circuited by national manhood's competitive individualism. Indeed, for Nelson, the promise of unity and fraternity held out by national manhood "never in fact did or even could exist" (204).

Hockey novels work to arbitrate gender identity in largely the same ways as they do national identity: by signifying within certain pre-existing frameworks of meaning (i.e., the hockey myth) and reinforcing these meanings through the repetitive rehearsal that Butler refers to as "coercive representation." Masculinity is seen as constituted for the most part by toughness, a corollary of which appears to be robust and expressive heterosexuality. Following the models of masculinity enacted by prominent hockey men such as Don Cherry, hockey novels maintain that a man's value consists primarily in his physical strength, tenacity, and willingness to battle. This individual toughness, however, appears most worthwhile and meaningful in the context of the team's fraternal unity. It is by dedicating personal skill and physical strength to the benefit and well-being of the team collective that individual players appear to derive a sense of significance and meaning. This model is essentially the same as that of national manhood for productive male citizenship, and the process of creating good hockey players appears easily transposed into the larger realm of civic responsibility. By acquiring the toughness and discipline necessary to succeed at hockey, then, young male protagonists are simultaneously seen to be equipped with the skills and discipline necessary to fulfill the requirements of productive citizenship. Probably the most obvious and extreme enactment of national manhood in civic terms is military service, and, as such, it is no coincidence that hockey novels often employ the metaphor of war in describing the game and the masculine fraternity it is seen to bring about.

As with Nelson's version of national manhood, hockey novels see the real and imagined fraternity of the dressing room both as a rationale for collective responsibility and as an area of respite from the pressures of individual effort. Furthermore, it is in the promise of the team (and to a lesser extent fan) *esprit de corps* that hockey novels see the idealized possibilities of national commonality and togetherness. If the real and imagined fraternities of the hockey dressing room provide a model by which national community can be imagined, hockey novels suggest that the toughness, strength, and collective-mindedness of individual players must contribute productively to the identity, direction, and well-being of the national whole. By suggesting the capacity of individual men to affect the national course, hockey novels appear to realize the central promise of national manhood and fulfill the desire of traditional masculinity for social utility and leadership through strength, focus, and individual responsibility.

A Nike television advertisement that aired during the 2007 Super Series provides an excellent illustration of national manhood's place within the Canadian hockey myth. The Super Series was an eight-game challenge between the Russian and Canadian national junior teams, organized in honour of the thirty-fifth anniversary of the Summit Series. Nike's advertising strategy for the Super Series was to highlight the intensive training and athletic conditioning Team Canada's athletes underwent in preparation – intimating, of course, the invaluable assistance of Nike gear throughout this process. The advertisement featured footage of Team Canada in training: strong and muscular young (white) men doing wind sprints, push-ups, lifting weights, tossing medicine balls, etc. Several shots featured these athletes experiencing visible pain and struggle; one shot depicted a player taking a spill during a team jog over rugged terrain. Interspersed throughout the montage of training footage were images of cheering Canadian fans wearing Team Canada jerseys, waving Maple Leaf flags, and painted in national colours. These jumpcuts between the team's training and their visibly nationalist fans draw a direct connection between male strength and national accomplishment. They create the impression that the young men of Team Canada recognize their responsibility to the national collective, their role in fulfilling an important narrative of unity and identity based on hockey victory that, in turn, must be secured through strength and fitness.

Although national manhood is in many ways an appealing ideology – it encourages men to internalize worthwhile values such as courage, self-sacrifice, and self-control, and offers a comfortable sense of moral certainty – it does present several significant problems. Nelson makes clear that the "process of identifying with national manhood blocks white men from being able ... to identify socioeconomic inequality as a structural rather than individual failure" and poses "a series of affective foreclosures that block those men's more heterogeneous democratic identifications and energies" (ix). In other words, national manhood works to reinforce existing socio-economic inequalities by making them appear impersonal and abstract, and, to borrow a phrase from Edward Herman and Noam Chomsky ([1998] 2002), works to "manufacture consent" among those who identify with it. As such, national manhood contributes to a version of Canadian identity that, again, has been resolutely white and male, a fact which has been particularly evident in hockey. While the idea that masculinity is constituted primarily by toughness has not been limited to Canada, it has been uniquely encouraged in this country and enshrined as part of our hockey myth. Many Canadian fans exhibit "a widely shared pride in 'our' boys' hardness and bravado, as if this was part of a preferred Canadian self-image: a symbolic reminder ... of the tough and courageous traditions of a northern frontier nation" (Gruneau and Whitson 1993, 187–8).

The hockey myth's symbolic insistence on masculine toughness through northernness bears uncomfortable resemblance to the ethnocentric nationalism of the Canada First Movement, a nineteenth-century crusade to absorb Canadian "ethnic differences" within an "anglo-Protestant norm" (New 2003, 83). The Canada First Movement saw northernness as the prime determinant of Canadian character and as "synonymous with strength and self-reliance" in contrast to southern climates, which purportedly bred "degeneration, decay, and effeminacy" (Berger 1966, 5). According to Canada First, only certain races – hearty, strong, industrious races – could survive in a demanding climate such as Canada's, and, consequently, it was believed that Canada would be spared from the "Negro problem" which troubled its southern neighbour (9). The vision of Canadian nationalism represented by Canada First, then, was founded on the idea that "because of the climate and because Canadians are sprung from ... the 'Aryan' family, Canada must be a pre-eminent power, the home of a superior race, the heir of both the historical destiny of the ancient Scandinavians and their spirit of liberty" (7).

As a game played on ice and snow, hockey readily came to be seen in the late nineteenth and early twentieth centuries as confirming the Canada First vision of Canadian identity: a hearty game sprung from the rugged north and played by hearty (white) Canadian men. Although the emerging rhetoric of cultural pluralism during Canada's Centennial era worked to move hockey away from the outdated and ethnocentric assumptions of Canada First,[1] hockey has remained, for the most part, a white male preserve. Again, this reality is reflected in the fact that hockey novel protagonists are almost uniformly white and male. Although the topocentric depictions of the game in Canadian hockey novels discussed earlier are neither overtly racist nor ostensibly exclusive, it should be remembered that the identity-by-northernness trope was once the centrepiece of a virulent and ethnocentric nationalist movement.[2]

A related offshoot of Canada First's blood nationalism was the idea that despite sometimes creating "monstrous behaviour in the normally mild men of Canada" (*Dawson City Seven*, 258), hockey actually contributes to Canadian peacefulness and tolerance by expunging harmful and violent male energies. This idea is referred to as "catharsis theory" in the literature of sport psychology, and has been largely discredited. Nevertheless, the idea that hockey works as a sort of collective release valve for male aggressive energy has frequently been used to defend the place of body contact and fighting in the game. Although this idea is expressed in several hockey novels, it has perhaps been stated most explicitly as a function of race by Hugh MacLennan: "To spectator and player alike, hockey gives the release that strong liquor gives a repressed man. It is the counterpoint of Canadian self-restraint, it takes us back to the fiery blood of Gallic and Celtic ancestors who found themselves minorities in a cold, new environment and had to discipline themselves as all minorities must" (quoted in Frayne 1990, 178). MacLennan's reference to the "fiery blood" of white ancestors ties immediately back to blood nationalist beliefs about the Canadian identity and context, while his assumption – in keeping with the release valve theory in general – denies men an important degree of agency and sees them, effectively, as prisoners to innate or inevitable violent impulses. In addition to presenting a limited and exclusive version of national belonging, then, national manhood encourages men to internalize harmful and reductive gender identities based in large part on strength, toughness, competition, and dominance.

MASCULINITY IN CRISIS

Before turning to the ways in which hockey novels rehearse and perform the values of national manhood, it is worth further historicizing the connection between national identity and the masculine toughness enacted in Canadian hockey. If the violence and aggression of early Canadian hockey grew out of European emulation of Aboriginal models of masculinity, the appeal of these identities can be traced to "a larger turn-of-the-[twentieth]-century masculine response to a perceived crisis of masculinity brought on by feminism, modernization, and widespread fears that boys and men were becoming 'feminized'" (Messner 1997, 25). When working-class men first began to participate widely in sports they were seen as "demonstrating masculine independence, respectability, and physical skill," values which became the chief components of masculine identity at a time when "artisanal skills were being devalued in the workplace and when employers committed to the principles of scientific management were seeking to extend their authority over their employees" (Howell 2001, 53). In other words, sport was seen in the late nineteenth and early twentieth centuries "as a strategy for 'defeminizing' men who no longer worked in physically challenging occupations" (Wamsley 2007, 75). The emergence of modern sport also responded to late nineteenth-century fears about the emasculation of men and the emerging feminist movement, typified by "the image of the 'New Woman' of the 1890s, whose major sins ... would seem to have been having a job, riding a bicycle, and ... all too obviously having two legs" (Braudy 2003, 339). The "homosocial cultural sphere" of sport, then, "provided men with psychological separation from the perceived feminization of society while also providing dramatic symbolic proof of the 'natural superiority' of men over women" (Messner 2007, 35).

Because concerns about the emasculation of men and boys were rooted in "the belief that the collapse of sexual differentiation would hamper procreation ... and thereby enfeeble the national future" (Braudy 2003, 338), the perceived masculinity crisis of the late nineteenth century was also seen as a matter of national well-being. It is hardly surprising, then, that during this period sport became integral to "a definition of [white] manliness that purported to ignore class, family, and wealth, interweaving the destiny of the new mass state with the physical condition of its male members" (341).[3] Team sports such as hockey "made the metaphoric relation between the well-trained individual body and national vitality even more explicit," and "by the 1870s and 1880s, personal fitness, team sports, and patriotism [had] formed a virtually unquestioned triad of male definition" (341). In other words, sport became an important part of the ideology of national manhood in the late nineteenth century, a way of encouraging and enabling individual men to cultivate personal strength and proficiency as a way of serving their nation.

Although sport was mobilized to reinvigorate the "manliness" of late nineteenth- and early twentieth-century men, masculine identities throughout the early twentieth century remained generally associated with wage-earning work. According to journalist Susan Faludi, such work provided the "truth on which a man's life could be securely founded" and out of which his authority grew (1999, 86). As Western societies began to enter the post-industrial era of the late twentieth century, men increasingly found themselves victims of "downward social mobility and unemployment" (144). During these years many industrial and labour-intensive jobs were outsourced to the developing world, corporate downsizing and restructuring trimmed the white-collar workforce, and many of the leader, protector, and provider roles on which masculine identities had traditionally been based became increasingly open to women. For many of the men affected by these developments, the breadwinner sense of security and authority collapsed into feelings of "shame" and the "suspicion that the world [had discredited their] claim to manhood, [found] it useless, even risible" (144). This trend perhaps became most evident during the so-called Great Recession of 2008–10, "in which three-quarters of the 8 million jobs lost were lost by men. The worst-hit industries were overwhelmingly male and deeply identified with macho: construction, manufacturing, high finance" (Rosin 2010). As Rosin notes, "some of these jobs will come back, but the overall pattern of dislocation is neither temporary nor random. The recession merely revealed – and accelerated – a profound economic shift that has been going on for at least 30 years, and in some respects even longer."

The result of the social changes described above, coupled with the critiques of masculinity offered by second-wave feminism throughout the 1970s, have led to the perception of a contemporary crisis of masculinity similar to that of the late nineteenth and early twentieth centuries. The sense that traditional masculinity has once again come under threat has given rise to a series of cultural movements in recent years that have attempted to reassert its value, such as Christian organizations like the Promise Keepers (who emphasize the traditional place of men as breadwinners and household leaders) and the spate of publications and seminars that sociologist Michael Messner refers to as the "mythopoetic men's movement" (which focuses on spiritual journeys and exercises "aimed at rediscovering and reclaiming 'the deep masculine'" nature of men [1997, 17]). Furthermore, the belief that traditional masculinity is under attack has led to "the ascendancy of a new and powerful figure" that literary critic David Savran refers to as "the white male as victim" (1998, 4), which, in hockey terms, has been mobilized by Don Cherry and by other polemical commentators such as David Adams Richards.[4]

In the same way that modern sport emerged from the crucible of late nineteenth-century concerns about emasculation and worker alienation, contemporary sport has often been supposed to address the late twentieth-century crisis of masculinity identified above. According to cultural critic Varda Burstyn, "just as the second half of the nineteenth century produced both the first wave of feminism and the consolidation of masculinism in sport, so the second half of the twentieth century ... has produced another great wave of feminism and several new stages in the evolution and hypermasculinization of sport and sport culture" (1999, 120). It is in the context of the late twentieth-century masculinity crisis, then, that Faludi explains the ascendance of American football as "a way of clinging to the idea that national destiny was still something played out by common men on a muddy field, even in an era dominated by skyboxes, television, and Astroturf" (1999, 158). For Faludi, "football was a workingman's way of resisting being sidelined, even as he sat in the stands. Here he might still believe himself a central 'player' in one of his culture's central dramas" (158). Journalist Franklin Foer has made similar claims about soccer fans who wed the game to violence, racism, and radical nationalism: "Deprived of traditional work and knocked off their patriarchal pedestals ... men desperately wanted to reassert their masculinity. Soccer violence gave them a rare opportunity to actually exert control. When these fans dabbled in racism and radical nationalism, it was because those ideologies worked as metaphors for their own lives. Their nations and races had been victimized by the world just as badly as they had been themselves" (2004, 13–14).[5] Both Foer's reading of soccer and Faludi's of football suggest that in the late twentieth-century crisis of masculinity occasioned by the transition to post-industrialism and second-wave feminism, the ideology of national manhood has increasingly appeared most viable when applied to sport. As lower- and middle-class men began to feel emasculated, obsolete, and increasingly disconnected from the sense of civic responsibility that had formerly been entailed by wage-earning work, aggressive sports such as football and soccer became one of the few remaining areas of culture in which traditional masculinity could be "legitimately" connected with national narratives and imagining. In Canada, of course, this has been especially true of hockey, and hockey novels respond to the late twentieth-century crisis of masculinity by reasserting traditional values, attitudes, plot trajectories, and (as will be seen) generic forms in the attempt to rehearse and enforce the nexus between national imagining and masculine toughness on which national manhood is premised.

HOCKEY VIOLENCE IN THE CANADIAN CONTEXT

When Bobby Bonaduce meets his prospective roommates in *The Good Body*, they judge by his assortment of visible scars that he is either "an axe murderer or a hockey player" (22). "I went to a fight last night," the familiar joke goes, "and a hockey game broke out." Hockey is the only team sport that allows for a context in which fighting can occur as "part of the game." Although fighting is technically illegal and always incurs a penalty, when players drop their gloves to fight, the referees and linesmen know to keep their distance until one or both of the combatants fall to the ice. Many fans applaud these fights, and coaches and players often view them as energizing a game. Because "breeding a culture of aggression or roughness in hockey" depends on "establishing a context wherein violent behaviours become discursively normalized" (Atkinson 2010, 22), representations of violent masculinity in Canadian hockey novels contribute directly to the ongoing tolerance of fighting within the game. While apologists for hockey pugilism defend the practice as "part of the game" and essentially harmless, fighting can have serious physical consequences such as concussions, lacerations, and broken bones. And in some extreme cases, hockey fights can actually result in death: in 2009 Don Sanderson, a twenty-one-year-old player for the triple-A Whitby Dunlops, died from injuries sustained in a hockey fight. Although fighting – which would be classified as borderline violence in Smith's typology of athletic violence – has been a major part of the way in which hockey continues to provide "a public platform for celebrating a very traditional masculine ideal" (Gruneau and Whitson 1993, 190), the game's basic level of brutal body contact has also been a way in which hockey suggests that masculinity is constituted by physical strength and toughness. As Robidoux notes, hockey players are "embodying specific qualities of one form of masculinity and establishing, at least esoterically, their male worth" simply by "fulfilling their occupational demands" in the "highly demanding physical competition" of the game (2001, 129).

True to the masculine identities that hockey was seen to represent throughout the late nineteenth century, many of the first organized contests were vicious and bloody affairs with fighting beginning on the ice and often spreading to fans and even referees. One Montreal newspaper went so far as to describe the early game as "a saturnalia of butchery" (quoted in McKinley 2006, 26). For example, the first Dominion Championship in 1886 was decided by forfeit when one team suffered so many casualties they were unable to continue, and in 1904 alone four players were killed in on-ice attacks. From its early days, then, "hockey actively traded on the popular enjoyment of an aggressive masculine physicality" and "this enjoyment has hung on at the core of the hockey subculture even as other attitudes in Canadian society have changed around it" (Gruneau and Whitson 1993, 181).[6]

While Gruneau and Whitson are correct to suggest that aggressive masculine physicality has remained a core element of Canada's hockey culture, the idea that the Canadian hockey identity consists in the "manly" values of toughness and physicality has been increasingly contested since the 1970s. Certainly the modest surge of scholarship and critical writing on the game in recent decades has contributed to a rising tide of opposition to borderline violence and the version of masculinity it is seen to represent, as, it would seem, have recent feminist studies of masculinity and sport. Several developments within the game itself, however, have simultaneously worked to unsettle the status of violence in hockey culture. When the creation of the WHA (World Hockey Association) in the early 1970s drew some of the most highly skilled players away from the NHL, it considerably diluted the talent pool of both leagues. Owners of this period were "unable to find players who could skate with the genuine stars" and as an alternative "reached out to people who could knock them down" (Simpson 1989, 219). The pioneers and perfecters of this goon-hockey ethos were the Philadelphia Flyers, known throughout the league as the "Broadstreet Bullies." Their tactics proved successful, and the Flyers won two Stanley Cups in the early 1970s by emphasizing intimidation and rough play rather than finesse or skill. Other teams began to follow the Philadelphia model by recruiting "enforcers," players who were expected to protect teammates and harry opponents through violence and fighting.

Throughout the early 1970s, the increased tolerance for roughness and aggression within the "acceptable" parameters (i.e., borderline violence) of North American professional hockey had a significant impact on the character of the minor league game as well. According to Simpson, "the call of parents to their male offspring to 'hit 'em' rang out in arenas from coast to coast" as "violence ... filtered down from the professional ranks of hockey to the minor-league levels" with the "sanctioned approval of coaches and officials" (220). Violence had become such a problem in minor league hockey by 1974 that the Minister of Community and Social Services at the time, René Brunelle, appointed a task force to investigate the issue. The resulting report, provided by Ontario's Attorney-General Roy McMurtry and titled an *Investigation and Inquiry into Violence and Amateur Hockey*, announced that many Canadian children were consciously emulating their NHL heroes in minor league and recreational hockey settings, and, to the shock of many Canadians, that a significant number of minor league coaches were actually teaching their players to cross-check, impede, and butt-end their opponents.

In some ways the McMurtry report provided the indictment of excessive hockey violence that the courts had repeatedly refused to deliver, and many fans began to demand the return of skill, finesse, and speed to the North American game. When the Montreal Canadiens swept the Philadelphia Flyers in the 1975–76 Stanley Cup series, it was widely recognized as a triumph of speed and finesse over thuggery and intimidation, an indication that North American professional hockey was to re-emphasize skill and technique. The point of all this is that the "goon boom" of the 1970s worked to raise critical awareness and debate about hockey violence to previously unparalleled levels (Simpson 1989, 217). Prominent players such as Wayne Gretzky and Mario Lemieux began to publicly question the place of borderline violence in the game throughout the 1980s (a fact that is reflected in MacGregor's *The Last Season*), and in 1992 then NHL president Gil Stein did the same. Gretzky especially became associated with the movement against borderline violence, although his involvement had more to do with securing NHL expansion than challenging harmful masculine identities. After being traded to the Los Angeles Kings, Gretzky "became all too aware of the game's image in the mainstream US media as a kind of wrestling on ice" (Gruneau and Whitson 1993, 186), and eventually came to believe that the best way to attract non-traditional audiences to hockey was to limit violent play and emphasize speed and skill.

Despite the rising tide of critical awareness and dissent throughout the 1980s and 90s, the NHL has done relatively little to remove borderline violence from the game. While on-ice aggression and physical contact have inarguably been scaled back since the 1970s and the league has recently taken steps to tighten boarding and charging calls and eliminate blindside hits, the orthodox wisdom of Canadian hockey culture remains for the most part that fighting and dangerous but "clean" hits are simply "part of the game." No person has been more single-handedly responsible for proselytizing this view in recent years than Don Cherry. Cherry is a former American Hockey League (AHL) player and NHL coach who, along with co-host Ron MacLean, conducts a weekly segment during *Hockey Night in Canada* called "Coach's Corner." Despite the fact that he only played one game in the NHL, Cherry has become Canada's most influential hockey personality, and, in the words of McKinley, "the moral guide for a generation of hockey players, their parents, and their coaches" (2006, 266). When the CBC conducted a survey to determine "the greatest Canadian" in 2004, Cherry polled a remarkable seventh-place finish (O'Sullivan 2004).[7]

Cherry's concerns are notoriously hockey, Canada, and "the code that makes a man a man" (Richard Harrison, "Coach's Corner"; in Harrison 2004, 50). Cherry is famous for, in the words of Richard Paul Knowles, his "aggressively bad grammar (consciously class-coded), his championing of old-fashioned and unfashionable causes such as the tolerance – or celebration – of fighting and violence in the sport, and above all his xenophobia and anti-feminism" (1995, 124). Furthermore, "it would appear, from the letters of support in newspapers across the country each time his job is threatened following a particularly offensive comment, that Cherry gives voice to the unspoken fears and anxieties of many 'ordinary,' English-speaking, working-class Canadians about such things as political correctness, feminism, 'the French,' the metric system, and immigration. He professes a studied ignorance of world events – 'the Soviets, or Russians, or whatever ya callem now' – and locates his moral and political centre in small-town Canada, where men are men, boys will be boys, and hockey remains the domain of the (white) male English-*Canadian* working class" (124–5). Cherry is especially notorious for his disdain of European players, often characterizing them as weak, cowardly, or unsportsmanlike. "The Europeans couldn't fight their way out of a wet paper bag," he once quipped, "the only fighting they do is with their wives" (quoted in McKinley 2006, 265). In addition to preaching his views from the national pulpit of *Coach's Corner*, Cherry has released a series of videos and DVDs entitled

Rock'em Sock'em Hockey that chronicle hockey's biggest hits and wildest fights. In *Salvage King, Ya!* Drinkwater actually gets into a fight with the specific idea that he will "make Don Cherry's video" (170). Although as Dowbiggin notes, Cherry's "hockey insights [have] grow[n] less consequential," he still wields a great deal of cultural capital: "as most minor hockey administrators will tell you, he saturates the debate on hockey in Canada at every level. NHL players report watching his *Coach's Corner* segments in the inter-missions of their own games. To underestimate him is fatal; to ignore him impossible" (2008, 131). While many academics and intellectu-als dismiss Cherry as self-parody or a sort of national court jester – Mordecai Richler, for instance, has derided him in *Maclean's* as "an appropriate model for cretins" (quoted in Dowbiggin 2008, 130) – Cherry remains massively popular among "ordinary Canadians" who appear to consume him for the most part at face value.

It is especially noteworthy that Cherry's ascension to hockey celeb-rity roughly coincided with the rise of Wayne Gretzky as a champion of skill and finesse in the Canadian game. Cherry, then, emerged as a belligerent defender of borderline violence and masculinity-as-toughness during a period in which these things were arguably more threatened than at any other time in hockey's history. His immense popularity testifies to the prominent position that borderline vio-lence continues to occupy in the game, and Cherry himself remains a complex and polarizing figure who is something of a litmus test on attitudes toward violence and masculinity. Although Cherry plays a minor role in Canadian hockey novels – a few mentions here and there – he might be seen as a model for the cultural work that the majority of these novels seek to accomplish regarding gender and violence.[8] If Canadian attitudes towards hockey violence in the last thirty or so years can be summed up by what Wayne Gretzky and Don Cherry represent, respectively, hockey novels side most consis-tently with Cherry. In fact, Cherry could be said to embody the cen-tral aspects of national manhood that the remainder of this chapter will trace.

Most of the novels to be discussed in this chapter are *Bildungsro-mans* that see the development of a youthful protagonist through hockey as both guaranteeing success in life and equipping the indi-vidual for productive service to the collectives of team and nation. By means of frequent sermonizing to young players about develop-ing strength, team focus, and fair play, as well as through his

championing of "good Canadian boys" (a category which he vari-
ably applies to hockey players, soldiers, and working-class labour-
ers), Cherry propounds a version of national manhood in which
adolescent development, civic responsibility, and personal strength
become inextricably linked.

Cherry also exemplifies the work that hockey novels tend to do in
adjudicating violence: he isn't so much a cheerleader for violence as
a referee who decides which forms are acceptable and which aren't.
While steadfastly encouraging clean hits and tough play, Cherry is
quick to condemn cheap shots, hits from behind, dirty stickwork,
and other "dishonourable" infractions. For Cherry, then, much of
the "code that makes a man a man" is the ability to perpetrate and
withstand brutal body contact and borderline violence while demonstrating discretion, self-control, and honour by avoiding quasi-
criminal and criminal violence. Hockey novels don't always draw
the same lines as Cherry, especially when it comes to Québécois and
European players, but most offer similar perspectives on the acceptability of brutal body contact and borderline violence. A more general way of saying this is that, like Cherry, hockey novels work to
distinguish between desirable toughness and excessive or dishonourable roughness. Indeed, the two most common milestones of
maturity in hockey *Bildungsroman* narratives are the willingness to
demonstrate toughness through fighting or the resolution to avoid
excessive roughness through self-mastery and restraint. Cherry can
also be said to reflect the military aspects of national manhood that
are emphasized in several hockey novels, frequently suggesting the
exceptional toughness and dedication of Canadian troops and publicly mourning fallen Canadian soldiers. Finally, as Cherry's aggressive disdain for feminism and the politically correct suggests, his
persona appears to respond directly to the late twentieth-century
"crisis of masculinity" that this study sees as underwriting the enthusiasm of Canadian hockey novels for traditional masculinity and
national manhood in the first place.

MAKING NATIONAL MEN: BECOMING A MAN
THROUGH HOCKEY VIOLENCE

Linda Christian-Smith's *Becoming a Woman through Romance*
explores the ways in which adolescent romance novels work to
"define feminine identity for young women readers" through codes

of romance, sexuality, and beautification (1990, 4). Many hockey novels work similarly to define masculine identity through toughness and violence, staging plots in which young male characters either learn the values of traditional masculinity and symbolically become men, or grow to recognize the difference between desirable toughness and excessive roughness and the value of maintaining this distinction (i.e., focus, responsibility, self-mastery, good citizenship, etc.). These novels tend to see the game as an adolescent proving ground, a crucible of challenge and competition that demands strength, skill, endurance, perseverance, and commitment, and teaches boys to be tough, stoic, focused, and collectively responsible. Hockey is valued, then, as a means to some particular moral or vocational end, and is often seen as the central component of a protagonist's *Bildungsroman* progression toward adulthood and maturity.

Literary critic Glenn Willmott has argued that English Canadian novels throughout the first half of the twentieth century often used the *Bildungsroman* form as a way of staging the possibilities of national development through the process of an individual character's growth and maturation. Among such novels, Willmott identifies "an isometry of nation and narration [which] authorizes the figure of the individual as a determining form, and authorizes his or her transition from youth to maturity as a determining paradigm, to carry, to plot out, and to resolve if possible [the] existential anxiety attending the making of a home, a belonging" (2002, 23). In other words, the early twentieth-century Canadian *Bildungsroman* not only suggested correlation between "the youth of a literature (primitive, naïve, but free, open to invention and development)... [and] the youth of its nation" (19), but overlaid a national significance on the *Bildungsroman* narrative of individual development. The cultural work of such novels, then, appears parallel with national manhood's project of encouraging individuals to cultivate personal talents and participate productively in the political and cultural marketplaces for the benefit of the larger national community.

The first Canadian novel to deal with hockey in any significant capacity is *Glengarry School Days* (1902) by Charles Gordon (pseudonym Ralph Connor). *Glengarry School Days* is a *Bildungsroman* and can be read as a "national allegory" in that it sees "the body of the nation [as] ... figured by means of the body of an idealized individual" (Coleman 2006, 130). In other words, *Glengarry School Days* proposes the moral development of its central character as a means of suggesting a connection between masculine toughness and national well-being and thereby establishing "a coherent image of a Canadian ideal" (130). The "Canadian ideal" proposed by *Glengarry School Days* is the figure of the Muscular Christian, one of four "regularly repeated literary personifications for the Canadian nation" that, according to Daniel Coleman, "mediated and gradually reified the privileged, normative status of British whiteness in English Canada" (6–7).[9] Muscular Christianity was a Protestant movement that sought to "reviralize the image of Jesus and thus remasculinize the church" (Kimmel 1996, 177), and one of the most significant results of the perceived masculinity crisis during the late nineteenth century. Organized sport was central to Muscular Christianity's crusade to "remasculinize" men and was seen as a proving ground in which men, especially young men, could develop the "Christian" values of strength, toughness, competition, determination, and self-mastery. Because of their "rules, chains of command, and strenuousity," organized sports were seen as "ideal teachers of duty and hard work" and "a means of channeling and dispersing those boyish energies (particularly sexual energies) which, if left unchecked, might result either in masturbation ('the deadly habit') or in other illicit behaviour" (Putney 2001, 16).

Charles Gordon is probably the most well-known Canadian proponent of Muscular Christianity. His fiction was immensely popular at the turn of the twentieth century, and sought to "guide individual readers into the modern world with their faith intact" (Karr 2000, 12). One of Gordon's earlier novels, for instance, *The Man from Glengarry* (1901), suggests a version of national manhood in which Christian values become associated with the emerging requirements of modern industry in the attempt to show, as one character puts it, "how the laws of the kingdom of heaven might be applied to the problems of labour" (258). The cultural work of Gordon's fiction, then, was not only to assert the value of Christian faith for a changing social and cultural order, but to produce workers and citizens whose values were amenable to the emerging industrial economy and its attendant labour requirements. Indeed, *The Man from Glengarry* traces the development of its central protagonist, Ranald Macdonald, as a man of virtue and self-mastery who ultimately dedicates his efforts to developing the Canadian West and bringing it into "the great Dominion reaching from ocean to ocean" (271). Although sport is seen as an important component in Ranald's moral development in *The Man from Glengarry*, athleticism in general and hockey in particular play a more central role in *Glengarry School Days* (1902).

Glengarry School Days is a collection of interrelated stories that focus on the moral and physical development of a young boy in Eastern Ontario in the 1860s, Hughie Murray. Over the course of these sketches, Hughie learns the importance of self-mastery, honesty, and bravery, largely from the example of his schoolteacher, Archie Munro, and his mother, Mrs Murray. In plot and generic terms, Hughie's moral development is thrown into question when Archie Munro leaves the school and is succeeded by several inadequate replacements, the final of which is John Craven, a cynical young man who shows an undue lack of interest in his teaching and his charges. The final episodes of *Glengarry School Days* focus not only on the completion of Hughie's maturation but on Craven's restoration to the masculine ideal represented by Muscular Christianity. The first real connection between Craven and his charges occurs during the winter months when the boys' schoolyard game of shinny moves to the ice and we are told that Craven becomes an "enthusiastic skater ... a whirlwind on ice" (272).[10] Several of the earlier sketches see athletic exercise as contributing to the development of manly virtues, so it is little surprise that Craven's athletic awakening marks the beginning of his gradual moral turnaround, which is ultimately brought to fruition by the inspiring influence of Mrs Murray. Soon a challenge is issued to an opposing school, Hughie is made captain of the team, and preparations begin for a big game. Craven eventually resolves "by the grace of heaven ... to try to be a man," further pledging that "I am going to play shinny with those boys, and if I can help them to win that match, and the big game of life, I will do it" (291). The shinny game, then, is seen as a microcosm, a proving ground for the development of manly strength and values that will be required in the "big game of life."

For Hughie, the substance of this test will be whether or not he can learn to control his temper. As he settles into the role of captain, Hughie is said to have "developed a genius for organization, a sureness of judgment, and a tact in management, as well as a skill and speed in play, that won the confidence of every member of his team" (296). In other words, Hughie has developed the necessary skills for success in the emerging modern workplace: he has become managerial, organized, and judicious.[11] Hughie's development is not complete, however, until he can demonstrate the necessary restraint that must accompany his physical strength. Before the big game Hughie tells his mother that "it's awful hard [not to fight] when a fellow doesn't play fair, when he trips you up or clubs you on the shins when you're not near the ball" (300). Throughout the game Hughie is harried by an aggressive opponent, but manages to show restraint and rally his teammates when all hope of victory seems lost. In the final minutes the aggressor breaks Hughie's leg with a dirty play, but rather than leave the game Hughie transfers to net, an action which in the framework of the story allows his teammates to tally the winning goal. Hughie's insistence on remaining in the game suggests the importance of team solidarity and collective responsibility; rather than leave his team a player short, Hughie is willing to play through the pain of his injury for the greater good of the team. The importance of not fighting is also underscored, and is suggested as a matter of moral propriety. As Craven tells the boys, "we entered this game with the intention of playing straight, clean shinny" (320), implying that fighting has no place in sport and emphasizing the values of honesty and directness. According to Clarence Karr, Gordon's fiction reflects both the "prevalence of violence in late-nineteenth-century society and the fervent desire of the middle class to repress it" (2000, 83). Gordon himself "revelled in competition but stopped far short of condoning violence," helping to establish "a church-sponsored league" in Winnipeg "expressly for the purpose of eliminating violence in sports" (83). After the game in *Glengarry School Days*, however, it appears that all bets are off, and Craven invites Hughie's assailant to fight within the more acceptable context of a formal challenge: "you cowardly blackguard, you weren't afraid to hit a boy, now stand up to a man, if you dare" (329). This final moment of the shinny episode vindicates Hughie's restraint, maintaining that justice, in this case retributive violence, will inevitably prevail, and suggests masculine physicality as the means by which this justice must be secured.

It is the final sketch of *Glengarry School Days* that makes the moral development of the shinny game most clear, in which a conversation between Craven and his uncle (a seminary professor) reveals that eleven of the Glengarry boys will be going into the ministry. "And judging by the way they take life," Craven tells his uncle, "and the way, for instance, they play shinny, I have a notion that they will see it through" (333). In *Glengarry School Days* success in shinny – the substance of which is voracious toughness tempered by propriety and self-restraint – portends well for moral success in life. Furthermore, the final sketch makes it clear that the boys have achieved manhood. Only a few pages earlier, Craven had referred to Hughie as a boy when fighting in his honour, but in the opening lines of the final sketch Hughie's uncle calls the Glengarry boys "men" (333). The shinny game, then, is not only a training ground but a rite of passage, validating the boys as men and proclaiming them ready both for modern life and moral living, the latter of which is particularly suggested by their vocational aspirations to the clergy.[12]

Glengarry School Days appears to have been the only novel published in Canada to significantly depict hockey during the period that historian Andrew Holman refers to as "the age of the school story (1890s–World War I) and the heyday of 'pulps' (1920–30)" (2009a, 54). By contrast, Holman's study of American juvenile hockey fiction throughout this period and the decade before the Second World War discovered "more than fifty boys' novels, and more than two hundred and fifty short stories that used ice hockey as a central vehicle" (56). Like *Glengarry School Days* itself, many of these mass-market hockey novels traded on "the transatlantic success" of Hughes' *Tom Brown's School Days* and functionally "prescribed ... norms for masculinity and gender roles and preached upright behaviour and attitudes" such as "selflessness, teamwork, pride in family and school, perseverance, fair play, moderation in all things, and respect for authority" (Holman 2009a, 55). According to Holman, these novels express "an ambivalence or duality" about Canada and Canadianness (61). On the one hand, "hockey was ... claimed as a quintessential American sport that, like football and baseball, bred American traits" (6). On the other hand, "hockey's Canadian roots were ... alluded to and characters' Canadian connections established them as authorities in the game" (61). In other words, these novels seem to suggest hockey as "speak[ing] for two nations" (61). The extent to which these novels celebrate Canadianness, however, remains limited in that the "best Canadians were those who were in transition; those who culturally or legally were *becoming* Americans and for whom the Canadian connection was either distant or past" (62; italics in original). Holman's findings suggest another noteworthy correlation with Canadian hockey writing, namely that the American juvenile hockey novels produced between 1890 and 1940 tend to represent the game as "wild, chaotic, [and] savage – a product of a frontier society and ... [reflection of] an elemental or 'natural' rusticity" (59). Furthermore, the "harshness of required conditions for play" is seen as leading to "the harshness of play itself" in that "these stories ... characterized the game as a violent, seemingly chaotic struggle, but one that has a 'natural order': the fittest players and teams survive and thrive" (59). Although many of the mass market American hockey novels produced throughout the early twentieth century must presumably have made their way into Canada as well, the market for homegrown Canadian hockey novels didn't exist until after the Second World War.

In addition to being a pioneer of the genre, *Glengarry School Days* can also be seen as a prototype for many subsequent Canadian hockey novels. Many of the first-wave children's hockey novels that were produced throughout the 1950s, 60s, and 70s follow the *Glengarry School Days* thematic of fair play, hard work, discipline, civic duty, and toughness as constituting manhood, and depict hockey as the rite of passage through which these values are best achieved. As Hewitt puts it in *Hello, Canada and Hockey Fans in the United States*, "no hockey game ever contributed to juvenile delinquency" (28). The players on the team in that novel, the Gloster Greys, are accordingly told that "we expect every boy, when off ice, to be as neat and well-dressed as his own funds will permit. He must be clean in appearance, speech and conduct so that all citizens may speak well of him and be proud of him" (35). The importance of education is also emphasized, as in Hewitt's *"He Shoots, He Scores!"* when a fictionalized Conn Smythe catches Mat Warren, the novel's young hockey-playing protagonist, reading Shakespeare's *Julius Caesar* at Maple Leaf Gardens and commends him for it: "I wish some of the people who say good hockey players are poor students could get a look at you right now ... there are teachers who say that sport and education don't combine. That's wrong" (100).

Beyond requiring good manners, dapper dressing, and attention to one's studies, early children's hockey novels demand hard work, discipline, toughness, and collective responsibility from young hockey-playing men. In addition to taking "time from his chores to put on his own skates, borrow a puck and stick, and whirl up and down the ice" (34) and "skat[ing] for hours in the open" to practice (44), part of Mat Warren's development on the way to becoming a professional hockey player in *"He Shoots, He Scores!"* is to overcome his youthful preference for "softer games where at least you don't lose your front teeth or break a leg" (22). Similarly, the protagonist of Young's *Boy on Defence*, Bill Spunska, works hard to stay on top of his high-school classes, improve his play through dedication and teamwork, and bring in some extra money for the family from a part-time job at a tobacco warehouse. Through perseverance, determination, and toughness, Spunska's hard work pays off: after "bulling his way up the ice" and enduring a vicious bodycheck from his antagonist, Spunska scores a spectacular goal in the final game and is rewarded for his effort by being drafted to the Maple Leafs and offered a generous salary that will ease his family's financial concerns (240). Indeed, "Spunska is honest, hard-working, polite, and self-disciplined – the all-Canadian boy" (Hollands 1988, 223).

Spunska's story continues in Young's *A Boy at the Leafs' Camp*, in which he learns to play "hard, strong, forceful, but never dirty" and to not feel guilty about injuring opponents as long as his checks are clean (1963, 246). Likewise, Andy O'Brien's *Hockey Wingman* (1967) tells the story of Danny Dooner, a boy who eventually makes the NHL through hard work, determination, well-roundedness (the narrative emphasizes the importance of getting a good education and follows Dooner through a degree at Loyola College), and toughness (which is demonstrated not only through hockey but by an episode in which Dooner becomes lost in a blizzard and skates all night on a frozen lake, as well as by an "interlude with bullets" in which he helps police foil a band of robbers). Although the above examples should be sufficient to illustrate the point, this thematic trajectory applies equally to other first-wave children's hockey novels such as T. Morris Longstreth's *The Calgary Challengers* (1962) and Frank Orr's Buck Martin books, *Buck Martin, Take Centre Ice* (1965) and *Buck Martin in World Hockey* (1966). As Hollands suggests, "the majority of [juvenile] Canadian sports heroes are characterized by their affection for hard work during team practice sessions. Off the ice rink or sports field, this enthusiasm spills over into the workplace, whether the job is creative or mundane (1988, 224).

In all of the preceding examples, toughness and work ethic are closely connected. The valorization of judicious toughness (i.e., toughness informed and tempered by fair play and good manners) is a central feature of Leslie McFarlane's hockey novels as well. Because most of the juvenile sporting and adventure stories available in Canada during the late nineteenth and early twentieth centuries featured British or American protagonists, McFarlane believed that

Canadian boys were growing up without any homegrown heroic role models and that "this probably explains why the adult, male Canadian today is a docile, modest fellow who knows his place and is never given to throwing his weight around" (quoted in Skinazi 2009, 110). The heroes in McFarlane's hockey stories are intended to fill this void and to offer Canadian boys a template for virtuous and heroic manhood. According to Karen Skinazi, McFarlane saw his stories as addressing "a time when Canada seemed to have no history, no culture, [and] no power" and believed "hockey to be big enough to fill Canada's holes" (110). Following roughly the same logic as the late nineteenth-century linkage between sport, masculinity, and nation, then, McFarlane believed his hockey stories could contribute to Canada's identity and well-being by moulding strong, virtuous, and civic-minded men. A good example of this sort of masculine heroism is the protagonist of McFarlane's "Too Slow to Count," Tim Cordell, "a short, wiry, 145-pound package of dynamite" whose underdog stature is perhaps intended to echo Canada's cultural relationship to Britain and the United States (*Squeeze Play*, 112). Despite not being overly big or skilful, Cordell helps his team win through tenacity, determination, and the refusal to give up against all odds. Even when his season is ended by a career-threatening injury, Cordell sits in the players' box "begging, imploring, cheering, [and] talking himself into a lather of perspiration" to inspire his teammates to victory" (120). When the final game rolls around and the team finds itself a player short, Cordell goes so far as to risk his future career by entering the play and thereby helping his side win the championship. As will be seen, this sort of self-sacrifice for the good of the collective is a central feature of national manhood and a substantial part of the way in which hockey novels conceive of civic duty.

But McFarlane's protagonists are expected to do more than just be tough, dedicated, and focused on the team. They are also expected to be honourable and to do the right thing at all costs. In "Squeeze Play," for instance, the protagonist Tim Kiernan is torn between going to the police to report a crime he wrongfully believes himself responsible for and the desire not to let his team down by missing the final game. In the end Kiernan's sense of civic duty prevails and he presents himself to the police, who unravel the misunderstanding and clear Kiernan's name in time to rush him by squad car to win the final game and fulfill his responsibilities to the team. Kiernan's last-minute heroics in the championship game secure him a spot on a "major league club" (48), and the message is abundantly clear: that sound moral behaviour is a necessary prerequisite to success. But while McFarlane took the idea that hockey builds character very seriously, he could also be somewhat tongue-in-cheek about it. At the beginning of *McGonigle Scores!*, for instance, the eponymous scout makes the following speech to some local prospects and their fathers: "hockey is the greatest game in the world. And when you play that game, remember this! You're a part of a team. Don't try to be the whole show. Don't try to be a star. You do right by the game and it will do right by you. Because I can tell you there isn't anything better than hockey for building character" (14). Immediately after McGonigle finishes this string of clichés (which basically summarizes the moral essence of McFarlane's hockey oeuvre), however, we discover that this stirring speech was written for McGonigle by the team's recruiting office and that the scout feels somewhat bashful about delivering it due to the fact that his own career wasn't particularly virtuous.

Another variation on the theme of emerging masculinity among the first wave of children's hockey novels is R.J. Childerhose's *Hockey Fever in Goganne Falls* (1973), which describes a misfit Midget A team that learns the importance of countering dirty play with stoic toughness. The star player in *Hockey Fever in Goganne Falls* is a soft-spoken Native boy named Jimmy Young Duck, who manages to score a championship-winning goal despite suffering a broken nose, several concussions, and having been knocked unconscious on three separate occasions throughout the game. Jimmy Young Duck is not only noteworthy for the outlandish violence he endures in order to establish and declaim his masculine toughness, but for the extent to which he represents the Centennial era push to align hockey with Canada's emerging pluralist identity. The ideological program of *Hockey Fever in Goganne Falls*, then, is the same as that of Young's *Scrubs on Skate*, another "school story" in the tradition of *Glengarry School Days* which, as discussed earlier, proposes the cross-cultural unity of a hockey team as a model for Canadian cultural pluralism. These stories maintain many of the gender and genre conventions set forth by *Glengarry School Days* but substitute the framing paradigm of "white civility" (Coleman 2006) for the emerging identity of cultural pluralism. Although the metaphor of national youth has hardly been applicable to Canada in the last three decades (the period in which most adult-oriented hockey novels were written), the *Bildungsroman* has remained the generic mode by which hockey novels tend to perform national manhood. In light of Willmott's characterization of the early twentieth-century Canadian *Bildungsroman*, the more recent adult- and young-adult-oriented hockey novels that form the basis of this study aren't so much anomalies in the mainstream of Canadian literature since the 1950s as they are anachronisms, hearkening back to an earlier generic and thematic way of conceiving both national and masculine identities.[13]

If *Glengarry School Days* can be said to respond to the perceived late nineteenth-century crisis of masculinity and to the cultural preoccupation with developing Canadian society and identity at that time, it stands to reason that the generic and thematic structures it enacts could be similarly applied to late twentieth- and early twenty-first-century anxieties about masculine and national identities. Furthermore, the re-enactment of such established conventions by contemporary hockey novels might be seen as a way of honouring tradition and affirming the hockey myth. It is entirely significant, then, that the Nike advertising campaign mentioned earlier chose to focus on Canada's national junior team rather than on the training regimes of returning NHL players. In effect, the narrative of national manhood supplied by the Nike ad is the same as that of *Glengarry School Days* trimmed of its overt Christianity. While the Glengarry boys' hockey victory equips them for moral service to the nation, Team Canada's act of service appears to be delivering the hockey victory itself. This distinction reflects Burstyn's suggestion that sport has become a "secular sacrament" (1999, 18) and Foer's contention that sport "allows men ... to join the [religious] tradition and institutions of their forefathers, to allay fears about abandoning history without having to embrace their forefathers' eschatology" (2004, 56).

Like *Glengarry School Days* and many of the adult-oriented hockey-novel genre's children's literature antecedents, both Paci's *Icelands* and Galloway's *Finnie Walsh* see hockey as a moral or vocational training ground, and both depict the possibility of becoming a man through hockey violence. The major challenge that Andrew Clark needs to overcome in his hockey maturation in *Icelands* is learning to demonstrate masculine toughness by participating in borderline violence. At one point in the story Andrew refuses to fight an opposing player and his coach tells him "you won't be playing Junior for long ... if you back down from scraps like that" (179). Later in the story Andrew has a chance to prove himself at a Junior B training camp, where he is challenged by a particularly aggressive player. Andrew's reaction is described as follows: "It felt like time had stopped. This was the wall his whole hockey career had been inching toward. That he had to do something. That he could no longer skate away. That if he wanted to go to a higher level in the game, there was no getting around this cold impenetrable wall of ice" (196). The challenge to fight is seen as a decisive moment: will Andrew remain in the childhood world of weakness or embrace the toughness required to move forward in the game and thus toward his successful future? The "wall" that Andrew confronts, however, is configured as more than just "this moron who was trying to shame him in front of his peers and the coaching staff" (196). Indeed, Andrew sees himself as up against the entire culture of hockey violence: "It was all the idiots, the goons, the loud-mouths. The morons who would just as soon break your wrists as smile at you. It was the different set of rules on the ice. It was Gordie Howe's elbows he had heard from his father. It was the Broad Street Bullies in the seventies. It was all the bench-clearing brawls and the enforcers and the rock'em sock'em mentality that game had spawned. It was all the cheap shots and career-ending injuries" (196). In essence, Andrew summarizes the culture of hockey violence that has been enshrined in Canada's hockey myth. He criticizes the fans who have encouraged (and ultimately financed) this culture, as well as the players who have perpetuated it by their complicity. Andrew also implicitly indicts the coaches and commentators who encourage borderline hockey violence, singling out Don Cherry with the phrase "rock'em sock'em." Nevertheless, Andrew believes that there is nothing he can do to alter the culture of the game, and so he decides to abandon his reservations and embrace this violence: "So, what the fuck! He dropped his gloves and barrelled into the wall, his fists flailing away" (196). As Blake suggests, "this is not a boiling-over but a reasoned process. Andrew gives himself over to the fight in the same way that we subjugate ourselves to the irrational rules of the game when we play hockey" or more generally assent to its cultural assumptions (2009, 79).

Just as Andrew isn't able to break down the figurative "wall" of hockey violence, he has little effect on the literal "wall" of his opponent in the fight. As he is nursing his injuries in the dressing room after the incident, waiting for his mother to arrive and bring him to the hospital, the Coach comes to tell him he has made the team: "Our scouting reports say you're a skilled player. And I've seen plenty tonight to confirm that. The only thing we weren't sure about was your moxie, your grit. Now we know" (198). It is his willingness, then, to demonstrate toughness by conforming to the established culture of the game that finally secures Andrew a spot on the roster, which in turn implicitly secures his university education and thus his broader prospects for productive citizenship. Upon making the team, Andrew's indignation about borderline violence immediately gives way to elation and a sense of accomplishment, and when he arrives at the hospital he "proudly" tells the Admitting nurse that he was in a "hockey fight ... [in which] I lost the battle, but I won the war" (198).

In addition to performing the process by which, presumably, many reluctant players are socialized into the culture of hockey violence, *Icelands* sees hockey as the means by which Andrew will secure his future in life beyond the game. Andrew's goal in the game is not to "[make] it in the NHL" but to "[get] a good education from hockey" (216). For Andrew, like Hughie Murray in *Glengarry School Days*, success in hockey can be parlayed into success in the "big game of life"; as the focalized narrative suggests about the university education that hockey will enable Andrew to get, "the rest of his future would spring from that" (216). Toughness, then, becomes Andrew's symbolic ticket into adulthood, and appears to equip him to fulfill the demands of national manhood for productive citizenship later in life. Although *Icelands* allows for the possibility of irony in Andrew's eventual acquiescence to hockey violence by positing his earlier critical perspective, the narrative's enthusiasm about Andrew's acceptance of hockey's cultural norms and the sense of belonging and possibilities for success this entails remains quite powerful. Taken straightforwardly, *Icelands* suggests that crossing the threshold from childish weakness to masculine toughness is what guarantees success in life. Such a representation could very easily influence readers to allay their concerns about borderline violence in hockey and to accept this culturally constructed value system as a natural and inevitable "part of the game." It is worth noting, however, that hockey-playing characters in other Paci novels, *The Italians* and *Black Madonna*, both eschew violence on principle. In *The Italians*, Bill Gaetano resents being "typecast" as a player who "stir[s] things up," and eventually addresses the matter by performing a violent "circus display" in which he pulls his opponent's sweater over his head, tackles him to the ice, and begins "laughing so loudly that, for all he knew, the other players crowding around must have thought him completely mad" (177, 178). As if this theatrical deviation from the anticipated fight is isn't enough to drive home his point, Gaetano makes the "grand dramatic gesture" of "bow[ing] clownishly" on the way to the penalty box (178). By performing this "circus display," of course, Gaetano communicates to the crowd what they are actually seeing during a hockey fight and invites them to think critically about this rather ridiculous spectacle. Unfortunately for Gaetano, however, his performance isn't enough to win either the coach or the crowd over to his way of thinking about hockey violence, and eventually Gaetano's refusal to fight in the playoffs makes him a scapegoat for the team's lack of success and ultimately gets him traded. Somewhat similarly in *Black Madonna*, Joey Barone refuses to fight while playing in an industrial league in which "fights were as frequent as the games" (43). For Barone, not fighting is a way of differentiating himself from other players in the league, "his only way of maintaining some measure of dignity in playing in a third-rate league with a bunch of has-beens" (43).

Similar to *Icelands'* depiction of becoming a man through hockey toughness is a passage in *Finnie Walsh* where Paul Woodward learns the value of toughness playing hockey with his friend Finnie: "I ended up blocking a lot of shots myself, accidentally, and once I got hit so hard in the stomach that I actually threw up. As soon as I was finished retching my guts out, I got back out there, though, because if Finnie wasn't going to break, then neither was I" (22). In addition to the values of perseverance and determination that Paul ostensibly acquires by playing through pain, he also learns to stand up for himself against aggressive opponents. These lessons, of course, are doubly applicable to hockey and the "big game of life." By conquering his fear of bigger opponents on the hockey rink, Paul learns not to let people push him around off-ice as well. Like many of his precursors in Canadian hockey novels, then, Paul's masculine toughness is both acquired and enacted through hockey. As an interesting counterpoint, Coady's *Saints of Big Harbour* plays with the expectation created by this familiar trajectory before ultimately rejecting its model of masculine coming of age through hockey violence. After being encouraged by his uncle Isadore to play dirty and to fight an opponent, the novel's protagonist Guy Boucher ultimately ends up leaving the game. Rather than confirming his manhood, then, it is participation in borderline violence that propels Guy toward *Saints of Big Harbour*'s alternative moment of achieved maturity, in which he finds the courage and self-determination to once and for all reject the overbearing masculinity of his violent and unpredictable Uncle Isadore.

Over the course of *Finnie Walsh*, Paul eventually decides to abandon his career in hockey to take over the sawmill and small commercial empire of Finnie's father. Although the "manly" values of confidence, determination, perseverance, and integrity that Paul learns playing hockey presumably contribute to his success after leaving the game, his participation in national manhood isn't primarily commercial or industrial. As noted earlier, the very act of Paul's leaving hockey is seen as a service to the game, a statement against the culture of greed that *Finnie Walsh* represents as profaning hockey and detracting from Canadian distinction. By opting for the workaday world of capitalist productivity, Paul is both applying the values he had learned playing hockey to a life of productive citizenship and performing an act of symbolic self-sacrifice that appears to work in the service of the national good. By foregoing a personally lucrative career in hockey to maintain the sanctity of the hockey myth itself, Paul enacts a version of national manhood in which civic responsibility appears more important than personal glory or gain. To phrase this in hockey terms, Paul has taken one for the team.

GOOD CITIZENS AND GOOD SOLDIERS: HOCKEY AS WAR

In civic terms, the ultimate expression of "taking one for the team" is military service. It is hardly coincidental that Andrew Clark uses the metaphor of war to describe his hockey injuries to the hospital Admitting nurse in *Icelands*. Military service, of course, is the most obvious expression of national manhood, and was central to the way in which this ideology became associated with athletic competition. As team sports were popularized and democratized throughout the nineteenth century they were often "emphasized as both a physical and moral preparation for war" (Braudy 2003, 339). Although the "model of military discipline, the rhythms of male bodies working together" was "crucial to the development of sports" throughout this time, "the increasing moralization of sports, the way in which individuals subordinated themselves and their ambition to the needs of the group and the code of fair play" was absolutely essential (341). The connection between sport and war has certainly been prominent in Canada, where "one of the most retold stories ... is the way the nation came of age because of the contribution of its soldiers in the First World War" (Dopp 2009, 88). According to Dopp, "though the success of the Canadians has been traditionally attributed to a number of factors, including the toughness and self-reliance embodied in the myths of the North and the small town, one of the factors was that, as soldiers of a 'new' nation, Canadians were thought to be less class bound and tradition bound than were the English and French, and so they were able to adapt to the rapidly changing circumstances of the modern battlefield – to go outside the traditional rules of combat" (88). Because of "its emphasis not just on toughness but also on speed and the ability to react quickly to changing circumstances," hockey can been seen as "the game that most closely embodies the kind of aggressive but adaptive masculinity traditionally ascribed to Canadian soldiers" (88).

Little has changed from this military model of duty and self-sacrifice about the ways in which athletic discourse conceives of individual responsibility to the sporting or national collectives. It should be noted, however, that while the comparison between hockey and war can be productive and illuminating, it has ossified into a rather tired cliché in contemporary hockey discourse. As Lorna Jackson suggests, this is largely because "broadcasters and players – who reportedly watch war films and listen to Winston Churchill to stoke for key games – take what should be a metaphor (in other words, a figurative comparison of two unlike things to enlarge the meanings of both) and treat it like a simple comparison: a hockey player is just like a warrior; a team is just like a squadron; losing a game is just like losing a battle. Same stakes, same heroes" (2007, 31). Hockey and war, of course, are not the same, a fact which is perhaps most apparent during wartime. While a significant number of players, both professional and amateur, saw combat during the First World War, those who enlisted during the Second World War were for the most part kept far away from active duty and seen primarily as contributing to "civilian and military morale" (Ross 2009, 112).

In hockey terms, to say a player has "taken one for the team" is to suggest they have made some sort of personal sacrifice for the greater good, allowed the collective to realize some goal or advantage at personal cost to themselves, often physical pain. For Hughie Murray,

Andrew Clark, and Finnie Walsh, becoming a man through hockey violence means establishing individual toughness, but it also means learning to deploy that toughness in the service of the team, and, by extension, in the service of nation through productive capitalist citizenship as they enter adulthood. While the inculcation of hockey values appears to enable broader success in "the big game of life," that success is seen, as least for Hughie and Finnie, as entailing self-sacrifice and service to the collective. In other words, the good citizens these novels attempt to produce bear striking resemblance to good soldiers. The same is true of Scott MacGregor in *50 Mission Cap*, although the military aspect of Scott's *Bildungsroman* development through hockey is made far more explicit.

50 Mission Cap follows Scott's coming of age as a hockey player and a man through the process of his learning to show leadership, occupy a privileged role in relation to coaches and management, and take more responsibility for his team's well-being than his peers. In hockey terms, Scott essentially has to learn the same lesson as Andrew Clark in *Icelands*: to stick up for himself and for his teammates by fighting aggressive opponents. At one point in the story, Scott is challenged to a fight, and thinks to himself: "If I didn't meet his challenge, it would be a let down to my team; we would have looked weak and easy to intimidate. If I dropped my hands, stayed submissive, drew a penalty, I would have gotten booed, called a wuss. And, if I chose to skate away, to turn my back without care, it would have been a shock and some might have even understood it as a statement, but hockey players don't do that sort of thing. It's part of the game, I told myself" (241). Like Andrew, part of Scott's maturation through hockey is learning to embrace the apparently indisputable fact that fighting is "part of the game." The need for toughness and conformity to existing cultural norms is seen here as both personal and collective. Scott certainly doesn't want to incur the individual shame of being called a "wuss," but he is also conscious that personal weakness reflects poorly on the team as a whole: if Scott were to back down from the fight, his team would appear "weak and easy to intimidate." At another point in the story Scott impresses a university scout and is offered a full-ride hockey scholarship on the basis of his collective-minded toughness: "we love your toughness," the scout tells Scott, "I knew you could score, but what really impressed me tonight was the way you stuck up for your teammate ... when he got banged around" (160). As with Andrew

Clark in *Icelands*, Scott's future beyond hockey and potential as a productive citizen appear secured by the university education the game will enable him to achieve.

Scott's willingness to sacrifice for the good of the team becomes the central theme of *50 Mission Cap*, the major symbol of which is the "50 Mission Cap" proposed by the novel's title. Early in the story Scott explains that "50 Mission Cap" is a "guitar-heavy rock song by The Tragically Hip that is played like an anthem between whistles at rinks across the land" (44). The song, a familiar Canadian hockey icon in and of itself, conflates Bill Barilko's Stanley Cup winning goal for the 1951 Toronto Maple Leafs and his subsequent disappearance while on a fishing trip that summer with the 50 Mission Cap, a commemorative hat that was given to Second World War pilots upon the completion of their fiftieth mission (after Barilko died, the Leafs didn't win another Stanley Cup until 1962, the year in which his body was discovered). An actual 50 Mission Cap enters the novel and assumes thematic importance by way of Scott's grandpa Joe, who supports his grandson by cheering him on at every game.

When Grandpa Joe dies early in the story after a long battle with cancer, he leaves behind a letter and a package for Scott. The letter tells the story of Grandpa Joe's time as a pilot during the Second World War, how on his fiftieth mission he had been hit by an enemy plane and needed to bail out. As the German pilot was coming in to finish him off, Grandpa Joe explains, his friend Frank Masters, "a good ol' Canadian boy from Kitchener," came "flying in to blow that Nazi to smithereens" (51). As a result, Grandpa Joe was able to eject safely while Frank Masters got shot down and suffered a crushed spine. As Grandpa Joe tells Scott in his letter, "[Frank Masters] had to spend the rest of his life in a wheelchair, all because he gave himself up to save me" (51). Possibly intended to echo Don Cherry, the identification of Frank Masters as "a good ol' Canadian boy" highlights the national basis of military fraternity and suggests the sense of civic responsibility that underwrites his sacrifice. Inside the package accompanying Grandpa Joe's letter is his 50 Mission Cap, which he hopes will bring Scott "friendship and the courage to do what's right when the time comes" (52). The Tragically Hip's "50 Mission Cap" happens to be "blaring from the speakers" (56) as the Kougars take the ice in their next game, and as the story continues Grandpa Joe's cap becomes a talisman of the team's success.

Although the 50 Mission Cap itself makes clear the connection between hockey and war, this association is supplied more directly several times throughout the novel: the players are said to "attack like infantry men" (5) and move together "like a squadron" (31), while Grandpa Joe's letter suggests that being in an aerial battle is "like [being on] a hockey team" in that the pilots are "supposed to look out for each other" (50). Scott's hockey education, then, is also a military education, the outcome of which is the strength and "courage to do what's right when the time comes." This opportunity "to do what's right" comes near the end of the story, when Scott discovers that one of his teammates is being sexually assaulted by the team's assistant coach, Clyde Parker. Plot events conspire to a showdown between Scott and Clyde, in which Scott attacks Clyde to defend his teammate, the strength for which he is seen to possess because of his hockey training and on-ice fights.

Although Scott's attack on Clyde earns him a suspension from the team, his actions are vindicated by the assurance of the local sports reporter that "you may have saved [your teammate's] life tonight. At the very least, you gave him a fighting chance. Be proud of that" (273). Scott's attack on Clyde, then, is thematically the same as Frank Masters' sacrifice for Grandpa Joe: an act of male fraternity arising from the military unity of the team and delivered through the exercise of hockey violence. In the final chapter, Scott makes a pilgrimage to Frank Masters' grave, during which he puts on the 50 Mission Cap and raises his hand to his temple before "whip[ping] it down in a salute" and "proudly walk[ing] on" (283). This final action solidifies the connection between hockey and war, and elucidates the pride Scott takes in his newly confirmed identity. By becoming a good hockey player, Scott has also become a good soldier, and, seemingly, a good national man.

Another hockey novel in which the game is explicitly seen to foster the military virtues of self-discipline and cooperation is *Hockey Night in the Dominion of Canada*. This is accomplished in large part by way of negative example through the character of Richard Laurence, the hired goon who eventually gets involved in the plot to assassinate Prime Minister Laurier. Laurence is a childhood companion of Cyclone Taylor, and early in the story participates (along with the other boys of Listowel) in imagining a connection between hockey and war: "one of the boys would pick up his stick and aim it at somebody like a rifle. The others would quickly follow suit, and soon the hockey game was transformed into a re-enactment of the Boer War" (7). After leaving Listowel, Laurence tries a stint in the army that ultimately fails because he "was more determined simply to fire a rifle than truly become a soldier" (218). In other words, Laurence is drawn to the violence of the army but not to the soldierly discipline and self-restraint that attempts to harness or channel this violence through proper avenues (i.e., in the service of the collective). Later in the story, after being discharged from the army, Laurence breaks a man's jaw for asking why he hasn't paid his union dues. Laurence explains to his victim that "I have no desire to join anyone's union ... I work only for my own benefit" (218). Again, Laurence is seen as dangerous because of his unwillingness to contribute to the good of the collective. His toughness, despite exemplifying the novel's preferred masculine ideal, remains dangerously individualistic. In hockey talk, Laurence is most certainly not a "team player."

The same is also initially true of Newsy Lalonde, who is told by his uncle not to "smile when you carry the puck" because "a hockey player should have no friends on the ice" (23). Lalonde's hockey individualism is seen in the same way as Laurence's refusal to unionize, ultimately ending in excessive and inappropriate violence: "He was filled with rage so intense that it felt as if his body were being consumed by fire. He had never before felt such anger. Seconds later, when the referee put the puck in play, Newsy Lalonde did not swing his stick at the tiny piece of rubber. Instead, he snarled and jammed his stick into the English boy's stomach" (26). Unlike Laurence, however, Lalonde eventually learns how to be a team player; in fact, this is essentially the lesson that all the Renfrew Millionaires need to learn after poor teamwork costs them their first game of the season. The players eventually realize that their aggregate individual talents aren't enough to achieve victory, and grudgingly learn to subordinate themselves to the greater good of the collective. This is, of course, an exercise in discipline and selflessness, the two values that Laurence and the young Lalonde most conspicuously lack. It is only when the Millionaires learn to play as team that they succeed on the ice, and it is ultimately through teamwork and cooperation that the players use their hockey toughness to foil the assassination plot against Prime Minister Laurier. In *Hockey Night in the Dominion of Canada*, then, the hockey team promotes a sort of military self-discipline and cooperation that is able profoundly to intervene in the national course. While the other novels discussed above merely suggest hockey as a preparation for good citizenship, *Hockey Night in the Dominion of Canada* actually dramatizes this possibility by enacting the nineteenth-century idea of sport in the service of national integrity and as an ongoing preparation for war. Physically strong from their hockey training and united by their cooperative teamwork (as well as the patriotism it represents), the Renfrew Millionaires easily go from hockey players to paramilitaries, serving their country by saving its prime minister, and, in the framework of the novel, ensuring the golden age of national progress that Laurier is seen to represent.

Not all hockey novels, however, are enthusiastic about the military aspects of national manhood. Although the narrative structure of Reddick's *Killing Frank McGee* (2000) suggests a linkage between hockey and war, the novel's content ultimately problematizes this comparison by way of vivid battle scenes and explicitly critical passages. *Killing Frank McGee* is the story of Frank McGee, "hockey's first superstar" (as he is described on the book jacket), who as a young man lost sight in one eye as result of a hockey accident and consequently played most of his career visually impaired. Despite this limitation McGee became a very effective player, and is probably best remembered for scoring 14 goals during the Ottawa Silver Seven's 23–2 route of the Dawson City Nuggets in the second of their 1905 Stanley Cup challenge games. Reddick's motivation for telling McGee's story was that the hockey hero's record of military service – he enlisted to fight in the First World War and was killed in action in September 1916 – is often treated as an "afterthought" in accounts of his life. The novel uses a dual narrative structure which switches back and forth between two characters who tell McGee's story from their own perspectives, Alf Smith (one of McGee's Ottawa Silver Seven teammates) and Private William Kinnear (based on Andrew Kinnear of Sackville, New Brunswick, whose name Reddick found in the registry of a British Military Cemetery). Smith supplies the hockey portions of McGee's narrative while Kinnear recounts his death in combat, and the structural intermingling of these two strands throughout the novel implicitly suggests that hockey and war are thematically related. There are moments when the connection is made more directly, such as in Smith's insistence that hockey, like war, requires "hands of iron and arms of steel, not only to shoot hard but more importantly to ward off the enemies when they come to get you or to get them yourself" (42). But Reddick doesn't push this comparison much further. While hockey is glorified and commemorated in *Killing Frank McGee*, war is depicted as "the depth of dismal disgrace, lives torn and dragged for no reason better than God and country, where any rational reality we ever knew no longer exists" (201).

A similar rejection of national manhood's military aspects occurs in *King Leary* where the eponymous protagonist finds himself fighting in the First World War battle of Vimy Ridge.[14] Leary initially conceives of the battle in hockey terms, remarking that "I played a game in my head whereby God was handing out Major Penalties, and I thought that if I just stayed crawling on all fours through the muck and didn't do anything wrong I'd be fine" (61). Eventually Leary does get hit with a bullet, however, which bounces off his helmet: "It dropped me like a sack of bricks, and I had a doozy of a headache for two or three days, but it wasn't that big a deal" (61). By contrast, in fact, Leary's war injury is seen as inconsequential compared with a hockey injury he receives a few years later when "the famous son of a bitch Sprague Cleghorn would two-hand my bean and split it open like a nut" (61).

The comedic disparity between Leary's war injury and Cleghorn's stick attack appears intended to parody the nineteenth-century belief that sport could serve as a training ground for war, especially as it was manifested in Canadian recruiting tactics during the First World War. According to McKinley, the War's recruitment campaigns frequently "drew from the amateur athletic ideal of the previous century and cast war as the ultimate game an athlete could play" (2006, 72). For instance, the president of the Canadian Amateur Hockey Association at the time, James Sutherland, suggested that "with every man doing his bit, Canada will raise an army of brain and brawn from our hockey enthusiasts the likes of which the world has never seen. The bell has rung. Let every man play the greatest game of his life" (quoted in McKinley 2006, 72). A recruiting advertisement for the 148th Battalion echoed these sentiments by depicting a beleaguered soldier somewhere on the battlefields of Europe imagining a spectator-filled hockey arena back in Canada and asking "Why don't they come?" The caption beneath the illustration poses a question to the soldier's compatriots: "why be a mere spectator here when you should play a *mans* [sic; *man's*] part in the real game overseas?"

These slogans depict war as a writ-large version of hockey, the ultimate "game" of "manly" strength and competition. Rather than equipping men to succeed in "the big game of life," these slogans suggest hockey as preparation for "the big game of war."[15]

Leary's flippant dismissal of his war injury as "no big deal" reverses the logic of these recruiting slogans entirely; for Leary, hockey is the "real" exercise in glory and toughness while war is little more than a confused and fearsome crawl through the muck. Quarrington's Leary refuses to get sentimental about his war experiences, despite offering fairly vivid descriptions of comrades dying and enemies conquered. When the Toronto Maple Leafs throw Leary a "big do" on the occasion of his seventy-fifth birthday, he consciously decides against wearing his war medals (61). *King Leary*, then, sees hockey and war as two very different things. While hockey proves to be everything promised by the recruiting slogans, war most certainly does not. Despite reinforcing the connection between masculinity and toughness, then, *King Leary* is a rare hockey novel in the *Bildungsroman* trajectory that doesn't lapse into "unhealthy nostalgia for a uniform" (Nelson 1998, 204).

CONTAINED CRITIQUE:
REPRESENTING THE 1970S "GOON BOOM"

It stands to reason that part of the cultural work of performing national manhood for the late twentieth and early twenty-first centuries must involve reckoning with the violent excesses of the 1970s. One hockey novel in particular, *Understanding Ken*, attempts to do just this, representing the experience of a child being socialized into the elevated violence of the "goon boom" as a way of recognizing that historical moment's excesses and thereby appearing to contain them. If hockey culture was inordinately violent in the 1970s, McCormack's narrative seems to suggest, these problems have been resolved in the progressive 1990s. By participating in the critiques of the 1980s and 90s against the roughness of the 1970s, *Understanding Ken* suggests a sense of achieved moderation that allows the ongoing connection between masculinity and hockey violence to appear acceptable and legitimate.

McCormack's historically contained critique of immoderate hockey violence in *Understanding Ken* works in two significant ways, the first of which involves a hockey-novel equivalent of the

Shakespearean fool. In Shakespearean drama, the character of the court fool or jester is often used to speak to the "truth" of a situation in ways not possible or politically prudent for other characters. Because the fool's remarks are packaged in the guise of madness, jest, or riddle, they are perceived in the framework of the play's fictional reality as amusing, unserious, and non-threatening to the established order. Indeed, the wisdom of the fool's insights is often more available and apparent to the audience than to the other characters in the play. Although the analogy isn't perfect, it is the unnamed narrator's mother who plays the role of the fool in *Understanding Ken*: despite being seen as both crazy and un-Canadian for her indifference to hockey, and frequently being dismissed as knowing nothing about the game, the narrator's mother manages to defy the conventional hockey wisdom of the 1970s several times in ways that would be likely to expose its folly to the 1990s reader.

Both of the prevailing hockey authorities in *Understanding Ken*, the narrator's father and coach, emphasize the elevated borderline violence of the day as a specifically Canadian hockey virtue. To be rough is seen as honourable and Canadian, while to be "fancy" and play with finesse is seen as soft, effeminate, and European. This is made explicitly clear, as the coach tells the narrator to "stop making those fancy-dancy drop passes. You're not Russian. You're a Canadian" (136). At one point in the story the narrator is insulted by an opposing goaltender, and starts a fight to avenge the insult. After the boy tells this story to his mother, she replies that the reason for the insult was that the goalie "didn't feel very good about himself inside." The narrator immediately responds by thinking, "doesn't feel good about himself! She doesn't understand anything about Canada!" (213). Again, the narrator's English-immigrant mother is coded as un-Canadian or "other." But the implication of the mother "not understanding Canada" is that a Canadian hockey player should be too tough to be lacking in self-esteem or confidence, or to perceive this deficiency in others. In "Canadian" hockey, the narrator implicitly suggests, the purpose of an insult is to intimidate or antagonize an opponent, and the only fitting response is to drop the gloves. In the framework of the narrative, however, it is the mother who appears most sensible, and readers in the late 1990s context of the novel's publication would recognize that the goalie's insult most likely does stem from poor self-esteem, as well as from an inclination to play the game within the parameters its culture dictates. While the mother seems foolish to her son, then, on the basis of his immersion in 1970s hockey culture, it is clear to the reader that she has actually assessed the situation quite correctly. The narrator's mother functions this way several times throughout *Understanding Ken*, exposing certain tenets of 1970s hockey culture as anachronistic and unreasonable and thereby troubling this hockey identity and its connection to national belonging. The mother's un-Canadianness is repeatedly highlighted throughout the novel in order to foreground her indifference to hockey, yet she is the character who most accurately assesses the hockey situations described above. If being Canadian means embracing the outdated goon-hockey ethos of the father and coach, the mother's sensible alterity signifies a modest and unobtrusive dissent.

A second way in which *Understanding Ken* works to trouble the place of violence in the game is by representing its detrimental impacts on the narrator. In effect, the story expresses the social and psychological pressures exerted on a young boy who is both an eager participant in the minor hockey culture of the 1970s and victim of that culture. Entirely focused on making it to the NHL, the narrator cultivates a disciplined regime of practice, study, and training that he hopes will hone his hockey skills to perfection. Although some of this pressure is self-imposed, a good deal also arises from the unreasonable and overly competitive expectations of the narrator's father and coach. The coach seems specifically intended to resemble the minor hockey situation described in the McMurtry report, and blatantly encourages his players to emulate the elevated borderline violence of the professional game at the time. In addition to the violent promptings of his coach, the unnamed narrator also faces constant pressure from his father, who launches into corrective admonitions laced with obscenities upon even the slightest mistake. As the novel progresses, the pressure to excel at hockey combines with the narrator's repressed feelings of inadequacy and his distress about his parents' divorce to make him tired and unstable. The psychological strain of the narrator's many concerns manifests itself in a passionate hatred of Ken Dryden, the former goaltender of his beloved Montreal Canadiens, who has opted to retire early and left the team in a slump. As these pressures continue to mount, the narrator increasingly retreats into a fantasy world of make-believe hockey scenarios and statistics, while in actual hockey games he experiences blank spells where he is oblivious to action or distracted by random thoughts about dinosaur bones or the French language.

In a sense, *Understanding Ken* traces the narrator's gradual progression from a healthy and balanced hockey toughness to an out-of-control hockey roughness that expresses itself both on and off the ice. Early on, the narrator is seen as disciplined and focused in his cultivation of hockey skill and physical strength, but as the story continues he appears increasingly unable to deal with the pressures that confront him. By the end of the story the narrator has started a brawl with an opposing team's goalie, physically panicked after his school principal mentions Dryden, and destroyed his father's television set with a slapshot following a Canadiens loss in the Stanley Cup finals. The moral/maturing lesson that the narrator learns at the end of *Understanding Ken*, then, fulfilling the novel's trajectory as a *Bildungsroman*, is that of moderation. By coming to understand Dryden's hiatus from hockey (by this point in the story Dryden has agreed to return for the following season), the boy manages to restore a balanced and proper perspective to his own hockey playing.

As the novel concludes, the narrator consciously decides not to join a beckoning road hockey game. While this closing gesture doesn't modify the narrator's professional hockey aspirations, it does recognize the benefit of "taking a little time off" (242). In other words, the narrator has gained a measure of maturity and self-knowledge that goes beyond the simple discipline of practice. He has learned to see the game in proper perspective, and realized the necessary measure of emotional and psychological detachment that allow for equilibrium. This lesson would seem to apply to the narrator's hockey toughness as well, in that it appears productive and beneficial when honed in moderation and tempered by restraint. It is only when the narrator's hockey toughness starts to spill over into excessive roughness that he runs into trouble. *Understanding Ken*, then, critiques the hockey culture of the 1970s not so much for its imbrication of masculine and national identities with hockey toughness, but for its tendency toward the harmful excesses represented by the narrator's father and coach. Hockey toughness can safely be both "manly" and "Canadian," *Understanding Ken* seems to suggest, when it is governed by restraint and proper perspective.

Understanding Ken aligns more closely with Nelson's account of national manhood than the other novels discussed in this chapter, in the sense that the unnamed narrator never really experiences the revitalizing fraternity of intra-team community that national manhood promises. Although the narrator fulfills his end of the national

manhood bargain through toughness, focus, training, and perseverance, *Understanding Ken* is a rare hockey novel in which the collectives of team and nation don't appear to warrant or justify these
efforts. The narrator is a social outsider who doesn't fit in with his
teammates and is ostracized because of his parents' divorce, and, as
such, never gets to experience the sense of team belonging which
other hockey novels appear to deliver as a "reward" for individual
effort. There is also, perhaps, a racial dynamic to the unnamed narrator's lack of belonging, in that his association with the "Negro
friend" mentioned earlier seems to mark him further as a social misfit. Although the friend is represented as playing pick-up hockey, he
is not a member of the narrator's minor hockey team, a fact which
communicates both class distinction and symbolic exclusion from
the white male fraternity of the game.

Because the narrator is represented as a social outsider, *Understanding Ken* offers empathetic appeal to male readers who feel
let down by national manhood or, as Faludi (1999) puts it, "stiffed"
by the changing gender assumptions and economic realities of the
1980s and 90s. Like the narrator of *Understanding Ken*, these men
were taught to "keep trying, keep pushing, and [that] when you keep
trying, everything goes the way it should" (*Understanding Ken*, 23).
Understanding Ken reflects, at least in part, the sense of futility and
injustice arising from the untruth of this maxim, and the cruel fact
that, contrary to national manhood's promises, hard work and dedication are not always rewarded with personal success and fraternal
belonging. Rather than offering readers an alternative ideology or
revised version of masculine identity, however, *Understanding Ken*
merely proposes a moment of respite and empathetic identification.
By suggesting the necessity of taking some time off, McCormack
allows his narrator a much-needed break but ultimately leaves him
enmeshed in the web of cultural forces and assumptions that will
work to make him a national man.

While the critiques of the 1980s and 90s against the excesses of
the 1970s did a great deal to rein in hockey violence and to challenge
the association between masculinity, toughness, and national identity, one important event during the 1970s themselves helped unsettle the place of violence in Canada's hockey myth: the 1972 Summit
Series. Historically speaking, it was the Summit Series that first
exposed Canadians to the undeniable fact that elite levels of hockey
were being played elsewhere in the world than North America. As a

result, NHL and especially WHA managers began to import European players who had been taught to emphasize speed, finesse, and skill rather than "Canadian" roughness, aggression, and intimidation. As Lundin notes in *When She's Gone*, "they changed everything, they brought the European style into Canadian hockey. Drop-passes, crossing over along the blueline, [Anders] Hedberg firing wrist-shots on his off-foot and on the fly, using the feet because in the summer they played soccer ... They showed us that skill could win games. Not intimidation. Pure skill" (19). In addition to importing the European style of play, however, the Summit Series also opened Canadian eyes to the declining state of the Canadian game. Despite celebrating Team Canada's victory as confirming Canadian hockey supremacy, many fans also realized that it was accomplished through violence and tenacity rather than skill. For many, the emblem of Canadian excess in the Summit Series was Bobby Clarke's infamous slash on the Russian superstar Valeri Kharlamov in Game 6.

Although hockey novels often work to mythologize the Summit Series as having "restored Canada's national pride" (*Finnie Walsh*, 36), several of these novels do address Clarke's slash on Kharlamov as a way of reckoning with the violent excesses of the 1970s. Again, by reacting against this moment of perceived excess, hockey novels attempt to contain its effects and recuperate the value and legitimacy of masculine toughness as it is expressed through hockey violence. Lundin has his narrator in *When She's Gone*, Mark, recall "switching allegiance in [Game 6 of the Summit Series] because of that one incident [Clarke's slash on Kharlamov] ... I tossed nationalism away then and there, I guess that made me a purist, at least until the Russians started the soccer-style bullshit of writhing around all over the ice every time someone hit them with a clean check" (178). Mark essentially echoes the thematic conclusion of *Understanding Ken* in this passage, suggesting that violence and toughness are inherently part of the game but must remain contained within certain acceptable parameters. Clarke's transgression is represented as a moment of excess, while the Russians, by contrast, are seen as guilty of insufficient toughness or violating the game's accepted cultural norms (faking injury is dishonourable and against the code). In the framework of *When She's Gone*, the latter certainly appears the greater crime.

Sedlack is equally critical of Clarke through the character of Fred Pickle in *The Horn of a Lamb*, calling the slash "a black mark on Canadian hockey" and concluding that "if you can't win honestly then don't be a jerk" (53). It is noteworthy, however, that while Fred disdains Clarke's slash on Kharlamov, he doesn't shy away from rough play himself. In fact, later in the novel we are told that "Fred liked skating with the older guys because he could play rough. A new player hadn't been baptized on Fred's rink until he'd been cross-checked into the snowbank from behind" (104). When read against Fred's opinion of Clarke, a familiar philosophy on hockey violence begins to emerge: that violence and aggressive play are part of the game – or, more specifically, part of the Canadian game – but that this applies only to a certain point (the line between borderline and quasi-criminal violence). Again, hockey novels work to referee some forms of violence as acceptable and others as excessive, apparently maintaining by this distinction the legitimacy of hockey violence and the nexus between masculine and national identities it represents.

Clarke's slash on Kharlamov also provides the context for an important insight in the unnamed narrator of *Understanding Ken*'s progression toward balance and maturity. The novel initially configures the Summit Series as a great triumph for Canadian hockey. When the narrator's mother's boyfriend tries to upset the narrator by claiming "the Russians are way better than the Canadians" because "the Canadians are dirty and they dump the puck into the corner and chase it like dogs," the narrator isn't bothered and thinks to himself "who won the series of the century with thirty-four seconds left? Ha-ha" (21). This affirmation of the Summit Series victory hints at the extent to which the narrator has been influenced by the examples of his father and coach, but the boyfriend's comment also points to a subtle leitmotif that runs throughout the novel. That the Canadian players chase the puck "like dogs" resonates with several instances in which the narrator likens himself to a dog and even prays to harness his dead dog's latent energy to improve his play. If the Canadians play like dogs, it would seem, then, being a dog is good enough for the narrator. It is not until later in the story that the narrator comes to see the Summit Series in a different light. Upon being censured in a local newspaper for sucker-punching an opposing player, the narrator begins to feel the injustice of his position and the hypocrisy of his hockey influences: "I was thinking about how everybody says, 'Play like the Philadelphia Flyers! Finish your damn checks!' The Flyers bite and kick and stick and have names like Mad Dog Kelly and Moose Dupont. Their captain, Bobby Clarke, with no front teeth, broke Kharlamov's ankle with his hockey stick just like a Nazi would. Why was that fine with everybody?" (209). In the end, the narrator of *Understanding Ken* comes to the same conclusion as the other characters who see Clarke's slash on Kharlamov as unacceptable and an emblem of Canadian excess.

In hockey terms, Clarke's slash is the ultimate expression of national manhood: a moment of hockey violence deployed against a "dangerous" opponent during a series that was seen as critical to the nation's identity and self-respect. Again, masculine physicality and strength appear to guarantee the well-being and direction of the national course. But at what cost? The narrator's identification of Clarke with Nazism is the most direct criticism of national manhood offered by Canadian hockey novels, suggesting, somewhat excessively, the extent to which national manhood both short-circuits democracy and is, at root, a "might makes right" ideology. The enforcer mentality blatantly contradicts the values of peacefulness and tolerance that Canadians have often seen as central to their national ethos, and hockey novels make little attempt to resolve this inconsistency except in a few isolated instances through the quasi-racist and agency-denying "release valve theory." Despite realizing the injustice of being taught to play like Clarke only to be sanctioned for doing so, the narrator of *Understanding Ken* is unable to move very far beyond the masculine identities rehearsed for him by his father and coach. Again, McCormack's ultimate conclusion is more to endure the failures and shortcomings of national manhood than to challenge this ideology's worthiness or viability, and, as such, *Understanding Ken* remains in step with the general work of hockey novels to consociate masculine toughness with national identity and productive citizenship.

5

Myths of Masculinity

THE HERO-PROTECTOR, OR,

THE HOCKEY *BILDUNGSROMAN* REVISITED

In a discussion of the NHL's 2000–01 "Every Player Has a Story" television advertising campaign, Kimberly Korol suggests "four primary mythologies of masculinity that exist within the [league]: the bully, the hero-protector, the sexual athlete, and the New Man" (2006, 181). Korol argues that the "Every Player Has a Story" campaign deliberately emphasized each of these four masculine mythologies as a way of "widen[ing] its audience and rekey[ing] the frame of hockey in order to compete for the fans' entertainment dollar" (184). By employing these apparently diverse mythologies of masculinity, then, the NHL consciously attempted to appeal to fans on a broader, more sophisticated level, mobilizing several specific narratives of masculinity that the game has often been seen to represent. Korol's four myths of masculinity apply equally well to the study of Canadian hockey novels, many of which enact these myths in the attempt to rehearse, prescribe, accommodate, or elaborate the identity of masculinity-as-toughness in relation to the current historical moment of perceived crisis.

Korol's explanation of the hero-protector myth is drawn from cultural critic Garry Whannel's discussion of masculinities and moralities in *Media Sport Stars*. Working from a wide array of allusions and archetypes, Whannel defines the heroic role as implying "exceptional courage and self-sacrifice and involv[ing] the idealization of a man of superior qualities or virtues" (2002, 40). According to Whannel, however, the idea of the heroic has been somewhat disrupted in the mechanized and industrial twentieth century. Because "travel and exploration have become less fascinating as much of the world is now accessible to tourists ... mechanization and speed have passed beyond the realm of individual heroics and are now thoroughly in the hands of science and technology ... [and] war heroism has [also] been undercut by the dominance of technology," a "gradual incorporation of sporting exploits into the pantheon of the heroic" has worked throughout the twentieth century to "[fill] the gap" (44).

During the same period in which athletic prowess came to be seen as demonstrating heroism, many literary and cultural texts began to react against the idea of the hero. Indeed, "the advent of postmodernity and the 'death of the (humanist) subject' [have] led many to question the very possibility of heroes" (Hughes-Fuller 2002, 108). This trend is demonstrated by the abundance of twentieth-century anti-hero protagonists in literature and film who appear marginalized, ineffectual, self-pitying, and more concerned with escaping their surroundings than improving them. This is not to say, of course, that literature and film have completely revolted against the idea of the hero. As Hughes-Fuller points out, the turn from the heroic in twentieth-century art has been a relatively "high culture" phenomenon (108). Indeed, popular representations of heroes and heroism abound, from comic books to action films to adventure novels.

Generally speaking, the hero-protector characters in Canadian hockey novels are those who fall within the hockey *Bildungsroman* trajectory. The message of the hockey *Bildungsroman* that personal effort should be deployed in the service of the collective is essentially that of the hero-protector myth as well, and in both cases the exercise of this responsibility appears to hang on masculine strength, toughness, and physicality. In the words of Korol, hero-protector masculinity "conquers evil, shields the less able, and safeguards all that is good and right" (2006, 181). The hero-protector myth, then, participates in the ideological work of the hockey *Bildungsroman* to produce and affirm good citizens via national manhood. The way in which this is most frequently accomplished is by representing heroism as a function of hard work rather than innate talent or skill.

Part of the twentieth-century uncertainty over heroes and heroism stems from an increasing democratization of the heroic. Despite the cultural suspicion that heroes no longer exist, heroic acts are still seen as possible, even prevalent. One recent example of this has been the widespread ascription of heroism to almost everyone affected in some way by the 9/11 terrorist attacks and their immediate aftermath. In many media accounts, the unfortunate bankers and brokers who perished in the Twin Towers became "heroic" for their contributions to American capitalism, while the firefighters who responded to the crisis became "heroes" simply by doing the work for which they were trained and paid, albeit under conditions of exceptional duress. Such responses to 9/11 suggest a link between heroism and the productive citizen ethos of national manhood. All it takes to be a hero, these narratives seem to suggest, is hard work, self-sacrifice (either chosen or incidental), and extraordinary circumstance. The example of the firefighters is particularly appropriate in that firefighting is often seen to embody many of the same aspects of traditional masculinity as hockey.[1]

The narrative of civic heroism surrounding the 9/11 firefighters is strikingly similar to the representations of heroism enacted by Canadian hockey *Bildungsromans*. In both cases, national well-being appears safeguarded, if not guaranteed, by masculine toughness, and heroism appears democratically available to anyone willing to work hard, privilege the collective, and, to perform, when called upon, their duties under the extraordinary circumstances of a national emergency or, at the risk of sounding trite, an important hockey game. The hero characters in hockey *Bildungsromans* are ostensibly "normal" people whose hockey training and masculine toughness enable them to rise to the occasion of a particular challenge. All of these characters make "heroic" stands in important hockey situations: Paul Woodward scores an unlikely Stanley Cup winning goal, Hughie Murray plays through pain and helps his team to win, and Scott MacGregor and Andrew Clark answer the challenge of aggressive opponents to fight. More significant, however, is the fact that these acts of hockey heroism become associated with the civic "heroism" represented by self-sacrifice and service to the collective in the "big game of life." Again, Paul Woodward rejects a lucrative NHL salary to maintain the "play-for-the-right-reasons" purity of the game, while Scott MacGregor sacrifices his place on the team to defend a teammate from a sexual predator. Both Andrew Clark and Hughie Murray parlay their hockey skills into futures of implied productive citizenship, and Hughie in particular exemplifies collective-mindedness through his vocational aspiration to the clergy. Although several of these characters are signalled as exceptional enough to occupy certain positions of minor privilege (Hughie Murray, for instance, is his team's captain, while Scott MacGregor serves as his team's alternate captain), their achievements are consistently seen as a function of hard work rather than innate giftedness or talent.

If popular notions of the heroic have moved into sport, they have done so in many ways as a "nostalgia for a purer, less compromised past" (Whannel 2002, 42) in which human beings are imagined as more connected to the elemental forces of nature, more dependent on physical strength for survival, and more convinced of certain moral absolutes that structured human conduct. In other words, the widespread cultural "longing for heroes and ... regret at the decline of heroes" (43) can be seen as consonant with the longing of the pastoral myth for childhood innocence and security. Although the "heroism" of the characters discussed above is arguably diminished by its apparent availability and certainly co-opted by its complicity in national manhood, the very idea of the hero hearkens back to an idealized time of childlike safety, stability, and moral certainty. Hockey *Bildungsromans*, then, might also be read as responding to the current moment of cultural and gender instability by evoking an earlier social state of imagined ideal order and security. In this context, the idea of the hero might involve "searching for a magical resolution of the contradictions of the present" (43–4). Quite simply, the "magical resolution" proposed by hero-protector characters in Canadian hockey novels is to combine the joy, innocence, and moral certainties of childhood with the discipline and responsibilities of adulthood. Such characters attempt to reassure readers of the continued viability of national manhood and traditional masculinity while offering nostalgic escape from the pressures and stresses these identities represent.

Probably the best example of the hero-protector's work to unite manly toughness with the innocence and moral certainties of childhood is the character of Mike Horseford in *Icelands*. Although Mike is technically a child, he is represented as having "grown up too fast" as a result of his alcoholic mother and absent father. Hockey becomes Mike's singular focus in life, the way by which he plans to "make something of himself ... and take care of his mom" (111). But while Mike considers hockey to be the "only way out" (111) of his troubled childhood and into a promising adult future, it also becomes a fantasy escape by which he can experience the childlike sense of innocence and security that circumstances have denied him. Mike often imagines himself as the star player for the Toronto Maple Leafs, the centerpiece in a "dazzling dreamland ... of ice and the wild excitement of fans" (88). Paradoxically, these fantasies are both an escape from "adult" pressures and a cause of these pressures, in that a great deal of Mike's worries and efforts relate to his desire for hockey success. This duality is captured throughout the novel by alternating descriptions of Mike's hockey stick as both a "weapon" and a "magic wand." The stick is a weapon in that Mike will use it to attain success, largely along the hockey *Bildungsroman* lines of achievement through discipline, toughness, and hard work.[2] But the stick is also a "magic wand" because it allows escape from these very pressures, admitting Mike to a fantasy world of childhood innocence and security that he never got to experience growing up. Hockey is seen as "a place where [Mike] could get bigger and bigger and still be a kid playing a kid's game. Almost, at times, a magical kingdom" (148). Despite being characterized as Mike's entrance ticket to adulthood, then, hockey heroism also provides an imaginary link to an idealized childhood that – like the nostalgic longing for an earlier social state of innocence and security represented by heroism itself – never really existed in the first place.

The fact that heroic narratives have become associated with sport during the same historical moment in which literary values have rejected the idea of heroism may help to account for the relative scarcity of hero-protector characters among the hockey novels most obviously intended for adult readers. With the noteworthy exceptions of *Icelands* and *Understanding Ken*, adult-oriented hockey novels tend to enact alternative forms of heroism to those based on physicality and toughness, or focus on protagonists who bear closer resemblance to the anti-hero than the hero. Although hockey novels are not particularly "literary" in their ambitions, the tendency of adult-oriented hockey novels to focus on anti-hero characters such as Batterinski, Bonaduce, Drinkwater, and Bayle can be seen as another strategy of legitimation. By focusing on anti-heroes rather than heroes, adult-oriented hockey novels ask to be taken seriously in that they appear to align with current literary tastes.

Mark Jarman hinted at this trend during his talk at the Canada and the League of Hockey Nations conference in Victoria, British Columbia, in April 2007 (see Jarman 2007), explaining that his original intent in *Salvage King, Ya!* was to tell the story of a star player, or, in other words, a hero. As Jarman got further and further into his early manuscript, he became increasingly unsatisfied with the heroic trajectory he had settled on. Eventually Jarman decided to transform Drinkwater, the protagonist of *Salvage King, Ya!*, into a journeyman player more concerned with keeping his place in professional hockey than with scoring game-winning goals. Although Jarman didn't identify the root of his dissatisfaction with the hero trajectory, his change certainly reflects the current literary preference for alienated anti-heroes over self-actualized hero-protectors. Heroic masculinity, then, as associated with toughness and collective responsibility, remains largely the domain of adolescent- and young-adult-oriented hockey novels, and this trend can perhaps be explained both by the desire of adult-oriented hockey novelists to be taken seriously and the easy congruence of democratically available heroism with the ideological work of national manhood.

BULLY MASCULINITY: *THE LAST SEASON*

To know the goodness and nobility of the hero, it is often necessary to witness the evil and underhandedness of a bully. The aggressive opponents who challenge Andrew Clark, Hughie Murray, and Scott MacGregor to fight are prime examples of bully masculinity, and illuminate the codependence between bully and hero. Minor and tertiary bully characters in Canadian hockey novels often work to define heroism by contrast. As Hughes-Fuller puts it in her discussion of Wayne Gretzky's and Eddie Shore's respective places within the hockey myth, "for every White Knight there must be a Black Knight" (2002, 134). Korol defines the bully as "the tough guy who will fight, gloves off, to defend his teammates and his honour" (2006, 181). While this is certainly the case, bully masculinity is not merely defensive. In hockey novels as well as the game itself, bullies are the aggressive players who harry and pester opponents through physical contact and intimidation. As noted earlier, such players are often known as enforcers and are seen as a sort of specialized labour, expected both to defend star teammates and intimidate skilled opponents.

By far the most prominent example of bully masculinity in Canadian hockey novels is the character of Felix Batterinski in *The Last Season*, whose name, as Blake points out, can be read literally as "The Happy Batterer" (2010, 40). According to *The Uninvited Guest* "enforcers were not born, they were made by their upbringings – made by their towns" (63), and in many ways *The Last Season* is about the social and cultural production of the bully, the ways in which Batterinski's coaches and supporters shape his identity by encouraging him to fight and play violently. Batterinski is certainly represented as a receptive subject, and as he begins to internalize the bully identity his coaches and supporters envision for him he starts to glory in the feeling of fighting and perceive his self-worth to be contingent on his ability to command fear and respect: "I knew it wasn't right, but it felt great. I could feel my defenseman [an opponent in a hockey fight] on my knuckles and when I touched them they stung with his jaw, just as I knew when he moved this week he would feel me and I would be with him, his better, for weeks to follow. He had my mark on him. I too had swelling and redness, but on the knuckles it shone with pride. Where his swelling made him less, mine made me more. I tried to feel his fear of me, and in trying this, my respect for myself grew. I went to the half-shattered mirror but saw no pimples. Just *Batterinski*, hulking in his pads, solid from blade to brushcut, a man oddly at ease while others about him panic" (21). Putting aside the obvious homoeroticism of this incident (an issue which will be returned to in the following chapter), this passage appears intended to suggest Batterinski's hyperborean superiority. Part of bully masculinity's appeal is the sense of power and dominance it seems to entail. If masculinity is contingent on toughness and physicality, the bully appears the most "manly" of men. He inhabits a reality in which might makes right, in which strength guarantees privilege and status. In a sense, Batterinski comes to see himself as above morality ("I knew it wasn't right, but it felt great") and above the petty weaknesses and distractions that trouble others ("a man oddly at ease while others about him panic"). In other words, Batterinski is represented here as the master of his own destiny in a way that could potentially provide enjoyment, reassur-ance, and an element of fantasy wish-fulfillment for adult male read-ers who perceive their masculinity to be threatened or marginalized.

While MacGregor initially sets up Batterinski's bully superiority as something for readers to enjoy, *The Last Season* begins to frus-trate this enjoyment as the story progresses. Because the bully appears the most "manly" of men, he is also an important site through which hockey novels demonstrate the necessity of "referee-ing" this identity by circumscribing the arena of its legitimacy. Bully characters in Canadian hockey novels often illustrate the limits of acceptability by transgressing them, and Batterinski is no exception in this regard. But rather than working as a foil for a more central or important hero character (who stays within the game's codes of acceptability and thus exemplifies desirable toughness and honourable propriety), Batterinski is the narrator and protagonist of *The Last Season*. The effect of this authorial decision is to put the reader inside the mind of the bully, fostering empathy, understanding, pathos, vicarious enjoyment, discomfort, and even repulsion in various turns. By initially inviting readers to empathize and identify with Batterinski's bully masculinity, MacGregor sets up a sophisticated critique of hockey violence that "goes too far," while implicating fans (i.e., readers) as part of the culture from which this excessive behaviour arises.

As with *Understanding Ken*, *The Last Season*'s critique is directed (and, this section will argue, limited) to the violent excesses of the 1970s. Toward the end of Batterinski's NHL career he takes a job as playing coach for a Finnish club, Tapiola Hauki, rather than accepting demotion to the North American minors. In plot terms this occurs at roughly the same time as the sea change in attitudes towards hockey violence during the late 1970s, and *The Last Season* supplies this contextual information by way of an article on Batterinski that is apportioned throughout the narrative. Written by a character named Matt Keening, the article explains that after Montreal's sweep of Philadelphia in the 1975–76 Stanley Cup series the goon hockey ethos of the Broadstreet Bullies was largely abandoned, and that with it went the relevance of players like Batterinski because "the fists no longer worked" (107). Batterinski himself remarks on the changing attitudes around this time, commenting that "things go in cycles. Right now hockey is all Gretzky and those damn Czechs, the Stastny brothers in Quebec, and the Swedes, and guys like Perrault and Dionne again. Five years ago it was all me and Hound Dog and Battleship and Bird and Schultzy and the Bullies. Cycles, round and round and round, like a whirlpool sucking dead-heads like me and Hound Dog down" (65). Whether these trends are cyclical (as Batterinski configures them) or linear, the fact remains that Batterinski's apparent agency and self-determination have evaporated in the changing cultural conditions of the late 1970s. Again, Gretzky, along with several others, notably European players, is seen as representing a triumph of skill and finesse that also signifies the obsolescence of physical players such as Batterinski. As the narrative shifts toward seeing Batterinski's skill set and gender identity as outmoded, he becomes an object of pity rather than prestige. As readers, then, we go from enjoying Batterinski's agency to discovering that it doesn't actually exist. For male readers who perceive their masculinity to be threatened by gender or vocational instabilities, Batterinski's incipient naivety about his security, self-determination, and moral legitimacy may well begin to feel uncomfortably familiar. In other words, as Batterinski's "masculine" superiority is increasingly called into question he becomes a casualty of changing societal attitudes and, potentially, an object of empathy for men who feel similarly emasculated or outdated. As the relevance of Batterinski's masculine toughness appears to evaporate, then, the readerly pleasure of the *Last Season* shifts from idealizing Batterinski to identifying with him. As with *Understanding Ken, The Last Season* ultimately fails to offer men who feel "stiffed" by the social and cultural circumstances of their time a viable alternative to traditional masculinity or a way to mitigate their personal investment in this obsolete and unproductive identity.

Part of the pathos that Batterinski evokes stems from the extent to which he tries to swim upstream against changing social and cultural currents. Rather than admit the obsolescence of his bully masculinity, Batterinski tries to apply his hockey-as-violence ethos to Tapiola Hauki. Upon Batterinski's arrival in Finland, the country's most respected columnist cautions that "no true Finnish hockey fan ... can condone hockey violence, but neither can he deny convincingly that Finnish hockey might gain much by a little infusion of aggression" (62). Batterinski soon finds out why this is the case upon meeting his team: "these guys are engineers and students and civil servants first, hockey players second. Hockey is more like a hobby to them" (68). What really bothers Batterinski, however, is the fact that Tapiola Hauki "all have their teeth. All of them, all of their teeth. And that says all anyone ever needs to know about European hockey, as far as this boy's concerned" (68). In the same way that Batterinski's injury becomes a mark of pride after the junior hockey fight, as quoted earlier, a missing tooth or two among the Finns would have indicated tenacity, physical toughness, work ethic, willingness to grind, fight, and play through pain – all the hockey virtues that Batterinski himself espouses and by default ascribes to Canadian hockey. In order to encourage the sort of toughness that Batterinski envisions as necessary to Tapiola Hauki's success, he institutes a system of monetary

rewards for violent and aggressive play. At first the ploy appears to
work: the players become more involved in the game, and Tapiola
begins to climb in the standings. Things eventually begin to unravel,
however, when Batterinski crosses the line between desirable toughness and excessive roughness in an incident at an exhibition game in
Sweden where he chases down an opposing fan who had spit on him
in the penalty box. Eventually the pay-for-aggressive-play system on
Tapiola Hauki comes to light, and the Finnish press accuses
Batterinski of "rewarding violence" (309). Canadian newspapers
pick up the story as well, and Batterinski becomes "a symbol overnight for what's wrong with Canadian hockey" (185).

Batterinski's pay-for-aggressive-play system is essentially an extension of North American professional hockey in the 1970s, another
way in which Batterinski's bully masculinity is represented by the
narrative to be defunct and obsolete. *The Last Season*, however, is
unique among hockey novels in that it consciously invites readers to
examine their place within a culture that economically rewards the
violent masculinity enacted in professional hockey. At one point in
The Last Season Batterinski is involved in an exhibition game
between the Soviet Red Army team and Broadstreet Bullies era
Philadelphia Flyers (of which Batterinski is a member). Upon finding
himself pinned against the boards by two linesmen, Batterinski sees
his fans through the glass, "fists pounding, mouths silently screaming toward mine, eyes bulging with thrill and desperate terror at the
same time ... I'd never been this close to my fans before, never seen
what they looked like. Never cared. But I saw now, and I knew finally that I was not Batterinski. *They* were" (215; italics in original).
This passage ostensibly portrays the realization that Batterinski's
bully identity has been constructed by the people he exists to entertain, that his violence is really their violence enacted vicariously. The
suggestion that Batterinski's violence is also that of his fans invites
readers to reconsider their own consumption of bully masculinity,
both in *The Last Season* and in hockey culture at large. The arena
glass is both mirror and window, affording Batterinski a view of his
fans that simultaneously reflects back on himself. In a sense, the
same is true of fictional representation: by staring at Batterinski
through the window of the novel, readers must consider the ways in
which his violence reflects on their own preferences and identities.
Cultural critic Cornell Sandvoss has suggested that "fans are fascin-
ated by extensions of themselves ... which they do not recognize as

such" (2005, 121). By asserting that fandom must be, at least on some level, indicative of the fan's own character, *The Last Season* forces readers to reckon with their complicity in hockey violence. By inviting readers into the mind of the bully, MacGregor alternately allows them to enjoy hockey violence and forces them to recoil from it, and, in doing so, to recoil from themselves.

What is most pathetic about *The Last Season* isn't Batterinski's inability to change, but the fact that the hockey world that created him turns its back on him in the end. In an emblematic moment upon returning to his hometown for the last time, Batterinski is dismayed to learn that they no longer allow body contact in minor hockey: "*No body contact!* Outlawed for all groups below bantam. Every two years it goes up a level. At that rate in eight more years it would reach the NHL. *No body contact.* Strike Schultz and Williams and Batterinski from the record books forever. We need more pages for Gretzky" (334; italics in original). As Batterinski becomes increasingly disillusioned with his enforcer identity, he finally seeks to understand why he is what he is. Rather than considering the hockey culture that produced him, however, he turns to the Polish heritage he has spent much of novel trying to diminish and reject. Batterinski's grandmother, Batcha, is a *càrovnica*, a Polish white witch, and throughout the story she harbours an unexplained hatred for Batterinski. As Batterinski attempts to piece together the puzzles of his heritage and identity, he determines that he is a *vjeszczi*, a sort of Polish vampire monster, signified by the fact that he was born with a caul. Batterinski reasons that Batcha's hatred of him is owed to the fact that the *vjeszczi* cure – grinding up the caul and feeding it to the monster – was never administered, and comes to attribute his hockey violence to the supposed monstrosity of his nature. In a desperate attempt to "cure" himself, Batterinski ingests a can of powder that he believes to be his caul. Instead, the powder turns out to be rat poison and causes Batterinski's death. In the end, then, Batterinski fails to recognize his monstrosity as culturally produced, believing it instead to be internally, "naturally" motivated. But while Batterinski dies believing that nature made him a monster, the reader is shown the "truth" of the situation by a final instalment of Keening's article, which ascribes the guilt of Batterinski's "suicide" to the "average fan": "who was it but the average fan who made of Batterinski a false god? And who turned from their worship when the god was cast down? Where were the cheers on Felix Batterinski's last lonely night on earth?" (360). In the end, then, readers are again confronted with the "truth" of their own implication in Batterinski's bully violence. Instead of nature, it is *we*, the readers and fans, who made Batterinski a monster, and this realization forces us to acknowledge and reckon with our own complicity in the culture of hockey violence.

If the readers and fans *are* Batterinski – that is, if his violence exists to vicariously satisfy our own – then we are ultimately responsible for encouraging him to embrace an identity that could only ever really prove to be hollow and destructive. By novel's end, Batterinski's apparent agency has been exposed for the social script it always was, and his violence is seen as a product of culture, a minor component of the elaborate pay-for-aggressive-play spectacle that was – and indeed in some ways remains – North American professional hockey. By forcing readers to reckon with their complicity in hockey violence, *The Last Season* places responsibility for this culture clearly on those who perpetuate it through economic and consumptive support. In terms of reader reception, however, *The Last Season*'s critique, like that of *Understanding Ken*, appears limited to the excesses of the 1970s. Because *The Last Season* is so thoroughly situated and historicized within the culture of the goon boom, it can't help but appear obsolete to the contemporary reader, a backward looking critique that has little to say now that the "excessive" violence of the 1970s has fallen out of favour. In this respect, it is easy to read *The Last Season* simply as an indictment of an outmoded hockey culture that encouraged players to internalize violent identities and a minor hockey feeder system that rehearsed and enforced these identities, a system that MacGregor has described elsewhere as "[verging] on insanity" (1997, 187). Although Batterinski's role as a bully protagonist offers readers the pleasures this identity entails (strength, dominance, control, etc.) to force them to recoil from its excesses and their complicity in them, *The Last Season*'s critique of hockey violence ultimately allows the connection between masculinity and toughness to emerge intact as long as it remains within "acceptable" levels.

THE NEW MAN: *THE GOOD BODY* AND *PUCK IS A FOUR LETTER WORD*

While the hero-protector helps perform the ideological work of national manhood and the bully works to contain hockey violence

within certain "acceptable" limits, the myth of New Man masculinity attempts to open up non-traditional identity possibilities for
hockey-playing men while maintaining toughness as a requisite
characteristic of masculine identity. Korol's myth of the "New Man"
is largely drawn from Whannel, who applies this label to "men who
had responded to and taken on board aspects of the critique of masculinity offered by feminism. Such men endeavoured to become
more involved with domestic labour and childcare. They got in
touch with their emotions and tried to combat their own sexism"
(2002, 75). Korol's characterization of the New Man also contains
elements of Savran's "sensitive male" (Savran 1998, 5), a category
that despite involving men in traditionally feminine pursuits "by no
means signals a repudiation of traditionally masculine goals" (125).
For Korol, then, the New Man "uses hockey as an outlet for the
conventional male needs, while still playing the role of caring, sensitive man" (2006, 182).

Two such characters in Canadian hockey novels are Bobby
Bonaduce in *The Good Body* and Willie Mulligan in *Puck Is a Four
Letter Word*, both of whom are distinguished as New Men by their
sensitivity, well-roundedness, and cultural mobility. They appear
intelligent, in touch with their emotions, respectful and appreciative
of women, and able to negotiate the range of social and cultural
circumstances in which they find themselves. Despite these apparently progressive values and abilities, however, both characters
ultimately subscribe to a version of masculinity based on strength
and toughness. In other words, Bonaduce and Mulligan appear to
accommodate traditional masculinity to the late twentieth- and early twenty-first-century contexts by establishing a rapprochement
with feminism without fully embracing its revisioning of gender
roles.[3] The effect of this mediation is to bridge certain perceived
cultural and gender distinctions in the attempt to open a wider range
of identity possibilities for hockey-playing men, thereby legitimating
(and, in the case of *The Good Body*, theorizing) the very idea of a
"hockey literature."

Interviewing Bill Gaston in *The New Quarterly*'s special issue on
hockey writing, Jamie Fitzpatrick suggests that "Canada has yet to
embrace and celebrate the hockey novel" because "fiction lovers
don't trust hockey and the hockey lovers don't trust fiction" (Gaston
2005, 95). Gaston responds to Fitzpatrick's comment in part by
asserting that "it's hard not to ignore statistics telling us that more

women than men are serious about literature, while more men than women are serious about hockey" (95). Whether or not this claim is true – Gaston doesn't cite the "statistics" to which he refers – his comment illustrates the fact that hockey and literature are often perceived to be gendered male and female, respectively. Together, then, Gaston and Fitzpatrick evoke several recognizable cultural "divides": the gap between "high" and "low" cultures (in which literature is associated with "high" culture and hockey with "low"), the Cartesian disconnect between mind and body (in which literature is associated with the mind and hockey with the body), and the idea that sport and literature are incompatibly gendered domains, all of which continue to work against the idea of hockey as a legitimate subject of "serious" writing. It is worth clarifying that the association of literature with femininity would seem to apply mainly to popular literature. According to Andreas Huyssen, the "Great Divide" between high art and mass culture has been animated by the prevailing "notion ... that mass culture is somehow associated with woman while real, authentic culture remains the prerogative of men" (1986, 47). All of this puts the aspiring hockey novelist in a potentially difficult position: if the game is gendered male (as Gaston and widespread societal opinion seem to believe) it appears incongruous with the putatively feminine domain of popular culture. At the same time, if hockey is associated with "low" culture and the body, it appears antithetical to serious literature, which, despite being putatively masculine, is associated with "high" culture and the mind.

Bonaduce's function in *The Good Body* is essentially to bridge these cultural divides. Probably the most obvious way this is accomplished is through his graduate studies in English literature and creative writing, which, beyond evincing his New Man masculinity, work in the novel to unite the ostensibly disconnected realms of "mind" and "body" and propose a vision for hockey writing that – contrary to the prevailing assumptions identified above – is simultaneously popular, masculine, and, to borrow Huyssen's term, "authentic" (i.e., legitimate, serious). Over the course of *The Good Body* Bonaduce produces his own hockey novel for a creative writing class, a device which allows Gaston to use Bonaduce as a mouthpiece for his own beliefs about literature. In this regard *The Good Body* is uniquely metafictional among hockey novels, and can in many ways be read as a hockey novel about how to write a hockey novel. When Bonaduce first arrives at grad school he is seen as a "body person," and is received with a mixture of curiosity and animosity, "body-people being exotic to head-people" (47). Bonaduce is initially critical of the "head-people" he meets at grad school, and in this respect *The Good Body* parodies what it sees as academic boringness, pettiness, pretentiousness, and tendentiousness. Gaston renders Bonaduce's grad-school colleagues and professors as caricatures that might feel uncomfortably familiar to anyone who has ever pursued graduate studies in literature (and likely in anything at all): the young female professor who sees herself "as a seventy-year-old guy from Oxford" (44), the grad student who spends all her time quibbling with the professor's syllabus, another grad student who is "especially good at belittling certain notions by pronouncing quotation marks around certain words and getting people to smile" (45–6), another grad student who loudly expounds on his intricate knowledge of steins while struggling to "[make] it through two beers in one sitting" (85), and yet another grad student who successfully defends a vacuous PhD dissertation entitled "*speculation* about *possible* uses of the *trapdoor* in *early versions* of *some* plays Shakespeare *might* have written" (142; italics in original).

Gaston represents Bonaduce as frustrated by the purposeful opacity of academic jargon, the hostility and pettiness of his colleagues, and the general lack of "humanness" that characterizes the gradschool experience (Gaston uses the word "human" several times throughout the novel to connote kindness, considerateness, decency, good humour, and straightforwardness). When Bonaduce first arrives at grad school he suggests that "all it was, really, was that these guys had worked up a decent act, all witty dash and brain-pizzazz" and that "the ordinarys in the cheap seats could see this" (45). After enduring his first seminar class (which he describes as an "ordeal"), however, Bonaduce decides that "he could maybe do this course if he got serious and learned the rules, and the meaning of 'postmodern,' and next time read the book" (46). In fact, Bonaduce goes so far as to suggest that "half the guys in any [hockey] dressing room he'd ever sat in could have ended up here [at grad school]" but "had for various reasons taken a different route, the body-route" (48).

For Bonaduce, the "body-route" merely demonstrates a different kind of intelligence to that of the "mind-route": "Language, simply, was a route not many [hockey players] took. Should he tell these loungers [his academic colleagues] that in 1968 Eric Nesterenko scored thirty-two goals for Chicago and published his first book of poems? But that would be falling into their trap, accepting their definition of intelligence. On the ice is where it really happened. The brilliance of some. All senses sparking, working at the widest periphery, aflame with danger and hope both, seeing the whole picture, the lightning fast flux of friends and enemies, the blending of opportunity and threat. Words didn't stand a chance here. Words were candy wrappers, dead leaves" (48). Although this passage valorizes bodily intelligence over the mental or verbal intelligence represented by poetry and literature in general, the example of Nesterenko actually signifies both sorts of intelligence and foreshadows what Bonaduce will become over the course of the story: a hockey player who is also a writer.[4]

The unity of body and mind demonstrated by both Nesterenko and Bonaduce is central to the theory of writing articulated in *The Good Body*. Early in the story when Bonaduce first returns home, he is prepared to disparage literature as something "perverse," an act of "indulgently gorging on words despite this dying world, the starving masses" (71). Bonaduce quickly undergoes a change of heart, however, after an epiphanic moment reading *Hamlet* while using the washroom: "sitting on the toilet, free of any pressure, free of having to do something *with* the stuff – maybe that was why it clicked" (71). In keeping with the set of beliefs that *The Good Body* endorses about academic approaches to literature, *Hamlet* becomes worthwhile and significant to Bonaduce when encountered outside the expectation of analysis and critique. Freed from the pressures of having to interpret, analyze, or criticize, Bonaduce sees the human condition as poignantly reflected in Shakespeare's play: "How could you not be cowed? Here you were perfectly described, here you were crawling between heaven and earth, a dirt-bound angel. Caught up in the demands of heaven, yet helplessly mired in earth's cruel gravities" (71). In other words, Bonaduce comes to the conclusion that "our struggle can seem only tedious until someone like Shakespeare renders it worthwhile" (71). Aside from the criticism that academic analysis strips art of its liveliness, its inspirational and empathetic power – "we murder to dissect," as Wordsworth puts it in "The Tables Turned" (1993, 136) – Bonaduce's appreciation of *Hamlet* importantly elucidates his own beliefs about art. "You read because people are in the terminal wing and your turn is coming" (71), Bonaduce suggests, and the implication is that art should describe something important, make life worth living, and give existential answers. In other words, art is always about the body, mortality, and the connection between abstraction and materiality. It is no coincidence, then, that Bonaduce comes to appreciate Shakespeare while using the toilet, an act which allows him to connect high art with the bodily realities of material existence.[5]

Beyond appearing to unify the ostensibly disconnected realms of mind and body, Bonaduce's decision to write a hockey novel implicitly broadens the subject matter of literature and thereby effaces some of the distinction between "high" and "low" cultures. This negotiation of Huyssen's "Great Divide" is another central tenet of Gaston's theory of literature. According to critic Marjorie Nicolson, part of the pleasure that readers derive from popular fiction is to "escape not from life, but from literature" ([1929] 1946, 113). For Nicolson, when we read popular novels "we have revolted from an excessive subjectivity to welcome objectivity; from long-drawn-out dissections of emotion to straightforward appeal to intellect; from reiterated emphasis upon men and women as victims either of circumstances or of their glands to a suggestion that men and women may consciously plot and consciously plan; from the 'stream of consciousness' which threatens to engulf us in its Lethean monotony to analyses of purpose, controlled and directed by a thinking mind; from formlessness to form; from the sophomoric to the mature; most of all, from a smart and easy pessimism which interprets men and the universe in terms of unmoral purposelessness to a rebelief in a universe governed by cause and effect" (113–14). Although Nicolson is referring specifically to detective stories, her characterization of the difference between high and popular literatures certainly resonates with the view put forward in *The Good Body*.

The Good Body is a conscious revolt against what it sees as the pretentiousness, "formlessness," "pessimism," and "Lethean monotony" of high literature (to borrow some of Nicolson's terms). At one point in the story Bonaduce expresses the desire to "hold the good mirror up" to hockey (117), and true to this dictum *The Good Body* is realist in mode and emphasizes the apparently mimetic connection between the fictionalized world of the novel and the real world of human existence. Gaston valorizes earnestness and humour while condemning seriousness and cynicism, and links this preference to literary straightforwardness as well. As Gordon Downie (2001, 10–11) puts it about hockey in general in his poem "The Goalie Who Lives across the Street": "No literary pretensions allowed. /

Two minutes for / 'I saw his blood, / a billowing crimson cloud / against the milk white ice.' / That's an infraction here." Although Gaston doesn't go so far as to affirm Richards' notion that "hockey is the non-intellectual impulse for life," he certainly shares Downie's belief that literary pretentiousness has no place in hockey (or hockey writing). As such, *The Good Body*, like the majority of hockey novels, remains conspicuously absent of aspirations to high literature. Furthermore, the grad-school scenes and caricatures work in many ways to deflate such devices as boring, pretentious, elitist, and ineffectual.[6] At one point in the story Bonaduce finds a way to work the word "postmodern" into a grad-school seminar presentation simply by saying "this book is not postmodern, but good old-fashioned storytelling" (235). This description clearly seems intended to apply to *The Good Body* as well, and perhaps to the writing of hockey novels in general. By rejecting the relativity and aesthetic complexity of postmodernism, *The Good Body* appears to deliver the "welcome objectivity" that Nicolson specifies in opposition to the "excessive subjectivity" of high literature. Furthermore, *The Good Body* associates being "postmodern" with the sort of cynicism that Bonaduce frequently condemns in his university-aged roommates: "You laugh at the purity of [musician] Del Shannon, it's your loss. Live your lives in a snarkier-than-thou postmodern house of mirrors, go ahead" (113).

By condemning the pessimism, pretentiousness, and inaccessibility of high literature, Gaston attempts to valorize the straightforwardness of popular literature. But while *The Good Body* values straightforwardness and offers many of the readerly pleasures that Nicolson associates with popular literature, it also acknowledges the danger that popular literature's reliance on convention might make it staid and predictable. Another way of saying this, perhaps, is that Gaston wants to write a novel that, to borrow from cultural critic Peter Swirski, is able "to identify and to satisfy a taste shared among a large number of people" while exposing the "world of semantic and cultural difference between the *lowest* and the *largest* common denominator" (2005, 5; italics in original). Simply put, *The Good Body* seems to suggest that working in the popular mode doesn't mean abandoning intellect or originality, and part of Gaston's purpose is to explore the difficulties of writing hockey in a way that is vibrant and engaging while remaining straightforward enough to avoid the "high" literature pitfalls of pretentiousness and inaccessibility.

For instance, when Bonaduce first begins contemplating his novel, he wonders what sort of story to write: "A pack of anecdotes? The exotic stuff? He'd seen a goalie's artery slashed. He'd seen teammates shit their pants during the game ... Or should he just write a stupid Rocky story about a guy who overcomes the odds? Everyone liked that crap, maybe even Jan [Bonaduce's professor]. Bill Spunska, clumsy immigrant, barely makes the team but scores the winning *yadda* with *yadda* left on the clock in the *yadda yadda* finals. Do you do the social comment? Team-as-microcosm thing? Modern gladiators, boxed vicarious bloodwar, testosteronic bugs in a bell jar. Do you write for an audience at all? Or do you just scribble for yourself and hope someone else gloms onto your heartbeat?" (116). This passage essentially catalogues the stereotypical conventions and plot trajectories frequently expressed in hockey narratives; in fact, the mention of Bill Spunska is a direct reference to the later two novels of Scott Young's juvenile hockey trilogy. Many recognizable moments from Canadian hockey novels are suggested by this list, if only in part or semblance, and these similarities highlight the difficulty of writing hockey without lapsing into bland conventions and familiar stereotypes. By acknowledging the dangers of convention and cliché, as well as the difficulty of "holding the good mirror up," Gaston recognizes the fundamental difficulty of producing hockey literature that is popular in appeal but fresh, vibrant, and intelligent in approach. Certainly *The Good Body* does take on many of the conventions of the hockey novel genre. It is essentialist about national identity (American fans are seen to specifically enjoy hockey violence and the game appears to guarantee Canadian cultural distinction), works to reinforce a version of traditional masculinity, and employs the familiar plot trajectory of an aging hockey protagonist coming to terms with his waning physical prowess. But this is perhaps the point: *The Good Body* doesn't attempt to disrupt convention so much as to use it in the production of what is simply and self-describedly a "good old-fashioned story."

If Gaston's writing of a "good old-fashioned story" rather than a "snarkier-than-thou postmodern house of mirrors" appears to unite the realms of mind and body and valorize popular fiction (both of which can be seen in turn as attempts to theorize and make possible the idea of a "hockey literature"), it is also perhaps, following Huyssen's suggestion that mass culture is associated with femininity, a way of branding the popular as sufficiently masculine. Again,

Bonaduce's New Man masculinity isn't a way of escaping conventional hockey identities and narratives so much as an attempt to
accommodate them to the current cultural moment. By incorporating the putatively feminine pursuit of literature into his masculine
identity, Bonaduce appears to respond to the critiques of feminism
and open up new identity possibilities for hockey-playing men while
maintaining and asserting the core masculine values of toughness
and strength (thus exemplifying Savran's claim, above, that despite
involving men in traditionally feminine pursuits New Man masculinity "by no means signals a repudiation of traditionally masculine
goals"). Contra the relativity, pretentiousness, and pessimism of high
literature, then, Gaston's adumbration of earnestness, optimism, and
straightforwardness in popular literature remains grounded in the
apparent solidity of the "good (masculine) body."

Like Bonaduce, Willie Mulligan in *Puck Is a Four Letter Word* is a
hockey-playing character who attempts to turn the game into literature. Willie is attributed with authorship of his narrative in the opening pages, although Orr doesn't exploit this device nearly as much
as Gaston. For the majority of the novel Willie functions simply as a
first-person narrator rather than a self-consciously metafictional
author–narrator combination. Furthermore, Willie's motivations for
turning hockey into literature are decidedly different than Bonaduce's,
as the opening sentences of *Puck Is a Four Letter Word* make clear:
"So what's a farmer named Willie Mulligan doing writing a book on
hockey? ... Simple. A New York publisher's big cash advance induced
my decision to 'go literary'" (1). Although Mulligan and Bonaduce
differ in their motivations, *Puck Is a Four Letter Word* implicitly proposes the possibility of a "hockey literature" in largely the same way
as *The Good Body*: by uniting the realms of mind and body, negotiat-
ing the gap between high and low cultures, and founding these medi-
ations on the apparent solidity of traditional masculine toughness.

While *The Good Body* sees academia as effete, elitist, and generally out of touch with "the ordinarys in the cheap seats," *Puck Is a
Four Letter Word* sees university education as integral to developing
the mental component of the mind–body unity it endorses. Both
Willie and his best friend, Hartley Laidlaw, are university educated,
and as a result are able effortlessly to negotiate the varied social
worlds that they routinely traverse, from locker room to publicity
press gala to small-town rural Ontario (where Willie is a farmer
in the off-season). At one point in the story the players attend a

publicity dinner with team management and financiers, and Willie complains that "I'm regarded as a jock, maybe not too bright, and the result is perfunctory chit-chat" (59). When Willie tells a marketing director and banking manager about his farm, the banker basically implies that it is an amateur operation. Willie retorts: "'Not quite,' I replied with some bite in my voice. 'I have a degree in animal husbandry and dairy science from Cornell University, 650 acres of prime Ontario farmland, 163 purebred Jersey cattle with 100 of them milkers, and a few hundred thousand worth of equipment. Starting from scratch, the outlay would be at least three million dollars'" (59). The banker promptly apologizes for being patronizing. Later in the story some of the younger players complain about having to attend another such publicity event, and Willie tells them to "use what's in your head" (174). He goes on to inform his teammates that a casual conversation with one of the teams' financiers once resulted in $8,500 worth of tractor tires, with the simple proviso that Willie and his brother (who co-manages the farm) would have to record certain performance details and send them to the manufacturer. Encouraged by Willie's example, the younger players try their luck and find they can negotiate class differences far better than expected.

The point of all this is that Willie's off-ice proficiency and intelligence allow him to work as a cultural mediator. In addition to being a skilled and knowledgeable farmer, Willie challenges hockey stereotypes by listening to jazz music and enjoying fine dining. Hartley Laidlaw does the same with his training as a lawyer, and, along with Willie, helps the players negotiate better free agency rights from the stingy and manipulative NHL owners. Furthermore, throughout the story Willie and Hartley work to educate some of the younger players on the team, teaching them about hockey but also encouraging them to be open-minded and articulate. For instance, one player who is particularly crass, belligerent, and undisciplined, Baby Joel, eventually manages to control his temper through Willie and Hartley's instruction, and toward the end of the story surprises them by using the word "antithesis" in conversation (274). This throwaway moment signifies, of course, a broadening of Baby Joel's identity horizons and privileges the New Man well-roundedness that *Puck Is a Four Letter Word* generally puts forward through Willie and Hartley. Another way of saying all this is that Willie and Hartley seem intended to address the problem that Young and Robertson propose through the character of Billy Duke in *Face-Off*, that "too often athletes are treated as hunks of meat with little or no academic potential" (1971, 2).

One of the central ways in which Willie's New Man intelligence and sophistication are expressed is through his refereeing of excessive hockey violence. "I don't like seeing blood on the ice," Willie quips at one point in the story, "especially when it's mine" (19). Later Willie comments that "it's distasteful to poke a man in the face with a bare fist and I wish they'd do away with [fighting]. But even more, I wish they'd stop shit like sticks in the face. An inch away from the eye is too close" (158). What Willie is doing in these passages is to draw relative lines of acceptability, and his belief that fighting (borderline violence) is more honourable than the cheap shot of a stick in the face (quasi-criminal violence) certainly echoes the conventional wisdom of hockey culture and traditional masculinity. Willie is somewhat exceptional among hockey novel protagonists, however, in that he doesn't see fighting and violence as "naturally" or inherently part of the game.

Willie's disdain for even borderline violence becomes most fully apparent by juxtaposition to the team's belligerent coach, Andy Jackson. Jackson is seen as a bad coach largely because he emphasizes physical contact over skill, and for his refusal to apply systematic play, scouting, or instruction to his role. In other words, Jackson is a bad coach because he refuses to think and teach, to exercise the kind of well-rounded intelligence that Willie and Hartley represent. Jackson is described by Willie as an anachronism, a relic from an era of hockey when roughness and aggression were enough to win. In many ways Jackson seems intended to parody hard-nosed hockey men such as Conn Smythe, the strong-willed and outspoken coach, manager, and president who presided over the Toronto Maple Leafs throughout the 1930s, 40s, and 50s, and whose coaching doctrine "if you can't beat 'em in the alley, you can't beat 'em on the ice" has become a hockey cliché (see Smyth with Young 1981). The idea of "beating 'em in the alley," in fact, is so well known that in *Salvage King, Ya!* Drinkwater makes fun of it without bothering to cite its origin: "The ex-goon coach actually gives a stirring speech without mentioning beating them in the alley. Instead he says, 'If I'm a gentleman and you're a gentleman, then who will milk the cow?' Such candour and metaphor. I see Pulitzers in his future" (94). Although Drinkwater mocks the phrase "beating 'em in the alley" as a cliché, he certainly ascribes to the idea on the ice: his hockey experience in *Salvage King, Ya!* is a litany of fighting, checking, grinding, and enduring injury. Drinkwater's Intended even goes so far as to describe the game as "a colder version of lions and Christians" (86). This is precisely the aspect of the game that the discerning hockey players in *Puck Is a Four Letter Word* disdain, and that coach Jackson, through his resemblance to Smythe and others like him, represents. At root, Jackson's ignorance is seen as a function of education. When it becomes clear to Willie and Hartley that Jackson is a terrible coach, they begin to take matters into their own hands by offering instruction to the younger members of the team. Angered by their interference, Jackson sarcastically retorts that "I'm sure lucky to have two genius college boys to tell me how to do things" (161). Within the framework of the narrative, of course, it is Willie and Hartley who appear sensible and intelligent, while Jackson – as well as the bully masculinity he represents – appears anachronistic and foolish.

While Willie dislikes borderline violence and would like to see it removed from the game, it becomes clear early in his career that he will have to tolerate and even perpetrate this level of violence to some extent. At one point in the story Willie recalls playing in a junior game before ever making it to the NHL, taking a particularly rough hit and hearing his mother yelling at him from the stands: "Why do you let that jerk push you around? Don't you know how to slash and spear?" (18). The moment is intended to be comedic, but the message remains abundantly clear: Willie will have to come to terms with the reality that to play hockey at an elite level, he needs to be willing, at least to some extent, to return violence with violence. It doesn't take Willie long to accept this fact after he is crosschecked from behind by another goon: "when I saw the kid laughing and heard the people cheering him, I went after him" (19). In other words, Willie is able to cultivate what Bonaduce describes as the basic level of toughness that "you need just to play the game" (*The Good Body*, 139), which sometimes involves sticking up for oneself against aggressive opponents.

Later in the story Willie is able to share this lesson with one of his Big Green teammates, Sven Stinquist, a Norwegian player who in addition to playing for the Big Green is completing a PhD in anthropology. Willie tells Sven that if opposing players take liberties with him on the ice he'll "have to return a certain amount," going on to explain that "I'm not very tough, but, at times, I'm forced to stick up for myself" (109). When Sven suggests that "fighting with fists has no place in sport" and wonders "why ... they allow it in professional hockey" (109), Willie explains that "those who run the league want [fighting] because they think the fans in the United States like to see fights. They also talk about the safety-valve factor, that if the players can't fight they'll use their sticks to get rid of frustrations. They see fighting as less dangerous" (109). Echoing the literature of sport psychology regarding catharsis theory, Sven immediately protests the NHL party line on violence because it detracts from player agency. Willie ends the discussion by agreeing with Sven, telling his friend that the players have made such arguments time and time again but that management has been unwilling to budge. It is clear, then, that Sven will need to learn the same lesson Willie had upon entering junior hockey: that playing the game requires a certain level of physical toughness and a willingness to stick up for oneself against aggressive opponents.

The above exchange between Willie and Sven is important because it suggests the extent to which hockey violence is a function of culture rather than nature. Most of the characters in the heroic trajectory discussed earlier must symbolically become men by learning to participate in borderline violence because it is naturally and inherently a fixed and immutable "part of the game." This is not the case in *Puck Is a Four Letter Word*. By emphasizing the extent to which the league allows and encourages hockey violence and by asserting the realistic possibilities of player agency and self-control, *Puck Is a Four Letter Word* challenges both the naturalness with which other hockey novels depict borderline violence and the boundaries by which many of these novels delineate acceptability from excess. Although it acknowledges hockey violence as a social construction, however, *Puck Is a Four Letter Word* ultimately maintains the requirement of mandatory toughness as a feature of the masculine identity expressed through hockey. Despite being cultural mediators and "genius college boys," the New Man characters in *Puck Is a Four Letter Word* must still be willing to drop the gloves and fight when circumstances require. Like *The Good Body*, then, *Puck Is a Four Letter Word* negotiates the distinction between high and low cultures and combines the realms of mind and body in such a way as to make room for a hockey literature that – while opening up a wider range of identity possibilities for hockey-playing men and thereby accommodating itself to changing societal attitudes about gender – remains ultimately rooted in "masculine" strength and physicality.

THE SEXUAL ATHLETE:
BUS RIDE AND THE UNINVITED GUEST

In an article on "The Aesthetics and Erotics of Hockey," Alison Pryer sees the game as a "ritualized gender performance, a celebratory, communal expression of heterosexual, heteronormative culture" (2002, 73). According to Pryer, the game is a "phallic drama" in which "a player must control his phallic stick well in order to shoot the small, seminal puck into a vaginal goal cavity" (74). Although Pryer concedes, quoting Freud, that "sometimes a cigar is just a cigar" (74), it occasionally seems applicable to pose such sexually suggestive readings of Canadian hockey novels as well. *Dawson City Seven*, for instance, characterizes Boston Mason's initial reaction to the game in markedly sexual terms. When Mason sees hockey for the first time upon arriving in Dawson City, he describes the game in terms of its violence: "men tore at each other with their elbows and sticks, frequently sending one to the ice who zigged when he should have zagged, without all his teeth left or with a badly swollen shin" (115). As Mason watches this spectacle from the sidelines, his skates already laced up and awaiting an opportunity to join the play, he feels an intense physical desire for action: "with my bird's-eye view of this carnage I felt the urgency you feel when you get excited physically, and I surged into the crowd when one poor soul limped to the side grimacing and holding his ankle" (115). The almost sexual release of Mason's "surge" into the play resolves the "physical excitement" aroused by the violent spectacle before him; in other words, Mason's first experience with hockey bears striking resemblance to an orgasm.

The idea of hockey as an erotic spectacle and activity is central to the myth of the sexual athlete. Korol's characterization of the sexual athlete mythology is drawn from Messner and Sabo, who suggest that "the phrase 'sexual athlete' commonly refers to male heterosexual virtuosity in the bedroom. Images of potency, agility, technical expertise, and an ability to attract and satisfy women come to mind" (1994, 36). According to Burstyn, the erotic appeal of the sexual athlete contains several aspects of heroic masculinity, one of which is the "physical bravery and muscularity [that] is associated with working and soldiering heroes" (1999, 37). When women don't recoil from violence in hockey novels (a plot device that will be discussed further in the following chapter), they are often depicted as sexually aroused by it. It is no coincidence, for instance, that in *Face-Off* Billy Duke has his first sexual encounter with the daughter of the family he is boarding with while playing junior hockey on the same night she comes to a game and watches him get into two fights and require stitches. In keeping with this pattern of violence appearing to qualify men for sexual "rewards," the exemplary novels to be discussed in this section – *Bus Ride* and *The Uninvited Guest* – both perform the myth of the sexual athlete by comparing the struggles of their hockey-playing protagonists to war. By learning to stand up to opponents, take competition seriously, and, indeed, to fight the battle of life as it confronts them metaphorically through sport, the central characters of these novels become symbolically worthy of the women they desire.

It should be noted from the outset that the sexual athlete is a particularly pernicious myth of masculinity when enacted in real-life sporting cultures. Many male athletes apply the expectations of athletic dominance and conquest to their relationships with women as well, and the result is that "dating becomes a sport in itself, and 'scoring,' or having sex with little or no emotional involvement, is a mark of masculine achievement" (Messner and Sabo 1994, 38). In this configuration "sexuality" easily becomes synonymous with "successful conquest" (Korol 2006, 192). By encouraging male athletes to see sexuality as a form of competition similar to sport itself, the idea of the sexual athlete has often resulted in the real-world sexual manipulation, abuse, and even rape, of women.

When Bill Underhill and Tony Chiello fight their respective hockey wars in *Bus Ride* and *The Uninvited Guest*, they are affirming the familiar dressing-room assumption that skill in sport somehow "naturally" translates into virility, potency, and sexual entitlement, potentially appealing to male readers who identify with these ideas in much the same way that real-life dressing-room banter about sexual conquest might. Part of the sexual athlete mythology, according to Burstyn, is the idea that "women become symbols in the masculine imagination of what men are fighting for (the rewards for their sacrifices)" (1999, 171). The "gladiator on the cover of *Sports Illustrated*," then, "is the symbolic warrior, the ideal male," while the "sex worker on the cover of *Penthouse* is his symbolic lover – his reward" (35). Both *Bus Ride* and *The Uninvited Guest* suggest the idea of women as a reward for athletic achievement through their depictions of female love-interest characters as happy sexual objects whose worth is determined largely by the prowess of their hockey-playing paramours. Both novels effectively see women as trophies, prizes to be won through male hockey heroism, and both represent their female characters as enthusiastically embracing this identity.

Bus Ride begins with an outdoor hockey game between the Point's Junior B team and that of a nearby town, Landsend. The teams are involved in a playoff series, the next game of which will be played in Landsend. Bill Underhill, the novel's protagonist and the Point's star player, has scored three goals but is being bothered by an opposing player, Danulchuck, who "had forty pounds on [Bill] and swung his weight recklessly ... like a berserk bruin with an assful of bees." Bill is initially reluctant to stick up for himself against his aggressor: "though he himself was tall and strong, he had not honed these muscles for the purpose of brawling" (10). As the game ends, Danulchuck hits Bill with a vicious elbow that knocks him to the ice and gives him a bloody nose. Although the crowd protests the hit, Danulchuck escapes without penalty or retribution. In generic terms, this plot structure is abundantly familiar: a tough but unaggressive adolescent protagonist deals with the excessive roughness of an opposing player. But Bill is soon confronted by another challenge, one less common in the framework of the hockey *Bildungsroman*.

The most popular and wealthy player on the team, Skip McKeough, has his own car and will drive to the next game at Landsend rather than ride the bus that will bring the team and many of the townsfolk to support them. Skip is well-known for his womanizing and underage drinking, and Bill is jealous of his sexual conquests, especially those with Lena, a girl whom Bill's mother had been "inclined to call ... 'a promiscuous little slut'" (22). Skip offers Bill the chance to ride along with him to the game in Landsend in order to "occupy" Lena while Skip works his charms on another girl he has been eyeing. Bill is certain that this date with Lena will result in sex, a prospect that thrills him greatly, but he is faced with the moral dilemma this poses in relation to his own girlfriend, Penny, whose sexual unavailability frustrates Bill immensely (we learn this in the following chapter). In a sense, the stage has been set: Bill will have to face Danulchuck again in the next game, and will have to decide whether or not to abandon his relationship with Penny for a fling with Lena.

In keeping with the military aspects of the hockey *Bildungsroman* identified earlier, Bill's hockey struggle is explicitly likened to his father's experience fighting in the First World War. When Bill eventually wins his hockey victory over Danulchuck by punching his opponent in the face, the triumph (which is explicitly characterized in military terms, as Bill is said to have "carved his way across No Man's Land" [110]), appears to qualify him for a sexual "reward" from Lena. Having won his "war," which is also, of course, the *Bildungsroman* moment of achieved maturity, Bill's decision is made: he sees himself as deserving what Peggy has withheld from him, and, as such, justified in his planned infidelity. Earlier in the story the narrative had described Bill fantasizing about Lena as if his thoughts were a "kind of theatre" in "Technicolour" and "3-D" (73). As the narrative "camera" zooms in across Lena's naked body and arrives between her legs, it reveals "a hockey net ... woven with pubic hair" and "goal posts in labular pink" (73). Aside from echoing Pryer's characterization of hockey eroticism, this fantasy sequence makes clear that Bill conceives of Lena's sexual availability in terms of his hockey prowess, an assumption that corroborates a comment from the narrator about minor hockey in the village: "to the victors, as they say, and the spoils of hockey in a village have always included bootleg beer and willing girls" (21). It is noteworthy, however, that Bill's violence against Danulchuck also seems to qualify him sexually from Lena's perspective; after the incident, she comes to visit him in the penalty box with "coy licentiousness in her voice and look" (109). Lena, then, appears an enthusiastic participant in the sexual athlete mythology, a willing and eager "reward" for Bill's hockey victory. Although events conspire to prevent Bill and Lena from consummating their desires, Bill seems to have symbolically "earned" her affections and learned the lesson that his father's war stories deliver about being a man: that "blood from our wounds [is] the only badge worth wearing" (172).

While *Bus Ride* attaches a narrative of sexual athleticism to the typical hockey *Bildungsroman* plot of becoming a man through hockey toughness (thus rendering the idea of the sexual athlete a "natural" part of Bill's maturation and development of masculine identity), *The Uninvited Guest* focuses on an adult character who had failed the test of hockey toughness in his youth but is later offered a second chance. Tony Chiello has many of the skills necessary for hockey success, but his professional hockey career ultimately fails because he is too short. As Tony grows older he becomes increasingly bitter about this fact, eventually taking a job as caretaker of the Stanley Cup as a way of compensating for never having won the trophy.[7] It is in this capacity that Tony embarks on a trip to Romania with Dragos Petrescu, the first Romanian-born player ever to win the Stanley Cup (Dragos plans to use his day with the Cup to bring it to his wedding). During the trip Tony becomes attracted to Dragos' sister, Diana, and learns about Romanian culture, specifically that the national passion for backgammon rivals that of Canada for hockey.

It is through backgammon that Tony is ultimately able to win a symbolic hockey victory and thereby demonstrate his worthiness of Diana's affections. At one point in the story backgammon is said to contain the "most essential elements of war. Unpredictability. Fate. Stupid luck" (219). Beyond reiterating the connection between military service and masculine toughness, the idea of random chance implied by this characterization evokes Tony's failure in professional hockey due to his height, an unplanned contingency for which no amount of training or strategy could compensate. The lesson Tony needs to learn in *The Uninvited Guest* is that his bitterness about not having made it in professional hockey is neither comely nor "manly." Diana believes that a man should not be "whining and sobbing about some lost thing, some nothing" (218–19), and makes it clear to Tony that he must learn to compete with stoic perseverance, discipline, and tenacity in the "ultimate struggle" of which every game is a representative component (131). By the end of the story Diana has set up an elaborate challenge to test Tony's resolve. She arranges to have the Stanley Cup taken from Dragos' wedding and hidden, offering Tony the following exchange: if he can defeat an exceptionally skilled backgammon player, the grandfather of Dragos' new bride, he will reclaim the Cup and receive a kiss from Diana.

Tony's struggle to embody the masculine ideal that both hockey and Diana require of him is most fully expressed by his desire to win the Stanley Cup. At one point in the story Tony asks Dragos what it takes to win the Cup, and Dragos tells him "[you must] make it so that hockey is the only thing to make you forget your greatest sadness. Allow hockey to replace the love and everyday affections of grandparents and the only real home you have ever known, to stand in for a language that slips away from you every day in a thousand unstoppable ways. Anyone can win your precious cup if they do just this one thing" (216). Dragos explains that he used hockey to compensate for the feelings of stress, inadequacy, frustration, and sadness that accompanied his immigration to Canada at a young age, but his comments convey a depth of perseverance and determination that perhaps imply Tony could have succeeded in hockey despite his short stature if only his commitment had been strong enough. When Diana poses her challenge at the end of the novel, Tony is given a symbolic second chance to win his Stanley Cup, and more importantly, to embody the masculine perseverance and toughness it takes to do so. When Tony accepts Diana's challenge, Dragos exclaims that "I recognize the look in his eye. I have seen this look in the locker room. This is the look of a man who will not leave here without the Cup. If he has to kill us all, he will take that cup, and whatever else he wants, back with him to Canada" (232). Dragos' addition of "whatever else he wants," of course, suggests Diana. As the game is about to begin, Diana whispers in Tony's ear: "Remember, he is not an old man. He is your opponent – your enemy" (232). As with Bill Underhill in *Bus Ride*, it is Tony's triumph over an enemy that simultaneously confirms his masculinity and entitles him to possess the woman he desires. But even more so than Lena's sexually suggestive approval of Bill's hockey violence, it is Diana who has set the terms of her erotic relationship with Tony. Diana seems to believe that in order to be worthy of her, Tony must exemplify the kind of masculine toughness that enabled Dragos to succeed in professional hockey. Although Tony's battle is in backgammon rather than hockey, it has been established earlier in the story by Dragos' father that the two games are remarkably similar (165). Tony's triumph, then, which is confirmed by the final chapter in which he prepares his home in Canada for Diana's coming and their impending marriage, is very much the triumph of the sexual athlete: it requires him to embody hockey toughness and rewards him for his efforts with both the Stanley Cup and the woman he desires. Certainly the fact that Tony and Diana end up getting married suggests their relationship to be more than the simply sexual connection expressed in the sexual athlete mythology, thus blurring a distinction that hockey novels tend to draw between "wives" and "groupies," which will be revisited next chapter. This variation aside, however, *The Uninvited Guest*, like *Bus Ride*, ultimately subscribes to the view that masculinity is constituted by competitiveness, perseverance, tenacity, and toughness, the demonstration of which through sportive victory somehow qualifies or entitles a man to possess the woman he desires.

Of the mythologies of masculinity discussed this chapter, the idea of the sexual athlete is most directly related to the process by which individual men become incorporated within the collective of the team. The idea that the game facilitates camaraderie and fraternity among men is an important component of the hockey myth, but it is necessary to recognize the extent to which this unity is predicated on certain compulsory behaviours and practices that often attempt to declaim masculinity in problematic and harmful ways. The sexual athlete mythology is one such way in which men appear to demonstrate their belonging within the culture of the team. Such beliefs and practices cause all sorts of trouble in the relationships they foster between men and women, and in the ways in which men conceive of their own gender identities and self-worth.

6

The Homosocial Dressing Room

The idea that hockey works to create camaraderie, trust, friendship, and solidarity among men is a frequent trope in Canadian hockey writing. From Dryden's description of the energy of the dressing room as a "kind of unremitting noise that no one hears and everyone feels" ([1983] 1984, 29) to Gaston's suggestion that "it's all about the beer [and] the boys" (2006) many commentators have remarked on the ability of the game to bring men together and foster social relationships. Gruneau and Whitson refer to this "discourse of team-as-community" as "the myth of community and social interdependence," and suggest that this myth is "ideological ... not because it is completely false, but because it is only partially true" (1993, 152). At its best, hockey can be a healthy and beneficial way for men to establish friendships and community in an often alienating and impersonal society. But hockey can work to divide as well as to unite. In the words of Robidoux, the "shared male experience of ... hockey [both] promotes segregation between men and women" and "segregates and devalues other men that do not fit within [its] hegemonic structure" (2001, 142). This is made evident in hockey novels primarily through the institution of the team, a homosocial community built in part around the exclusion of women and gay men and maintained through certain expected behaviours and attitudes that appear intended to declaim masculinity and thereby guarantee belonging.

According to Eve Kosofsky Sedgwick, the term homosocial "is a neologism, obviously formed by analogy with 'homosexual,' and

just as obviously meant to be distinguished from 'homosexual'"
(1985, 1). Sedgwick suggests, however, that homosociality encom-
passes (rather than differs from) homosexuality, and that sexual
identity positions should actually be seen as a continuum between
the socially normative (heterosexuality) and the socially prohibited
(homosexuality). If "heterosexual" and "homosexual" are poles on a
spectrum rather than discrete and essentially opposed categories,
there must necessarily be some space of confusion and instability
between these positions. According to Sedgwick, "for a man to be a
man's man is separated only by an invisible, carefully blurred,
always-already-crossed line from being 'interested in men'" (89).
The existence of this blurred and medial territory results in what
Sedgwick calls "homosexual panic," the heteronormative regulation
of male–male relationships that has structured the discourse of modern Western societies.

With only one exception to be discussed momentarily, hockey novels attempt to portray homosexual and heterosexual as discrete and
essential categories that can be fully understood, identified, and – in
the case of homosexuality – appropriately marginalized. In other
words, hockey novels consistently repress their anxieties over sexual
instability and the possibility of homoerotic attraction between "heterosexual men." This repression is particularly evident in passages
such as the one discussed last chapter where Batterinski relishes the
male–male physicality of an on-ice fight. The pleasure Batterinski
takes from this encounter, *The Last Season* insists, is combative rather than sexual, and appears to confirm his heterosexual identity
rather than call it into question or complicate it. Messner and Sabo
suggest, however, that "the salient social meaning of ... images of
male power and grace [in sport] lie not in identification with violence
... but rather in narcissistic and homoerotic identification with the
male body," and, as such, "perhaps the violence represents a denial of
the homoeroticism in sports" (1994, 96–8). Although Batterinski's
enjoyment of violent physical contact with another man appears to
declaim his heterosexual toughness, it also trades on a homoerotic
pleasure that *The Last Season* subconsciously or deliberately denies.
By attempting to foreclose on the homoerotic subtexts of male–male
physicality and dressing-room camaraderie, hockey novels refuse to
recognize that "people's sexual desire[s]" can rarely ever be "even
momentarily ... transparent to themselves" (Sedgwick 1990, 26). In
doing so these novels remain firmly in step with hockey culture itself,

which is powerfully homophobic and coercively heteronormative. By denying the continuum of desire between heterosexual and homosexual and positing this distinction near the centre of their construction of masculine toughness, hockey novels perpetuate the caustic attitudes and beliefs that continue to structure the culture of the game. For instance, the NHL remains the only major North American professional sports league in which no active or former player has publicly come out as a homosexual.

There are, however, small signs that hockey's culture of coercive heteronormativity may be changing. Brendan Burke, the student manager of the Miami University hockey team and son of Toronto Maple Leafs general manager Brian Burke (a famous proponent of "pugnacity, testosterone, truculence, and belligerence"), announced his homosexuality publicly in November 2009, prompting widespread discussion in the hockey community about the ugly reality of homophobia within the game. Burke had been a promising goaltender before becoming a student manager for his university team, but quit playing over concerns about exposing his sexual orientation to his teammates. By validating hockey homophobia in the minds of readers and reinforcing this harmful status quo through coercive repetition, hockey novels help to maintain a culture that is harmful to the developing identities of gay youth and which undoubtedly ends up deterring young people such as Burke from playing the game.[1] It is worth noting that several hockey texts in other genres have been more progressive on the issue of hockey and homosexuality than the adult-oriented hockey novels discussed in this study. For instance, the film *Breakfast with Scot* (Lynd 2007) depicts an openly gay former NHL player who adopts a young boy along with his male partner, while Bidini's *The Five Hole Stories* includes a story in which a thinly veiled doppelgänger for the former NHL goaltender Grant Fuhr challenges the sexual strictures of hockey culture by fantasizing about his teammate "Wayne Bradley" (an obvious reference to Wayne Gretzky): "the butterfly goalie and the all-time all-star moving together in a total representation of male love, our passion cascading across the fag-hating frozen tundra" (2006, 34).[2] As Blake suggests of Bidini's Wayne Bradley story, these texts "are unique in hockey fiction because [they] directly [portray] homosexual attraction ... [and invite] us to reconsider the assumption that masculinity is a 'package deal' that includes heterosexuality" (2010, 83).

Only one adult-oriented hockey novel, Michael Markus' self-published *East of Mourning* (2001), explicitly reflects Sedgwick's continuum of desire between homosexual and heterosexual, but does so quite sinisterly in its approving depiction of an inappropriate relationship between a young player and his minor league hockey coach. *East of Mourning* is narrated by Brian, a thirty-year-old man with no ambition or prospects until he meets Kyle Clark, a ten-year-old player on a minor league hockey team that Brian grudgingly ends up coaching. According to Brian's description of Kyle, the boy "glows with a special grace, a perfect, timely mix of genes, personality and intangibles" (5). Acting on his disturbing obsession with Kyle and the nihilistic philosophy that life is "an accident ... on the floor of the universe" (61), Brian begins a long process of earning Kyle's trust and manipulating situations and circumstances so as to gradually turn the boy against his family and friends. As the following passage illustrates, Brian and Kyle's relationship is intensely and inappropriately physical even in its early stages: "'Are you coming on to me?' I asked in a husky voice, clutching a hand to my chest. Kyle laughed and murmured, 'Oh baby, oh baby.' He blew into my ear. 'You're making me crazy.' 'You are crazy.' I grabbed his wrist and flipped him over on his back onto the bed. We wrestled; mattress springs squealing and bedclothes flying. It was always good to hear Kyle laugh. Everything was all right again" (106). Such homoerotic encounters are a major part of the process by which Brian builds his relationship with Kyle and simultaneously turns the boy against other important people in his life, and *East of Mourning* is uncharacteristically up-front about this fact for a hockey novel. Later in the story when Kyle has become a teenager, several characters have a discussion about homosexuality and Kyle concludes that being gay might actually be preferable to being straight. What is apparent to readers throughout this exchange, if not to Kyle himself, is that Kyle has actually been exploring the complexity of sexual identities and his openness to homosexuality all along through his physical relationship with Brian. The novel ends with Brian arranging a set of circumstances which cause Kyle's mother to commit suicide and Kyle to murder his own father; unaware that Brian has orchestrated these events, Kyle turns to him to salvage the situation and ends up being legally adopted by Brian. Again, *East of Mourning* is disturbingly optimistic about this outcome: in the end, Brian has found a way to maintain his inappropriate relationship with Kyle indefinitely and, by way of Kyle's prospects in professional hockey, appears to have secured his own financial well-being in the process.

The issue of homoerotic attraction is addressed more progressively in one young-adult-oriented hockey novel, Diana Wieler's *Bad Boy* (1989). *Bad Boy* is the story of a self-confident gay player, Tusla Brown, who quietly pursues a relationship with another closeted teammate. When Tulsa's best friend, the novel's protagonist A.J. Brandiosa, discovers this secret relationship he begins to question his own sexuality. As A.J. struggles with feelings of confusion and denial that he might be sexually attracted to Tulsa, he becomes increasingly violent on the ice. Again, homoerotic violence appears to repress the possibility of homoerotic attraction. As A.J. feels less and less certain about his sexual identity, it is "the love song descending from the stands" whenever he gets in a fight that provides him with the illusion of stability and control (115). *Bad Boy* clearly implies a connection between A.J.'s repressed homoerotic attraction to Tulsa and the pleasure he takes in perpetrating on-ice violence; furthermore, the possibility that A.J. might act on his feelings is finally brought to light after the friends get into a physical fight. When A.J. finally confesses his sexual attraction to Tulsa, Tulsa replies that A.J.'s curiosity is different from his own confirmed homosexuality and refuses to explore a physical relationship. But while A.J. affirms this as the best course of action, he explicitly acknowledges that it is also an act of repression: "I know what you said about you and me not being the same, Tul[sa]. But I can't risk it. I can't ever have the chance to know, for sure" (179). Although the novel ends, then, with A.J. pursuing a heterosexual relationship with Tulsa's sister (a plot strand that has also been developed throughout the novel), *Bad Boy* recognizes the continuum of desire between homosexual and heterosexual and insists that sexual identities are far more complicated than most adult-oriented hockey novels are willing to acknowledge.

Eliding the unacknowledged subtext of homoerotic attraction that informs the homosocial relationships depicted in adult-oriented hockey novels is the appearance of heightened Platonic camaraderie and friendship between players. In addition to the "narcissistic and homoerotic identification with the male body" that Messner and Sabo identify, much of the appeal of hockey and other violent sports resides in the continued resonance of the "masculine" values they appear to enact and the promise of idyllic male community they frequently propose. This study's use of the word homosocial, then, includes both the unacknowledged erotic subtexts that hockey novels attempt to repress and the signification of idealized male community that they intend to convey, in which "relationships ... [exceed] mere friendship" but are "more of a brotherly kind of bond" (Robidoux 2001, 143). Probably the most striking feature of the factional rebellion that some of the players wage against management in Craig's *The Pro* is that despite "[defying] hockey's most basic creed" of supporting one's team at all costs, there is no animosity between the two camps of players: "yesterday the group had been cut off, divorced from the rest of the team by their stand. Yet, strangely enough, there had been no basic hostility in the dichotomy. They had been divided, but even in their division there had been a basic bond of unity, woven in many different places and through many different days and nights, that had still held them loosely together" (253). The myth of the team-as-community, then, appears to be so powerful that it trumps all other considerations, a highly idealized social bond based on loyalty, camaraderie, integrity, and trust.

In *Leisure Life: Myth, Masculinity and Modernity*, his study of a particular group of British working-class men, "the lads," sociologist Tony Blackshaw found that these men have reacted to the changing social and gender orders of the late twentieth century by creating for themselves a "leisure-life" world of homosocial community in which an aggressive form of traditional masculinity is enacted and asserted as ultimately valuable. Writing from the perspective of the lads, with whom he identifies to some extent, Blackshaw notes that "we have seen one comforting myth after another taken apart ... we have ... learned to close our shutters to guard against ... the intricate cogs of our masculine realism from being damaged. We have suffered setbacks of all kinds; but still we emerge intact ... because we keep our own narratives alive" (2003, 92–3). Despite feeling burdened, then, and sometimes compromised by the "all-consuming shapes that were women, love, cohabitations, marriages, divorce, children, financial responsibilities, the continual threat of unemployment and increasing public and private regulation," the lads perceive themselves as being enfolded within the "feeling of 'home,' of belonging, of happiness" supplied by their leisure-life world of male fraternity and solidarity (92, 93).

Blackshaw's account of the lads is instructive toward the function of the "team" in Canadian hockey novels as a way of preserving and enacting traditional masculinity. The majority of hockey novels appear directed at men whose masculine identities, like the lads, have been called into question or compromised by the perception of changing social and gender orders in the late twentieth and early twenty-first centuries. In the same way that the homosocial leisure-life world of the lads appears to "keep [their] own narratives alive," hockey novels suggest male community and solidarity as a way of reinstating certain "comforting myths" about masculine identity. The role of the team in Canadian hockey novels, then, is to provide individual men with purpose, direction, and camaraderie, the sense of "home, belonging, and happiness" that exists among the lads, and to propose traditional masculinity as the dominant value system of this collective. Rather than the unity of the "erotic, social, familial, economic, and political realms" that Sedgwick proposes (1985, 3), hockey novels, like the lads, view these spheres of male experience as separate and distinct, privileging the social realm of camaraderie, fraternity, and interdependence above the others because it appears to preserve masculine identity and guarantee belonging. In other words, hockey novels see the social relationships men foster through the game as a bulwark against instability and uncertainty in the other facets of their lives. Part of the pleasure that hockey novels potentially offer male readers, then, is to escape from such stresses in their own lives by vicariously participating as a member of the fictional team, partaking imaginarily in its unifying struggles, triumphs, goals and values, and, effectively, becoming "one of the guys."

To say all of this another way, the myth of the team-as-community appears to deliver the idealized male fraternity promised by national manhood, which suggests male community as both the rationale and reward for individual toughness and effort. The prospect of warm, brotherly fraternity is seen to justify the individual's hard work to fulfill his "manly" responsibilities to the varied collectives of family, corporation, nation, etc., while simultaneously appearing to grant respite from the pressures these efforts entail. The same is true of the national manhood enacted by hockey novels, in which the homosocial community of the team apparently gives players a reason to compete while enabling the masculine toughness this competition requires.

At one point in the *The Good Body* Bonaduce describes his teammates as "red and white warriors, tall and anonymous in their helmets and face cages ... they yipped, hollered, and punched each other's shoulders, a nervous herd urging itself to become something carnivorous" (217). By "urging [themselves] to become something carnivorous" the players – described here as "warriors," a significant characterization given that national manhood is often enacted and imagined through military service – affect a sort of aggregate strength in which the entire team can participate. Each individual appears empowered to compete in the upcoming game by his belonging in the collective and his shared stake in the team's energy and enthusiasm. *The Good Body* similarly sees the institution of the team as a mechanism for managing pain. According to Bonaduce, hockey is like war in that "a soldier's biggest fear is fear of cowardice" (140), the possibility of not measuring up to the expectation of masculine toughness and strength. The potential problem of cowardice, however, is apparently overcome by the individual's need for belonging and acceptance among his teammates: "It's harder to show pain than it is to just sit on it," Bonaduce suggests, when you're "on the bench surrounded by the guys" (140). In other words, the social sanction incurred by expressing weakness within the context of the team is actually worse than the bodily discomfort of enduring pain, and in this way, according to Bonaduce, the individual's "pain is absorbed by the team" (140). Thus, "the good body" in Gaston's novel is not only a masculine corporeal body but a corporate body in which individual men participate both to manage pain and experience pleasure (i.e., belonging, fraternity, solidarity, etc.).

Beyond enabling individuals to compete, the idea of hockey homosociality as a sort of *esprit de corps* purports to justify competition in the first place. At one point in *The Horn of a Lamb* Fred Pickle suggests that "hockey is not about scoring goals and dreaming of the NHL, just like the old wars were not about soldiers fighting for their countries or their moms or their wives – they fought and died for each other, the men who were with them every step of the way in the gas and explosions and the terrible things they had to see and it is wrong to say that being on a hockey team is just like that, buh, buh, it's as close as you'll get" (300). By seeing homosocial fraternity as the real reason for soldiering, and privileging this sort of brotherly community as, in a way, the apex of masculine experience, Fred suggests male collectivism as the rationale for individual effort. As with Blackshaw's characterization of the lads, Fred's description of hockey as an analogue for war subsumes all other spheres of existence (familial, political, economic, etc.) beneath the social and suggests the primacy of male–male friendship. The collective of the team, then, becomes "the basic unit of [the] world" and "accords each [player] his sense of ontological security" (2003, 53). This, of course, is precisely the ideological swindle of national manhood, in which individual men are encouraged to work and sacrifice in the service of the collective on the promise of an idealized and unrealizable masculine fraternity as their reward. As Nelson suggests of national manhood and Robidoux notes of professional hockey, the myth of masculine community and fraternity is constantly short-circuited by the competitive individualism of the capitalist marketplace and the hockey dressing room, respectively. At the end of the day, "the struggle for success in hockey appears to overwhelm any notion of fraternity, making the profession much more individualistic than the usual portrayal [i.e., the myth of community]" (2001, 144).

EXCLUSIONS I: WOMEN

Beyond promising an idealized and unrealizable degree of community and fraternity, the myth of social interdependence appears founded on the exclusion or marginalization of those who don't "belong," namely women and gay men. This section will discuss the exclusion of women. Probably the most straightforward way in which sport has functioned to promote the "gender dominance of men" (Burstyn 1999, 28) has been through the maintenance of athleticism as a masculine ideal. Despite the recent gains of high-school- and college-level women's sport throughout the 1960s and onward, as well as the increasing range of recreational athletic options available to women in contemporary society, "there is still a dynamic tension between traditional prescriptions for femininity and the image presented by active, strong, even muscular women" (Messner 2007, 38). The qualities and characteristics necessary for successful athletic competition are still predominantly associated with men and masculinity. By representing the game as a male preserve, hockey novels work to rehearse and establish the "undeniable 'fact' that there is at least one place where men are clearly superior to women" (38). Even the representations of New Man masculinity discussed last chapter – which appear on some level to incorporate the critiques of feminism and allow for broader identity possibilities among hockey-playing men – tend to see the game itself as one area of culture in which traditional gender roles still apply.

The word "homosocial" obviously implies insularity, and hockey novels support the hegemonic identification of masculinity with athleticism quite straightforwardly by banishing women and femininity from the game. Probably the most explicit articulation of this principle is Batterinski's simple assertion in *The Last Season* that "hockey [is] the masculine game." For Batterinksi, hockey demonstrates masculinity more than other sports because "only hockey has it all: the basic skill level required, strength, quick thought, imagination, body contact, [and] conquest" (70). By asserting "strength" and "thought" as masculine attributes, this passage implicitly marks their opposites, weakness and emotion, as feminine. The point of keeping women out of hockey, then, is to maintain a space in which the traditional male attributes of toughness, physicality, stoicism, rationality, and technical proficiency appear safe from the emasculating influences of "feminine" weakness and emotion, thus apparently maintaining the potency of traditional masculinity, the "superiority" of men, and reassuring male readers who identify with these ideas. This is often accomplished simply through throwaway details. Later in *The Last Season*, for instance, Batterinski calls into question the masculinity of his Tapiola Hauki teammates because of their scent: "You wouldn't smell cologne in the dressing room of the Broad Street Bullies. But now, kissing the inside of my sweater as I pull it down, that is what I do smell: perfume. It makes me want to puke" (96). The implication, of course, is that perfume – ostensibly a marker of femininity – implicitly detracts from the masculine toughness of the players. In fact, to push this slightly further, Batterinski's impulse "to puke" suggests the abjection of femininity, an actual physical revulsion from it.

Another such moment occurs in *Salvage King, Ya!*, when Drinkwater perceives his masculinity as compromised by a similar intrusion of the feminine. During one of the coach's motivational speeches ("we want pitbulls, not poodles, we want physical play!"), Drinkwater notices that when he fastens the strap on the side of his helmet, the motion is "exactly like a woman putting on an earring" (94). After this thought occurs, Drinkwater notes that "I try to do it a different way, but somehow just don't feel quite as brutal" (94). Later in *Salvage King, Ya!* Drinkwater receives a cut to the face and the referee puts a tampon on it to stop the bleeding: "The referee … puts something on my cut. 'Hey, what is that?' 'A tampon.' 'A tampon? You put a tampon on my face?' 'Sure, they're efficient at soaking up blood; any First Aid course will tell you that.' Logical or not, I don't like a tampon on me" (217). The reason Drinkwater doesn't want a tampon soaking up his blood, of course, is that he feels somehow compromised by the femininity it represents. All these examples, then, suggest moments in which masculine toughness is interrupted or diminished by the intrusion of unexpected items or thoughts associated with femininity (perfume, affixing an earring, a tampon).

One hockey novel in particular, *Dawson City Seven*, explicitly works to exclude femininity from the game and from athleticism in general. Although Reddick's narrator, Boston Mason, specifically professes not to be "anti-female," his learning to skate is characterized as a reaction against the "female yakking" of his mother and eight sisters (12). Yakking, of course, ostensibly represents the sort of emotional and sentimental effusiveness that hockey novels see as anathema to masculinity. Later in the story when Mason plays his first hockey game, it is expressly out of "the necessity to exert myself physically, to punish my body or someone else's for all the wrongs I believed had unjustly cascaded upon my shoulders" (114). In other words, Mason is characterized as needing to work through his frustrations physically rather than by talk, a stereotypically masculine response that aligns with his disdain for feminine "yakking." Of course, part of the (typically implicit) work of hockey novels in general is to accommodate masculine toughness to the realm of language and literature, and, as such, *Dawson City Seven* could be read on the whole as an attempt to code "yakking" as comfortably and sufficiently masculine, albeit less self-reflexively and deliberately than *The Good Body*.

One particularly interesting moment in *Dawson City Seven* occurs when women transgress the boundaries of the novel's narrowly established gender categories in order to actually participate in hockey. Not surprisingly, the women's game quickly becomes an object of ridicule for the novel's male characters: "The women's game gave us an opportunity for much comic relief, for Crazy Norman Watt – as a surprise to everybody – came onto the ice to referee it in a dress and hat, the hat decorated with chrysanthemums. On his shoulder he twirled a sunflower-patterned parasol. This caused an uproar with our crowd – with everybody – and we called to him as Miss Watt, and Doc noted he never did see such a helpful referee before, Crazy Miss Watt helping up any players who fell down close to him" (210–11). The supposed humour of this scene arises from the putative incongruity between women and hockey. Rather than supporting the women in their efforts to inhabit the physical realm that Mason had privileged earlier in his narrative, the male characters react with scorn, derisive parody, and even (in the case of Norman Watt) by taking physical liberties with the female players. In a sense, the women in *Dawson City Seven* are allowed to play hockey merely to show how ridiculous they are for wanting to do so. The reaction of the male characters to this episode, of course, is also a strategy of containment. By ridiculing the women's game, *Dawson City Seven* doesn't force or encourage its reader to reckon with the breakdown of gender distinctions that the prospect of female hockey players proposes.[3]

Even when hockey novels allow women to participate in the game or enjoy it as spectators, they typically propose limits on the extent of this involvement. Women can enjoy hockey and even excel at it, hockey novels seem to suggest, as long as they are differentiated from men by their weakness (signified by the inability to tolerate even brutal body contact, the lowest level in Smith's typology of athletic violence) or by their lack of passion for the game. In *Hockey Night in the Dominion of Canada*, for instance, Cyclone Taylor is surprised to learn that his girlfriend Thirza Cook is a proficient figure skater, and, more astonishingly, a hockey player as well. Their second date is a trip to one of Thirza's games: "[Taylor] had no idea what to expect from a women's hockey game. He knew there were lots of women's leagues around the country now, but he had never actually seen a woman play the game. He envisioned skirts and knee socks and giggling girls chasing the puck playfully across the ice. He had the uniforms just about right, but the rest of his vision couldn't have been more wrong. The women's game was played every bit as seriously as the men's. There was not as much contact – the women didn't wear much padding – but the action was fast and exciting. Taylor soon found himself cheering for Thirza almost as wildly as the fans who usually screamed for him" (110). Taylor soon overcomes his patronizing and chauvinistic assumptions, learning to appreciate and respect the women's game and Thirza's proficiency at it. Rather than the occasion for ridicule that women's hockey becomes in *Dawson City Seven*, *Hockey Night in the Dominion of Canada* suggests a fast-paced, vibrant, and exciting competition. But while the women's game in *Hockey Night in the Dominion of Canada* is played with skill and seriousness, it remains apparently inferior to the men's game because it lacks body contact. Later in the story the narrator informs us that Thirza no longer attends Cyclone Taylor's games, because she cannot tolerate the roughness of men's hockey: "As she had found herself more and more attracted to him, she had found his hockey games less and less enjoyable. The violent nature of the sport seemed so out of keeping with the man she knew" (224). What separates Thirza from Cyclone Taylor when it comes to hockey, then, isn't so much skill as the ability to perpetrate and withstand violence. If Thirza's hockey proficiency appears to threaten the inherent masculinity of hockey, this threat is contained by the suggestion of her feminine weakness and inability to tolerate violence. Similar moments in which female characters profess distaste for rough play or concern for the safety of hockey-playing men occur in *The Good Body*, *Salvage King, Ya!*, and *Puck Is a Four Letter Word*, functionally suggesting that "feminine" weakness has no place in hockey and signifying "masculine" toughness by contrast. In *Puck Is a Four Letter Word*, for instance, Willie's girlfriend Clarice, an otherwise competent, athletic, confident, and strong-willed woman, watches Willie play hockey and later tells him "I was so worried ... I don't know if I can watch you play again. It's so violent" (159).

Beyond excluding women from hockey on the basis of their apparent weakness, adult-oriented hockey novels tend to represent female characters as unable to fully grasp the glory of the game. In *Finnie Walsh*, for instance, when Finnie invites Joyce Sweeney, a girl who both Paul and Finnie are secretly attracted to, to watch the boys play hockey, she surprises them by responding that she would rather play than watch. The boys are clearly impressed with Joyce's skill, but are astounded after the game when she tells them she won't join them again because she isn't very interested in hockey. This episode seems to signify that while a female can play and even be good at hockey, it takes a male to truly love and appreciate the game. From the mother in *Understanding Ken* to the Intended in *Salvage King, Ya!* to Grace Wheeler in *The Age of Longing* to Leah in *The Good Body*, many of the female characters in Canadian hockey novels simply cannot grasp the game's importance as a male passion, a way of life, and, indeed, in some cases, an existential answer. According to *Heroes*, the consequences of this can be dire: as noted earlier (chapter 1, pp. 44–6), it is Patty Bayle's inability to love hockey in the way that her father and brother do which eventually appears to bring about her suicide.

While hockey novels don't require women to adulate or even understand hockey, they do require women to recognize and respect the game's importance to men. This idea is especially important in *Icelands* and is expressed through the novel's central female characters, Lina and Karen. Although Lina spends a good deal of time at the arena watching her son, Andrew, play, she isn't particularly interested in hockey. Over the course of the novel Lina becomes bitter about the game's importance to the men in her life, eventually retreating from these relationships and becoming increasingly unhappy. Karen, on the other hand, is able to learn the "necessary" lesson that relating to men requires accepting and respecting the importance of hockey in their lives. Throughout the story Karen doesn't get the kind of love and support that she needs from her father, Vince, because Vince feels he doesn't understand women and spends most of his time at the rink supporting his son. After a series of turbulent incidents including a suspected pregnancy and a drug overdose, Karen eventually comes to the realization that she needs to stop resenting her father and accept him the way he is: "there were certain things, she knew, that he could never understand about her. But she had to accept that. Just like she couldn't understand his hockey" (206). As Karen learns to accept her father's inability to express his emotions, she also learns to appreciate his love for hockey. As the novel ends, Karen imagines her own children playing hockey, being coached by her father. At first she can't believe she would ever marry a hockey player, but the final line of the novel – "or could she?" – certainly leaves the possibility open if not suggesting its inevitability. Karen, then, ultimately learns the lesson about relating to men that Lina could not: that the masculine love for hockey is unchangeable and must be accepted. Inasmuch as Lina is the only character who ends the story unhappy, *Icelands*, like *Heroes*, suggests unfortunate consequences for women who can't learn to like hockey or at least accept the game's importance and apparent inevitability to Canadian men. It is also worth noting the extent to which the novel's conclusion restores the secure, patriarchal family structure that potentially links back to ideas about national continuity and stability. By associating hockey with this sort of patrimony, or, in the case of the character Mike Horseford, proposing the game as compensation for its absence and instability, *Icelands* sees hockey as the solidly masculine foundation on which the larger social units of family and nation should ultimately be built.

Perhaps predictably, the first wave of children's hockey novels are equally invested in traditional gender roles as their adult-oriented successors. For instance, a passage from McFarlane's *McGonigle Scores!* explaining why Mrs Beckett refuses to watch her son play hockey is almost identical to the passages from adult-oriented hockey novels quoted above that attempt to signify feminine weakness: "'I couldn't stand it,' she explained. 'I wouldn't want to see him get hurt'" (121). Probably the best example of this theme among first-wave children's hockey novels, however, is McFarlane's "They Didn't Know Hockey," which is premised entirely on the idea that "most girls didn't understand very much about hockey" and in fact relies on this idea to fuel the reader's enjoyment of the story (*Leslie McFarlane's Hockey Stories*, 116). Dan Howley is a talented player on his local team, but faces pressure from his girlfriend Mary to score goals rather than set up opportunities for his teammates. Mary's interest in motivating Dan isn't to help him achieve personal glory or realize his talents to the fullest; instead, "Mary's desire to stir [Dan] up a little may have been due to her objection to marrying a man who didn't earn any more than eighteen dollars a week, and to her conviction that Dan could be making a great deal more if he capitalized on his hockey ability" (116). Mary's desire to marry a man with money is implicitly related to her lack of understanding of hockey culture, in which the sort of selfishness she encourages contravenes the best interests and collective spirit of the team. Nevertheless, Dan gives in to Mary's request and changes his style of play to pass less and shoot more. Finally during the last game of the season Dan realizes the error of his ways and begins passing again, which allows his team to win the championship. As usual in McFarlane's hockey stories, good moral character is rewarded: after the championship game Dan meets a professional scout who had earlier dismissed him as a puckhog but expresses interest in signing him upon learning that Dan is actually an excellent playmaker. The intended humour, of course, is that as a woman Mary didn't know what she was talking about when it comes to hockey. In fact, if she hadn't tampered with Dan's style of play he would have been signed as a professional much sooner. As the story ends, Dan tells the scout about his plans to be married, prompting the scout to inquire "is your girl a hockey fan?" (138). Dan replies "Sure. But she doesn't know a whole lot about the game" (138).

While first-wave children's hockey novels generally attempt to perpetuate traditional gender roles and exclude women from the game on the basis of "feminine" weakness or lack of knowledge, the second wave of children's hockey novels produced throughout the 1990s and 2000s are full of female players who are both skilful and tough. In fact, it is in their depictions of the relationship between women and hockey that adult-oriented hockey novels differ most significantly from their contemporary children's counterparts. For instance, the best player in MacGregor's *Screech Owl* series is Sarah Cuthbertson, a female player who is so talented that when the Screech Owls participate in the famous Quebec Peewee International Hockey Tournament she matches former NHL superstar Guy Lafleur's record of seven goals in one game (*The Quebec City Crisis*). Furthermore, Sarah is the only one of the Screech Owls to make it to the highest level of the game, becoming the captain of the Canadian Olympic team and "the greatest hero the town of Tamarack had ever known" (*The Screech Owls' Reunion*, 15). Beyond being a highly skilled player, Sarah is said to get "as big a kick out of checking players as she did out of scoring goals" (*The Quebec City Crisis*, 26). Sarah is represented as being so tough, in fact, that MacGregor once received a letter from a young male reader who, commenting on the disproportionate number of injuries that Sarah seems to endure in the early novels, suggested that "I think you're hurting Sarah too much." MacGregor agreed that this was indeed the case, and explains his rationale as follows: "I had done it because I want to portray Sarah as a real hockey player, and because she's a girl, I want to demonstrate that she has courage, every bit as much courage as any male player throughout history, but I'd gone overboard" (MacGregor 1998). Although the issue of Sarah's femininity (as well as that of the team's other female players) comes up from time to time in the *Screech Owls* novels, the presence of female players on the team is for the most part represented as normal and unremarkable.

Other children's hockey novels have been more direct in their portrayals of female protagonists who manage to succeed in hockey despite the cultural sexism that continues to structure the game. For instance, Heather Kellerhals-Stewart's *She Shoots, She Scores* – which was written in 1975 and is an exception among the first wave of children's hockey novels – is the story of a young Edmonton girl who wants to play hockey but encounters all sorts of social barriers that threaten to keep her from the game. Jacqueline Guest's *Hat Trick* and *Rookie Season* (2000) also explore the gender politics of girls' hockey from the perspective of female protagonists and in light of the obstacles and difficulties that many young women face upon entering the game, even – in the case of *Rookie Season* – those who choose to play on all-girls teams. Sigmund Brouwer's *Chief Honor* (1997) is the fictional story of the first female player in the Western Hockey League, who has to clear her name after being framed for steroid use in a discriminatory attempt to discredit her play. And Gordon Korman's *Slapshots* series depicts Alexia Colwin, the first female player in the local league and one of the best. Alexia is gritty, tenacious, the captain of her team, and capable of throwing "a body check that would have derailed a train" (*The Stars from Mars*, 48). Two of the *Slapshots* books in particular focus on the challenges Alexia faces as a girl playing among boys. In Slapshots 2 of the series, *All-Mars All-Stars* (1999), Alexia is omitted from the league's all-star team because she is a girl and later refuses to join on principle when public pressure causes the league to reconsider their decision. Similarly in Slapshots 4, *Cup Crazy* (2000), the league uses an archaic municipal law disallowing women from "hold[ing], or otherwise wield[ing], a length of wood exceeding three feet, with the exception of mops, brooms, and butter churns" (11) as grounds to prohibit Alexia from playing, although the team eventually manages to circumvent this rule in time for the final game by supplying Alexia with an aluminum stick. All of these books build powerful pathos for their maligned female players, and rely heavily on their young readers' senses of justice. By making it abundantly clear that women can play the game well and that gender discrimination isn't fair, these novels challenge the idea that hockey should be a male preserve.

The discrepancy between children's and adult hockey novels on the issue of women in the game conveys a fairly simple message: that young girls might play (and even succeed in) hockey, but that when the game gets serious (read: adult), it's time for women to step aside and let men do their thing. Stenson's *Teeth* demonstrates this troublesome idea in a throwaway moment when a hockey-mad ten-year-old girl complains about her physical maturation that "I guess I'll get breasts soon" and the narrator informs us that this is "a negative development, an impediment in her struggle to be as good as any boy in the most male of all arenas: the hockey rink" (48). This passage is intended to be funny, but quite explicitly conveys the message that young girls are welcome in hockey while women are not. Although children's hockey novels can at times be didactic in their

treatment of hockey and gender – a characteristic of children's literature in general – they create valuable space for women within the
game that adult hockey novels consistently attempt to deny. This is
important cultural work, and can have profound real-world consequences in the lives of young readers. As it happens, one of my recent
Canadian literature students, Ricki-Lee Gerbrandt, was a reader of
hockey novels in her childhood and went on to achieve a high level
of success in the game as a player. When I asked Ricki-Lee how reading hockey novels had affected her attitude toward the game, she
suggested that they were both important in normalizing the idea of
her involvement and inspiring in terms of what they helped her feel
capable of accomplishing. Ricki-Lee was kind enough to oblige my
curiosity further by writing up a short account of her experience in
the game and as a reader of hockey novels, which is reproduced as
an appendix to this study. Although this account is only one reader's
experience, it goes a long way toward demonstrating the positive
real-world outcomes that healthy and progressive representations of
hockey culture can have.

EXCLUSIONS II: GAY MEN

Probably the most obvious reason why homosexuality is forbidden
within the team community is that it presents the possibility that
team membership might "feed the homoerotic imagination and provide homoerotic contact" (Pronger 1990a, 195), thus disrupting the
brotherly (read: Platonic) familiarity and comfort on which team
unity appears to be based. Although hockey novels exemplify homosexual panic by attempting to repress the possibilities of homoerotic
desire, the perceived threat to team community isn't primarily homoerotic. In the words of Burstyn, "homophobia [in sporting cultures]
is often strongly motivated by men's fear of the 'feminine' qualities
– softness, weakness, dependency, sexual receptivity – that are dis-
claimed in violent sport and displaced onto homosexual men" (1999,
203). The primary "threat" of homosexuality, then, is the same as
that posed by women, that the team's masculine toughness might be
somehow diluted or compromised by allowing homosexuals. It is
important to recognize that hockey novels exclude women from the
game on the basis of what they represent as an essential category
(weakness, emotion, delicacy, etc.), and that these same characteristics are often attributed to homosexual men. As Messner and Sabo

note, "'fag,' 'girl,' and 'woman' are insults that are used almost inter-
changeably" in male sporting cultures, and "through this practice,
heterosexual masculinity is collectively constructed by denigrating
homosexuality and femininity as 'not-male'" (1994, 47).[4]

A good example of how the exclusion of weak and effeminate men
appears to contribute to the team's homosocial fraternity occurs in
The Last Season during an episode in which Tapiola Hauki acquires
a particularly weak player, Matti, who has been released by another
team for his lack of effectiveness. Matti, whose weakness as a player
is described as stemming from "fear" (162), plays his first game for
Tapiola Hauki during an exhibition match against a Swedish elite-
league team. After the game gets off to a bad start for Tapiola,
Batterinski berates his teammates during the first intermission. When
Matti questions Batterinski's anger, he is instantly kicked off the
team, an act which appears to expurgate the unacceptable weakness
and cowardice that Matti represents. Matti's alienation from his
teammates, however, is far from over at this point in the story.

On the airplane back to Finland after the game, Batterinski is
sleeping when he is unexpectedly awoken by a slap from Matti.
Batterinski reacts: "I am startled. I have been hit by a man, kicked by
a man, choked, bit-speared, tripped and nearly knifed by a man. But
slapped? I can do nothing but laugh. 'You think this is funny,
Batterinski?' Matti asks. 'Not really,' I say. 'That's about what I
would expect of your type – a woman's slap'" (172). Batterinski
subdues Matti almost effortlessly, binds him with athletic tape, and
passes him off to another player to deal with. When the plane touch-
es down in Finland, the team owners' representative, Erkki, is waiting for Batterinski near the luggage carousel. Erkki is shocked when
he sees Matti arrive through the carousel door among the team's luggage: "Matti, taped, twisted, and terrified as he rises on the rubber
treadmill and rolls down the steel plates, circling twice before Erkki,
alone, hauls him off like a flopping, massive muskie. No one moves
to help as we gather up our equipment and depart, for the first time
a true team" (173). It is by marginalizing and humiliating a weak
and explicitly effeminate player, then, that Tapiola Hauki is first said
to become a "team." Batterinski makes it abundantly clear that there
is no place on his team for weakness or fear, and his highly public
and almost ceremonial way of drawing this line not only referees the
terms of team belonging but allows the remaining players to participate in this identity. Matti's treatment by his former teammates

reduces him to the level of object (he arrives with and is treated as baggage) and subhumanity (he is characterized as "a flopping, massive muskie"). By refusing to help Matti off the carousel or release the athletic tape that binds him, the players implicitly declare him unworthy of their allegiance, accept and enact the masculine toughness that Batterinksi's "Canadian" hockey vision requires of them, and in doing all this constitute themselves "for the first time" as "a true team." Beyond signifying weakness, the need to forcibly marginalize Matti indicates the power of the threat he represents to the team's masculine stability. In other words, the binding of Matti is an unacknowledged moment of homosexual panic, a coercive and disciplinary action against someone who implicitly proposes that hockey homosociality may in fact complicate or transgress the boundaries of "acceptable" platonic camaraderie.

While Matti isn't explicitly identified as homosexual, his association with "feminine" weakness could certainly be seen to imply this in the gender and sexual binaries that hockey novels consistently draw. Several other hockey novels depict homosexual characters who appear to be excluded from the team community on the basis of their "feminine" weakness. In *King Leary*, for instance, the sexual orientation of Leary's son, Clarence, is initially established through his writing of poetry that at one point in the story Leary describes as "queer stuff" (210). Poetry is often associated with sensitivity, emotionality, and effusiveness, all of which are ostensibly feminine attributes in the gender binary drawn by hockey culture. The same principle is later applied to Clarence's athleticism, in that he is said to "[skate] like a girl" (48). To tell someone they skate like a girl, of course, is one of the worst insults in the male-dominated domain of hockey, and trades on the long-standing cultural association between masculinity and athleticism. To skate "like a girl" is to skate with slowness, uncertainty, and lack of proficiency, or, even more anathema to the expectations of hockey masculinity, with the daintiness and finesse associated with figure skating. Quite interestingly, the hockey-playing women in Hedley's *Twenty Miles* exhibit this sort of disdain for figure skaters and the version of femininity they represent as a way of broadening feminine identity and opening up new possibilities for women within the game. In *Twenty Miles*, to skate "like a girl" is to skate like a hockey player.

At one point in *King Leary* the title character recalls a Maple Leafs Christmas skating party from his time as coach, to which Clarence

– much to Leary's shame – arrived wearing white figure skates (i.e., women's skates). Despite his women's skates, Clarence quickly impresses the hockey players in this flashback episode by performing his father's trademark hockey move, the St Louis Whirlygig, and then executing an additional figure-skating style manoeuvre that the players soon begin to emulate. None of the hockey players are able to complete Clarence's move, and Leary's narration notes that "amidst all the chuckling and cackle" occasioned by their failed attempts, "I heard one of the players say, 'Not bad for a *queer*'" (214; italics in original). Even in this apparent moment of belonging, then, Clarence remains an object of contempt and exclusion because of his homosexuality (which, again, is expressed through his women's skates and figure-skating style). The word "queer," of course, is intended as an insult in this context, and serves as a strategy of containment: it marks Clarence as "other" to the team and dismisses his skating accomplishment as unworthy or unremarkable, something to be attempted in parody or jest but not to be taken seriously or deemed important.

Although Leary's outlandish disdain for Clarence's "queer" tendencies ultimately suggests an ironic stance toward the novel's depiction of homosexuality and hockey culture, it is worth noting that Clarence's homosexuality doesn't appear to seriously "threaten" or disrupt the homosocial fraternity of the team, because it announces itself clearly and can thus be belittled and contained. The same is true of Lannie Leroux, the Kougars' flamboyantly gay former owner in *50 Mission Cap*. As with Clarence, Lannie's homosexuality is explicitly announced by his association with femininity. During his time as owner of the Kougars, Lannie is said to have "attend[ed] games in his most outlandish outfits, even wearing shoulderpads underneath a ballgown once" (17). *50 Mission Cap* sees this behaviour as so shameful that it is said to have brought about the resignation of the team's general manager, whose parting comment was that "no twenty-five-thousand-dollar-a-year job is worth this kind of humiliation" (17). Lannie is also characterized as a completely incompetent owner, "fir[ing] coaches at whim, trad[ing] players if they didn't score when he wanted them to, [and] even instruct[ing] the sound operator to play 'In the Navy' by the Village People during the opening skate" (17). Given that the novel works to mythologize the Tragically Hip's "50 Mission Cap" as a Canadian hockey icon, the throwaway detail about Lannie's musical preference for the Village People – a thinly veiled reference to gay culture – is particularly illuminating. Posited at the end of a complaint about Lannie's managerial ineptitude, the mention of "In the Navy" both further suggests Lannie's ignorance of hockey and expresses this ignorance as a "natural" function of his homosexuality. No explanation is given, of course, as to why "50 Mission Cap" is more appropriate than "In the Navy" as a musical accompaniment to the team's opening skate, or why Lannie's behaviour is so particularly humiliating; rather, *50 Mission Cap* assumes these "truths" to be self-evident to hockey initiates, the novel's obvious target readership.[5]

Early in *50 Mission Cap* it is revealed that Lannie (who has sold the team but still owns their arena), is planning to evict the Kougars in order to demolish the arena and construct a bizarre theme-park tribute to himself (again, this "dangerous" eccentricity appears to stem from his homosexuality). The arena issue becomes one of the many problems that Scott MacGregor has to deal with over the course of the story, but the situation is eventually resolved when Scott is able to placate Lannie with the prospect of nominal involvement in the team by way of a bequeathed award. In *50 Mission Cap*, then, Lannie's overt homosexuality also makes his danger to the team manageable. Because Lannie's homosexuality announces itself openly and apparently, his "threat" to the team amounts to little more than a disruptive nuisance that is defused or contained by Scott's manipulation and – at other points in the story – through outright scorn. The manageability of Lannie's announced homosexuality, however, works by contrast to suggest the danger of another character's concealed homosexuality. Worse than the bad managerial decisions and potential eviction from the arena that stem from Lannie's homosexuality is the pedophiliac abuse that results from that of Clyde Parker, the Kougars' assistant coach. Clyde's homosexuality is more dangerous than Lannie's because it isn't easily detected. Although homosexuality and pedophilia are by no means synonymous, *50 Mission Cap* uses Clyde to suggest the "threat" of unannounced homosexuality and its potential to disrupt or undermine the homosocial unity of the team. In the end, however, Clyde's homosexuality is ultimately revealed, and "paid for" with the severe beating discussed earlier in chapter 4.

Both *King Leary* and *50 Mission Cap* suggest an apparent need to announce, disclose, or discover homosexuality so that its "threat" to the team might be reckoned with and contained. This tendency may reflect and express cultural anxieties about gay athletes "passing" as straight. According to sports ethicist Brian Pronger the homophobia of real-life sporting cultures often makes it necessary for gay athletes to conceal their sexual orientation, an experience that leads them to see sexuality not "as what one *is*" but as the "ways in which one *acts*" (1990b, 145; italics in original). The possibility that gay men could "pass" as straight calls attention to the performative nature of gender, which in turn appears to threaten the essentialist categories by which hockey novels understand sexual identity. By representing gay men as *obviously* gay (i.e., associated with femininity) or by seeing homosexuality as a fixed and stable category that can be discovered and reckoned with (i.e., diminished, demonized, or, in the case of Clyde Parker, given criminal connotations), these novels resist the possibility that sexual identities are more fluid and flexible than the hockey myth's rigid concept of masculinity acknowledges.

Another novel that significantly appears to require full disclosure of a character's concealed homosexuality is *The Divine Ryans*. In a sense, homosexuality quite literally haunts *The Divine Ryans* through the character of Donald Ryan, Draper Doyle's deceased father, whose ghost appears periodically throughout the story in the attempt to communicate something with young Draper Doyle. Early in the story we are told that Draper Doyle has entirely forgotten the events surrounding his father's death, a phenomenon that Uncle Reginald refers to as his "missing week" (8). When the repressed memories of Draper Doyle's "missing week" are eventually revealed, we learn that Draper Doyle had walked in on Donald Ryan having sex with another man shortly before his death. Unlike the depictions of homosexuality discussed above, however, *The Divine Ryans* doesn't see Donald Ryan's homosexuality as disqualifying him from hockey.

Over the course of the novel the reader essentially learns that Donald Ryan's relationship with his son had been based in large part on their shared love of hockey, one noteworthy feature of which is a secret code system whereby Donald transmits hockey scores to Draper Doyle the morning after a game. The eventual revelation of Donald's homosexuality does nothing to detract from or diminish these moments, and hockey apparently remains an important part of Donald Ryan's existence in the afterlife: his ghostly apparition always carries a hockey puck, and during the novel's dream-sequence climax, a Virgilian descent into the underworld of Reg Ryan's funeral home, it is by placing pucks on his father's eyes that Draper Doyle symbolically comes to terms with his passing and secures his "rest" in the afterlife.[6] What Donald Ryan's ghost wants to communicate with Draper Doyle turns out to be the existence of a suicide note that Donald had left for his son using their secret code for transmitting hockey scores. The note confirms Draper Doyle's discovery of his father's homosexuality, and enables him to use this knowledge to gain freedom for himself, his mother, and his sister from the Divine Ryans' overbearing matriarch, Aunt Phil. *The Divine Ryans*, then, is an exception among hockey novels in that although it requires homosexuality to be disclosed and reckoned with, this reckoning doesn't involve censure or exclusion from hockey. Rather than excluding him from the homosocial fraternity of hockey culture, Donald Ryan's homosexuality works to alienate him from his staunchly Catholic family. As such, *The Divine Ryans* challenges the gender and sexual identities that other hockey novels work to associate with the game in much the same way that it defies the myth of French–English unity through hockey discussed earlier in chapter 3.[7]

MAKING THE TEAM: HAZING

One of Robidoux's conclusions about the undisclosed AHL (American Hockey League) franchise he studies in *Men at Play* is that the team maintains an internal "standard of behaviour that tends to function outside perceived social norms and conventions" (2001, 126). Because players "are socialized and validated for acting within these so-called norms," they tend to "find strength and solace in [the team] environment" (126). This sense of "strength and solace," of course, is much of the basis for the team-as-community myth. Robidoux also discovered, however, that belonging in the team collective requires conforming to its assumptions and expectations, a process that can "strip players of their individuality and immerse them in a collective whole with a belief system, world view, and values that are often counterproductive to personal development" (126).

The process of belonging in the team can be seen, in Foucault's terms, as "an uninterrupted, constant coercion" (1979, 137) that continuously works to replicate its assumptions, police its boundaries, and enfold its subjects. Simply by being in and around the team, by participating in its behaviours and fulfilling its expectations, individual players are confirming and conforming to the pre-existing standards of knowledge and power that govern team culture. In other words, belonging involves subjecting oneself to the values and discipline of the team collective. Again, this is another way in which national manhood works to short-circuit democratic impulses and energies among its adherents. As Foucault notes, the disciplined body is also a "docile" body that can be "subjected, used, transformed, and improved" (136).[8] The homosocial community of the team, then, often works to incorporate its members and replicate its assumptions through various forms of social discipline and certain "compulsory" behaviours. By representing such coercions as natural, inevitable, and, indeed, beneficial, hockey novels themselves operate as disciplinary forces that attempt to perform and reproduce the versions of masculinity that are often enacted in real-life hockey cultures.

Probably the most straightforward and obvious way in which individual men are incorporated into the team collective is through ritual initiation, or "hazing." Formal initiation rituals are used by many male fraternities, gangs, and secret societies for the purpose of "creat[ing] a structured space in which men [can] feel individually reconstructed within the abstract identity of ... brotherhood" (Nelson 1998, 185). These "fraternal ritual[s]" offer "men a formally and emotionally focused time during which they [can] experience themselves as part of a controlled male body" (185). Blackshaw emphasizes the importance of such rituals as a means of accepting and incorporating individuals into the leisure-life world of the lads, a process which in their case typically involves perpetrating violence against "somebody worth hurting" (2003, 51). In hockey culture, young players and rookies are often subjected to humiliating, degrading, and even abusive "punishments" by veteran players, the stoic acceptance of which is seen to "earn" their place within the team. Rodiboux's research found that, as with the lads, ritual initiations in hockey are perceived as a "necessary procedure in the process of achieving group solidarity" (2001, 109). In fact, Robidoux goes so far as to suggest that "rookie participation in these [hazing] events can be interpreted as an example of sacrificing oneself for the sake of the team" in that "the group dynamic takes precedence over individual identity" (109).[9]

The issue of hazing represents a unique challenge for Canadian hockey novels. Because these novels are generally realist and purport to portray the hockey world "as it actually exists," it would seem inevitable that at least some of the accounts offered by hockey novels must include depictions of hazing. The difficulty of such representations, however, is that they threaten to undermine the ordered and controlled ways in which hockey novels attempt to legitimate traditional masculinity. Public awareness about hazing rituals and their harmful effects on young male players has been growing in Canada over the last decade or so, largely due to several important journalistic investigations into the matter. In 1996 journalist Laura Robinson teamed with the CBC's *Fifth Estate* program to produce a documentary entitled "Thin Ice," which was essentially an *exposé* of the prevalence and severity of hazing in the Canadian junior game (Scott 1998). Robinson's book *Crossing the Line* was published two years later, and further examines "ritual and the sexually abusive initiations of rookie players" (1998, 8). Both of these accounts paint disturbing pictures of Canadian junior hockey culture, and highlight the extent to which hockey hazing can be abusive, psychologically damaging, and can work to reproduce "deviant behaviour [among] many victimized players" (8).

Although hockey hazing has been increasingly challenged in recent years, it remains a widespread practice in Canadian hockey culture. True to their realist agendas, several hockey novels do reflect this fact. Unlike "Thin Ice" or *Crossing the Line*, however, these novels have no interest in sordid realism or critique. Rather, they attempt in various ways to contain or downplay the troubling consequences of hazing and install this practice as a harmless, even natural, way in which young men are incorporated into the fraternity of the team. Another way of saying this is that these novels accommodate hazing to the literary conventions of the *Bildungsroman* in such a way as to render this practice simply another aspect of the initiation into manhood and team membership. When Mike Horseford, for instance, complains about going into the "sweatbox" in *Icelands*, a ritual in which rookies are locked together naked in the washroom of the team bus for the duration of a ride, his mother, Paula, simply smiles and answers that "boys will be boys" (211). When the narrator of *Understanding Ken* sees two junior hockey players who have been stripped naked, completely shaved, strapped down to tables, and left out on the rink with hot muscle cream rubbed on their genitalia, he accepts this simply as a matter of "what they do on the junior team" (134). By characterizing these hazing rituals as the good-natured and "natural" phenomenon assumed by Paula Horseford or the inevitable rite of passage anticipated by the narrator of *Understanding Ken*,

these novels belie the damaging emotional and psychological consequences such practices inflict. Rather than the sadistic and abusive
forms of social discipline that these behaviours can be, hazing is
represented as both natural (i.e., proper and unavoidable) and relatively harmless. The same could be said of *The Horn of a Lamb*,
which deals particularly with hazing and represents the practice as
problematic only when it transgresses the established structures of
hockey power and threatens to "go too far" by inflicting lasting
physical harm. As with other harmful aspects of the myth, then,
hockey novels tend to affirm the status quo on hazing and invite
their readers to do the same.

DECLAIMING MASCULINITY: HOMOPHOBIA

While hazing rituals such as those described above work as a formal
"means of legitimizing power as it is perceived within the hockey
environment" (Robidoux 2001, 118), there are less formal ways in
which the institution of the team works to impose social discipline
on its members. To be accepted within the culture of the team, individual players are expected to engage in various performative decla-
mations of masculinity that work to express and encourage "the
illusion of an interior and organizing gender core" (Butler 1990,
173). According to Messner and Sabo, belonging in male athletic
cultures is often predicated on overt "sexism and homophobia," the
expression of which functions as "one of the key bonds to the male
peer group" (1994, 50). As with homoerotic violence, homophobic
speech and actions attempt to repress or deny the possibility of
homoerotic attraction between teammates. But this is exactly the
point: by engaging in sexist and homophobic "words, acts, and gestures" (Butler 1990, 173), male athletes ostensibly assert their heterosexual toughness and thereby secure or advance their social
standing within the team. In addition to excluding certain identities
from hockey culture and thereby defining the team by what it is
avowedly *not*, then, sexism and homophobia function as compulsory requirements for team belonging, another form of social discipline by which hockey-playing men are subjected to the game's
established identity assumptions. As with the practice of hazing, of
course, men can choose not to participate in these attitudes and
behaviours, but to do so is to risk isolation, exclusion, or, in career
terms, "ruined ... chances of success" (Messner and Sabo 1994, 50).

Hockey novels generally fail to recognize the harmful consequences of sexist and homophobic behaviours, representing these
things instead as normal, even "natural," mechanisms by which team
unity is created and masculine toughness ensured. This section will
address the problem of homophobia. According to Sedgwick, "'male
bonding' ... in our society ... [is] characterized by intense homophobia, fear and hatred of homosexuality" (1985, 1). This is especially
true of sporting cultures, in which, as Kirk Bohls and Mark Wangrin
rather playfully put it, "athletes revel in being one of the guys, not
one of the gays" (1997, 167). The extent to which each player is
permitted to belong as "one of the guys," in fact, appears at least
partially dependent on the performative assertion that he is not "one
of the gays." Generally speaking, these apparently requisite declara-
tions of homophobia are expressed in hockey novels (and hockey
culture in general) in two seemingly contradictory ways.

First, hockey men appear to declaim their heterosexual masculinity through explicitly homophobic comments and behaviour. This
should certainly be evident from the earlier discussions of characters
such as Clarence, Lannie, and Matti, but two brief episodes from
Dawson City Seven serve to further elucidate the point. Both episodes occur as side stories from the central plot, told by one of the
Dawson players, Doc McLennan, in the effort to entertain his teammates during their cross-country journey. In the first story, McLennan
recalls scoring an important goal before hearing "people screaming,
and when I turn here's fat François Lafrançois sliding across the ice
– he's a big, fat, round guy with wide, wild eyes – he slides over,
throws his arms around my neck and gives me this big, sloppy kiss
right on my lips – right on my lips! – all the while doing his French
gibberish because whenever he gets excited he forgets he's in
English Canada, and sure enough we get a penalty for delaying
the game" (154). Aside from posing an interesting moment for
French–English relations, this episode suggests what is framed in
McLennan's narrative as "a penalty for kissing" (154).[10] The actual
penalty, of course, is for delay of game, but *Dawson City Seven*
makes it abundantly clear that the real transgression is Lafrançois'
celebratory kiss. Indeed, part of the point of the story is to referee
the boundaries of hockey propriety. Although there are many
"acceptable" forms of affectionate physical contact between players within the culture of the game, kissing isn't one of them and
McLennan's narrative makes this abundantly clear by associating it

with "excessive" fatness, wildness, sloppiness, and even Frenchness (thus aligning sexism with xenophobia). Hockey initiates, of course, will already be aware that male–male kissing is taboo in hockey culture, and as such the story works to foster homosocial camaraderie among the Dawson teammates based of their mutual recognition of this "fact" and their shared contempt for Lafrançois' transgression (this knowledge and attendant sense of belonging, of course, potentially extend to the reader as well). The intended humour of the passage, it would seem, trades on the fact that no serious harm has befallen the team's staunch heterosexual toughness: Lafrançois' "homosexual" excess has been openly recognized as such, and can thus be contained by the other players' scorn and by the apparently due punishment of a penalty.

Later in *Dawson City Seven* Doc McLennan tells another story that allows the team to "bond" through their shared contempt for homosexuality. In this story, McLennan describes a former hockey roommate who once insisted on making a hotel bed he had slept in the night before. The climax of the story occurs upon McLennan's realization that his own unmade bed would convey the appearance that the players had slept together. The implied homosexuality of this prospect, of course, is clearly intolerable despite existing only in appearance, and poses a dilemma for McLennan as to what should be done to set things "straight." The efficacy of the story hangs on the apparently obvious fact that something *must* be done to resolve this intolerable situation, and the listening players appear united by the shared recognition of McLennan's predicament and the anticipation of an interesting dénouement (again, the shared contempt for homosexuality appears to underwrite the team's sense of community). One possible resolution, of course, would be for McLennan to dispel the appearance of homosexuality by making his own bed as well, but the narrative forecloses on this possibility through a teammate's "twinge of disgust" (244). In other words, the feminine connotation of bed-making – a domestic labour – is itself associated with homosexuality, and McLennan is therefore seen to be facing a non-choice. The story concludes, then, in what is apparently the only way possible, when McLennan informs his teammates that "I tore that [made] bed all to hell!" (244).

Both of these episodes from *Dawson City Seven* suggest the importance of declaiming heterosexual masculinity through the performative denunciation of homosexuality, and both appear to deliver community and camaraderie through their collective rehearsals of homophobia. A second (and apparently paradoxical) way in which hockey novels express homophobia is through physical intimacy between teammates. Anyone who has ever watched a hockey game will have some sense of what this entails: players tapping each other on the rear to celebrate a skillful play or embracing after an important goal, etc. Although, as Lafrançois' kiss illustrates, there are unwritten rules and assumptions that govern the sorts of physical contact that are acceptable and unacceptable, physically intimate behaviour among teammates tends to become more pronounced in the players' off-ice relationships, a fact which, as noted above, both expresses a high degree of fraternal community and represses latent homoerotic desire (Messner and Sabo 1994, 51; Burstyn 1999, 178).

Robidoux addresses the seemingly paradoxical coexistence of dressing-room homophobia and physical intimacy in his discussion of "mock sexual interaction" between players (2001, 138). According to Robidoux, the high level of physical familiarity that players exhibit with one another doesn't signify homoerotic attraction so much as the players' "desire to fulfill the macho image expected of them as hockey players" (139). In Robidoux's reading, then, mock sexual interaction between teammates such as "grabbing another man's testicles," expresses an established "trust" between players that works to "[maintain] masculinity by superficially assuming a role that subverts the tough, macho exterior that is, in reality, being expressed" (138, 139). In this sense, homosexual innuendo and physical intimacy among players functions as a sort of parody, a way of performing that appears to "[undermine] the strictly heterosexual notion of masculinity, while [at the same time] keeping ... masculinity up front" (139). Thus, when Peka gives Batterinski a "small special tap on the rear" to celebrate a goal in *The Last Season* (165), these characters seem to be demonstrating an established heterosexual trust that is substantiated throughout the novel by their obviously asexual friendship. The public expression of this heterosexual trust through physical intimacy apparently works to "further [establish these characters'] idyllic level of security in themselves as men" (Robidoux 2001, 139).

A similar moment occurs in *The Good Body* when Bonaduce envisions his teammates coming to "whack [him] on the ass" to celebrate a good pass (173), an action that appears to entail the same spirit of homosocial bonding and camaraderie that Bonaduce effects later in the story by making gay jokes in the dressing room (250). Paradoxically, then, the function of explicit homophobia and that of physical intimacy among teammates are in some ways the same: to declaim the team's heterosexual masculinity, and to propose this identity as a central pillar of team unity and belonging. While Robidoux acknowledges the extent to which "grabbing another male's genitals is a multivalent gesture, capable of withstanding a multiplicity of interpretations," he maintains that it is important to "resist reading this behaviour as an expression of sexual desire" because "such a reading, while likely true in individual cases, refuses to acknowledge the voices of the actual individuals involved ... who claim to be heterosexual" (2001, 138–9). What Robidoux doesn't recognize in taking player comments about physical intimacy at face value, however, is the fact that – as Butler points out – people's sexual desires are seldom entirely apparent or easily comprehensible even to themselves. By appearing to declaim robust heterosexuality, moments such as Batterinski's "small special tap on the rear" and Bonaduce's "whack on the ass" consciously attempt to deny the possibility of homoerotic desire between teammates while unconsciously exploring and enacting such desires in one of the few ways deemed acceptable within the culture of the game.

SEXUAL SCHIZOPHRENIA AND THE TRAFFIC IN WOMEN

While sporting cultures tend to see homosexual men as objects of scorn, derision, and parody, women are often seen as objects of exchange. Cultural anthropologist Gayle Rubin has written about what she calls "the traffic in women," the set of social values, assumptions, and practices that construct men as "sexual subjects – exchangers – and women [as] sexual semi-objects – gifts" (1975, 176). The purpose of this sexual economy, according to Rubin, "is that it expresses, affirms, or creates a social link between the partners of an exchange ... [and] confers upon its participants a special relationship of trust and solidarity" (172). Rubin's claim about the "traffic in women" appears especially applicable to hockey culture, in which men frequently "bond" through objectifying banter about female bodies, bragging about sexual conquest, and, in some extreme cases, through the actual sharing of sexual partners, both willing and unwilling (Robinson 1998).

As noted in chapter 5, regarding the sexual athlete mythology, sporting cultures often encourage men to apply the athletic ideals of dominance and competition to their relationships with women as well. In the same way that scoring goals in a hockey game, then, becomes a mark of social distinction among teammates, the "sexual conquest" of women becomes a way of "gaining status in the male peer group" (Messner and Sabo 1994, 47). When several teammates tell the narrator of *Understanding Ken* that his father's girlfriend has "big tits," the boy asks them in response: "So what? What's that got to do with hockey?" (86). What the prepubescent narrator remains slightly too young to know is that the objectification of women has a great deal to do with hockey, at least as it is enacted on a daily basis in arenas across the country. This social dynamic has led feminists and sport sociologists to refer to the athletic dressing room as a "rape culture," a "sex-segregated" and "male-dominated" domain that "displays a high degree of hostility to, and contempt for, women" (Robinson 1998, 5). While it is important to qualify, as Messner and Sabo do, that the "rape culture" of the athletic dressing room "is probably, in most cases, just a rhetorical performance" that "does not necessarily reflect or cause actual physical aggression against women" (1994, 51), it is also important to recognize the extent to which simply performing such acts gives them power and suggests them as natural. According to Butler, linguistic performatives "[accumulate] *the force of authority through the repetition or citation of a prior and authoritative set of practices*" (1995, 205; italics in original). Thus, injurious speech "works its injury precisely through the accumulation and dissimulation of its force," its establishment of "linguistic community with a history of speakers" (206). A more extreme way of phrasing this, perhaps, is that the performative function of injurious speech is such that "the word and the deed are one" (219). Inasmuch as performance references "a prior and authoritative set of practices" and thereby constitutes assent for and involvement in these practices, hockey novels participate in the objectification and depersonalization of women simply by performing these ideas and suggesting their "naturalness" as a means of male bonding.

A good illustration of how the "traffic in women" appears to create community and camaraderie among men occurs during a throw-away moment toward the end of *King Leary*, in which the young hockey sensation Duane Killibrew and his girlfriend Hallie spirit

Leary away from a television commercial he is supposed to be film-
ing in order to visit the new Canadian Sports Hall of Fame. As these
characters enter Killibrew's car, Leary notes that "Hallie ... takes off
her buckskin jacket, [and] slings it over her shoulder" (224). What
follows is one of several moments in the novel where Leary, the narrator, addresses the reader directly: "this lady's got bubs, brother, but
I don't have the time to tell you about it" (224). In addition to illustrating the extent to which hockey novels appear directed toward a
male audience, Leary's comment suggests the extent to which the
homosocial camaraderie of the team is promoted by the traffic in
women. Leary's ogling of Hallie's breasts appears here as a normal,
even "natural," aspect of male behaviour, and apparently presents
him, as narrator of the story, with an opportunity to engage his reader. Leary's address to the reader as "brother" is particularly informative, extending the fraternity of hockey belonging on the basis of
shared appreciation of a woman's body. This throwaway moment,
of course, also works to referee the terms of hockey masculinity and
team belonging, not only excluding men who wouldn't appreciate
the female body (i.e., homosexuals) but also those who would be
troubled or offended by this sort of objectification.

The effect of this and other such objectifying moments in Canadian
hockey novels is essentially to propose two different categories of
women, groupies and wives. Groupies, or as Fred Pickle refers to
them in *The Horn of a Lamb*, "puck bunnies or fuck bunnies depend-
ing who [is] within earshot" (106), are "women who ... are attracted
to [hockey-playing] men mostly for their bodies and the fact that
you have to pay to watch them play" (*The Good Body*, 214).[11]
Many hockey novels mention groupies as a category or include
groupie characters as part of the traffic in women and as a way of
conveying the sexual athlete mythology. Because the promiscuity
this often occasions remains at the borderline of social acceptability,
hockey novels tend to see such behaviour as a sort of temporary
phase through which hockey-playing men must "naturally" pass.
While promiscuity and the pursuit of sexual relationships as a form
of conquest may appear acceptable within hockey culture itself,
hockey novels ultimately require their protagonists to "settle down"
within the framing confines of loving and monogamous marriage,
thus apparently appeasing the expectations of society at large. It is
hardly coincidental, then, that *Puck Is a Four Letter Word*, *The
Uninvited Guest*, *Dawson City Seven*, *Hockey Night in the Dominion*

of Canada, Icelands, Finnie Walsh, and *Saved* all conclude in some way on the generically comic note of a wedding, or that other hockey novels such as *King Leary* and *50 Mission Cap* stress the importance of fidelity and commitment within romantic relationships, or that marriage and stability are what Batterinski tragically longs for in *The Last Season* and Doug Burns hopes to achieve in *Teeth*.

The double standard of male behaviour that hockey novels alternately propose toward groupies and wives (objectification versus respect, erotic attraction versus love and companionship) promotes what Messner and Sabo call a pervasive "sexual schizophrenia" among men (1994, 41). Advocating a version of male sexuality that seeks to "integrate eroticism with love and commitment," Messner and Sabo condemn the models of masculinity enacted in athletic cultures and the sexual athlete myth (41). Hockey novels, however, appear to want it both ways. By suggesting that men must "settle down" within the loving and emotional relationships implied by traditional marriage, hockey novels seem to acknowledge the "genuine [male] need for intimate relationships" that also "[meet] women's expectations and satisfy their emotional needs" (41). But by representing a certain category of women as superfluous sex objects and endorsing the idea that male bonding based on the objectification of women is somehow normal or natural behaviour, hockey novels also encourage men to degrade and disrespect women through the pursuit of sexual conquest and cheap eroticism. By propounding the myth of the sexual athlete and perpetuating the traffic in women as a means by which homosocial camaraderie is produced, hockey novels encourage unhealthy attitudes and behaviours toward women and again, generally speaking, attempt to ensure "the gender dominance of men" (Burstyn 1999, 28).

THE EXCEPTION THAT PROVES THE RULE: *ICED*

If the homosocial community of the team works in Canadian hockey novels to enable masculine toughness, justify individual effort on behalf of the collective, exclude those who "don't belong," and reproduce its assumptions and power structures through expectations of certain compulsory behaviour that is often abusive, homophobic, and/or sexist, one hockey novel in particular explicitly defies these trends: Judith Alguire's *Iced*. *Iced* is a lesbian hockey novel published by a lesbian feminist press, New Victoria Publishers.

Despite occupying what would seem to be a fairly narrow market niche, however, *Iced* targets a broader audience than the majority of hockey novels by attempting to accommodate readers who may not be familiar with the game and its prevailing culture. For instance, *Iced* is the only adult-oriented hockey novel discussed in this study to include a glossary of hockey terms and an explanatory diagram of a rink. *Iced* also goes to great lengths to explain certain details about the game that other hockey novels take to be self-evident or common knowledge, and supposes its readership doesn't have a basic understanding of the game's argot, technical aspects, or cultural assumptions. Alguire's express purpose in reaching beyond established hockey fans to those less familiar with the game is to polemically confront the "male-dominated sportsworld" (174) and the ways in which it exploits and marginalizes women.

 Iced is narrated by Alison Guthrie, a former amateur player turned coach of the "Toronto Teddies," one of the inaugural franchises in the fictional Women's Professional Hockey League (WPHL). The novel essentially follows Alison's struggles to negotiate the male-dominated world of professional sport, attend to the various professional and personal needs of her team, and to conceal her own romantic feelings for one of her players, Molly Gavison, a former Olympic speed skater who has fallen from glory because of an abusive father and molesting coach. Until Hedley's *Twenty Miles* was published in 2007, *Iced* was the only adult-oriented Canadian hockey novel written by a woman, focused on a female protagonist, and in which women played hockey on any serious basis. The novel confronts what Alguire perceives to be the problems with the men's game in that most of the episodes suggest in some way the harmful consequences of masculine toughness or condemn the objectification of women that other hockey novels tend to normalize. One of the players, for instance, has to deal with an abusive husband, while two others discuss their history of mistreatment by men before eventually discovering their sexual love for each other.

 Alison is critical of men's hockey for its roughness and aggression, and expresses this opinion in an ongoing exchange with a friend's daughter, Mandy, who wants to grow up to play in the NHL. Alison explains to Mandy that women's hockey is "better" and that she should "play on the girls' team ... [because] the best players are on the girls' teams" (29). Later Alison suggests to Mandy that the WPHL is better than the NHL because "we play a different game ... I like to think we play the game the way it was intended to be played ... a game where a good small player can still be a hero" (81). Alison's meaning here is essentially that the women's game "prizes agility and quickness, not strength and power as the men's game does" (Scanlan 2002, 237), a point re-emphasized later in the story when Alison elaborates on the difference between men's and women's hockey: "men love to mix the metaphors of sex with sport, of sport with sex, of sport and sex with war and battle. Our game is purer, less psychologically extreme" (119). This passage, of course, keys in on some of the themes discussed in the last three chapters: the compulsory expectation of masculine toughness, the imbrication of male athleticism with sexuality via the sexual athlete myth, and the comparison of hockey to war that is central to the ideology of national manhood. By suggesting women's hockey as an alternative to men's hockey, a "less psychologically extreme" and therefore implicitly more healthy and moderate exercise, Alison suggests that for women, hockey is just a game, a game to be played with skill, intensity, joy, and competitiveness, but, at the end of the day, just a game. Rather than freighting the game with the host of social meanings and expectations that men do, *Iced* suggests that women play for the purer reasons of fun, enjoyment, exercise, and fellowship. Alison is eventually able to win Mandy over to her way of thinking about hockey, and by the end of the novel we learn that Mandy is now "playing for an all-girls team" (197).

One of the major obstacles that Alison has to deal with in her capacity as coach is a series of exploitative and objectifying behaviours from the team ownership and league management. These include a rival team that plays in figure-skating costumes to enhance the sex-appeal of their hockey "product," a hockey pin-up girl calendar and other debasing promotional ventures, a disruptive and undesirable trade that is brought about to cover up the inappropriate sexual advances of another team's owners toward a player, and a directive from the Teddies' owners to suppress the news that an attractive young player has recently come out of the closet as a lesbian. Although some of these episodes are exaggerated and implausible,[12] their point is clearly to emphasize the "many hardships and struggles" that women's hockey has faced in its more than a century of existence (Avery and Stevens 1997, 14). As each new challenge arises, Alison stands firm and protects the dignity of her players and the women's game at all costs. She is eventually fired over an altercation with the team's owners, only to find she has become something of a feminist celebrity because of her work with the Teddies. Alison's life soon fills up with lectures, media appearances and the like, in which she speaks out against the "male-dominated sportsworld" and advocates for women's sport, thus thematizing the cultural work of *Iced* itself.

In addition to challenging the identity of masculine toughness and the idea of the game as a male preserve, *Iced* takes on the assumption of compulsory heterosexuality that prevails among other hockey novels. The Teddies dressing room is seen as a "dyke" domain, where heterosexuality is permitted but is by no means the norm. The all-female community of the Teddies hockey team is seen as a safe and supporting environment that even the heterosexual players enjoy for its feminine solidarity and its absence of "condescending male[s]" (83). Women's hockey itself, then, is represented largely as a lesbian concern, a fact that is illustrated by Alison's comment before the first game of the WPHL championship series: "a quick glance told me that every woman hockey player and every dyke in Ontario was in the stands" (135–6). Women involved in elite-level sports have often been subjected to the "sexual suspicion" of lesbianism, an assumption that has frequently resulted in the "enforcement of a 'feminine image' by ... coaches, administrators, and sponsors of many women's leagues" (Bremner 2002, 8). According to physician and Olympic wrestler Kyla Bremner, female athletes who do not perform traditional femininity to counter the assumption of their homosexuality "risk being expelled from teams, losing scholarships, or being generally ostracized by the sporting community" (8). It is perhaps surprising, then, that a novel so concerned as *Iced* with overturning prevailing assumptions about gender identities and sport actually works in this regard to reinscribe another pervasive stereotype about female athletes. Despite quite rightly objecting to the enforcement of "feminine images" on its female characters, *Iced* also reinforces the problematic assumption that most female athletes are lesbians. While this characterization is certainly in keeping with the gender and political agendas of *Iced* as a lesbian novel, it inadvertently belies the "systemic intolerance" and actual discrimination frequently encountered by real-life lesbian athletes (Fusco 1997, 172).

Given both Alguire's position as the first adult-oriented female hockey novelist and the weight of opinion and assumption against which she was writing, it is understandable that her posture is somewhat aggressive and polemical. *Iced* challenges the male-dominated and heternormative inertia of hockey culture in ways that are forthright and necessary, and its work to encourage people – especially young children like Mandy – to value women's participation in hockey and idealize female athletes as heroes is valuable and beneficial. One potential problem with Alguire's approach, however, is her interest in distinguishing the women's game from the men's along the lines of skill versus strength. Because women's hockey has been "effectively stigmatized as an inferior form of the 'real' game" (Adams 2009, 133), apologists for women's hockey have often attempted to extol the virtues of their game by differentiating it from men's hockey along exactly these lines. But as Charlene Weaving and Samuel Roberts argued in their paper at the Hockey on the Border conference in June 2010, making such distinctions between the men's game and the women's game actually ends up entrenching normative gender assumptions. Focusing on the prohibition against bodychecking in women's hockey (the major structural distinction that informs the differences – both real and perceived – between the two games), Weaving and Roberts conclude that "the current regulations are immoral, and, ultimately sexist." According to Weaving and Roberts, "it is quite evident that the restrictions under which women are permitted to play reproduce social norms. By righting this wrong ... physical sports, specifically hockey, should serve as a device to encourage a change from traditional gendered expectations of women in sport." Whether by rule variations or character generalizations, the impulse to differentiate the men's game from the women's is ultimately unproductive. This study has been intensely critical of the ways in which hockey novels work to configure the game as essentially masculine, but the solution is not to identify or privilege some imaginary category of the essentially feminine as an alternative. Men can be skilled and women can be tough, and both of these attributes are – and should be seen as – necessary and gender-neutral qualifications for playing the game well. The way forward toward a truly gender-neutral view of hockey, then, is to remove the structural and representational forces that maintain normative assumptions about gender. This concern aside, *Iced* is to be commended for its pioneering role in critiquing the gendered aspects of the hockey myth, and can be seen as having paved the way for several more recent hockey novels whose critiques perhaps suggest the shape and direction of things to come.

NEW DIRECTIONS: *TWENTY MILES, THE PENALTY BOX,*
THE CHECKOUT GIRL, AND *THE PENALTY KILLING*

As of this writing, the four most recent adult-oriented hockey novels
are Hedley's *Twenty Miles*, O'Connor's *The Penalty Box*, Zettel's
The Checkout Girl, and McKinley's *The Penalty Killing*, and all of
these work in some way to address various shortcomings of the
hockey myth. *Twenty Miles* is the second adult-oriented Canadian
hockey novel written by a woman and featuring a female protagonist, and challenges the idea of hockey as a male preserve by opening
up space for women within the culture of the game. Hedley's novel
deals with many of the familiar themes of the hockey genre: the
importance of hockey to small-town Canada, the pastoral myth
(expressed by a Christmas Day skate on a frozen pond), the ways in
which the game structures and mediates family relationships, and
the tendency to mythologize hockey heroes (which, at least in part,
involves imaging a hockey-playing identity for the "non-mythical
hockey goddess" Isobel Stanley, "the daughter of Lord Stanley, as in
the Stanley Cup" [80]). Furthermore, *Twenty Miles* incorporates
both of the plot trajectories that consistently structure the hockey
novel genre: as the story of Isabel Norris's struggle to live away from
home, adjust to university life, and fit-in with her new teammates
(the fictional Winnipeg University Scarlets) *Twenty Miles* can be
read as a *Bildungsroman*, while the novel's major plot conflict is
essentially a retirement narrative in which Isabel wrestles with her
growing doubts about hockey, an uncertainty which leads her to
leave the game, her team, and her university education for a time
before eventually returning.

In terms of gender roles, *Twenty Miles* works to challenge the idea
that the aggressiveness and physical toughness necessary to play the
game are "masculine" qualities. This is made evident early in the
story during the team's tryout, in which Isabel hits another player,
Hal, with a solid bodycheck and sends her sprawling to the ice.
Twenty Miles maintains the distinction that bodychecking is forbidden in women's hockey – Isabel quickly apologizes that she had
played minor hockey with boys and had been taught to "play the
body" – but this isn't seen to detract from the toughness, physicality,
and aggression of the women's game. When Hal gets up after Isabel's
hit she is furious, not due to the pain but because, as she puts it, "I
was just laid out by a fucking Barbie doll" (18). It is the "Barbie

doll" version of femininity in which women are valued primarily for their attractiveness and passivity that *Twenty Miles* explicitly rejects, and throughout the story the Scarlets condemn this identity as it is enacted by other female characters (figure skaters, Hooters waitresses, etc.).[13] As a team, the Scarlets evince an alternative femininity based on toughness and team fraternity, but ostensibly absent the more problematic aspects of these identities. For example, lesbians are openly accepted in the Scarlets' dressing room, and the most ominous hazing ritual depicted in *Twenty Miles* consists of a relatively harmless evening of dinner and drinking in which the rookies are forced to wear outlandish ball gowns and make-up (a device that both ironically dramatizes the version of femininity the novel rejects and exemplifies the logic suggested earlier that hazing rituals establish identity by performing its "other"). In other words, *Twenty Miles* implicitly addresses some of the problems this study has identified in other hockey novels as growing out of the expectations of masculine toughness. This isn't an attempt, however, to associate these problems specifically with masculinity or to assert the purity of the women's game. Rather, *Twenty Miles* conceives of hockey in relatively gender-neutral terms, creating a space for women within the game by rendering it – and the toughness it requires – as equally open to both men and women.

Like *Twenty Miles*, *The Checkout Girl* attempts to create space for women within the culture of the game. This thematic is less explicit in the novel itself, however, than in the promotional write-up from Signature Editions (2008), which announced in large typeface near the top that "Hockey's Not Just For Boys!" The gender politics of *The Checkout Girl* are subtler than this press release seems to indicate, and Zettell isn't particularly overt or polemical about women's participation in hockey. In fact, the novel explicitly rejects this approach when the protagonist, Kathy Rausch, and her friend Darlyn dismiss the budding 1970s feminism of Darlyn's mother as impersonable and overly ideological: "She thinks hockey is men being boys and the boys are play-acting war. She thinks all contact sports are deliberate staged acts of belligerence that mimic war. That they're displays of patriarchal dominance put on for other men to see – pissing contests, she calls them. They're also reminders to women about who has the strength and power in the world ... That's the way she talks now, Kathy ... Those are the kinds of things she tells us. Dad looks confused and sad and goes into the basement.

He pulls his chair right up to the TV screen and tries to keep the volume very, very low when he's watching *Wide World of Sports*, hoping Mom doesn't hear so he won't get another lecture " (136).

One of the problems that Zettel seems to have with these sorts of ideas is that they throw the proverbial baby out with the bathwater. Rather than reject sports entirely as an arena of male domination, *The Checkout Girl* represents hockey as an unobtrusively normal component of feminine identity. The critique here, however, is of Darlyn's mother more than her ideas, in that her approach appears overly preachy and makes her unpleasant to live with. In fact, despite rejecting the idea that sports are unredeemable, *The Checkout Girl* implicitly endorses Darlyn's mother's critique of patriarchy in several ways, probably the most obvious being a disturbing scene in which Kathy is raped by her former boyfriend. Kathy's immediate response to this traumatic violation is to reassert her composure and sense of self by going to play hockey at a local outdoor rink (which could also be seen as an implicit affirmation of the pastoral myth). While acknowledging the harmful patriarchal beliefs and actions that hockey culture can encourage, then, *The Checkout Girl* also recognizes the potential for the game to function as a site of healing in which such violence can be undone. Zettell's working title while writing the novel was "The Bobby Orr Guide to Becoming a Woman," which interestingly gestures to the gender politics involved in adapting the hockey *Bildungsroman* to a woman's experience. The change to *The Checkout Girl*, however, is more reflective of the finished product, in which hockey does less to determine the emerging adult identity of Zettell's protagonist than her job as a grocery store checkout girl. Aside from the main character's interest in Bobby Orr, hockey doesn't ultimately play a central role in *The Checkout Girl*. In fact, the book could be more accurately described as a skating novel than a hockey novel, as the protagonist spends a good deal of time skating and dreams of earning a living by skating as well.

On the issue of women's involvement in the game, *Twenty Miles* and *The Checkout Girl* can be situated within a growing trend among Canadian sports novels in the late 2000s to depict strong and athletic female characters. Angie Abdou's *The Bone Cage* (2007)[14] and Samantha Warwick's *Sage Island* (2008), for instance, both focus on female protagonists for whom swimming is a central component of personal identity. While *Sage Island* sees swimming as the means by which a young woman finds herself, *The Bone Cage* explores the feelings of loss and uncertainty that many high-performance athletes experience when they can no longer compete at the most elite levels of their sport. Also in this vein is Arley McNeney's *Post* (2007), in which a national team women's wheelchair basketball player is forced to end her career due to hip-replacement surgery and forge a new identity for herself outside the game. All of these novels adopt roughly the same approach toward female athleticism as *Twenty Miles* and *The Checkout Girl*, depicting strength, competitiveness, and determination as gender-neutral values and assuming – rather than arguing – that female athleticism is both normal and natural.

Gender is a central issue in *The Penalty Box* as well, although masculinity is the focus rather than femininity. Despite working in several ways to mythologize hockey as Canadian, *The Penalty Box* is unique in the way it explicitly – almost didactically – sets out to portray some of the negative consequences of masculinity-as-toughness. *The Penalty Box* is narrated by Kyle Callendar, a former NHL player attempting to recover psychologically from the sexual abuse he has been subjected to by one of his coaches in junior hockey. Throughout the process of reckoning with this traumatic experience, *The Penalty Box* represents the "masculine" need to be tough as working against the emotional vulnerability and trust that are necessary for Kyle's healing. By explicitly criticizing the game's culture of silence surrounding incidents of sexual abuse, recognizing that putting "the Team above all else" is dangerous and unhealthy (159), and acknowledging that socialization in hockey culture can lead men to view women as sexual objects, *The Penalty Box* encourages readers to challenge the terms of the myth and question the ways the game works to construct gender identities. Due in part to the revelation in April 2010 that hockey's most notorious sex offender, Graham James, the former coach of the Swift Current Broncos in the Western Hockey League, had been quietly pardoned by the Canadian Parole Board in 2007, and in part to the appearance of a memoir by former NHL star Theoren Fleury alleging that he was one of the players abused by James, there has been growing public scrutiny surrounding the issue of sexual abuse in hockey. *The Penalty Box* contributes to this emerging awareness and encourages cultural change within the game as the solution to hockey's code of silence on these issues. Furthermore, such a novel might also encourage participants in hockey culture to be more in touch with and up-front about their emotions and experiences in the game, and to resist the pressure toward what sports sociologists call "deviant overconformity" within the culture of the game. Beyond condemning the way in which hockey culture has silenced victims and facilitated abuse, the *Penalty Box* is also critical of national manhood. Kyle spends much of the story trying to come to terms with his emotionally distant and unsupportive father, a man described as "a soldier following his own set of rules. Bring order to the home, a strong work ethic to his boy. Fight the ultimate Canadian battle, the necessary failure. Surrender is not an option" (59).

Like *The Penalty Box*, *The Penalty Killing* works to expose several negative consequences of hockey's disciplinary and coercive culture. For instance, McKinley's protagonist Martin Carter, a former professional player whose career has been ended by a traumatic injury, is critical of the "sexual antics [that] went on between players on the road" in which "it was not uncommon for a couple of them to pick up a keen female fan or two and share them back at the hotel" (225). *The Penalty Killing*'s most sustained critique, however, is directed at the compulsory heterosexuality that continues to structure hockey culture. Although Carter is avowedly heterosexual and pursues several female love-interest characters throughout the novel, he resents the fact that during his time as a player "the team tried to make him date actresses and show up at clubs on the arms of babes ... so people wouldn't think he was gay" just because he "didn't do the groupie thing ... and didn't think peeler bars were the height of human accomplishment" (217–18). One of the key pieces of evidence in the novel's complex murder-mystery plot is a secret video featuring a star player in McKinley's fictional Continental Hockey League performing oral sex on another of the league's star players. Both of the players' teams are anxious to destroy the tape, and one of the players involved even attempts to attack Carter and his partner in the investigation, Gracie Yates, a newspaper reporter covering the Vancouver team, in an attempt to obtain the video. When Carter and Yates outwit and subdue the aggressive player, he pleads with them to give him the video and insists that he is not a "fag" (224). The video is potentially damaging, of course, because of the extent to which homosexuality remains forbidden in hockey culture. As Yates suggests, "it scares them to death, doesn't it, the idea that one of their almighty hockey stars could be gay?" (217). Carter replies that "the [Continental Hockey League] just denies they exist – no gay players, no gay fans" (217). But beyond questioning hockey's attempts to deny and repress homoerotic attraction between players, *The Penalty Killing* suggests the potential for serious violence as a consequence of this denial and repression. The novel's mystery plot begins with an on-ice fight between the two players involved in the sex video. As the story progresses, it becomes clear that the erotic encounter between the two was the reason for the fight and that one of the players involved had been taunting the other by calling him a "fag." As in other hockey novels, this passage suggests borderline and quasi-criminal violence as a way of declaiming heterosexual masculinity within the game. But unlike other hockey novels, *The Penalty Killing* doesn't attempt to erase, deny, or even problematize homoerotic attraction between players. By depicting the stakes of being "outed" in hockey culture and suggesting the lengths to which players may go in their attempts to convey heterosexual toughness – one of the players involved in the fight is seriously injured and almost loses his life – *The Penalty Killing* criticizes hockey's culture of coercive heternormativity.

As noted earlier in chapter 2, *The Penalty Killing* is also exceptional among Canadian hockey novels in its suggestion that American fans are equally entitled to hockey as their counterparts north of the border. The point of calling attention to the fact that *Twenty Miles, The Checkout Girl, The Penalty Box,* and *The Penalty Killing* all work in some way to challenge the long-standing assumptions of the hockey myth is to underscore the fact that the adult-oriented hockey novel genre is relatively young and in the early stages of its development. Perhaps these most recent hockey novels signal the shape and direction of things to come. As more and more hockey novels are written it seems reasonable to suggest that the genre will be broadened beyond rendering the game as Canadian and masculine in the reductive and homogenizing senses identified in this study. If the first wave of adult-oriented English Canadian hockey novels respond to the perceived late twentieth- and early twenty-first-century crises of national and masculine identity by nostalgically hearkening back to an imaginary past, perhaps the second wave will envision a broader and more inclusive future. Freed from the assumption that the game must offer a sort of master narrative about what it means to be Canadian and male, hockey storytelling may yet become a consistently productive way of performing and exploring the identities to which we collectively and individually aspire.

While many of the hockey novels discussed in this study appear to limit or contain toughness within certain acceptable parameters, they simultaneously work to normalize and reinforce the very identities that result in roughness and excess. By supposing that masculinity must be constituted by toughness, hockey novels invite the lapses into excess depicted, for instance, in Bonaduce's purposefully breaking an opponent's leg during a game in *The Good Body*, or, to use a real-life example, by Todd Bertuzzi's career-ending hit on Steve Moore. By encouraging men to objectify women in the "hockey context" of dressing-room banter and groupies, hockey novels potentially foster the chauvinism and perceived sexual-entitlement that in real-life worst-case scenarios has led to abuse and even rape. Scanlan is correct to suggest that excessive hockey violence "requires synchronicity – tacit agreement among those who watch, those who play, and those who govern play" and that "owners and players, coaches, fans, and referees are all complicit in creating an atmosphere in rinks that paves the way for hockey violence in its myriad forms" (2002, 280–1). But while there may be no single cause or obvious solution to excessive hockey violence, working to move prevailing attitudes about masculinity away from physical toughness would go a long way toward addressing the problem.

Hockey novels are correct to want to referee violence, but don't appreciate the extent to which this must also involve reconsidering the ways in which they define masculinity. To say this another way, hockey novels attempt to treat the symptoms rather than the disease. What is required is a full-scale shift in cultural attitudes and assumptions. This does not necessarily mean resolving the perennial skill versus strength binary in any definitive way, or, as sports sociologist Nancy Theberge has suggested, encouraging social assumptions about athletic excellence away from valuing "power and force" (2000, 154). Rather, power and force should continue to be seen as integral parts of the game, but be divorced entirely from our ideas about gender. Practically speaking, this might mean stricter enforcement of the rules (which, to be fair, the NHL has implemented following the 2004–05 lockout), the abolition of "clean" but dangerous hits (which the NHL took an important step toward in its decision to penalize head shots near the end of the 2009–10 season), harsher penalties for fighting, and the removal of the non-contact rules from women's hockey that currently work to distinguish it from men's.

More abstractly, the divorce of masculinity from toughness would mean encouraging players and fans to see the game in gender-neutral terms. Certainly the simple efforts of discipline and self-control that hockey novels often emphasize can go a long way toward limiting violence and aggression, a fact that becomes particularly evident every spring when certain NHL players seem to magically acquire a sense of restraint in time for the playoffs. But while the moderating impulse among Canadian hockey novels is commendable, it fails to recognize the root of the problem. Rather than constituting or contributing to a player's masculine identity, stopping an opponent with a clean bodycheck should be seen as part of the gender-neutral requirements of the game, a purely physical act that can be accomplished effectively by both men and women. None of this is to deny or downplay the importance of even the contained critiques offered by novels such as *Understanding Ken* and *The Last Season*. But, generally speaking, hockey novels work to reinscribe rather than challenge the harmful assumption that masculinity must be contingent on strength, dominance, and competition. Such representations, of course, relate back to ideas about the performance of masculine toughness as being very near to the heart of national identity. As long as these attitudes toward nation and gender remain untroubled in the myths and narratives that surround Canadian hockey, the various problems and exclusions that have often attended "Canada's game" will remain firmly in place.

Conclusion

There is a story about a NASA scientist sifting through the reams of data generated by the first moon landing and remarking "some day we'll put a poet up there and find out what it's really like." Although we have yet to put a poet on the moon, the novels discussed in this study have taken Canadian literature somewhere that once seemed equally unlikely: the hockey rink. While the genre of literary hockey writing remains relatively young, we have reached a moment at which hockey novels can no longer be marginalized or ignored within the Canadian canon or dismissed forthright on the basis of their "superficial" subject matter. Hockey novels are here to stay, and have a great deal to tell us – both for better and for worse – about the game's place in Canadian culture and the ways in which it continues to referee identity.

This study began by suggesting my personal sense of the hockey myth's appeal. I love the game, the "swift and skilled delight of speed" that comes from playing and the "rapid pouring / of delight out of self" that hockey brings among fans and spectators (Al Purdy, "Hockey Players"; 1996, 58, 57). Like many Canadians I've been raised with the game, a process that has along the way involved learning to feel at home within its narratives and assumptions. Hockey novels often reproduce these conventional ideas about what the game means and how it should be played, and in this sense they appear very realistic: by representing hockey as we are accustomed to seeing it and corroborating the thoughts that we are often encouraged to have about it, the novels discussed in this study appear to confirm what many Canadians believe they already know. Indeed, this feeling of authenticity is one of the primary ways in which hockey novels attempt to appeal to their readers. Entering a fictional world that affirms one's values and beliefs can be immensely comforting, especially if those values and beliefs appear to be under attack in other areas of culture and society. The danger in reading hockey novels is that we might suppose their authentic-feeling depictions of the game to be the way things actually are and should be. It is easy to fall into the NASA scientist's assumption that literature helps us get at the "truth" of things, and that the "truths" conveyed in hockey novels are natural and inevitable and therefore appropriate, indisputable, and unchangeable.

At an historical moment in which Canada appears to have no overarching narrative or binding principle of unity, hockey novels attempt to provide these things by way of the game itself. In doing so, these novels respond both explicitly and implicitly to the general sense of crisis that permeates identity discourse in Canada, as well as to the attendant idea that lack of a binding and distinctive national culture has resulted in increased globalization and Americanization. During a period in which nationalism is often perceived to be exhausted and ideologically suspect, then, hockey novels wage an aggressive rearguard campaign to foster Canadian patriotism and preserve the idea of hockey as a cultural monolith. This is not to say that hockey novels are explicitly interested in dredging up Canada's ongoing linguistic or constitutional schisms. Rather, these novels attempt the cultural work of inculcating national identity following the terms of the hockey myth itself: through suggestions of ontological inevitability (i.e., hockey as religion), by positioning the game alongside Canadian history, by invoking pastoral nostalgia and mythologizing the game's connection to nature, and by romanticizing cultural processes such as the game's mediation of social relationships and technological processes such as radio and television broadcasts.

Hockey novels are also somewhat invested in the idea that the game works to unify Canadian peoples, although this unity tends to be expressed on an interpersonal level rather than intercultural. Furthermore, the unity conveyed by hockey novels is rather homogenous: despite some depiction of Natives and other minorities, the range of racial and cultural difference these novels explore is relatively limited. Finally, hockey novels attempt to suggest the Canadianness of the game quite straightforwardly by mythologizing hockey's cherished moments and hallowed heroes. This process, of course, is highly selective: while the 1972 Summit Series is frequently discussed as a defining national moment, no mention is made of the 1974 Summit Series – which Canada lost – or the so-called "Miracle on Ice" in which Team USA overcame the heavily favoured Russians in the 1980 Olympic hockey semifinals to accomplish one of the greatest upsets in hockey history (perhaps to be expected, this noteworthy moment *is* mythologized in an American hockey novel, Falla's *Saved*).

Canadian hockey novels are equally selective in their hagiographic accounts of hockey heroes: while there are plenty of references to Wayne Gretzky, Bobby Orr, Rocket Richard, and other Canadian greats, the main context in which hockey stars from other nations appear is as worthy but ultimately defeated adversaries (Vladislav Tretiak and Valeri Kharlamov, for example). Furthermore, there is no celebration of female hockey heroes such as Hayley Wickenheiser, Abigail Hoffman, or the Preston Rivulettes, to name just a few possibilities. The need to gloss these references illustrates the extent to which hockey continues to be publicly commemorated and memorialized as a male domain: Wickenheiser is a three-time Olympic gold-medal winner for Canada and possibly the greatest female player ever, Hoffman is a former Canadian track and field athlete and advocate for women's advancement in sport who caused considerable controversy as a young girl when she disguised herself as a boy in order to play organized hockey, and the Preston Rivulettes were a women's team who lost only 2 of the 350 or so games they played throughout the 1930s. Hockey has inarguably been played and enjoyed by Canadian women for as long as it has by Canadian men, but hockey novels give very little indication that this has been the case. Rather, hockey novels consistently deny the place of women in the game as an attempt to bolster a traditional version of masculinity that has been increasingly called into question during the last thirty or so years.

As the tenets of traditional masculinity – hard work, determination, perseverance, strength, toughness, breadwinner provision, and responsibility to the collectives of family and nation – become less and less applicable in post-industrial society, violent sports such as hockey have often been seen as the last area of culture in which these values appear legitimate and effective. Growing out of nineteenth-century assumptions about the relationship between sport, masculinity, and national well-being, hockey appears to maintain the idea that a man's worth is dependent on physical toughness and that by deploying this toughness in the service of the collective he might legitimately contribute to the nation's well-being. These ideas are made manifest particularly where hockey novels depict the game as a proving ground in which boys become men and in their frequent consociation of hockey with war. They are also evident in the attempts of hockey novels to preserve the myth of heroic masculinity, and to a lesser extent in several other mythologies of masculinity by which hockey novels attempt to appeal to readers, prescribe certain gender identities, and accommodate traditional masculinity to the moment in which these novels were produced (the bully, the sexual athlete, and the New Man).

Such representations attempt to reassure readers that masculine toughness can still be effective and powerful by contributing productively to the nation's destiny and well-being, protecting the weak, and ensuring that justice prevails. When Bayle's father watches Dave "Tiger" Williams win a fight in Robertson's *Heroes*, he is able to "nod his head with the satisfaction of knowing that at least for tonight – at least at Maple Leaf Gardens tonight – fairness and justice ruled the world once and for all, that the bad guys weren't going to get away with anything they shouldn't, and that the good and honourable were guaranteed the standing ovation they so rightly deserved" (186). As Blake notes, this passage propounds an obvious untruth: Tiger Williams wins the fight because he is a better fighter, not because the cosmic register of justice and propriety somehow favours the Maple Leafs (2010, 120). But while the exaggeration and blatant partisanship of Bale's father create ironic distance, Robertson himself has suggested the extent to which someone like Bayle's father, a blue-collar labourer whose own life seems governed by unfairness and anonymity, can earnestly hold such views: "Saturday night when someone's picking on one of the smaller Leaf team-mates and Tiger Williams steps in, that's the only kind of integrity he sees all week. It's real" (quoted in Blake 2010, 120). By constructing a fictional reality in which male toughness and aggression seem to ensure that things remain as they "should be" in at least one area of culture, the appreciation felt by Bayle's father for Tiger Williams is an excellent example of the cultural work hockey novels undertake toward traditional masculinity itself. Furthermore, by suggesting hockey as the only place in which masculine stability (and therefore truth and justice, etc.) prevails, hockey novels – like the adulation of Bayle's father of

Hockey Night in Canada – ascribe the game with disproportionate and unreasonable levels of importance.

As part of their project of preserving traditional masculinity, hockey novels frequently disqualify women from the game on the basis of purported weakness. Because women aren't strong enough to participate in the violence that characterizes the men's game, these novels suggest, they are unable to play "properly" or fully appreciate the game. Even among hockey novels that to some extent take on board feminist critiques of traditional masculinity, physical toughness remains the one characteristic that irrevocably separates the sexes. Beyond keeping women out of the game, this characterization contributes to the ways in which hockey novels categorize women. While – in keeping with the obligations of traditional masculinity – wives and girlfriends need to be protected and provided for, groupies and "puck bunnies" appear to exist entirely for the sexual gratification of "deserving" male athletes. The problem of inordinate or unmanly weakness also appears to define gay men as an essential category and – along with the unacknowledged "threat" of homoerotic attraction that hockey novels consistently repress – precludes the possibility that gay men might play the game or participate in the masculine fraternity of the team.

Although the institution of the team often appears to establish friendships and mediate relationships between men, the idyllic male community promised by the myth is disrupted both by the game's culture of competitive individualism and by the coercive requirements of belonging, a fact which hockey novels rarely acknowledge. Furthermore, real-life athletic cultures are regulated through certain compulsory attitudes and behaviours that function to declaim masculinity and thereby guarantee membership, and many hockey novels endorse this culture of enforced conformity despite the fact that the game's rituals of belonging often demand participation in harmful and degrading hazing rituals and encourage men to see women as sexual objects. Several of the most recent hockey novels, however, challenge various aspects of the game's disciplinary culture, from the assumption that hockey is a male preserve to the culture of conformity that has often allowed for the abuse and manipulation of players by coaches and management.

The danger in all of this, of course, is that readers might internalize the harmful and problematic assumptions they encounter in hockey novels or allow these depictions to confirm what they think they already know about the game. In the area of national identity, this might mean encouraging readers to accept a limited view of Canadianness which at best fails to accept cultural difference and at worst descends into vulgar ethnocentrism or chauvinist patriotism. It may also involve elevating hockey's role in the minds of readers beyond any reasonable expectation of what the game might hope to accomplish in Canadian society and at the expense of other valuable institutions and pursuits. In terms of gender, readers may come away from hockey novels confirmed in the inherited wisdom that border-line violence is "just part of the game" and that it constitutes a definitive part of masculine identity. Heterosexual male readers might be left with exclusionary attitudes toward women and gay men, as well as the belief that it is somehow okay to see women as sexual objects and the perception that masculinity is at least in part contingent on performing this view in one's speech and actions. Female readers might accept and internalize the role of sexual object that hockey culture foists on them, and, along with gay men, may also be discouraged about their possibilities for participating in the game. Although it should never be supposed that readers lack agency or the capacity to think critically about the content they consume, novels inarguably have the potential to influence the ways in which we see the world. While some hockey novels employ irony at times to create critical distance from their subject matter or to inject humour, the genre as a whole is predominantly invested in the sort of earnestness and straightforwardness championed by Gaston in *The Good Body*. Generally speaking, readers are meant to take the representations they encounter in hockey novels at face value and to go along uncritically with the ideas being put forward. Again, this desire to referee identity originates in anxiety over the perception of crisis that has attended both nation and gender in late twentieth- and early twenty-first-century Canada. Hockey novels, however, don't intend to be retrograde or harmful in their depictions of nationhood and masculinity, but to hearken back to an era in which these things seemed more stable and coherent, and duty, morality, and social order appeared more straightforward and comprehensible.

By all accounts, Gary Cheevers of the Boston Bruins was the first NHL goaltender to decorate his mask. During the 1967–68 NHL season, Cheevers took a puck in the face during practice and used the incident as an excuse to head to the dressing room to take a break. Noticing a dent in the surface of Cheevers' mask where the puck had struck, one of the Bruins' trainers jokingly painted a scar. Cheevers took to the idea and began adding new scars to the mask whenever he was hit in the face, inadvertently beginning a long tradition of mask decoration among goaltenders. This tradition is a somewhat curious development in hockey culture: although goalies have always been seen by their teammates as lone wolves and peculiar characters (see Randall Maggs' 2008 poetic treatment of Terry Sawchuk for an exploration of this), the practice of mask painting allows the goalie to differentiate himself from his teammates in a way that would seem anathema to hockey culture. A goalie's mask allows for a degree of individuality and self-expression that is typically forbidden in hockey culture, or at least subsumed within the coercive process of belonging to the team. Alone among hockey players, the goalie is allowed to express himself creatively during actual play and is differentiated from his teammates in this way.

The practice of mask decoration offers a somewhat unlikely way of thinking about the cultural work hockey novels undertake and their relation to the game itself. What mask decoration does, of course, is to apply the artistic impulse to the game. In a sense, each and every hockey novel does the same thing by exploring what it means to render the game in aesthetic terms and by proposing that the realms of body and mind are not as incompatible as often thought. But while by its nature a decorated goalie mask defies the team's uniformity, hockey novels tend to fall readily in line with the norms and assumptions of the game's culture and the myth. In this sense, the decorated mask occupies a position to which hockey novels might productively aspire: rather than affirming the game's status quo and working within its constricting parameters, hockey novels should be artistic outliers that stand apart and creatively question. Another function of the decorated goalie mask is to protect, and, to push an already tenuous metaphor slightly further, hockey novels might reasonably be expected to do the same. The effect of Cheevers' stitch-faced mask is to dramatize the harmful consequences of being hit in the face with a puck while diminishing this danger in reality. At their best, hockey novels should work in somewhat the same way: by fictionalizing the harmful aspects of hockey culture in such a way as to encourage critical distance and thereby work against these things in real life.

This book has recognized the appeal of the hockey myth while working to analyze and expose the mechanisms by which it has been propagated and encouraged. For the critical reader, the process of consuming hockey novels is one of alternately enjoying the game's appeal and recoiling from its deficiencies. As such, this book has taken a position of critical support for the novels it discusses. Although this study has focused particularly on their limitations, it should be made clear that there is much to be admired and enjoyed about Canadian hockey novels. Many are in various ways resonant, entertaining, engaging, and acutely descriptive of the game's myriad details and sensations. As the genre matures, hockey novels will grow to embrace and expand on these finer qualities while exposing, opposing, and defying the limiting terms of the hockey myth. Story and narrative are wonderful ways by which we can celebrate, explore, and make sense of the game, and the hope of this study is that our collective vision for both hockey and hockey writing will become increasingly more expansive, inclusive, generous, and enthralling.

Appendix

The following was written by Ricki-Lee Gerbrandt, a student in one of my Canadian Literature courses at the University of Western Ontario, about her experience growing up as a hockey player and reader of hockey novels.

I have played hockey for as long as I can remember. I grew up in Northwestern Ontario, and my home town of Kenora (population 15,500) is a small Canadian hockey town. We have dozens of public outdoor hockey rinks, three indoor hockey rinks and dozens of private rinks scattered in people's backyards and lakes. I grew up with an ice rink in our backyard on the lake. In the summer I shot pucks against a tarp in the garage. I played girls hockey until my second year of peewee when I also joined the boys hockey league, and was the first ever girl in my hometown to play boys hockey with checking. That year I was in grade 8, and played in the girls league, the boys league, and for the high-school team (I began playing girls high-school hockey when I was still twelve years old and in grade 6). During the summers around this time I travelled to Thunder Bay to play for an triple-A travelling team representing Northern Ontario. At the age of fourteen I moved to Kelowna, British Columbia, and became the only girl in the Pursuit of Excellence Hockey Academy where I played with twenty-six boys ages twelve to sixteen. We practiced on ice two hours per day, did off-ice training for one hour, and spent another hour in hockey skills class. I was the first female graduate from the Pursuit of Excellence Hockey Academy but numerous other women have graduated since, many of whom went on to play for university and Canadian national teams. When I was fifteen years old I played in an double-A midget boys tournament, and was the youngest player to try out for the Edmonton Chimos of the National Women's Hockey League (NWHL). I was invited back for training camp and given a full article review in the *BC Hockey News*. I moved to Ottawa for grade 12 and played junior women's hockey for the National Capital Competitive Program Junior Raiders, a Junior affiliate for Ottawa's NWHL team, before moving back home to graduate from high school and play double-A midget boys hockey for the Kenora Thistles (where I was the only girl on the team) as well as boys house-league and girls high-school hockey. During my university studies I played varsity hockey for the Western Mustangs in 2006–7.

My favourite hockey novels growing up were the *Screech Owls* series by Roy MacGregor and the *Slapshots* series by Gordon Korman. I started reading the *Screech Owls* when I was in grade 3. That year my family had moved to Kenora from Winnipeg and it was also the first year I registered for hockey. I finished the *Screech Owls* books as fast as I could read them, which was pretty much as fast as my mom and I could travel the two hours back and forth to Winnipeg to buy them at the bookstore. I would eagerly wait for each new book in the series to come out. The *Screech Owls* series, for me, was probably like the *Harry Potter* series has been for kids today. When I was young I would stay up all night reading them. When I was a little older and could read faster, I would have them finished before my family had left the bookstore. The *Screech Owls* series represented the ideal life for me. The mystery plot lines aside, the novels portrayed a life dedicated to hockey. The town, the players, and all the characters bonded over the game, dedicated their lives to pursuing dreams of the Olympics and NHL. In one of the books, the character Sarah plays in the Olympics. Not only was the best player a girl (Sarah) but she was the only one to make it far in the game. The male players end up in various other careers, never reaching the NHL. This hugely impacted my perception and appreciation for hockey. Reading these novels greatly influenced me to go beyond gender limits in the game. Reading about a character who succeeds in a male-dominated league made me realize I could do the same. The *Screech Owls* series takes place in peewee, which is the level at which I switched to boys hockey and became the first girl in Kenora to do so. At that time I wasn't aware of the difference between the fictional world portrayed in the novels and reality. I definitely thought that it was possible for me to succeed, like Sarah, in a boys league. My peewee and bantam years playing boys hockey were my most fun and memorable years. I was the only girl in the league and in all the tournaments we travelled to. I was named Assistant Captain each year, and was the second leading scorer on my team. I played with twenty boys who thought video games and farting were the most epic experiences in life. Although I wasn't so keen on either, I can say that some of my best friends today are my teammates from my first year playing boys hockey. The *Screech Owls* series, particularly the character of Sarah, made me realize that I didn't need to be constrained, simply because I was a girl. Playing boys hockey helped me develop as a player, and I know I definitely wouldn't have gone as far in my hockey career if I hadn't switched leagues. I was lucky to have extremely supportive parents and a dad who was willing to fight through political barriers and deal with the complaints of parents who felt girls shouldn't play. My mom was also a huge influence in supporting my future dreams and ambitions. She bought every *Screech Owls* book for me, and told me I could accomplish any dreams and goals that the characters I was reading about had.

I also read Gordon Korman's *Slapshots* series. I immediately fell in love with the main character, Chipmunk, an aspiring sports journalist. I began reading these when I was ten years old and in grade 5. One of the characters, Alexa, a power forward, went through similar experiences I had in playing boys hockey. She was criticized by opposing teams' parents. In one of the books, *All-Mars All-Stars*, Alexa doesn't get chosen for the all-star team even though she is second best in the league. This reminds me of hearing some parents complain because the coaches gave me more ice team than their sons, in addition to playing special teams. After some outrage from her team, Alexa is allowed to play on the all-star team but chooses not too, saying she had to wash her hair. I haven't read this novel for probably ten years, but I will never forget that line. The grittiness of the player, her absolute dedication and toughness showed me I could be tough and gritty regardless of my gender. Her experiences represented some of the realities I would face, and the discrimination I was exposed to. The only thing I didn't like about the *Slapshots* novels was the fact that Alexa wore figure skates. I was very offended. I have never worn figure skates, and although most people refer to them as "boy's skates," I have been advocating the term "hockey skates" my whole life. I didn't think such an amazing player, like

Alexa, should be resigned to wearing figure skates, simply because she is a girl.

Alexa is a great role model because she is fierce, a talented player, and very determined. I remember really identifying with her character on many levels. She was one of the best in the boys league, yet she still had to fight for her right to play. These novels are right about the game discriminating based on gender. This wasn't a battle I had to fight outright, but my parents, especially my dad, had to defend my presence to league officials and coaches. I was lucky to be drafted by an amazing coach, who is now a close family friend. During my whole hockey life playing with boys I had to undergo many additional challenges because I was a girl. Similar to Alexa, I was often targeted in games. I was harassed on the ice by opposing teams, with both sexually and physically threatening messages. (The hockey novels I read did not deal with sexual harassment, but the female characters were often physically and emotionally harassed). I fractured my foot in peewee after the captain of an opposing team aimed two consecutive slap shots at me. While this discrimination was discouraging, I had a support network of coaches, parents, and teammates that made the harassment seem immature and ridiculous. I learned to stick up for myself at an early age, and I can definitely say my experiences playing boys hockey have had a tremendous influence on my personality. The longer I played, the more I was accepted. In fact, one of my favourite childhood pictures is of my team and I, all crammed into a hot tub at a hotel during a tournament. It shows a group of rowdy twelve-year-old peewee players, and me, right in the middle, wearing a bright pink bathing suit and not looking out of place at all.

Notes

INTRODUCTION

1 The title of a conference held in April 2005 in Plymouth, Massachusetts, Canada's Game?: Critical Perspectives on Ice Hockey and Identity, calls into question the legitimacy of this assumption. The conference featured papers from many different disciplines and perspectives, several of which challenged the idea of a symbolic connection between hockey and Canadianness.

2 This study's treatment of multiculturalism deals more with the myth of multiculturalism than the practice, by which is meant the range of cultural meanings that the "mosaic" identity seems intended to convey: the idea that Canada is a tolerant society which actively celebrates difference and diversity, that this tolerance is underwritten by a history of embedded pluralism, and that the Canadian "mosaic" distinguishes us culturally from the American "melting pot." The work of Eva Mackey, Himani Bannerji, and others has exposed the extent to which the actual practice of Canadian multiculturalism attempts to "institutionalize, constitute, shape, manage, and control difference" and to which "the power to define, limit and tolerate differences still lies in the hands of the dominant group" (Mackey [1999] 2002, 70).

3 Kidd and Macfarlane's The Death of Hockey is not to be confused with an updated hockey manifesto of the same name by Jeff Klein and Karl-Eric Reif, The Death of Hockey, Or: How A Bunch of Guys With Too Much Money and Too Little Sense Are Killing the Greatest Game on Earth (1998).

4 A similar articulation of Richards' hockey nationalism occurs in his novel Nights below Station Street (1988) through the character of

Adele: "she saw how some of her friends – and some radio and television commentators – started to lose heart in the Canadian team [during the 1972 Summit Series], and even took to ridiculing it. At her young age, she did not understand that criticism of your own in Canada was often considered fashionable expertise" (1988, 79). The narrator continues that "for Adele who had always loved hockey," the Summit Series "was the one spiritual happening she could think of. It might have seemed silly to a few, but the greater majority of Canadians thought like she did" (80).

5 Szeman makes this claim with the caveat that there exists "an enormous gap between the actual content of Canadian literary texts and the ways in which they were interpreted during this period" (2003, 163). For Szeman, "it is the discourse of Canadian literary criticism [rather than literature itself] that seems to require the production of a homogenous national space" (162). While he acknowledges that there are some Canadian novels which sustain nationalist readings, Szeman suggests that these readings have arrived largely uninvited and indicate the extent to which literary criticism (again, rather than literature itself) has "safe-guarded *and* produced" the "nation's soul" (198; italics in original).

6 The story behind *Amazons: An Intimate Memoir by the First Woman Ever to Play in the National Hockey League* is rather unlikely. When DeLillo first wrote the novel, his publisher at the time, Knopf, declined to publish *Amazons* but allowed him to take it elsewhere under the condition that it must be published pseudonymously. After *Amazons* was picked up by Holt, Rinehart, and Winston publishers (who actually hired a woman to pose as Cleo Birdwell, the novel's supposed author and "first woman ever to play in the National Hockey League"), several critics recognized DeLillo's style and exposed him as author. The novel went out of print in the mid-1980s, and DeLillo has never allowed it to be republished despite considerable interest (see Howard 2008). In a recent *New York Times Book Review* article "In Search of the Great American Hockey Novel," Keith Gessen complains about the "marginal place of hockey in the world of American letters" (2006, 27) but praises *Amazons* for its descriptions of American cities and travelogue flavour: "DeLillo's subject," Gessen suggests, has always been America, in the broad sense ... and here, via hockey, he gets close to what Cleo [the narrator of *Amazons*] calls 'the schizy, dark heart' of it" (27).

7   As Karen Skinazi notes, Leslie McFarlane's hockey novels were "mostly revisions of pieces he had written for *Sport Story* [magazine] in the 1930s" (2009, 117). *Sport Story* was published from 1923 to 1943 by Street & Smith, a New York-based publisher of pulp fiction and dime novels.

8   The term "hockey novels" is used throughout this study to refer to the adult-oriented Canadian hockey novels that comprise its central focus. When children's hockey novels or other hockey texts are being discussed, this will be clearly specified.

9   One of the major ways in which hockey novels attempt to be realistic is by incorporating real hockey players and events in their fictional narratives. The significance of this gesture, of course, is to create a feeling of correspondence between the real and fictional hockey worlds, a device which delivers the pleasures of familiarity and situatedness to readers who are also fans of the game. Another effect of this gesture is myth-making: by fictionalizing real players and events, hockey novels suggest certain moments and personalities from hockey's past as significant, contribute to their established cultural meanings or supply them with new ones, and ask readers to receive them in certain ways (as glorious, infamous, "Canadian," etc.).

10 Other strategies of legitimation are generally evident across the genre as well, such as the almost invariable reference in Canadian hockey novels to some "high culture" author such as Shakespeare or T.S. Eliot, to name the two most frequent. For example, Adrian Brijbassi's *50 Mission Cap* contains a scene in which members of the local junior hockey team are forced to explicate *The Waste Land* in a high-school English class and by doing so realize new insights into the character of one of their teammates.

11 *King Leary* was nominated and defended by musician and hockey commentator Dave Bidini. In addition to his non-fiction writing about the game, Bidini has himself authored a collection of hockey short stories, *The Five Hole Stories* (2006), and contributed to a volume of hockey short stories edited by Quarrington entitled *Original Six* (1996).

12 The best-seller lists at Amazon.ca are "unscientific" both because they update hourly and because they don't factor multiple editions into a novel's total sales. Sales figures for novels are very difficult to track down, as BookNet Canada – an industry research firm that tracks sales data and trends – only makes specific results available to booksellers and publishers. Publishers, it would seem, are equally reluctant

to divulge this information, as my inquiries about hockey novel sales figures have gone largely unacknowledged.

13 Hughes-Fuller has argued elsewhere that anxiety about the game's place in Canadian society may account for the somewhat frequent presence of ghosts and other gothic elements in hockey literature. Aside from participating in a Canadian tradition of gothic writing, Hughes-Fuller sees these texts as proposing an interesting paradox: while Freud conceived of the gothic as *unheimlich* ("un-home-like"), one of the "framing narrative[s] of [Canadian] identity is that our 'country is winter' and home is where the hockey is. Perhaps there is a tension between this most familiar of myths and the fear that, as discourse, it may turn out to be unsustainable? If so, then the presence of gothic elements in hockey texts also speaks to the 'in-between space' that is Canada, and the anxiety this ambiguity produces" (Hughes-Fuller 2010, 260–1).

14 Mason examines responses to the FoxTrax puck, a regular hockey puck implanted with a computer chip to allow sensors throughout the arena to display its location as a red streak across television screens. The FoxTrax puck was introduced and briefly used by the Fox television network during the 1996 NHL season. Designed to make viewing easier for entry-level fans, the new puck quickly raised the ire of established hockey watchers. Much of the Canadian criticism directed toward the FoxTrax puck cast it as an example of American ignorance and greed spoiling "Canada's game."

15 While Rosin writes specifically about the United States, it is reasonable to suggest that many of these trends apply equally to Canada.

CHAPTER ONE

1 *When She's Gone* uses italics rather than quotation marks to designate speech, which have not been reproduced for reasons of style and clarity. Unless otherwise noted, quoted passages from this novel have been de-italicized.

2 In 1977 Tom Sinclair-Faulkner published an essay entitled "A Puckish Reflection on Religion in Canada" in response to a sportswriter who had characterized hockey as "the nearest thing to extant religious fanaticism in the country today" (Frank Moritsugu, quoted in Sinclair-Faulkner 1977, 384). Sinclair-Faulkner argued that hockey constitutes an "ecclesia," the characteristics of which are "its own doctrine, its own priesthood, its own judicial system, and [being] 'ecclesiastic'" or

constituted by a body of believers who have been "called-out, set over against the rest of the world" (388). Sinclair-Faulkner's explanation of hockey doctrine is particularly interesting for my purposes here, in that it expands beyond the simple codified regulations of professional hockey to include "popular books about hockey, the ritual pep talks before and during games, special team rules laid down by coaches and managers, stories and anecdotes which circulate among the players and fans, commentary and interviews in the news media" (391). According to Sinclair-Faulkner, the ultimate signification of these doctrinal texts and rituals is that "in the hockey cosmos one is Canadian, one is manly … [and] one is excellent" (390). In other words, Sinclair-Faulkner's idea of hockey doctrine is roughly approximate to my characterization of the hockey myth.

3   On the issue of national priorities and exclusions, Angie Abdou's *The Bone Cage* suggests the effects of hockey's prominence on athletes in other Canadian sports when Digger, an Olympic wrestler for Canada, complains that "he'd be a national hero instead of just another unknown amateur athlete" if he had been born in "one of the countries that appreciates wrestling" (22). Despite his high level of success as a wrestler, Digger goes so far as to question his choice of sports and suggest that "maybe [he] should have stuck with hockey like his dad always said" (22).

4   Beyond its critical stance toward hockey violence, *Saints of Big Harbour* is also an outlier in its treatment of hockey-as-religion. Although Coady depicts spectators at the arena cheering the name of a player who has viciously attacked an opponent as being "like heaven-crazed fundamentalists calling on their Lord and Saviour" (2002, 60), the comparison is blatantly ironic in its contrast between the sacrificial violence inflicted on Christ and the malicious violence of the hockey game.

5   West's painting itself configures Canadian history in accordance with religious iconography, depicting Wolfe's death according to the pictorial conventions of the Lamentation of Christ. By maintaining this convention in his imitation of West's painting, Carroll puts Lundin in the place of Christ in *The Deth of Wulf*, a gesture that seems to indicate both the purity, innocence, and sacrificial betrayal of Winnipeg Jets fans by their team's owners and the relationship between Canadian fans and the exploitive forces of "American" capitalism in general.

6   The route taken by the Nuggets in *Dawson City Seven* brings the team from Dawson to Whitehorse by sled, Whitehorse to Skagway,

Alaska by train, Skagway to Seattle, Washington by boat, Seattle to
Vancouver by train, and, finally, Vancouver to Ottawa by train.
According to *Hockey: A People's History* (CBC 2006), the actual
Nuggets were able to travel directly from Skagway to Vancouver by
boat. A more radical discrepancy occurs in Wayne Simpson's (1989)
chapter on hockey history, which traces the route as Dawson to the
Athabasca River by dogsled, the Athabasca River to Edmonton by
boat, and Edmonton to Ottawa by train.

7 Almost exactly the same joke is made in Jack Falla's *Saved*: "We char-
tered into Montreal on Friday after the practice. It's a short flight, so
we were in our hotel, the Queen Elizabeth, by early afternoon. The
Queen E is home to one of Canada's oldest restaurants – the Beaver
Club, a name dating back to the day when Montreal's chief industry
was the fur trade. 'I made dinner reservations for us at the Beaver
Club,' Cam told me as we got off the bus. Bruno Govoni overheard
him. 'Why would anyone want to eat at a strip joint?'" (2007, 88).
Although this passage does more to indicate Govoni's particular values than the novel's perspective on women, it is reasonable to see the
moment as an intentional allusion to *Puck Is a Four Letter Word* as
Falla mentions Orr – the author of *Puck Is a Four Letter Word* and a
fellow hockey journalist – in the acknowledgments of *Saved*.

8 The shack is named after Eddie Shack, who played in the NHL from
1958 until 1975. According to the creator of several hockey history
websites, Joe Pelletier, Shack was known for his "magnetic personality,
desire and fearlessness," as well as his "incredible combination of
toughness, leadership, character, and showmanship" (2006a). Shack
was so popular in his day that he became one of the few professional
hockey players to inspire a song, "(Clear the Track) Here Comes
Shack" by Douglas Rankin and the Secrets.

9 The character of King Leary is loosely based on Francis "King"
Clancy, who played for the Ottawa Senators from 1921 to 1930 and
for the Maple Leafs from 1930 to 1937. One of the NHL's "most popular fan attractions during the 1930s," Clancy was "a paradox in
motion … feisty, fast, and pugilistic on the one hand, but fun-loving,
skilled and soft-spoken on the other" (Simpson 1989, 202).

10 Use of the word "strategy" here isn't necessarily intended to imply
deliberateness.

11 Although neither Hewitt nor Young are overly obtrusive in their
patriotism, both *Hello, Canada and Hockey Fans in the United States*
and *That Old Gang of Mine* see winning a gold medal in Olympic

hockey as an act of service to the nation. An interesting counterpoint occurs in Arley McNeney's *Post* (2007) when the narrator, Nolan Taylor, wins Olympic gold for Canada in women's wheelchair basketball and yet remains focused on a recent romantic disappointment in her personal life rather than on any larger sense of national glory or even the personal thrill of victory. As Taylor puts it, "I remember that game – that it existed – but I don't remember winning … They played 'O Canada' and when someone put a gold medal around my neck, I used it as an excuse to cry" (427).

CHAPTER TWO

1 A telegraph machine was used during the 1896 Stanley Cup challenge between the Montreal Victorias and the Winnipeg Victorias to convey the action of the game live from Montreal to fans back in Winnipeg.

2 Hewitt actually makes a cameo appearance in his own hockey novel *"He Shoots, He Scores!"* when the protagonist and his father attend a playoff game at Maple Leaf Gardens. With what might otherwise seem like a surprising degree of detail, the father tells his son to "take a look at that long, open gondola away up on the far side. That's where Foster Hewitt's hockey broadcasts begin. From here it doesn't look very roomy, yet it's thirty-four feet long. It's as high above the ice as the top of a five-storey building. I'll bet it wasn't a very comfortable perch on the night when Foster described that Boston–Toronto game that went 164 minutes overtime" (6–7).

3 The idea that an iconic sporting event can contribute to national unity and identity is suggested in Carol Shields' *Small Ceremonies* (1976), but of football rather than hockey. A novel which defines irony as "observation … acid-edged with knowledge" (125), *Small Ceremonies* uses its own acid-edged observation to poke fun of the attempts of Canadian literary criticism to map out a national character and identity, particularly those versions proposed by Frye and his acolytes which portray the Canadian sensibility as a response to a hostile and antagonistic natural world. This occurs primarily through the character of Furlong Eberhardt, a rather pompous and disingenuous author whose work is said to be "definitively Canadian" and to represent the "most nearly complete flowering of the national ethos in the middle decades of the century" (140). During one episode in *Small Ceremonies* Eberhardt schedules a book-launch party to be held on the same day as the Grey Cup, which causes another character to note that for

someone who "embodies the national ethos … [Eberhardt] is fairly casual about the folkways of his country" (50). In part, the implication of this passage is to undermine and expose literary pretentiousness (a project which hockey novels also undertake); when the blunder is revealed and the book launch rescheduled Shields' narrator confesses "[relief] that I would not have to admit we put football before literature in this house" (51). But the passage also indicates that the championship game of the Canadian Football League (CFL) contributes as much, if not more, to national character and identity as the work of a supposedly definitive Canadian author. As the only entirely Canadian professional sports league involved in one of the four major North American team sports, the CFL is well-suited to Shields' purpose here: while Canadian franchises compete alongside American ones in the National Basketball Association, Major League Baseball, and NHL, the CFL is a uniquely Canadian alternative to the all-American National Football League. Although *Small Ceremonies* depicts the Grey Cup as an important national institution, then, this suggestion must ultimately be taken in the context of Shields' somewhat ironic stance toward the idea of a definitive national character and identity. Furthermore, it should be noted that while the CFL remains relatively popular in Canada, Shields' depiction of the event's prominence was perhaps more accurate in the 1970s.

4 Gretzky has proven to be a remarkably complex public figure in the aftermath of the trade. Despite working abundantly to "grow" the sport in America, Gretzky has remained in many ways the "face" of Canadian hockey. His recent involvement with Hockey Canada as executive director testifies to this, while his work as head coach of the NHL's Phoenix Coyotes – formerly the Winnipeg Jets – from 2005 to 2009 demonstrates his commitment to the NHL's agenda of American expansion.

5 Kerry Fraser's missed call on Gretzky during the 1993 conference final remains infamous among Maple Leaf fans, to the point that Fraser dedicated an entire chapter of his autobiography (Fraser 2010) to the incident and addressed it publicly in a column for TSN on the event's eighteenth anniversary (Fraser 2011).

6 This particular complaint, of course, is no longer relevant given the relocation of the Atlanta Thrashers to Winnipeg and the club's adoption of the Jets name prior to the 2011–12 NHL season. Although the new incarnation of the Jets has been widely regarded among Canadian fans as a patriotic reclamation, the league's permission to move the Thrashers from Atlanta to Winnipeg was based almost entirely on

economics and is in many ways emblematic of Canada's relative strength during the financial crisis of the late-2000s. If Canada's economy remains strong and stable compared with that of its southern neighbour in the long term, it is entirely possible that other struggling American franchises will receive the NHL's blessing to seek out greener financial pastures in Canadian markets, such as Quebec City and Hamilton. Should this be the case, it will be interesting to see whether or not the perception of "the game in crisis" abates somewhat in Canadian hockey rhetoric. Since Canadian hockey novels seek in large part to guarantee the status of hockey in Canadian culture, perhaps the number of new hockey novels being produced will decline if our national grip on the game appears to become more secure.

7 In both cases it was the arena issue that eventually precipitated the team's relocation. In the NHL of the 1990s, teams were increasingly relying on amenities such as luxury boxes and priority seating to generate operating revenue. Both Quebec and Winnipeg launched bids to receive new publicly funded arenas similar to those being built in many American expansion cities at the time, but both campaigns ultimately failed.

8 *Teeth* is exceptional here in its willingness to place part of the blame on Canadian regionalism. Eventually the unnamed Western Canadian prairie city is able to get its NHL team, but only because there are no other bidders on "a failing franchise, wilting in the heat of a southern US city" (16–17) – a prescient notion, given the fate of the Atlanta Thrashers. Despite reversing the pattern of NHL teams migrating from Canada to the USA that hockey novels more commonly depict, *Teeth* is concerned about the struggles and viability of small-market Canadian teams in the early 1990s. Even after arriving in Canada, the team – which is named "the Bisons," thereby suggesting its unnamed locale to be Winnipeg as the same appellation applies to the University of Manitoba's athletic teams – struggles to be successful and faces constant rumours of further relocation.

9 *McGonigle Scores!* was republished in 2006 by Key Porter in an edition that was edited and introduced by McFarlane's son and prominent hockey commentator Brian McFarlane, who has been criticized for failing to change "a couple of racial comments that may have been acceptable when the book was originally published in the 1960s" (Bergen 2006). Key Porter has also released a collection entitled *Leslie McFarlane's Hockey Stories*, which gathers some of McFarlane's previously uncollected stories and was also edited and introduced by Brian McFarlane.

10 *Face-Off* was turned into a feature film of the same name, in which Scott Young made a brief cameo as a reporter (McCowan 1971).

11 The backlash against the Ottawa Silver Sevens (and by proxy, the centralist/federalist ethos that they surely represent) might also be read as suggesting a Canadian unity that is more regional than national in character. Given the totalizing myth-making tendencies of *Hockey Night in the Dominion of Canada* and *Dawson City Seven*, these characterizations might be seen as moments of slippage that expose the simplifying aspirations of the myth and gesture both toward the complex nature of identity and the reality of complicated ways in which Canadians have experienced hockey as "variously connected to the local community, to broader 'communities' of loyal fans who follow professional teams, and finally, to an imagined national community" (Gruneau and Whitson 1993, 200). Hockey didn't, of course, abandon small-town Canada after the outflow of elite players diminished the competitiveness of regional teams throughout the 1910s and 20s. Instead, the game remained an important community activity because of the long Canadian winters and its ability to "cut across occupational, religious, and ethnic divisions" (205). When many small communities built indoor arenas throughout the 1940s, 50s, and 60s, hockey became the "[focal point] of a gregarious intracommunity and intercommunity culture that ... represented the friendliness and togetherness of small-town Canada" (205). As Dryden and MacGregor suggest in *Home Game*, hockey "was, for many, a means of off-season fitness for the rigours of farming, the driving force behind the building of community centres, the way in which widely separate communities connected with each other" (1989, 20–1). Another way of saying this is that throughout the same period in which elite professional hockey had been relegated to Toronto and Montreal (the only Canadian cities that could sustain NHL franchises), the small-town idylls enacted by hockey novels actually existed to some degree in real life. It is perhaps reasonable to suggest, then, that the historical movement of high-calibre hockey away from small towns helped to establish and entrench the pastoral myth of recreational small-town hockey as being more authentic or pure than profit-driven big-city professional hockey.

CHAPTER THREE

1 Dryden played for the Canadiens from 1971 until 1979, with the exception of the 1973–74 season which he sat out due to a contract dispute. During his relatively brief career, Dryden helped lead

Montreal to six Stanley Cups and was one of Team Canada's goalies in the 1972 Summit Series.

2 "The Hockey Sweater" was first written in 1979 for a collection of short stories entitled *Les enfants du bonhomme dans la lune*, and was translated into English by Sheila Fischman that same year (appearing in *The Hockey Sweater and Other Stories*). In 1980, Carrier collaborated with illustrator Sheldon Cohen to produce an animated short film based on the story, *Le chandail de hockey / The Sweater*, which won honours in nine international film competitions. In 1984 Carrier and Cohen produced a children's picture book version of the story in both French and English.

3 It should be noted that *Two Solitudes* does align with the myth-making tendencies of other hockey novels in its attempt to render hockey as an aesthetic experience. Paul's characterization of hockey players as "the best artists this country ever turned out" resonates with a general tendency among hockey novels to describe the game in terms of its poetry, artistry, or beauty. Though pleasing and part of the legitimate purpose of art, this device functions to remove hockey from its social, political, and historical contexts (or, in other words, to mythologize).

4 For further discussion of minority involvement in Canadian hockey see George and Darril Fosty 2004, Cecil Harris 2004, Robert Pitter 2006, Garth Vaughan 2002, and Robidoux 2002b.

5 This plot device is undoubtedly intended to criticize the state of labour relations in the NHL during the early 1980s when *Puck Is a Four Letter Word* was published. During this time Alan Eagleson, the corrupt and ineffectual head of the NHL Players Association, frequently worked with NHL management against the players' demands for salary disclosure and a functional free agency system. For a thorough discussion of this situation, see Bruce Dowbiggin's (2006) *Money Players*.

6 Following largely the same logic as Kroetsch's narrator in *The Studhorse Man*, Bidini argues that the idea of Canadian multiculturalism was first experienced and internalized through hockey, specifically Phil Esposito's prominent role in the 1972 Summit Series: "He was the first Italian. Before him, you never saw Italians on television in Canada. It was all British and Irish ... The closest you got was Stan Mikita. Stan was a man of colour. He was Czech, but he looked Asian. But that was it. Until Espo became the de facto captain of Team Canada, hockey was all Conachers and Smythes and Clancys. But Espo was no cake Loyalist. No: he looked and sounded different and, by seeing him every day on television and in the newspapers, you could tell that Canada's face was changing" (2000, 193–4).

Notes to pages 140–1

7 A similar moment of apparent maternal ignorance occurs in Stan
Dragland's *Peckertracks* (1978), after the young protagonist Percy
Lewis attends a hockey game with a girl he is attracted to, Ginny
Barber. At one point in the game an opposing player is pinned against
the boards near where Percy and Ginny are sitting, and someone from
the crowd reaches out to grab his stick. In an act of indiscriminate
retaliation, the player swings his stick blindly into the crowd and hits
Ginny on the arm causing her to fall over. Percy finds himself "torn
between helping Ginny and watching what's going to happen on the
ice" (94), a detail which acknowledges the dangerous appeal that
hockey violence can hold. Soon the guilty player is expelled from the
game and the play continues, but "the spark has gone out of the
game" and "the hockey is very clean" (95). When Percy gets home,
news of the incident has already reached his mother who asks her son
"what in Heaven's name goes on at those hockey games? Somebody
hit Ginny with a stick? Her mother's really up in arms. Grown men! If
that's what hockey's all about you'd better stay home from now on"
(95). While there is undeniable truth to the mother's suggestion that
grown men shouldn't be behaving like this, Percy dismisses the incident as a natural (and therefore permissible) part of the game which
his mother wouldn't be capable of understanding: "There's not much
use trying to explain. His mother never goes to hockey games, so she
doesn't understand how the emotions get involved" (95). While
Peckertracks doesn't claim any special position for hockey in
Canadian society and represents other sports such as golf, curling,
baseball, and basketball with equal or greater prominence, hockey is
seen as the only athletic activity in which such excessive and indiscriminate violence appears to be okay.

8 Although *Understanding Ken* is self-conscious in its critique of excessively rough play, McCormack doesn't seem to offer a narrative stance
outside the totalizing view that Canadian identity is inextricably
linked to hockey culture. In other words, *Understanding Ken* depicts
unhealthy attitudes toward violence to critique them, but doesn't
appear to do the same regarding issues of national identity. Although
the obvious unreliability of McCormack's child narrator perhaps calls
into question the association between hockey and national identity
that he frequently draws, part of the narrator's development in
Understanding Ken is to learn to reject excessive violence. By contrast,
his beliefs about the Canadianness of hockey are left untroubled and
appear firmly intact by novel's end.

9 In addition to *The Uninvited Guest*, two exceptional novels that portray hockey as a means by which immigrant/outsider characters symbolically become Canadian are Paci's *The Italians* and *Black Madonna*.
Both novels are set in Sault Ste Marie, Ontario (although *The Italians*
fictionalizes the name as Marionville), and both explore intergenera-
tional conflicts within the Italian-Canadian community between parents and grandparents who want to preserve their cultural heritage
and children faced with pressure to assimilate. *The Italians* focuses on
the Gaetano family, the youngest son of whom, Bill, loves hockey so
much that "he dreamed it, ate it, lived it day in and day out" (38)
despite his parents' disapproval. Indeed, on the ice Bill is said to have
"achieved a sense of belonging, of being wanted and admired, which
he never got at home. He felt somewhat alien in a house filled with
Italians" (40). Beyond measuring his distance from his Italian family,
hockey helps Bill fit in at school better than either of his siblings: "He
had learned at an early age that his prowess in the sport made many
people take notice of him. His school friends looked up to him, and
his teachers, at least those who were fans of the game, treated him
with deference. It seemed to make him less Italian" (40). But *The
Italians* isn't entirely optimistic about hockey's negotiation of cultural
difference. When Bill makes it to the NHL playing for the Chicago
Blackhawks, he encounters a great deal of discrimination which,
despite becoming accustomed to "he still found difficult to bear. It
wasn't so much that he felt himself insulted, for he didn't think of
himself to be that 'Italian.' He felt those insults were aimed at his
father. It was as if each time someone called him a Wop or a DP or a
Dago they were calling to question everything that his father had
accomplished in the new country" (112). While hockey allows Bill to
be valued and appreciated in Canadian society, it also reveals the fact
that the rest of Bill's family hasn't been so welcome. Bill's transforma-
tion "from being a second-generation Italian ... [to] 'the hockey star'"
(150), then, doesn't entirely disconnect him from his cultural heritage,
and at the end of the day the coexistence of these identities remains
somewhat uneasy. Hockey features less prominently in *Black Madonna*,
but a similar thematic emerges when the protagonist, Joey Barone,
wants to leave home to play Junior hockey but his traditional Italian
father objects: "The scouts had seen him play and had confidentially
told him there'd be no worry about making the team. And if he made
the team, there'd be a good chance of playing professional hockey,
which was his life-long dream. But his father had looked hurt beyond

measure. His eyes downcast, his voice wavering, Adamo had said, 'You want to leave home because of this?'" (17). Joey ends up staying in Sault Ste Marie, and rather than getting a shot at realizing his dream in the big leagues ends up playing below his potential in a local Industrial League. According to McKinley's description of Paci in *Hockey: A People's History*, the theme of assimilation through hockey arises from the author's experience growing up in an Italian immigrant family: "as the son of working-class immigrants, Paci couldn't expect new hockey gear from his parents whose sporting allegiance was to soccer, but he persuaded them to buy him a pair of second-hand skates from the Salvation Army. As generations have done before him and since, Paci felt freedom and power on the ice, but he also felt that playing hockey was his true passport to the new world" (192). In Paci's own words, "for us immigrant kids, hockey is the game we all want to excel in because it's the Canadian game. Hockey makes us different from our parents – it sets us apart. Playing hockey makes us feel that we belong in the new country" (quoted in McKinley 2006, 192).

CHAPTER FOUR

1 The world's fair in Montreal during Canada's Centennial year, Expo '67, was the "moment in which the nation 'came out' to the world, and to itself, in what was perceived as its new progressive and pluralist form" (Mackey [1999] 2000, 59). One of the government pamphlets distributed at Expo '67, *Change Comes to Canada*, worked specifically to position hockey within the emerging myth of pluralism as a game that all Canadians participate in and enjoy regardless of race, sex, or class. For subsequent commentators who emphasize the game's northernness, then, such as Kidd and Macfarlane and Beardsley, hockey's connection to the Canadian winter is seen as part of what makes it available to all Canadians.

2 A Hockey Canada television advertisement that aired during the 2008 IIHF (International Ice Hockey Federation) World Junior Hockey Championship featured the slogan "Hockey First," eerily – though no doubt unintentionally – echoing "Canada First."

3 It is worth noting that the emergence of modern sport had a great "democratizing" effect, if, as cultural critic Leo Braudy observes, "you happened to be white" (2003, 341).

4 Nelson notes that "'white' manhood as an institution has [recently] conceded some space in the public and civic arenas, to those people formerly constituted as legal others – 'minorities' and 'white' women. But as the recent dismantling of affirmative action programs and their replacement with 'new' civil rights laws designed to 'protect' white men, and intensified national border phobias have demonstrated, such concessions have done nothing to dislodge or displace the referential power of 'white' manhood, whether we agree that such men are privileged or 'equally' victimized" (1998, 28). In other words, although many of the men who identify with the ideas of national manhood perceive themselves as not having benefited consistently from it, the hegemonic power of this ideology remains relatively intact.

5 Foer offers this reading as an "obvious explanation" for soccer violence and hooliganism, but does so as a preface to another less obvious theory, "an ethos of gangsterism – spread by movies, music and fashion – [that] conquered the world ... gangsterism and its nihilistic violence had become fully globalized" (14–15).

6 The Canadian taste for and tolerance of hockey violence is perhaps best illustrated by the relative immunity hockey players have enjoyed from prosecution for on-ice attacks. Several incidents of criminal hockey violence made their way to the courts throughout the early twentieth century, which repeatedly acquitted offending players while simultaneously ruling that hockey was "in need of help from the law to prevent manslaughter from becoming an integral part of the game, and to punish those who transgressed" (McKinley 2006, 28). In other words, these rulings regularly suggested the immanent necessity of controlling and containing hockey violence while simultaneously exonerating its most flagrant and visible perpetrators. According to Lawrence Scanlan, this cycle has perpetuated itself in subsequent cases since the early twentieth century where on-ice incidents have been ultimately decided by courts of law. The result has been, according to Scanlan, that hockey violence has been "doubly protected – by amnesty and amnesia" (2002, 58). Amnesty, of course, refers to the relative impunity that offending hockey players have enjoyed in these trials, while amnesia evokes the striking lack of Canadian cultural memory for hockey's violent past. While many Canadians can readily identify players such as Marty McSorley or Todd Bertuzzi whose on-ice antics have recently earned them court appearances, far fewer would be likely to recognize the name of Allen Loney who in 1905 was charged

with murder as the result of a hockey scrum. According to Scanlan, the general lack of awareness about hockey's violent past means that present-day players are "prisoners of hockey's violent past" (261).

7 This survey was completed as part of a television show that invited Canadians to determine the "greatest Canadian" through two rounds of interactive voting. First, Canadians were invited to nominate their personal choices for the honour, and, second, once these results were in, celebrity personalities appeared on the program to make the case for each of the top entries before a second round of voting (Cherry's cause was championed by professional wrestler Brett "the Hitman" Hart). Not counting Cherry, 10 of the top 100 "greatest Canadians" were hockey players, the highest ranking of these being Wayne Gretzky who finished in tenth place. It should be noted that Radio-Canada did not take part in the series, likely reducing francophone input.

8 Probably the most significant role that Cherry plays in a Canadian hockey novel is in Scott Young's *That Old Gang of Mine*, which portrays a Cherry doppelganger named Farley Fitzgerald. Fitzgerald's role as an ersatz Don Cherry is to transform Peter Gordon's unlikely group of players into a competitive unit, which he does with great success as Canada ends up winning the gold medal.

9 *Glengarry School Days* resonates with Thomas Hughes' *Tom Brown's School Days* and *Tom Brown at Oxford*, Victorian novels modelling the Muscular Christianity espoused by Thomas Arnold during his time as head of Rugby (a prominent British public school). Arnold believed that education should be focused not only on learning but on character-building and the production of Christian gentlemen, and the reforms he instituted to this end had a profound effect on the English educational system.

10 Although *Glengarry School Days* doesn't specifically use the word "hockey," it suggests a tactical shift in the move from shinny to shinny on ice. Craven's coaching is said to arise from his knowledge of lacrosse, of which "the same general rules of defense and attack could be applied to shinny" (285). *Glengarry School Days*, then, also fictionalizes a development in the evolution of the game, bringing together the formative influences of shinny and lacrosse.

11 In his role as captain, Hughie "set[s] himself to resolutely banish any remaining relics of the ancient style of play," in which "every one rushed to hit the ball with out regard to direction or distance, and the consequence was, that from end to end of the field a mob of yelling, stick-waving players more or less aimlessly followed in the wake of

the ball" (297). Again, the move toward system and strategy can be seen to reflect the modernizing developments in industry and labour around this time.

12 Although this study remains critical of Gordon's construction of masculinity in *Glengarry School Days*, the novel's appeal should also be recognized. Donald Hall's experience of *Tom Brown's School Days* resonates with my own reading of *Glengarry School Days*, and I quote it here as an attempt to suggest the readerly pleasures that Gordon's novel seeks to supply: "the novel was morally compelling as well as repugnant. Its celebration of resiliency, determination, comradeship, and hard-fought, successful struggles against overwhelming odds struck chords deep inside me. I could not help but wish that pluck and hard work would lead always to earthly and heavenly rewards, that social harmony was finally attainable by living in accordance with broadly defined, simply stated rules" (Hall 1994, 4).

13 To supplement this qualification it is worth noting that several hockey novels appear congruent with Theresia Quigley's claims in *The Child Hero in the Canadian Novel* about child protagonists throughout the 1970s and 80s. *Bus Ride*, for instance, exhibits the 1970s tendency to see childhood as "a prison-like state from which the child tries to escape at the earliest possible time," while *The Last Season* could certainly be said to fit Quigley's 1980s rubric of "childhood re-examined as a necessary means toward wholeness" (Quigley 1991, 6; although "wholeness" isn't ever achieved for Batterinski, it is the insight into his childhood that allows the reader to understand the violence of his adulthood). The point of this aside is to suggest that in some ways Canadian hockey novels are not as far removed from the literary mainstream since 1950 as this study has suggested they are in relation to national identity.

14 Vimy Ridge is often mythologized as a "defining moment for Canada, when the country emerged from under the shadow of Britain and felt [itself] capable of greatness" (T. Cook 2004). In an episode of "Coach's Corner" that aired shortly before Remembrance Day 2008, Don Cherry both contributed to this myth and associated it with hockey by showing pictures from the attack on Vimy and suggesting the soldiers' bravery and sacrifice as a testament to Canadian honour and toughness (CBC 2008b).

15 The association between hockey and military service remains remarkably current, as evidenced by Canada's then Chief of Defence Staff General Rick Hillier's May 2008 visit to Canadian Forces in

Afghanistan with the Stanley Cup and nineteen former NHL players who participated in ball-hockey games against Canadian soldiers.

CHAPTER FIVE

1   It is hardly coincidental that "popular men's sports emerge[d]" in the post-9/11 milieu "as significant symbols that the nation had experienced an attack but had not sustained a fatal blow" (Staurowsky 2010, 64). An excellent example of this in the Canadian context was the "Tickets for Troops" game played in November 2007 between the Edmonton Oilers and Chicago Blackhawks at Edmonton's Rexall Place. For the "Tickets for Troops" event, which marked the culmination of a philanthropic campaign organized in partnership between the Oilers and the pharmacy chain Rexall in support of the Canadian Forces, season ticket holders were asked to donate their seats to military personnel from CFB Edmonton. According to Jay Scherer and Jordan Koch, the narratives produced in this event worked to "optimistically promote the war in Afghanistan, the Canadian Forces, and the Conservative Party of Canada," emphasize "the post-9/11 solidarity of [Canada and the United States]," associate "soldiers and their families, military leaders, and Conservative politicians with affective national symbols [i.e., hockey]," and "[promote] ... personalized and patriotic representations of these interest groups as 'ordinary Canadians'" (2010, 10, 12).

2   Braudy notes that "a frequent Anglo-Saxon word for male human beings ... is *wæpned* (weaponed)," and goes on to explain the linguistic association between maleness, heroism, and weaponry in medieval cultures: "though *wæpen* could also mean 'penis,' we should remember that only a particular class of men had the wealth and the social sanction to carry weapons, and so the interplay between the words for 'man,' the words for 'man of high rank,' and the words for 'warrior' has a long history" (2003, 5; italics in original). *Icelands* is by no means the only hockey novel to characterize the stick as a weapon, a metaphor that – if inadvertently – evokes the connection signified by the word *wæpned* between maleness, strength, heroism (i.e., high rank and responsibility), and sexual virility (which will be returned to later in this chapter in regard to the sexual athlete myth).

3   One potential effect of this characterization might be to appeal to readers beyond the white male audience to which hockey novels appear primarily directed. According to Gaston, *The Good Body* was

particularly successful with female readers: "I don't know why, but a large proportion of women connected to this book. I got quite a few responses from older women in particular, one a letter from a retired nurse in Florida who said it was her favourite, most moving book of all time" (Gaston 2005, 96).

4 Although Gaston reasserts the claim that Nesterenko published a book of poetry in his hockey memoir *Midnight Hockey* (2006, xi), I haven't been able to find any other reference to this publication (neither the Worldcat database of books and other materials in libraries worldwide or the Hockey in Print database maintained by David McNeil at Dalhousie University have any record of such a book [see McNeil 2004]). Gaston's claim in the above passage that Nesterenko scored 32 goals in the 1968 NHL season slightly stretches the truth: Nesterenko actually amassed 32 *points* in 1968–69, of which only 15 were goals. Perhaps Gaston is similarly "stretching the truth" in his claim about Nesterenko's publication of a book of poetry. If any NHLer were to have produced a book of poetry, Nesterenko would have been a likely candidate. According to Pelletier, Nesterenko "would frequent theatres and operas, the symphony and art museums," and "even took some part time university literature courses" (2006b). After his career in hockey Nesterenko spent time working as "a disk jockey, a stock broker, a travel broker, a freelance writer, a university professor, and a ski instructor" (2006b). Furthermore, Nesterenko did "odd jobs such as driving a loader and diesel Cat in the arctic… [and] even tried his hand at acting – he played the father in the Rob Lowe hockey movie *Youngblood*" (2006b). Given his wide range of interests and abilities, it seems entirely plausible that Nesterenko might have published a book of poetry. But if Gaston is "stretching the truth" in the interests of making a point, his suggestion of Nesternko as a hockey player who bridged the perceived divide between mind and body certainly makes sense. Although his book wasn't yet published when *The Good Body* was written, Gaston could just as well have referred to former NHL defenceman Sheldon Kannegiesser as another hockey player who also writes poetry. Kannegiesser's *Warriors of Winter: Rhymes of a Blueliner Balladeer* (2009) tells the story of his NHL career from 1967 to 1979 in a poetic style inspired by Robert Service. Kannegiesser repeats many of the familiar themes in literary hockey writing; for instance, writing about the unique cultural position the game occupies in Canada from the perspective of the nation itself (and echoing the sentiment that

Canada's game can't be bought), Kannegiesser suggests that "my
resources I'll share for a price that seems fair / but hockey's my heart
and my soul" ("The Series of '72," in 2009). Kannegeisser's poetry is
largely intended to be humorous, as the title of a poem about being
sent down to the AHL (American Hockey League) Hershey Bears in
Hershey, Pennsylvania indicates: "They Sent Me Down to Chocolate
Town." Another interesting example of the sort of literary negotiation
of the mind/body dualism that Gaston explores – albeit from the
opposite trajectory as Nesterenko and Kannegiesser – is George
Plimpton's *Open Net* (1985). Plimpton was an author who carved out
a rather curious literary niche as a "participatory journalist" throughout the 1960s and 70s by training with various professional sports
teams and writing books about the experience. *Open Net* is the story
of Plimpton learning the position of goaltender with the Boston
Bruins and actually playing in one of the team's preseason games.
Although Plimpton's writing is engaging and vibrant, his physical talents weren't quite on par with those of Nesterenko, Kannegiesser, or
even the fictional Bonaduce: "I stepped out onto the ice in my goaltender's skates like the frightened rat, Chuchundra, in Rudyard Kipling's
Rikki-tikki-tavi, who never dares to come into the middle of the room
… taking crotchety steps as I tried to dredge out of my past even the
simplest fundamentals. I had forgotten everything … how to stop …
to skate backwards. I had always assumed that once one had learned
to skate, it was inevitably there – however awkwardly one did it …
like bicycling, or remembering how to play 'Chopsticks,' or swimming, or folding a sheet of paper to build a glider. But all that was left
of my skating past, with its crazy abandon, was that I still sagged over
onto my ankle bones" (3).

5   A similar attempt to unite the realms of mind and body through
hockey and Shakespeare occurs in McKinley's *The Penalty Killing*
when Martin Carter looks at a picture taken during his second year as
a professional hockey player: "He was wearing his green-and-gold St
Pats home uniform in the club dressing room and reading a book:
The Sonnets of William Shakespeare. The photo had been set up by
the photographer, and Carter had been too college arrogant to see it
as anything other than him, the scholar athlete, telling the world that
he was not to be taken for just another toothless, puck-chasing grunt.
He had book learning. He was different" (26–7). By suggesting the
possibility of other ways to interpret the photograph (as a joke,

perhaps?), McKinley's combination of Shakespeare and hockey is less straightforward and less earnest than Gaston's.

6 In his defence of *King Leary* for the 2008 Canada Reads competition Dave Bidini referred to Canadian literature as "encased in … tweedy austerity" (quoted in CBC 2008), a quip that operates on the same logic as Gaston's valorization of popular literature – specifically the popular hockey novel – as being more authentic, accessible, and vibrant than high literature.

7 The position of "keeper of the Cup" was created in 1995 and is filled by three Hockey Hall of Fame employees whose job it is to accompany the trophy everywhere it goes (the practice of allowing every Stanley Cup-winning player a day with the Cup was also started at this time). *The Uninvited Guest* fictionalizes the history of this job, however, representing it as having been created in 1952 after the Cup inexplicably went missing for several months. It is the role of keeper of the Cup that drives much of the plot action in *The Uninvited Guest*, both through the characters of Tony and his predecessor, Stan Cooper.

CHAPTER SIX

1 Brendan Burke was killed in a car accident in February 2010.
2 *Breakfast with Scot* was the first film to receive permission from the NHL and the Toronto Maple Leafs to use the Maple Leaf logo, jerseys, and other items relating to the club. The next film to do so, Mike Myers' *The Love Guru* (Schnabel 2008), depicts a black hockey player, Darren Roanoke, whose dismay over being abandoned by his wife adversely affects his play. After being helped by Myers' character, the titular love guru, Roanoke leads the Toronto Maple Leafs to win the Stanley Cup. Like the depiction of a homosexual hockey player in *Breakfast with Scot*, the character of Darren Roanoke works to broaden the range of "normal" and "acceptable" hockey identities along racial lines. While the Leafs are to be commended for allowing their brand to be used in such progressive ways, there's probably a joke somewhere in all of this that racism and homophobia will have been abolished long before the Leafs win another Stanley Cup.
3 It should be noted that Mason's ideas about gender don't appear to stem from his characterization as a man of his time (Mason narrates the story as an old man in 1962, with the bulk of the story actually occurring in 1904–5). Throughout the narrative, Reddick has Mason

specifically defuse certain outdated beliefs and assumptions about gender that could also be attributed to periodization. At one point, for instance, Mason recalls telling one of his friends that "women can't even vote … [so] they'll never be allowed to drive automobiles" (42), but immediately retracts the content of this assertion by expressing shame at having said this. Similarly, Mason repeatedly asserts the platitude that men don't cry throughout his narrative, but by the end of the story admits that shedding tears can be a healthy expression of sadness and loss (314–15). By working to modify or retract certain outdated assumptions about gender while leaving others solidly in place, *Dawson City Seven* upholds the idea of hockey as an exclusively male preserve, one final sector of culture in which masculinity remains safeguarded from the emasculating influences of feminine weakness and emotion.

4 It is worth distinguishing here between the effeminate man (i.e., the homosexual), whose "weakness" appears to threaten the team's collective strength and unity, and the New Man, who appears as a concession to changing societal attitudes about gender by incorporating certain "feminine" values without disturbing the core assumption of masculine toughness.

5 "In the Navy" is presumably inappropriate for hockey culture because it calls attention to the potentially homoerotic nature of military bonding and to the performative nature of military masculinity (which, for the Village People, is expressed as a sort of masculine drag), both of which would appear to threaten the Platonic masculine stability on which the idea of a team is founded.

6 For more on this and other psychoanalytical aspects of *The Divine Ryans* see Sugars (2004) and Méira Cook (2004).

7 These aren't the only ways in which *The Divine Ryans* steps outside of the generic conventions of the popular hockey novel. Johnston's narrative defies several of the trends discussed in this study by offering an adolescent anti-hero protagonist whose *Bildungsroman* development doesn't pertain directly to hockey or get realized through his involvement in the game. Furthermore, *The Divine Ryans* seems to ridicule the ideas of team unity and masculine *esprit de corps* that are central to national manhood, inasmuch as Draper Doyle is never fully enfolded in the fraternal belonging of the hockey team (on which he remains an outsider and a third-rate player) or Father Seymour's "Number" (a troupe of orphans who are ostensibly "fathered" by Draper Doyle's uncle through instruction in boxing and choral music).

8 It is important to recognize the extent to which belonging in the culture of team ultimately remains a "voluntary submission" (Robidoux 2001, 119). Objectively speaking, individual men will always have the freedom to forego hazing rituals and endure the social sanction this inevitably incurs. This is not, however, an easy decision, as men who choose to symbolically refuse membership in the collective by avoiding initiation typically face ostracism, exclusion, and persecution that, in some cases, has actually driven players from the game (126).

9 The fact that hazing rituals typically involve nudity and often contain markedly homoerotic elements has led Laura Robinson (1998) and others to read these rituals as expressions of homoerotic desire. Although this study doesn't foreclose on the possibility of such a reading, it doesn't see homoeroticism as the primary signification of either real-life hazing rituals or novelistic depictions thereof. Rather, hazing rituals attempt to incorporate individuals into the team collective by dramatizing what they are ostensibly *not*: weak, powerless, effeminate, homosexual, etc. It should also be remembered that nudity has "very different significance for [hockey] players than for society at large" (Robidoux 2001, 113), and, as such, hazing rituals could also be read to perform certain "normal" aspects of hockey culture as a way of symbolically enfolding newcomers within that culture.

10 Reddick's decision to tell this story through a character named McLennan could be a subtle allusion to Hugh MacLennan's *Two Solitudes*, a novel that, as discussed earlier in chapter 3, sees hockey as unifying the French and English elements of Canadian culture. *Two Solitudes* famously takes for its epigraph Rainer Maria Rilke's suggestion that "Love consists in this, / that two solitudes protect, / and touch, and greet each other," and offers this dictum as a model of coexistence for the "two solitudes" of Canadian culture. Applied to *Dawson City Seven*, of course, Rilke's words appear ironic in that Reddick's narrative forbids "love" between teammates – in this case French and English – from being expressed through "touch," or at least through "inappropriate" touch that intimates homoerotic attraction.

11 Falla's *Saved* similarly suggests that hockey players describe puck bunnies as "puck fucks" and notes that "screwing a puck fuck is about as hard as hitting an empty net" (23). Working from the testimony of a woman who was gang-raped by six Junior hockey players, Robinson points out that the term "puck bunny" is highly derogatory because it implies the way in which groupies are "passed around" between teammates "like a puck" (1998, 147).

12 Although the point that women's sports have often been promoted on the basis of their sex appeal is quite valid, it is inconceivable to imagine a professional women's hockey team playing in "tutus ... white and sparkled with silver spangles ... necklines plunging to reveal ample bosom" and without helmets so as not to conceal the players' faces (42). This is true simply for the outlandishness of the outfits, but also for the cultural sexism that refuses to tolerate serious injury to female hockey players. Bodychecking was removed from the international women's game in 1990 after a public outcry over the number of players sustaining serious injury, a fact which has been the "centerpiece of the construction of women's hockey as an alternative to the men's game" (Theberge 2000, 116). While Alguire's WPHL does allow for body contact, Alison explicitly maintains that the women's game is more about skill than strength.

13 Hal's characterization of Isabel as a "Barbie doll" is initially intended as an insult, but as Isabel makes the team and gains the respect of her teammates they nickname her "hockey Barbie" as an ironic gesture to the version of femininity they collectively reject.

14 *The Bone Cage* was a finalist for Canada Reads 2011, and was defended by former NHL enforcer Georges Laraque.

Bibliography

Novels and stories discussed in the book are cited by author and title; secondary literature (films, newspaper articles, critical studies, etc.) are cited by author and date.

NOVELS AND STORIES DISCUSSED

Abdou, Angie. *The Bone Cage*. Edmonton, AB: NeWest, 2007.

Alguire, Judith. *Iced*. Norwich, VT: New Victoria Publishers, 1995; Toronto: Women's Press, 1995.

Armstrong, Jeannette. *Slash*. 1985. Penticton, BC: Theytus Books, 1988.

Brand, Dionne. *What We All Long For*. Toronto: Vintage Canada, 2005.

Brijbassi, Adrian. *50 Mission Cap*. Victoria, BC: Trafford, 2001.

Brouwer, Sigmund. *Chief Honor*. Lightning on Ice 6. 1997; Victoria, BC: Orca, 2008.

– *Thunderbird Spirit*. Lightning on Ice 3. 1996; Victoria, BC: Orca, 2008.

Callaghan, Morley. *The Loved and the Lost*. Toronto: Macmillan, 1951.

Carrier, Roch. "The Hockey Sweater." Pages 77–81 in *The Hockey Sweater and Other Stories*. Trans. Sheila Fischman. Toronto: Anansi, 1979.

Childerhose, R.J. *Hockey Fever in Goganne Falls*. Toronto: Macmillan, 1973.

– *Winter Racehorse*. Toronto: Peter Martin, 1968.

Clarke, Austin. *The Question*. Toronto: McClelland & Stewart, 1999.

Coady, Lynn. *Saints of Big Harbour*. Toronto: Doubleday, 2002.

Craig, John. *The Pro*. Toronto: Peter Martin, 1968.

Degen, John. *The Uninvited Guest*. Roberts Creek, BC: Nightwood Editions, 2006.

DeLillo, Don [pseud., Cleo Birdwell]. *Amazons: An Intimate Memoir by the First Woman Ever to Play in the National Hockey League.* Toronto: Lester & Orpen Dennys, 1980.

Dragland, Stan. *Peckertracks.* Toronto: Coach House, 1978.

Falla, Jack. *Saved.* New York: St Martin's Press, 2007.

Galloway, Steven. *Finnie Walsh.* Vancouver: Raincoast Books, 2000.

Gaston, Bill. *The Good Body.* Vancouver: Raincoast Books, 2004.

Gordon, Charles [Ralph Connor]. *Glengarry School Days.* 1902; Toronto: McClelland & Stewart, 1975.

– *The Man from Glengarry.* 1901; Toronto: McClelland & Stewart, 1969.

Guest, Jacqueline. *Hat Trick.* Halifax, NS: Lorimer, 1997.

– *Rookie Season.* Halifax, NS: Lorimer, 2000.

Gutteridge, Don. *Bus Ride.* Ailsa Craig, ON: Nairn Publishing House, 1974.

Haliburton, Thomas Chandler. *The Attaché; or, Sam Slick in England.* London: R. Bentley, 1843; New York: Stringer & Townsend, 1856.

Hayward, Steven. *The Secret Mitzvah of Lucio Burke.* Toronto: Alfred A. Knopf, 2005.

Hedley, Cara. *Twenty Miles.* Toronto: Coach House, 2007.

Hewitt, Foster. *"He Shoots, He Scores!"* Toronto: Thomas Allen, 1949.

– *Hello, Canada and Hockey Fans in the United States.* Toronto: Thomas Allen, 1950.

Jarman, Mark Anthony. *Salvage King, Ya!* Vancouver: Anvil Press, 1997.

Johnston, Wayne. *The Divine Ryans.* Toronto: McClelland & Stewart, 1990; Toronto: Vintage Canada, 1998.

Kellerhals-Stewart, Heather. *She Shoots, She Scores.* Toronto: Women's Press, 1975.

King, Thomas. *Green Grass, Running Water.* Toronto: Harper Perennial, 1993.

Kinsella, W.P. *The Iowa Baseball Confederacy.* Don Mills, ON: Collins Publishers, 1986.

– *Shoeless Joe.* New York: Ballantine Books, 1982.

Korman, Gordon. *All-Mars All-Stars.* Slapshots 2. Toronto: Scholastic, 1999.

– *Cup Crazy.* Slapshots 4. Toronto: Scholastic, 2000.

– *The Stars from Mars.* Slapshots 1. Toronto: Scholastic, 1999.

Kroetsch, Robert. *The Studhorse Man.* 1969. Edmonton: University of Alberta Press, 2004.

Longstreth, T. Morris. *The Calgary Challengers.* Toronto: Macmillan, 1962.

Lundin, Steve. *When She's Gone.* Winnipeg, MB: Great Plains Publications, 2004.

MacGregor, Roy. *The Last Season*. Toronto: Penguin, 1983.

– *Mystery at Lake Placid*. Screech Owls 1. Toronto: McClelland & Stewart, 1995.

– *The Quebec City Crisis*. Screech Owls 7. Toronto: McClelland & Stewart, 1998.

– *The Screech Owls' Northern Adventure*. Screech Owls 3. Toronto: McClelland & Stewart, 1996.

– *The Screech Owls' Reunion*. Screech Owls 20. Toronto: McClelland & Stewart, 2004.

MacLennan, Hugh. *Two Solitudes*. Toronto: Macmillan, 1945.

Markus, Michael. *East of Mourning*. Victoria, BC: Trafford, 2001.

McCormack, Pete. *Understanding Ken*. Vancouver: Douglas & McIntyre, 1998.

McFarlane, Leslie. *Breakaway*. Toronto: Methuen, 1976.

– *The Dynamite Flynns*. Toronto: Methuen, 1975.

– *Leslie McFarlane's Hockey Stories*. Ed. Brian McFarlane. Toronto: Key Porter, 2005.

– *McGonigle Scores!* Ed. Brian McFarlane. 1966. Toronto: Key Porter, 2006.

– *Squeeze Play*. Toronto: Methuen, 1975.

McKinley, Michael. *The Penalty Killing*. Toronto: McClelland & Stewart, 2010.

McNeney, Arley. *Post*. Saskatoon, SK: Thistledown Press, 2007.

Miller, Gloria. *The Slapshot Star*. Winnipeg, MB: Pemmican Publications, 2001.

Mitchell, W.O. *The Black Bonspiel of Willie MacCrimmon*. Toronto: McClelland & Stewart, 1993.

O'Brien, Andy. *Hockey Wingman*. New York: Norton, 1967.

O'Connor, Larry. *The Penalty Box*. Toronto: Kellom Books, 2007.

Orr, Frank. *Buck Martin, Take Centre Ice; The Exciting Life in Junior 'A' Hockey*. Toronto: Musson, 1965.

– *Buck Martin in World Hockey*. Toronto: Musson, 1966.

– *Puck Is a Four Letter Word*. Toronto: Methuen, 1982.

Paci, F.G. *Black Madonna*. Ottawa: Oberon, 1982.

– *Icelands*. Ottawa: Oberon, 1999.

– *The Italians*. Ottawa: Oberon, 1978.

Quarrington, Paul. *King Leary*. Toronto: Doubleday, 1987; Bantam-Seal Book, Toronto: McClelland & Steward-Bantam, 1988.

– *Logan in Overtime*. Toronto: Doubleday, 1990.

– (ed.) *Original Six: True Stories from Hockey's Classic Era*. Toronto: Reed Books, 1996.

Reddick, Don. *Dawson City Seven*. Fredericton, NB: Goose Lane Editions, 1993.

– *Killing Frank McGee*. Burnstown, ON: General Store Publishing House, 2000.

Richards, David Adams. *Nights below Station Street*. Toronto: McClelland & Stewart, 1988.

Richler, Mordecai. *The Apprenticeship of Duddy Kravitz*. London: André Deutsch, 1959; Markham, ON: Penguin, 1985.

– *Barney's Version*. Toronto: Alfred A. Knopf, 1997.

– *The Incomparable Atuk*. 1963. McClelland & Stewart, 1989.

Ritchie, Rob. *Orphans of Winter*. Hamilton, ON: Seraphim Editions, 2006.

Robertson, Ray. *Heroes*. Toronto: Dundurn, 2000.

Sedlack, Robert. *The Horn of a Lamb*. Toronto: Anchor Books, 2004.

Shields, Carol. *Small Ceremonies*. 1976. Toronto: Penguin, 1996.

Stenson, Fred. *Teeth*. Regina, SK: Coteau Books, 1994.

Thomas, Audrey. *Coming Down from Wa*. Toronto: Viking, 1995.

Tracey, Grant. *Parallel Lines and the Hockey Universe*. Clifton, VA: Pocol Press, 2003.

Wagamese, Richard. *Keeper'n Me*. Toronto: Doubleday, 1994.

Walsh, Ann. *Shabash!* Toronto: Sandcastle, 1994.

Warwick, Samantha. *Sage Island*. Victoria, BC: Brindle & Glass, 2008.

Wieler, Diana. *Bad Boy*. Toronto: Groundwood, 1989.

Wright, Richard B. *The Age of Longing*. Toronto: HarperPerennial, 2001.

Young, Scott. *Scrubs on Skates*. Toronto: McClelland & Stewart, 1952.

– *A Boy at the Leafs' Camp*. Toronto: Little, Brown & Co., 1963.

– *Boy on Defence*. 1953. Toronto: McClelland & Stewart, 1988.

– *That Old Gang of Mine*. Toronto: Fitzhenry & Whiteside, 1982.

– and George Robertson. *Face-Off*. Toronto: Macmillan, 1971.

Zettell, Susan. *The Checkout Girl*. Winnipeg, MB: Signature Editions, 2008.

Zweig, Eric. *Hockey Night in the Dominion of Canada*. Toronto: Lester Publishing, 1992.

SECONDARY LITERATURE

Abdel-Shehid, Gamal. 2000. "Writing Hockey thru Race: Rethinking Black Hockey in Canada." In *Rude: Contemporary Black Canadian Cultural Criticism*, ed. Rinaldo Walcott, 69–86. Toronto: Insomniac Press.

Abdou, Angie. 2010. Review of *Now Is the Winter: Thinking about Hockey*, ed. Jamie Dopp and Richard Harrison. *ARETE* (Sport Literature Association listserve), 25 March.

Adams, Carly. 2009. "Organizing Hockey for Women: The Ladies Ontario Hockey Association and the Fight for Legitimacy, 1922–1940." In *Coast to Coast: Hockey in Canada to the Second World War*, ed. John Chi-Kit Wong, 132–59. Toronto: University of Toronto Press.

Althusser, Louis. 1971. *Lenin and Philosophy and Other Essasys*. Trans. Ben Brewster. London: NLB.

Anderson, Benedict. 1991. *Imagined Communities: Reflections on the Origin and Spread of Nationalism*. Rev. ed. London: Verso.

Associated Press. 2010. "Pocklington Blames Lawyer in Case." ESPN website. 27 May. http://sports.espn.go.com/nhl/news/story?id=522702 (accessed 25 August 2011).

Atkinson, Michael. 2010. "It's Still Part of the Game: Violence and Masculinity in Canadian Ice Hockey." In *Sexual Sports Rhetoric: Historical and Media Contexts of Violence*, ed. Linda Fuller, 15–29. New York: Peter Lang.

Auden, W.H. [1940] 1996. *Another Time*. London: Faber & Faber.

Aulakh, Raveena. 2010. "Rapture on Yonge St as Fans Celebrate Hockey Gold." *Toronto Star*, 28 February. On-line 8 March 2010. http://www.thestar.com/news/gta/article/772997--rapture-on-yonge-st-as-fans-celebrate-hockey-gold

Avery, Joanna and Julie Stevens. 1997. *Too Many Men on the Ice: Women's Hockey in North America*. Victoria, BC: Polestar Books.

Bannerji, Himani. 2000. *The Dark Side of the Nation: Essays on Multiculturalism, Nationalism, and Gender*. Toronto: Canadian Scholars' Press.

Barthes, Roland. 1972. *Mythologies*. Trans. Annette Lavers. New York: Hill & Wang.

Beardsley, Doug. 1987. *Country on Ice*. Winlaw, BC: Polestar.

Beaty, Bart. 2006. "Not Playing, Working: Class, Masculinity, and Nation in the Canadian Hockey Film." In *Working on Screen: Representations of the Working Class in Canadian Cinema*, ed. Malek Khouri and Darrell Varga, 113–33. Toronto: University of Toronto Press.

Bentley, D.M.R. 1992. *The Gay/Grey Moose: Essays on the Ecologies and Mythologies of Canadian Poetry, 1690–1990*. Ottawa: University of Ottawa Press.

Bergen, Jonine. 2006. Review of *McGonigle Scores!* CM Magazine 12, no. 8 December. http://www.umanitoba.ca/cm/vol13/no8/mcgoniiglescores.html (accessed22 July 2010).

Berger, Carl. 1966. "The True North Strong and Free." In *Nationalism in Canada*, ed. Peter Russell, 2–26. Toronto: McGraw-Hill.

Bhabha, Homi K. 1990. "Introduction: Narrating the Nation." In *Nation and Narration*, ed. Homi Bhabha, 1–7. London and New York: Routledge.

Bidini, Dave. 2000. *Tropic of Hockey: My Search for the Game in Unlikely Places.* Toronto: McClelland & Stewart.

– 2006. *The Five Hole Stories.* Victoria, BC: Brindle & Glass.

Blackshaw, Tony. 2003. *Leisure Life: Myth, Masculinity, and Modernity.* London: Routledge.

Blake, Jason. 2009. "'Just Part of the Game': Depictions of Violence in Hockey Prose." In *Canada's Game: Hockey and Identity*, ed. Andrew Holman, 65–80. Montreal and Kingston: McGill-Queen's University Press.

– 2010. *Canadian Hockey Literature.* Toronto: University of Toronto Press.

Bohls, Kirk and Mark Wangrin. 1997. "Athletes Revel in Being One of the Guys, Not One of the Gays." In *Taking Sport Seriously: Social Issues in Canadian Sport*, ed. Peter Donnelly, 167–71 Toronto: Thompson Educational Publishing.

Braudy, Leo. 2003. *From Chivalry to Terrorism: War and the Changing Nature of Masculinity.* New York: Alfred A. Knopf.

Bremner, Kyla. 2002. "Gender, Sexuality, and Sport." *Canadian Woman Studies* 21, no. 3: 6–11.

Bumsted, J.M. 1998. *A History of the Canadian Peoples.* Toronto: Oxford University Press.

Burstyn, Varda. 1999. *The Rites of Men: Manhood, Politics, and the Culture of Sport.* Toronto: University of Toronto Press.

Butler, Judith. 1990. *Gender Trouble: Feminism and the Subversion of Identity.* New York: Routledge.

– 1995. "Burning Acts: Injurious Speech." In *Performativity and Performance*, ed. Andrew Parker and Eve Kosofsky Sedgwick, 197–227 New York: Routledge.

Callaghan, Morley. [1942] 2003. "The Game That Makes a Nation." Repr. in *Words on Ice: A Collection of Hockey Prose*, ed. Michael P.J. Kennedy, 24–7. Toronto: Key Porter Books.

Candelaria, Cordelia. 1989. *Seeking the Perfect Game: Baseball in American Literature.* New York: Greenwood Press.

Carraghe, James. 2001. "Good, Not Great." Review of *The Divine Ryans*. *Amazon.ca*. Amazon.ca, 19 February. http://www.amazon.ca/Divine-Ryans-Wayne-Johnston/dp/0676971849/ref=sr_1_1?ie=UTF8&s=books &qid=1280582079&sr= 8–1 (accessed 29 August 2010).

Carrier, Roch. 2003. Introduction to *Backcheck: A Hockey Retrospective*, 28 January. Library and Archives Canada. http://www.collectionscanada.ca/hockey/index-e.html (accessed on 15 February 2007).

Cawelti, John. 1976. *Adventure, Mystery, and Romance: Formula Stories as Art and Popular Culture*. Chicago: University of Chicago Press.

CBC (Canadian Broadcasting Corporation). 2006. *Hockey: A People's History*. DVD. Toronto: CBC. (Produced by Susan Dando, Hubert Gendron, and Mark Starowicz.)

– 2008a. "It's Down to Three Books on Canada Reads." CBC website. 28 February. http://www.cbc.ca/arts/books/story/2008/02/08/canada-reads-thursday.html (accessed 6 May 2008).

– 2008b. "Coach's Corner." Television broadcast. Commentator Don Cherry, host Ron MacLean. 8 November. Montreal: CBC Sports Archives.

– 2009. "Paul Henderson Has Scored for Canada." CBC digital archives website, 1 September. http://archives.cbc.ca/sports/hockey/clips/1005 (accessed 25 August 2011).

Charland, Maurice. 1986. "Technological Nationalism." *Canadian Journal of Political and Social Theory* 10, nos 1–2: 196–221.

Cheah, Pheng. 2003. "Grounds of Comparison." In *Grounds of Comparison: Around the Work of Benedict Anderson*, ed. Jonathon Culler and Pheng Cheah, 1–20. London: Routledge.

Christian-Smith, Linda K. 1990. *Becoming a Woman through Romance*. London: Routledge.

Coleman, Daniel. 2006. *White Civility: The Literary Project of English Canada*. Toronto: University of Toronto Press.

Cook, Méira. 2004. "On Haunting, Humour, and Hockey in Wayne Johnston's *The Divine Ryans*." *Essays on Canadian Writing* 82: 118–50.

Cook, Tim. 2004. "The Battle of Vimy Ridge, 9–12 April 1917." *WarMuseum.ca*, 14 September. Canadian War Museum. http://www.civilization.ca/cwm/vimy/index_e.html (accessed 20 May 2008).

Cruise, David and Alison Griffiths. 1991. *Net Worth: Exploding the Myths of Pro Hockey*. Toronto: Viking.

CTV. 2010. "2010 Gold Medal Game Is the Apex of TV Viewing in Canada as Legend of '72 Summit Series Finally Laid to Rest." CNW website, 12 March. http://newswire.ca/en/releases/archive/March2010/12/c9483.html (accessed 25 August 2011).

Culler, Jonathon. 1975. *Structuralist Poetics: Structuralism, Linguistics and the Study of Literature*. London: Routledge & Kegan Paul.

– 2003. "Anderson and the Novel." In *Grounds of Comparison: Around the Work of Benedict Anderson*, ed. Jonathon Culler and Pheng Cheah, 29–52. London and New York: Routledge.

Davey, Frank. 1993. *Post-national Arguments: The Politics of the Anglophone-Canadian Novel since 1967*. Toronto: University of Toronto Press.

Dopp, Jamie. 2009. "Win Orr Lose: Searching for the Good Canadian Kid in Canadian Hockey Fiction." In *Canada's Game: Hockey and Identity*, ed. Andrew Holman, 81–97. Montreal and Kingston: McGill-Queen's University Press.

– and Richard Harrison. 2009. Introduction to *Now Is the Winter: Thinking about Hockey*, ed. Jamie Dopp and Richard Harrison, 7–18. Hamilton: Wolsak & Wynn.

Dowbiggin, Bruce. 2006. *Money Players: The Amazing Rise and Fall of Bob Goodenow and the NHL Players Association*. Toronto: Key Porter.

– 2008. *The Meaning of Puck: How Hockey Explains Modern Canada*. Toronto: Key Porter Books.

Downie, Gordon. 2001. *Coke Machine Glow*. Toronto: Vintage.

Dryden, Ken. [1983] 1984. *The Game*. Don Mills, ON: Totem; originally published by Macmillan.

– and Roy MacGregor. 1989. *Home Game: Hockey and Life in Canada*. Toronto: McClelland & Stewart.

Earle, Neil. 1995. "Hockey as Canadian Popular Culture: Team Canada 1972, Television and the Canadian Identity." *Journal of Canadian Studies* 30, no. 2: 107–23.

Evans, Christopher and William Herzog II, eds. 2002. *The Faith of 50 Million: Baseball, Religion, and American Culture*. Louisville, KY: Westminster John Knox Press.

Faludi, Susan. 1999. *Stiffed: The Betrayal of the American Man*. New York: William Morrow.

Fiske, John. 1989. *Reading the Popular*. Boston: Unwin Hyman.

Flaherty, David H. and Frank E. Manning, eds. 1993. *The Beaver Bites Back: American Popular Culture in Canada*. Montreal and Kingston: McGill-Queen's University Press.

Foer, Franklin. 2004. *How Soccer Explains the World: An Unlikely Theory of Globalization*. New York: HarperCollins.

Fosty, George and Darril Fosty. 2004. *Black Ice: The Lost History of the Coloured Hockey League of the Maritimes, 1895–1925*. New York: Stryker-Indigo.

Foucault, Michel. 1979. *Discipline and Punish: The Birth of the Prison*. Trans. Alan Sheridan. New York: Vintage Books.

Francis, Daniel. 1997. *National Dreams: Myth, Memory, and Canadian History*. Vancouver: Arsenal Pulp Press.

Fraser, Kerry. 2010. *The Final Call: Hockey Stories from a Legend in Stripes*. Bolton, ON: Fenn Publishing.

– 2011. "The Anniversary of You-Know-What for Leaf Fans." TSN website. 27 May. http://www.tsn.ca/blogs/kerry_fraser/?id=367030 (accessed 5 September 2011).

Frayne, Trent. 1990. *The Tales of an Athletic Supporter*. Toronto: McClelland & Stewart.

Frye, Northrop. 1971. *The Bush Garden: Essays on the Canadian Imagination*. Toronto: Anansi.

Fusco, Caroline. 1997. "Lesbians and Locker Rooms." In *Taking Sport Seriously: Social Issues in Canadian Sport*, ed. Peter Donnelly, 172–7. Toronto: Thompson Educational Publishing.

Galloway, Steven. 2006. "He Doesn't Shoot, But He Does Score." *Globe and Mail* (Toronto), 22 July, p. D4.

Gaston, Bill. 2005. "Slash, Spear, Elbows Up: A Conversation with Bill Gaston." Interview with Jamie Fitzpatrick. *New Quarterly: Canadian Writers and Writing* 94: 95–8.

– 2006. *Midnight Hockey: All about Beer, the Boys, and the Real Canadian Game*. Toronto: Anchor Canada.

Genosko, Gary. 1999. "Hockey and Culture." In *Pop Can: Popular Culture in Canada*, ed. Lynne Van Luven and Priscilla Walton, 140–50. Scarborough, ON: Prentice Hall Allyn & Bacon Canada.

George, Rosemary Marangoly. 1996. *The Politics of Home: Postcolonial Relocations and Twentieth-Century Fiction*. Cambridge: Cambridge University Press.

Gessen, Keith. 2006. "In Search of the Great American Hockey Novel." *New York Times Book Review*, 19 February, p. 27.

Gillmor, Don. 2005. "Hockey: The Great Literary Shutout." *The Walrus* 2, no. 1: 88–93.

Gittings, Christopher. 2002. *Canadian National Cinema*. London: Routledge.

Goldie, Terry. 1989. *Fear and Temptation: The Image of the Indigene in Canadian, Australian, and New Zealand Literatures*. Montreal and Kingston: McGill-Queen's University Press.

Greenblatt, Stephen. 1990. "Culture." In *Critical Terms for Literary Study*, ed. Frank Lentricchia and Thomas McLaughlin, 225–32. Chicago: University of Chicago Press.

Gruneau, Richard and David Whitson. 1993. *Hockey Night in Canada: Sport, Identities, and Cultural Politics*. Toronto: Garamond Press.

Gubar, Susan. 2006. *Rooms of Our Own*. Urbana, IL: University of Illinois Press.

Gumbrecht, Hans Ulrich. 2006. *In Praise of Athletic Beauty*. Cambridge, MA: Belknap Press.

Gzowski, Peter. 1981. *The Game of Our Lives*. Toronto: McClelland & Stewart Limited.

Hall, Donald. 1994. "Muscular Christianity: Reading and Writing the Male Social Body." In *Muscular Christianity: Embodying the Victorian Age*, ed. Donald Hall, 3–13. Cambridge: Cambridge University Press.

Hardy, Stephen and Andrew Holman. 2009. "Periodizing Hockey History: One Approach." In *Now Is the Winter: Thinking about Hockey*, ed. Jamie Dopp and Richard Harrison, 19–35. Hamilton: Wolsak & Wynn.

Harris, Cecil. 2004. *Breaking the Ice: The Black Experience of Professional Hockey*. Toronto: Insomniac Press.

Harrison, Richard. 2004. *Hero of the Play*. 10th-anniversary ed. Toronto: Wolsak & Wynn.

Herman, Edward and Noam Chomsky. [1998] 2002. *Manufacturing Consent: The Political Economy of the Mass Media*. New York: Pantheon.

Hewson, Kelly. 2009. "'You Said You Didn't Give a Fuck about Hockey': Popular Culture, the Fastest Game on Earth and the Imagined Canadian Nation." In *Now Is the Winter: Thinking about Hockey*, ed. Jamie Dopp and Richard Harrison, 187–203. Hamilton: Wolsak & Wynn

Hiebert Alton, Anne. 2002. "*The Hockey Sweater*: A Canadian Cross-Cultural Icon." *Papers: Explorations into Children's Literature* 12, no. 2: 5–13.

Highway, Tomson. 1989. *Dry Lips Oughta Move to Kapuskasing*. Saskatoon, SK: Fifth House.

Hobsbawm, Eric. 1983. Introduction to *The Invention of Tradition*, ed. Eric Hobsbawm and Terrance Ranger, 1–14. Cambridge: Cambridge University Press.

Hollands, Robert. 1988. "English-Canadian Sports Novels and Cultural Production." In *Not Just a Game: Essays in Canadian Sport Sociology*, ed. Jean Harvey and Hart Cantelon. Ottawa: University of Ottawa Press.

Holman, Andrew. 2009a. "Frank Merriwell on Skates: Heroes, Villains, Canadians and Other Others in American Juvenile Sporting Fiction, 1890–1940." In *Now Is the Winter: Thinking about Hockey*, ed. Jamie Dopp and Richard Harrison, 53–67. Hamilton: Wolsak & Wynn.

– 2009b. Introduction to *Canada's Game: Hockey and Identity*, ed. Andrew Holman, 3–8. Montreal and Kingston: McGill-Queen's University Press.

Howard, Gerald. 2008. "The Puck Stopped Here: Revisiting 'Cleo
Birdwell' and Her National Hockey League Memoir." *Bookforum.com*,
December–January. http://www.bookforum.com/inprint/014_04/1406
(accessed 7 July 2010).

Howell, Colin. 2001. *Blood, Sweat, and Cheers: Sport and the Making of
Modern Canada*. Toronto: University of Toronto Press.

Hughes-Fuller, Patricia. 2002. "The Good Old Game: Hockey, Nostalgia,
Identity." PhD diss., University of Alberta.

– 2010. "Gothic Night in Canada: Global Hockey Realities and Ghostly
National Imaginings." In *How Canadians Communicate III: Contexts
of Canadian Popular Culture*, ed. Bart Beaty and Derek Briton, 259–80.
Edmonton: Athabasca University Press.

Huyssen, Andreas. 1986. *After the Great Divide: Modernism, Mass
Culture, Postmodernism*. Bloomington: Indiana University Press.

Hyatt, Craig and Julie Stevens. 2009. "Are Americans Really Hockey's Vil-
lians? A New Perspective on the American Influence on Canada's National Game." In *Canada's Game: Hockey and Identity*, ed. Andrew Holman,
26–43. Montreal and Kingston: McGill-Queen's University Press.

Jackson, Lorna. 2007. *Cold-Cocked: On Hockey*. Emeryville, ON:
Biblioasis.

Jackson, Steven. 1994. "Gretzky, Crisis and Canadian Identity in 1988:
Rearticulating the Americanization of Culture Debate." *Sociology of
Sport Journal*. 11, no. 4: 428–46.

Jackson, Steven and Pam Ponic. 2001. "Pride and Prejudice: Reflecting on
Sport Heroes, National Identity, and Crisis in Canada." In *Sport and
Memory in North America*, ed. Stephen Wieting, 43–63. Portland, OR:
Frank Cass Publishers.

Jarman, Mark Anthony. 2007. Reading from *Salvage King, Ya!* At the
Canada and the League of Hockey Nations Conference, Victoria, BC,
April.

Karr, Clarence. 2000. *Authors and Audiences: Popular Canadian Fiction in
the Early Twentieth Century*. Montreal and Kingston: McGill-Queen's
University Press.

Kannegiesser, Sheldon. 2009. *Warriors of Winter: Rhymes of a Blueliner
Balladeer*. North Bay, ON: Wind & Lion Publishing.

Kennedy, Michael P.J. 1998. "Hockey as Metaphor in Selected Canadian
Literature." *Textual Studies in Canada* 12: 81–94.

– 2005. "I Am Hockey." In *Going Top Shelf: An Anthology of Canadian
Hockey Poetry*, ed. Michael P.J. Kennedy, 19–22. Surrey, BC: Heritage
House.

Kidd, Bruce. 1983. "Skating Away from the Fight." In *Sports and the Humanities: A Symposium*, ed. William Baker and James Rog, 180–99. Orono, ME: University of Maine at Orono Press.

Kidd, Bruce and John Macfarlane. 1972. *The Death of Hockey*. Toronto: New Press.

Kimmel, Michael. 1996. *Manhood in America: A cultural history*. New York: Free Press.

Klein, Jeff and Karl-Eric Reif. 1998. *The Death of Hockey, or: How a Bunch of Guys With Too Much Money and Too Little Sense Are Killing the Greatest Game On Earth*. Toronto: Macmillan.

Knowles, Richard Paul. 1995. "Post-, 'Grapes,' Nuts and Flakes: Coach's Corner as Post-Colonial Performance." *Modern Drama* 38 (spring): 123–30.

Korol, Kimberly Tony. 2006. "Marketing Multiple Mythologies of Masculinity: Television Advertising and the National Hockey League." In *Horsehide, Pigskin, Oval Tracks and Apple Pie: Essays on Sports and American Culture*, ed. James A Vlasich, 180–99. Jefferson, NC: McFarland.

Lynd, Laurie, dir. 2007. *Breakfast with Scot*. DVD. Toronto: Scot Pictures. (Performed by Tom Cavanagh, and Noah Bernett.)

McCowan, George, dir. 1971. *Face-Off*. Videorecording. Scarborough, ON: Agincourt Productions.

MacGregor, Roy. 1997. "No Room for Late Bloomers in Canada." In *Taking Sport Seriously: Social Issues in Canadian Sport*, ed. Peter Donnelly, 187–8. Toronto: Thompson Educational Publishing.

– 1998. Profile by Dave Jenkinson. *Canadian Review of Materials*. (Based on an interview conducted 31 May 1998.) http://www.umanitoba.ca/cm/profiles/mcgregor.html (accessed 22 June 2010).

– 2006. Foreword to *Artificial Ice: Hockey, Culture, and Commerce*, ed. David Whitson and Richard Gruneau, vii–x. Peterborough, ON: Broadview Press.

Mackey, Eva. [1999] 2002. *The House of Difference: Cultural Politics and National Identity in Canada*. Toronto: University of Toronto Press; originally published by Routledge.

McKinley, Michael. 2000. *Putting a Roof on Winter*. Vancouver, BC: Greystone Books.

– 2006. *Hockey: A People's History*. Toronto: McClelland & Stewart.

McNeil, David. 2004. *Hockey in Print: A Bibliography of Writing on Hockey*. Dalhousie University website. http://www.hip.english.dal.ca/credits.php (accessed 30 August 2011).

Maggs, Randall. 2008. *Night Work: The Sawchuk Poems*. London, ON: Brick Books.

Mandel, Eli. 1977. "Modern Canadian Poetry." In *Another Time*, 81–90. Erin, ON: Press Porcépic.

Mandelbaum, Michael. 2004. *The Meaning of Sports: Why Americans Watch Baseball, Football, and Basketball, and What They See When They Do*. New York: Public Affairs.

Mason, Dan. 2002. "'Get the Puck Outta Here!': Media Transnationalism and Canadian Identity." *Journal of Sport and Social Issues* 26, no. 2: 140–67.

– 2006. "Expanding the Footprint? Questioning the NHL's Expansion and Relocation Strategy." In *Artificial Ice*, ed. David Whitson and Richard Gruneau, 181–99. Peterborough, ON: Broadview Press.

Messner, Michael. 1997. *Politics of Masculinities: Men in Movements*. Thousand Oaks, CA: Sage.

– 2007. *Out of Play: Critical Essays on Gender and Sport*. Albany, NY: State University of New York Press.

Messner, Michael and Donald Sabo. 1994. *Sex, Violence and Power in Sports: Rethinking Masculinity*. Freedom, CA: Crossing Press.

Mitchell, Mike. 1995. "Lacrosse: A Gift for People of Canada." Canadian Lacrosse Association, January. www.lacrosse.ca/nationalsport.html (accessed 3 August 2006).

Morris, Timothy. 1997. *Making the Team: The Cultural Work of Baseball Fiction*. Urbana, IL: University of Illinois Press.

Morrison, Scott. 1988. "Keep Superstar in Canada NDP Appeals." *Toronto Star*, 10 August, p. A4.

Morrow, Don. 1989. "Lacrosse as the National Game." In *A Concise History of Sport in Canada*, ed. Don Morrow and Mary Keyes, 45–68. Toronto: Oxford University Press.

– 2002. "Paul Quarrington's Hockey Schtick: A Literary Analysis." In *Putting It on Ice: Hockey in Historical and Contemporary Perspective*. Vol. 1: *Hockey and Cultural Identities*, ed. Colin Howell, 111–18. Halifax, NS: Gorsebrook Research Institute, St Mary's University.

– and Kevin Wamsley. 2010. *Sport in Canada: A History*. 2nd ed. Don Mills, ON: Oxford University Press.

Nelson, Dana. 1998. *National Manhood: Capitalist Citizenship and the Imagined Fraternity of White Men*. Durham, NC: Duke University Press.

New, W.H. 2003. *A History of Canadian Literature*. 2nd ed. Montreal and Kingston: McGill-Queen's University Press.

Nicolson, Marjorie. [1929] 1946. "The Professor and the Detective." In *The Art of the Mystery Story*, ed. Howard Haycroft, 110–27. New York: Grosset & Dunlop.

O'Sullivan, Guy, dir. 2004. *The Greatest Canadian*. Television show. Toronto: Canadian Broadcasting Corporation.

Pelletier, Joe. 2006a. "Eddie the Entertainer." *Toronto Maple Leafs Legends*. On-line. http://mapleleafslegends.blogspot.com/2006/05/eddie-entertainer.html (accessed 17 February 2008).

– 2006b "Eric Nesterenko." *Chicago Blackhawks Legends*. On-line. http://blackhawkslegends.blogspot.com/2006/05/eric-nesterenko.html (accessed 13 May 2008).

Pitter, Robert. 2006. "Racialization and Hockey in Canada: From Personal Troubles to a Canadian Challenge." In *Artificial Ice: Hockey, Culture, and Commerce*, ed. David Whitson and Richard Gruneau, 123–42. Peterborough, ON: Broadview Press.

Plimpton, George. 1985. *Open Net: A Professional Amateur in the World of Big Time Hockey*. Guilford, CT: Lyons Press.

Pound, Ezra. 1952. *Guide to Kulchur*. Norfolk, CT: New Directions.

Pronger, Brian. 1990a. *The Arena of Masculinity: Sports, Homosexuality, and the Meaning of Sex*. New York: St Martin's.

– 1990b. "Gay Jocks: A Phenomenology of Gay Men in Athletics." In *Sport, Men, and the Gender Order: Critical Feminist Perspectives*, ed. Michael Messner and Donald Sabo, 141–52. Champaign, IL: Human Kinetics Books.

Pryer, Alison. 2002. "The Aesthetics and Erotics of Hockey." *Canadian Woman Studies* 21, no. 3: 73–76.

Purdy, Al. 1996. "Hockey Players." In *Thru the Smoky End Boards: Canadian Poetry about Sports & Games*, ed. Kevin Brooks and Sean Brooks, 57–8. Vancouver: Polestar.

Putney, Clifford. 2001. *Muscular Christianity: Manhood and Sports in Protestant America, 1880–1920*. Cambridge, MA: Harvard University Press.

Quarrington, Paul. 2007. "Staying in the Game: Paul Quarrington Launches His 'Not the First Book Off' Campaign." *Canada Reads*, Blog Archive, 11 December. On-line. http://www.cbc.ca/canadareads/2007/12/staying_in_the_game_paul_quarr.html (accessed 18 February 2008).

Quigley, Theresia. 1991. *The Child Hero in the Canadian Novel*. Toronto: NC Press.

Richards, David Adams. [1996] 2001. *Hockey Dreams: Memories of a Man Who Couldn't Play*. Toronto: Anchor Canada.

Rigby, Brenda. 2001. "Oh the Memories." Review of *Finnie Walsh*, by Steven Galloway. *Chapters.indigo.ca*. Chapters.indigo.ca. http://www.chapters.indigo.ca/books/Finnie-Walsh/9781551923727-item.html?ref=DS%3a Review%3aguest (accessed 29 July 2010).

Robidoux, Michael. 1997. "Artificial Emasculation and the Maintenance of a Masculine Identity in Professional Hockey." *Canadian Folklore Canadien* 19, no. 1: 69–87.

– 2001. *Men at Play: A Working Understanding of Professional Hockey*. Montreal and Kingston: McGill-Queen's University Press.

– 2002a. "Imagining a Canadian Identity through Sport: A Historical Interpretation of Lacrosse and Hockey." *Journal of American Folklore* 115, no. 456: 209–25.

– 2002b. "The Subaltern Framework of Aboriginal Hockey: *Gnoseology* and Thinking Along the Borders." In *Putting It on Ice: Hockey in Historical and Contemporary Perspective*. Vol. 1: *Hockey and Cultural Identities*, ed. Colin Howell, 29–33. Halifax, NS: Gorsebrook Research Institute, St Mary's University.

Robinson, Laura. 1998. *Crossing the Line: Violence and Sexual Assault in Canada's National Sport*. Toronto: McClelland & Stewart.

Rollin, Roger B. 1989. "Against Evaluation: The Role of the Critic of Popular Culture." In *The Study of Popular Fiction: A Source Book*, ed. Bob Ashley, 16–22. Philadelphia: University of Pennsylvania Press.

Ron. 1999. "The Divine Ryans." Review of *The Divine Ryans*. *Chapters.indigo.ca*. Chapters.indigo.ca.http://www.chapters.indigo.ca/books/The-Divine-Ryans-Wayne-Johnston/9780676971842-91078-Review.html (accessed 29 July 2010).

Rosin, Hanna. 2010. "The End of Men." *Atlantic*, July/August. http://www.theatlantic.com/magazine/archive/2010/07/the-end-of-men/8135/ (accessed 7 July 2010).

Ross, J. Andrew. 2009. "Arenas of Debate: The Continuance of Professional Hockey in the Second World War." In *Coast to Coast: Hockey in Canada to the Second World War*, ed. John Chi-Kit Wong, 86–131. Toronto: University of Toronto Press.

Rubin, Gayle. 1975. "The Traffic in Women." In *Toward an Anthropology of Women*, ed. Rayna Reiter, 157–210. New York: Monthly Review Press.

Sandvoss, Cornell. 2005. *Fans: The Mirror of Consumption*. Cambridge: Polity Press.

Saul, John Ralston. 1997. *Reflections of a Siamese Twin: Canada at the End of the Twentieth Century*. Toronto: Viking.

Savran, David. 1998. *Taking It Like A Man: White Masculinity, Masochism, and Contemporary American Culture*. Princeton, NJ: Princeton University Press.

Scanlan, Lawrence. 2002. *Grace under Fire: The State of Our Sweet and Savage Game*. Toronto: Penguin.

Scherer, Jay and Jordan Koch. 2010. "Living with War: Sport, Citizenship, and the Cultural Politics of Post-9/11 Canadian Identity." *Sociology of Sport Journal* 27, no. 1: 1–29.

Schnabel, Marco, dir. 2008. *The Love Guru*. DVD. Los Angeles:Paramount Pictures. (Performed by Mike Myers, Jessica Alba, and Romany Malco.)

Scott, Cece. 1998. Review of *Crossing the Line: Violence and Sexual Assault in Canada's National Sport*, by Laura Robinson. *Quill and Quire*. September. On-line. http://www.quillandquire.com/reviews/review.cfm?review_id=1035 (accessed 16 October 2011).

Sedgwick, Eve Kosofsky. 1985. *Between Men: English Literature and Male Homosocial Desire*. New York: Columbia University Press.

– 1990. *Epistemology of the Closet*. Berkeley: University of California Press.

Sheppard, Robert. 2002. "Party Time." *Maclean's* 11 March: 24–7.

Signature Editions. 2008. Press sheet for *The Checkout Girl*, by Susan Zettell. Winnipeg, MB: Signature Editions.

Simpson, Wayne. 1989. "Hockey." In *A Concise History of Sport in Canada*, ed. Don Morrow and Mary Keyes, 169–229. Toronto: Oxford University Press.

Sinclair-Faulkner, Tom. 1977. "A Puckish Reflection on Religion in Canada." In *Religion and Culture in Canada/Religion et Culture au Canada*, ed. Peter Slater, 383–405. Toronto: Canadian Corporation for Studies in Religion.

Skinazi, Karen. 2009. "The Mystery of a Canadian Father of Hockey Stories." In *Canada's Game: Hockey and Identity*, ed. Andrew Holman, 98–124. Montreal and Kingston: McGill-Queen's University Press.

Smith, Michael. 1983. *Violence and Sport*. Toronto: Butterworths.

Smythe, Conn with Scott Young. 1981. *If You Can't Beat 'Em in the Alley*. Toronto: McClelland & Stewart.

Staurowsky, Ellen. 2010. "Reflections on Sport in the Aftermath of 9/11." In *Sexual Sports Rhetoric: Historical and Media Contexts of Violence*, ed. Linda Fuller, 63–75. New York: Peter Lang.

Stoat, Chris. 2007. "Rooted in Time and Place." Review of *The Good Body*. *Amazon.ca*. Amazon.ca, 5 September. http://www.amazon.ca/Good-Body-Bill-Gaston/dp/0887849601/ref=sr_1_1?ie=UTF8&s=books&qid=1280583758&sr=1-1 (accessed 29 July 2010).

Sugars, Cynthia. 2004. "Notes on a Mystic Hockey Puck: Death, Paternity, and National Identity in Wayne Johnston's *The Divine Ryans*." *Essays on Canadian Writing* 82: 151–72.

Surette, Leon. 1982. "Here is Us: the Topocentricism of Canadian Literary Criticism." *Canadian Poetry: Studies, Documents, Reviews* 10 (spring/summer): 44–57.

Swirski, Peter. 2005. *From Lowbrow to Nobrow*. Montreal and Kingston: McGill-Queen's University Press.

Szeman, Imre. 2003. "The Persistence of the Nation." In *Zones of Instability: Literature, Postcolonialism, and the Nation*, 152–98. Baltimore, MD: Johns Hopkins University Press.

Theberge, Nancy. 2000. *Higher Goals: Women's Ice Hockey and the Politics of Gender*. Albany, NY: State University of New York Press.

Thiessen, Cherie. 2005. "Fool for Love." Review of *The Secret Mitzvah of Lucio Burke*. *January Magazine*. http://januarymagazine.com/fiction/secmitzvah.html (accessed 6 August 2010).

TSN. 2010. "Oh Canada! 80 Percent of Canadians Watch Gold Medal." *TSN*, 1 March. On-line. http://www.tsn.ca/nhl/story/?id=312025 (accessed 3 March 2010).

Van Sloten, John. 2010. "Hallowed Be Thy Game." *Vancouver Sun*, 24 February. http://www.vancouversun.com/sports/Hallowed+game/2606303/story.html (accessed 13 July 2010).

Vanessa. 2001. "Makes Me Proud to Be Canadian." Review of *Finnie Walsh*. *Chapters.indigo.ca*. Chapters.indigo.ca. http://www.chapters.indigo.ca/books/Finnie-Walsh/9781551923727-item.html?ref=DS%3aReview%3aguest (accessed 29 July 2010).

Vaughan, Garth. 2002. "The 'Colored' Hockey Championship of the Maritimes." In *Putting It on Ice: Hockey in Historical and Contemporary Perspective*. Vol. 1: *Hockey and Cultural Identities*, ed. Colin Howell, 25–7. Halifax, NS: Gorsebrook Research Institute, St Mary's University.

Wamsley, Kevin. 2007. "The Public Importance of Men and the Importance of Public Men: Sport and Masculinities in Nineteenth Century Canada." In *Sport and Gender in Canada*. 2nd ed., ed. Kevin Young and Philip White, 75–91. Oxford: Oxford University Press.

Watson, Sheila. 1974–75. "What I'm Going to Do." *Open Letter* 3, no. 1: 181–3.

Weaving, Charlene and Samuel Roberts. 2010. "Checking in: An analysis of the (lack of) body checking in women's hockey." Paper presented at the Hockey on the Border conference. Adam's Mark Hotel. Buffalo, NY, 3–5 June.

Whannel, Garry. 2002. *Media Sport Stars: Masculinities and Moralities*. London: Routledge.

Whitson, David and Richard Gruneau. 2006. Introduction to *Artificial Ice: Hockey, Culture, and Commerce*, ed. David Whitson and Richard Gruneau, 1–25. Peterborough, ON: Broadview Press.

Willmott, Glenn. 2002. *Unreal Country: Modernity in the Canadian Novel in English*. Montreal and Kingston: McGill-Queen's University Press.

Wordsworth, William. 1993. "The Tables Turned." In *The Norton Anthology of English Literature*. 6th ed. Vol. 2, ed. M.H. Abrams et al., 135–6. New York: W.W. Norton.

Index

Orr, Bobby, 90, 100, 258, 266
Orr, Frank: *Puck Is a Four Letter Word*, 55, 59, 75, 124–5, 206–10, 282n7, 287n5
Ottawa Silver Seven, 53–4, 105, 177, 286n11

Paci, F.G.: *Black Madonna*, 58, 170, 289–90n9; *Icelands*, 48–9, 58–60, 77–8, 81, 167–9, 171, 189, 190–1, 231–2, 243; *The Italians*, 169–70, 289n9
pastoral myth. *See* northernness; nostalgia
Philadelphia Flyers, 153
Plimpton, George: *Open Net*, 296n4
Pocklington, Peter, 91
Ponic, Pam, 30
Pronger, Brian, 240
Pryer, Alison, 39, 211
Purdy, Al: "Hockey Players," 264

Quarrington, Paul: *King Leary*, 23, 28, 70–1, 77, 178–9, 237–8, 249–50, 279n11, 282n9; *Logan in Overtime*, 57, 61, 82
Quebec Nordiques, 97
Quigley, Theresia, 293n13

race: and hockey, 63, 88, 93, 122–43, 147–8
radio. *See* technology, importance of
railroad. *See* technology, importance of
Reddick, Don: *Dawson City Seven*, 23, 53–4, 58–9, 87, 105, 211, 228–9, 245–7, 281–2n6, 286n11, 297–8n3, 299n10; *Killing Frank McGee*, 177–8

Renfrew Millionaires, 51, 104, 176
Richard, Maurice, 25, 118–20, 266
Richards, David Adams: *Hockey Dreams*, 16–17; *Nights below Station Street*, 277–8n4
Richler, Mordechai, 156; *The Apprenticeship of Duddy Kravitz*, 21, 131–3; *Barney's Version*, 134–5; *The Incomparable Atuk*, 133–5
Ritchie, Rob: *Orphans of Winter*, 64–5
Roberts, Samuel, 255
Robertson, Ray: *Heroes*, 44–7, 82, 84–6, 90–2, 96, 267
Robidoux, Michael, 6–8, 218, 226, 241–2, 247
Robinson, Laura, 243, 299n9, 299n11
Rosin, Hanna, 32–3, 150, 280n15
Rubin, Gayle, 248

Sabo, Donald, 211–12, 219, 235–6, 244, 249, 251
Salt Lake City Olympics, 3–4, 17, 18, 139
Sanderson, Don, 152
Sandvoss, Cornell, 196–7
Savran, David, 150, 199
Scanlan, Lawrence, 291–2n6
Sedgwick, Eve Kosofsky, 218–19, 245
Sedlack, Robert: *The Horn of a Lamb*, 69–70, 106–9, 184, 225, 244, 250
Shack, Eddie, 69, 282n8
Shehid, Gamal Abdel, 126
Shields, Carol: *Small Ceremonies*, 283–4n3
Simpson, Wayne, 9, 80, 104, 120, 153–4, 282n6, 282n9